Advancing IT Audits Through Integrative Approaches and Emerging Technologies

Manish Gupta
University at Buffalo, SUNY, USA

John Walp
University at Buffalo, SUNY, USA

Raj Sharman
University at Buffalo, SUNY, USA

IGI Global
Scientific Publishing
Publishing Tomorrow's Research Today

Vice President of Editorial	Melissa Wagner
Director of Acquisitions	Mikaela Felty
Director of Book Development	Jocelynn Hessler
Production Manager	Mike Brehm
Cover Design	Jose Rosado

Published in the United States of America by
IGI Global Scientific Publishing
701 East Chocolate Avenue
Hershey, PA, 17033, USA
Tel: 717-533-8845
Fax: 717-533-7115
Website: https://www.igi-global.com E-mail: cust@igi-global.com

Library of Congress Cataloging-in-Publication Data

Names: Gupta, Manish, 1978- editor | Walp, John, 1967- editor | Sharman, Raj editor
Title: Advancing IT audits through integrative approaches and emerging technologies / [edited by] Manish Gupta, John Walp, Raj Sharman.
Description: Hershey, PA : IGI Global Scientific Publishing, [2026] | Includes bibliographical references and index. | Summary: "The book explores the integration of modern technologies such as AI, automation and machine learning into IT auditing. This publication delves into specialized practices within sectors like healthcare and offers insights into transitioning from legacy systems to cloud-based environments"-- Provided by publisher.
Identifiers: LCCN 2025023882 (print) | LCCN 2025023883 (ebook) | ISBN 9798337330785 hardcover | ISBN 9798337348896 paperback | ISBN 9798337348902 ebook
Subjects: LCSH: Information technology--Management | Information technology--Auditing | Auditing, Internal--Technological innovations | Artificial intelligence--Industrial applications
Classification: LCC HD30.2 .A344 2026 (print) | LCC HD30.2 (ebook) | DDC 658.4/038--dc23/eng/20250728
LC record available at https://lccn.loc.gov/2025023882
LC ebook record available at https://lccn.loc.gov/2025023883
British Cataloguing in Publication Data
A Cataloguing in Publication record for this book is available from the British Library.

Table of Contents

Detailed Table of Contents

As organizations deepen their reliance on third-party vendors to drive innovation and operational flexibility, the landscape of Third-Party Risk Management (TPRM) has become increasingly intricate and vulnerable to cyber threats, regulatory violations, and operational disruptions. This study presents a comprehensive review of how Artificial Intelligence (AI), particularly Natural Language Processing (NLP) and Large Language Models (LLMs), are transforming the TPRM ecosystem. By automating the analysis of vendor communications, compliance audits, legal contracts, and security assessments, AI-driven tools enabling real-time monitoring, predictive risk scoring, and anomaly detection at an unprecedented scale. The paper investigates a range of academic and industrial solutions and compares their effectiveness in automating assessments and enhancing transparency. Ultimately, the research advocates for building adaptable, interpretable, and secure AI systems that can support enterprise-wide risk governance in an evolving third-party ecosystem.

Artificial intelligence and its usage are rapidly growing. Various business functions have already started utilizing the benefits of AI for their tasks. With time, the complexity of information systems is also increasing, leading to extensive audits. As a result, conventional audit practices require additional manual checks to ensure the effectiveness of controls. Integrating AI with audits would provide relief to auditors by automating repetitive tasks. Core AI technologies and their application potential in the audit process are discussed in the following study. The focus of the paper mainly lies on how we can improve the audit reporting process through the implementation of various AI/ML solutions, automating the process and enabling auditors to deliver audit reports quickly. This implementation needs to be regulated to ensure the reliability of AI systems is maintained; hence, an overview of the major AI standards is discussed in the paper.

This study pertains to the impact of new emerging technologies—Artificial Intelligence (AI), blockchain, and cloud computing—on the auditing process. Based on case studies and literature reviews, it explains how each of the foregoing technologies enhances audit quality, real-time assurance, fraud detection, and evidence integrity. AI enables high-frequency data analysis to detect fraud and anomalies in a more efficient manner. Cloud computing enables real-time collaborative auditing but raises data privacy and regulatory compliance issues. Blockchain offers tamper-evident audit trails via smart contracts but suffers from interoperability challenges. The paper presents a visionary sketch of the signs of these technologies and gives recommendations to auditors, educators, and policymakers.

This chapter addresses the digital transformation of the healthcare sector as it moves from on-premises legacy infrastructure to the cloud. The drivers are enhanced scalability, lower costs, and real-time analysis of data for providing improved patient care. Despite the benefits, the transformation raises issues about the confidentiality, integrity and availability of patient data, as if patient data is compromised, companies face HIPAA and GDPR investigations. Without proper security controls, breaches may occur, causing financial loss and reputational damage to organizations. This chapter covers compliance regulations, most critical risks, migration plans, and emerging AI/ML technologies combined with key security principles for optimal best practices. The chapter also provides a checklist for migrating to the cloud to allow healthcare organizations to walk through each phase of the migration process and ensure operational resilience and regulatory compliance for ease of practical implementations.

The proliferation of multi-cloud environments, driven by the need for flexibility, redundancy, and cost efficiency, has introduced new challenges in managing security, compliance, and risk. This chapter explores integrative approaches to auditing within multi-cloud infrastructures, highlighting frameworks, tools, and methodologies necessary to ensure robust security and regulatory alignment. It examines key components such as identity and access management, data encryption, network security, and continuous monitoring. Additionally, the chapter outlines auditing practices for security and compliance, referencing international standards like NIST and GDPR. Risk mitigation strategies are discussed through real-world case studies, including risk assessment models and continuity planning. The discussion underscores the need for cohesive auditing mechanisms to address the complexity and fragmentation inherent in multi-cloud systems. By adopting a holistic audit perspective, organizations can safeguard critical assets, meet compliance demands, and build resilient digital ecosystems.

This chapter presents a comprehensive strategy for auditing IT application portfolios to mitigate risks, enhance governance, and drive strategic optimization. Targeted at IT auditors, risk professionals, and enterprise architects, it integrates frameworks such as CISA, COBIT, ITIL, SOC 2, NIST, and ISO 27001 to guide practices in inventory validation, business alignment, cost-effectiveness, technical risk, and cloud readiness. Structured tools like checklists, the TIME model, and dashboards support a systematic audit process. A hypothetical case study illustrates practical application across multi-industry and multi-region settings, demonstrating how audit-driven insights can uncover redundancies, improve lifecycle health, and strengthen operational resilience. This chapter per the authors emphasizes that a well-governed

Preface

In an era marked by increasing technological disruption and heightened regulatory complexity, the field of IT auditing is undergoing a profound transformation. The days of static audit checklists and retrospective reviews are rapidly giving way to a dynamic landscape powered by artificial intelligence, cloud-native infrastructure, real-time monitoring, and strategic risk governance. With this edited volume, *Advancing IT Audits Through Integrative Approaches and Emerging Technologies*, we aim to provide a panoramic view of how the practice of auditing is being reimagined to address modern operational realities—across industries, infrastructures, and geographies.

The genesis of this book emerged from a shared observation: while technological innovations such as AI, blockchain, and multi-cloud environments are radically redefining the contours of modern enterprises, the frameworks and methodologies governing IT audits have struggled to evolve in tandem. This volume seeks to close that gap. Each chapter in this collection explores a distinct yet interwoven dimension of the emerging audit ecosystem, offering both theoretical insights and practical tools. From the automation of third-party risk management to the ethical auditing of generative AI systems, the book engages with the central challenge of building trust and accountability in increasingly complex digital environments.

We are proud to present contributions from a diverse set of scholars and practitioners across academic institutions and industries. The collective expertise captured here speaks to a growing recognition: that effective auditing is no longer just a function of regulatory compliance, but a strategic capability vital to organizational resilience and innovation. The voices in this volume represent a critical step forward in establishing a next-generation dialogue around audit methodologies—one that is adaptive, inclusive, and technologically grounded.

CHAPTER OVERVIEWS

Chapter 1: Next-Gen 3rd Party Cybersecurity Risk Management Practices: AI Enablement

Aneesh Krishna and Moksh Gupta (University at Buffalo, United States)

This chapter explores how AI technologies—especially NLP and large language models—are revolutionizing Third-Party Risk Management (TPRM) by automating vendor assessments, compliance audits, and anomaly detection. Krishna and Gupta present a comparative study of academic and industrial AI-driven solutions that support real-time risk scoring and decision-making, emphasizing the importance of adaptable, interpretable systems for enterprise-wide cybersecurity governance.

Chapter 2: Enhancing Audit Reporting Through AI-Powered Solutions

Tanisha Ahuja and Aanchal Ahuja (University at Buffalo, United States)

Ahuja and Ahuja delve into how AI and machine learning can transform the audit reporting process by automating manual checks and accelerating reporting timelines. The chapter outlines core AI technologies applicable to audit environments and emphasizes the importance of compliance with emerging AI standards to ensure audit accuracy and system reliability.

Chapter 3: Impact of AI on Audit and Assurance

Mahesh Thaluru, Moksh Gupta, Zishen Liao, Tianyi Zhang, and Raj Sharman (University at Buffalo, United States)

This chapter investigates AI's profound influence on corporate audits, from enhancing risk assessment to enabling predictive fraud detection. Thaluru and colleagues analyze the shift from traditional audits to scalable, real-time AI-driven models, while also addressing critical concerns like data privacy, bias, and audit ethics.

Chapter 4: Auditing Generative AI

Asmita Jain, Zayan Shaheen, Dollie Juneja, and
Anuja Ulhe (University at Buffalo, United States)

Jain and team present a comprehensive framework for auditing Generative AI systems using COSO and COBIT 5, focusing on ethical, security, and operational risks. The chapter introduces methods for assessing AI model integrity and compliance, offering practical solutions for emerging governance and legal challenges posed by GenAI.

Chapter 5: Innovative Auditing Practices – Evidence from Emerging Technologies

Dollie Juneja (University at Buffalo), Abinash Jena
(SMBC), Manish Gupta (M&T Bank), and Raj Sharman
(State University of New York, United States)

This chapter highlights how AI, blockchain, and cloud computing are reshaping auditing practices. Drawing on real-world cases, Juneja and colleagues discuss the benefits and limitations of each technology, offering actionable insights for improving audit quality, fraud detection, and evidence integrity.

Chapter 6: Managing Risks and Ensuring Compliance in Healthcare Cloud Migration

Nishanth Holla Raghavendra and Vijay Kumar Banoth (University
at Buffalo, State University of New York, United States)

Raghavendra and Banoth examine the healthcare sector's shift to cloud computing, discussing the regulatory, operational, and security challenges involved. The chapter provides a practical migration checklist and explores how AI/ML technologies can enhance compliance, data integrity, and patient data security in a highly regulated environment.

Chapter 7: Multi-Cloud Environments – Auditing for Security, Compliance, and Risk Mitigation

Varanasi Rahul, N Sathyanarayana, Muralidhar L B, Y Fathima (JAIN University, India), and Shilpa R (RJS Institute of Management Studies, India)

This chapter presents a detailed approach to auditing complex multi-cloud infrastructures, addressing key issues like identity management, data encryption, and compliance with international standards. Through case studies and risk models, the authors advocate for unified audit strategies that ensure security, continuity, and regulatory alignment.

Chapter 8: Auditing IT Applications for Risk Management and Strategic Optimization

Varun Razdan, Aman Modi, Dinesh Kanna Aranganathan, Manish Gupta, and Raj Sharman (State University of New York at Buffalo, United States)

Razdan and colleagues propose a structured auditing methodology for IT applications, leveraging frameworks like COBIT and ISO 27001 to align audits with organizational strategy. Using tools such as the TIME model and dashboards, the chapter illustrates how strategic audits can uncover inefficiencies and support modernization efforts.

Chapter 9: Data-Driven IT Audits in Higher Education – Leveraging Big Data and AI for Enhanced Governance and Compliance

Tshepo Maota and Audrey Legodi (University of South Africa)

Maota and Legodi assess how six South African HEIs are utilizing AI and big data in IT audits to drive governance and digital transformation. Their analysis reveals disparities in adoption maturity, highlighting the need for improved data literacy, formal governance structures, and region-specific audit strategies to build institutional resilience.

Chapter 10: Ensuring Compliance in Cloud Native Assurance & IT Audits

Harini Shankar (Technology, United States)

Shankar reimagines compliance in cloud-native environments by advocating for built-in, automated governance via Infrastructure as Code and Policy-as-Code. The chapter emphasizes the importance of cultural and skillset shifts alongside technology to ensure compliance is seamlessly integrated into agile development processes.

Chapter 11: Fortifying Municipal Governance – Leveraging IT Audits and Disruption Management for Sustainable Public Services

Tshepo Maota (University of South Africa)

This chapter examines how IT audits and AI-powered disruption management can transform municipal governance in South Africa. Using global best practices and municipal audit data, Maota identifies systemic gaps and offers recommendations to institutionalize digital oversight, enhance resilience, and foster citizen-centric, tech-enabled governance.

We would like to express our deepest gratitude to the contributors whose scholarship and commitment made this volume possible. Their willingness to engage with complex and often uncertain terrain speaks to the importance of collaboration and intellectual rigor in this fast-moving field. We also thank our institutional partners for their support in facilitating research and fostering dialogue around emerging audit practices.

A special acknowledgment is due to the students and early-career researchers who have contributed their perspectives to this volume. Their voices are especially vital as we imagine what IT auditing will look like not just in five years, but in fifty. Their curiosity, adaptability, and fluency with digital systems signal the next wave of innovation and stewardship in audit and governance functions.

Finally, we invite you—the reader—to approach this volume as both a reference and a provocation. Whether you are an auditor, a technologist, a policymaker, or an educator, we hope you find in these chapters both actionable insight and inspiration. The future of auditing is being written now. Let us write it thoughtfully, collaboratively, and with an unwavering commitment to transparency and trust.

Chapter 1

Next-Gen 3rd Party Cybersecurity Risk Management Practices: AI Enablement

Aneesh Krishna
https://orcid.org/0009-0002-3882-1501
University at Buffalo, SUNY, USA

Moksh Gupta
University at Buffalo, SUNY, USA

ABSTRACT

As organizations deepen their reliance on third-party vendors to drive innovation and operational flexibility, the landscape of Third-Party Risk Management (TPRM) has become increasingly intricate and vulnerable to cyber threats, regulatory violations, and operational disruptions. This study presents a comprehensive review of how Artificial Intelligence (AI), particularly Natural Language Processing (NLP) and Large Language Models (LLMs), are transforming the TPRM ecosystem. By automating the analysis of vendor communications, compliance audits, legal contracts, and security assessments, AI-driven tools enabling real-time monitoring, predictive risk scoring, and anomaly detection at an unprecedented scale. The paper investigates a range of academic and industrial solutions and compares their effectiveness in automating assessments and enhancing transparency. Ultimately, the research advocates for building adaptable, interpretable, and secure AI systems that can support enterprise-wide risk governance in an evolving third-party ecosystem.

DOI: 10.4018/979-8-3373-3078-5.ch001

INTRODUCTION

In today's hyper-connected and increasingly digitized business environment, organizations are more reliant than ever on third-party vendors, cloud platforms, service integrators, and digital suppliers to maintain operational efficiency and competitive edge. While such partnerships offer immense flexibility and innovation, they also introduce intricate cybersecurity and regulatory risks. A single vulnerability in a third-party system can ripple across the entire enterprise, exposing organizations to data breaches, service disruptions, compliance failures, and reputational damage. Recent statistics highlight that more than 60% of data breaches originate from third-party vendors, underscoring the urgent need for robust Third-Party Risk Management (TPRM) strategies (Simmons and Miller, 2022).

Traditional TPRM approaches are predominantly manual, relying on static assessments, periodic reviews, and subjective risk scoring. These outdated methods fail to match the speed and complexity of today's dynamic threat landscape. Enter Artificial Intelligence (AI): a transformative force that has fundamentally redefined how organizations assess, monitor, and respond to third-party risks. AI technologies, particularly Natural Language Processing (NLP), Machine Learning (ML), and Robotic Process Automation (RPA), enable real-time, automated, and data-driven risk evaluations. This paper delves into the transformative impact of AI in TPRM, offering a comprehensive synthesis of academic literature, industrial frameworks, and commercial platforms, including the latest advancements since our previous version.

Among AI's most powerful contributions to TPRM is its ability to conduct continuous, real-time monitoring across structured and unstructured data sources. Platforms powered by ML and NLP can now extract risk signals from a multitude of sources such as security audits, SOC reports, legal documents, vendor responses, threat intelligence feeds, social media, and even dark web content. These systems significantly enhance the ability to identify latent risks, generate dynamic risk scores, and trigger automated mitigations. For instance, vendors like BitSight and Interos offer AI-powered dashboards that aggregate over 100 proprietary data sources to compute vendor security ratings in near real time, enhancing proactive decision-making and visibility into multi-tier supply chains.

The rise of Retrieval-Augmented Generation (RAG) frameworks has further enhanced TPRM capabilities. Tools like AgraBOT developed by IBM integrate Information Retrieval with LLM-based question-answering systems to automate Third-Party Security Risk Management (TPSRM) assessments. Unlike static questionnaires, AgraBOT leverages semantic search and in-context learning to generate evidence-backed assessments from large corpora of vendor documents. This significantly reduces the burden on human evaluators while ensuring audit-ready traceability and explainability. Complementing this, NLP bots have been employed to automate sentiment analysis and risk classification of vendor responses, offering practical enhancements in onboarding and compliance workflows.

In addition to these structured implementations, the research landscape has also embraced innovative methodologies. For example, the AIRMF framework applies machine learning models to Distributed Agile Software Development (DASD) environments, automating risk detection across geographically distributed teams. Studies like COREQQA and ProveRAG represent significant advances in AI-driven legal and vulnerability assessment, respectively. COREQQA aligns vendor responses with GDPR mandates using RoBERTa-based QA systems, while ProveRAG enhances CVE analysis through real-time data retrieval and self-critique, achieving over 99% accuracy in exploitation detection

The integration of supply chain topology into risk modeling has also emerged as a frontier advancement. Hu et al. (2022) demonstrate how digital supply chain interconnectivity—captured via graph-based metrics such as centrality and systemic relevance—can improve cyber risk prediction models. Their machine learning framework incorporating network-level features saw a statistically significant uplift in AUC scores, indicating the growing value of ecosystem-aware risk intelligence.

Commercially, the TPRM landscape is expanding rapidly. Established vendors such as ComplyScore and FICO have integrated AI modules to support document analysis, real-time compliance mapping, and ESG risk profiling. Meanwhile, newer platforms like ActiveFence and CalypsoAI extend these capabilities by focusing on AI governance, LLM prompt protection, and runtime vulnerability scanning. These developments highlight the shift from static compliance reporting to real-time, context-aware, and explainable risk management systems.

However, this evolution is not without challenges. Many AI systems still operate as "black boxes," raising concerns around explainability, fairness, and regulatory compliance. Adversarial threats such as prompt injection, data poisoning, and hallucinated responses remain critical risks in AI-driven TPRM. Ethical issues, particularly regarding data privacy and model bias, also demand attention. As organizations deploy these tools at scale, the need for robust governance frameworks, standardized model validation, and human-in-the-loop (HITL) systems becomes paramount.

To address these issues, researchers and practitioners are converging on explainable AI (XAI), federated learning, and reinforcement learning from human feedback (RLHF) as potential solutions. These approaches promise to balance automation with accountability, ensuring that AI-generated insights remain transparent, verifiable, and legally defensible. Federated learning, for instance, allows global AI model training without compromising local data privacy—an increasingly important capability in multi-jurisdictional enterprises.

This paper synthesizes the current landscape and future trajectory of AI-enabled Third-Party Risk Management. Section 1 provides an extensive review of academic literature covering cybersecurity applications, AI methodologies, and compliance automation. Section 2 conducts a comparative evaluation of three AI-based implementations: the NLP Bot for textual analysis, AgraBOT for security assessments via RAG, and the AIRMF framework for DASD environments. Section 3 explores additional studies, including innovations such as supply-aware risk modeling and retrieval-augmented vulnerability analysis tools like ProveRAG. Section 4 investigates industry solutions, both established and emerging, including BitSight, ComplyScore, Interos, and AI governance platforms like ActiveFence. Section 5 discusses ongoing challenges and research gaps, offering insights into building future-ready TPRM systems. Together, these sections chart a path for developing secure, explainable, and scalable AI frameworks tailored to modern third-party risk ecosystems.

1. LITERATURE REVIEW

In today's highly interconnected digital environment, third-party vendors and partners play a central role in the functioning of most organizations. However, these partnerships also introduce significant cybersecurity risks. Recent data breaches — such as those affecting Target (via HVAC vendor access) and SolarWinds — underscore the threat that third-party relationships can pose. According to a Deloitte study, over 80% of organizations experienced a third-party incident in recent years, and many lacked robust tools for monitoring and assessing these partners in real-time (Deloitte, 2023). Traditional third-party risk management (TPRM) techniques rely heavily on manual assessments, compliance audits, and periodic reviews — approaches that are often reactive and inadequate for rapidly evolving cyber threats.

Artificial Intelligence (AI), particularly machine learning (ML) and deep learning (DL), offers promising capabilities to automate and enhance TPRM. AI can ingest large-scale, dynamic data, detect anomalies, prioritize threats, and offer predictive risk assessments. This literature review surveys existing AI applications in cybersecurity and critically examines their extension into third-party risk scenarios. The application of AI in cybersecurity has been steadily increasing. Early models employed supervised ML techniques for malware detection, spam filtering, and intrusion detection systems (IDS). Over time, this evolved into more sophisticated unsupervised learning and deep learning architectures capable of detecting zero-day threats and anomalies in complex datasets (Sharmeen and Hassan, 2018). Several key developments form the basis of AI's potential in TPRM include Anomaly Detection and Threat Intelligence Correlation. AI systems trained on network activity can flag unusual behaviors that indicate threats. This is crucial for third-party access monitoring where behavior baselines differ from internal users (Glisson et al, 2021). AI models can synthesize data from threat feeds, dark web monitoring, and vendor behavior to identify compromised entities (Kim et al, 2023). NLP enables the analysis of vendor documents, certifications, policies, and legal contracts to assess security posture at scale (Ma and Zhao, 2020). According to a comprehensive IEEE survey, hybrid AI systems combining rule-based engines with learning algorithms offer a balance between explainability and adaptability — a key requirement for regulatory and legal TPRM needs (Scarfone and Mell, 2021).

Despite its utility in cybersecurity, specific applications of AI in TPRM are relatively nascent but growing rapidly. AI's contribution to TPRM can be categorized into four main areas:

1.1. Vendor Risk Profiling

AI-driven tools aggregate data from public sources (e.g., news, financial reports, legal cases) and private repositories to generate dynamic risk scores. These scores can reflect not only cybersecurity posture but also ESG (Environmental, Social, Governance) factors that affect vendor trustworthiness. Machine learning algorithms can adapt these scores over time as new information arises (Tamersoy et al, 2021).

1.2. Continuous Monitoring and Real-Time Alerts

Traditional TPRM frameworks relied on annual or quarterly assessments. AI enables continuous risk monitoring by automating data collection from attack surface monitoring tools, domain/IP reputation scores, and behavioral logs of third-party access. AI systems can autonomously correlate patterns and issue alerts when a vendor shows signs of compromise or risky behavior (BitSight Technologies, 2022). One of the most successful implementations of this is in platforms like BitSight and SecurityScorecard, which utilize AI models to provide real-time, external assessments of vendors' security posture (Lee, 2023).

1.3. Third-Party Access Behavior Analytics

With Zero Trust becoming a popular model in cybersecurity, AI plays a role in behavior analytics of users — including third-party users. Using behavioral baselines and time-series analysis, AI can detect subtle deviations in access patterns, such as lateral movement or privilege escalation attempts from third-party accounts (Yu et al, 2020).

1.4. Policy Automation and Compliance Mapping

Many organizations must ensure that vendors comply with specific regulations like GDPR, HIPAA, or NIST. NLP and AI-enabled document analysis can scan vendor security documents, map controls to frameworks, and flag non-compliance or outdated policies. This automation dramatically reduces manual audit workload and helps in onboarding vendors faster (Zeng and Wang, 2022).

The existing literature highlights several critical methodologies in cybersecurity, NLP, and TPRM. Jide et al. proposed an automated methodology for evaluating security and privacy risks in chatbot-based messaging platforms, particularly focusing on Discord, where the lack of user permission checks poses significant vulnerabilities. Their research reveals that over half of Discord chatbots request administrative privileges, with minimal privacy protections in place (Edu et al, 2022). Similarly, Marco et al. emphasize the role of NLP in Cyber Threat Intelligence (CTI), outlining how NLP-driven techniques such as data crawling, relationship extraction, and collaboration improve threat detection. However, they also acknowledge challenges related to data quality and ethical concerns (Arazzi et al, 2023). Delia et al. explores the intersection of algorithms and human behavior in auditing, introducing the Auditor-Governing-the-Loop (AGL) approach to understand how AI systems impact auditing processes. Their findings suggest the need for further research into human-algorithm interactions and updates to educational programs to align with evolving audit technologies (Tiron-Tudor and Deliu, 2022). Lastly, Unal et al. focus on Cyber Third-Party Risk Management (C-TPRM), a growing field that assesses cybersecurity risks associated with external partners. Their study compares various C-TPRM assessment methods, highlighting inconsistencies in security scoring and the emergence of non-intrusive techniques like penetration testing for more reliable risk evaluations (Keskin, 2021). These studies collectively underline the evolving role of AI and NLP in cybersecurity, risk management, and compliance auditing.

Traditional approaches to risk management in DASD are often manual and heavily reliant on human expertise (Schön, 2020). This makes them inefficient in addressing the dynamic and fast-paced nature of distributed agile environments. Research has identified several risk factors inherent in DASD projects, such as Group Awareness risk, External Stakeholder collaboration risks, Technology setup rusks, and Project Management Risks (Shrivastava and Rathod, 2015). However, these studies often fail to propose comprehensive or automated solutions. While some tools have introduced semi-automated processes using software agents or basic analytics, they do not address the complexity or scalability required for managing risks in DASD projects effectively (Odzaly et al, 2018).

The advancements in Generative AI, large language models (LLMs), and sophisticated NLP techniques have led to a growing number of applications in domains that demand deep, domain-specific expertise (Ahmed et al, 2023)(Aktas et al, 2023). In particular, areas like supply chain management and cybersecurity have seen parallels with AI-based Third-Party Risk Management (TPRM) solutions, especially in tracking and managing risks and vulnerabilities. Closely aligned with our work (Li et al, 2023) (Abualhaija et al, 2022), the proposed COREQQA system serves as a question-answering (QA) tool designed to analyze legal compliance documents in accordance with European regulations, such as GDPR. COREQQA leverages an Information Retrieval approach to identify the N-most relevant instances related to a given query and then generates responses using RoBERTa-QA, a powerful LLM tailored for question answering tasks.

Hu et al. (2022) demonstrate that supply chain characteristics—such as vendor interconnectivity and digital dependencies—can significantly enhance cyber risk prediction when integrated into machine learning models. Their findings show a 2% improvement in AUC, emphasizing the value of externally observable features in TPRM. This supports the need for AI-driven, supply-aware risk frameworks that account for systemic exposure across digital ecosystems.

ProveRAG introduces a novel vulnerability analysis system that combines real-time data retrieval with LLMs and a self-critique mechanism to enhance the accuracy and reliability of CVE assessments. Achieving over 99% accuracy in identifying exploitation strategies, ProveRAG demonstrates how retrieval-augmented AI systems can support compliance, improve third-party vulnerability detection, and provide evidence-backed cybersecurity insights (Fayyazi et al., 2024).

The integration of Generative AI and Retrieval-Augmented Generation (RAG) into TPRM has enabled the automation of compliance audits, document reviews, and risk identification tasks. These technologies improve accuracy, reduce manual workload, and enhance traceability, especially when analyzing regulatory documents. However, challenges such as data source reliability, AI model bias, and transparency call for stronger governance and emerging safeguards like blockchain integration (Arora & Ramteke, 2024).

2. COMPARATIVE STUDY

2.1. NLP Bot for Third-Party Risk Management

In response to the increasing complexity and criticality of third-party engagements across industries (Aliane and Zakariya, 2023), NLP-based bots have emerged as a revolutionary solution to TPRM methods. NLP-bot technology leverages advanced natural language processing algorithms to effectively sift through massive volumes of unstructured textual data, including contracts, agreements, and social media conversations, to proactively identify financial risks, security threats, and regulatory violations (Tounsi and Temimi, 2023). Traditional TPRM frameworks often struggle with complex architectures and manual-intensive procedures, increasing the probability of errors. NLP Bots significantly streamline these processes by automating risk detection, thereby increasing accuracy, efficiency, and the capacity for proactive risk mitigation (Tounsi and Temimi, 2023). The 2023 EY Global Third Party Risk Management Survey found that 90% of organizations are investing in enhancing the effectiveness of their TPRM programs, with 61% of risks stemming from cybersecurity and digital threats. This shows how NLP has contributed to efficient and dynamic TPRM practices across organizations (Sadgrove, 2016).

The NLP Bot's integration with Robotic Process Automation (RPA) platforms is particularly noteworthy, as it allows automated and swift responses by issuing alerts or notifications when unauthorized access attempts or significant risks are detected (Đ and Tran, 2021). Sentiment analysis has proven especially useful, providing insights into third-party interactions by gauging sentiments and detecting concerns embedded in communications, thus enabling informed decision-making (Sharma and Jain, 2020).

Table 1. Dataset Sample

Vendor	Question	Answer	Comment	Acceptability
Vendor A	What security measures do you have in place?	Our security measures include …	Regarding data encryption…	Neutral
Vendor B	How often do you conduct security audits?	We conduct audits quarterly	NaN	Acceptable
Vendor C	What is your contingency plan for outages?	Our contingency plan includes …	Needs further clarification	Not Acceptable

Sourced from (Mohta et al, 2024)

The initial dataset was developed with input from Risk Analysts, who compiled a list of security questions for third-party vendors and gathered their responses, as shown in the table above. The "Acceptability" column represents the response generated by the NLP bot using a sentiment analysis algorithm. Each Question, Answer, and Comment is classified into Neutral, Acceptable, or Not Acceptable (Mohta et al, 2024). However, adopting NLP Bots in TPRM is not without challenges. Issues such as prompt injection attacks, malware distribution, dataset poisoning, and risks of data breaches and leaks necessitate robust cybersecurity measures (Jo, 2019). Despite these concerns, the technology's benefits—enhanced risk visibility, greater efficiency, and superior decision-making capabilities—substantially outweigh its drawbacks. The application of NLP technology in TPRM holds considerable promise for the future, especially with the continual advancements in NLP, such as transformer models (e.g., GPT-4), poised to further boost bots' analytical precision in complex risk-related tasks (Mohta et al, 2024).

Practically, NLP bots have found diverse applications, including vendor evaluation, cybersecurity assessments, continuous monitoring of compliance, preparation for business continuity (e.g., backups, contingency planning), and awareness training programs. Empirical studies utilizing datasets comprising assessment questions, vendor answers, and analyst comments indicate the effectiveness of NLP in classifying vendor responses, thus providing clear criteria for acceptability and enhancing TPRM practices significantly (Mohta et al, 2024) (Aliane and Zakariya, 2023).

2.2. AgraBOT

AgraBOT, developed by IBM Research, is another sophisticated approach to optimizing Third-Party Security Risk Management (TPSRM) assessments, primarily addressing the challenges of timeliness, scalability, and subjectivity inherent in traditional TPSRM processes. Framework dramatically reduces assessment times from days to minutes, a crucial advancement given growing number of third-party engagements organizations must evaluate (Toslali et al, 2024).

Figure 1. AI architecture

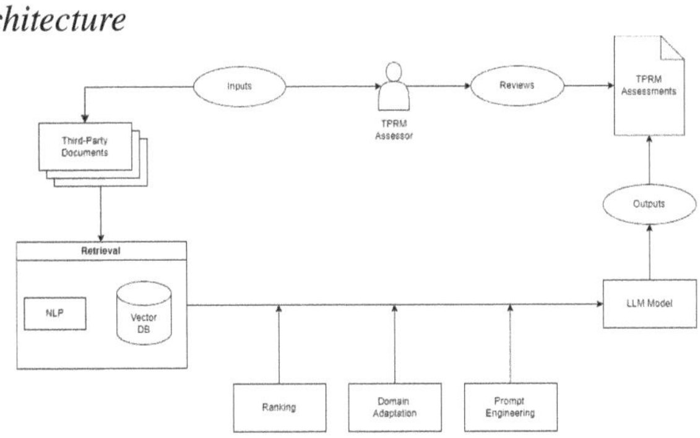

Adapted from source (Toslali et al, 2024)

Above figure shows AgraBOT's AI framework is designed using a RAG approach, integrating (Information Retrival) IR and (Large Language Models) LLM-based question answering to enhance TPSRM assessments (Gao et al, 2023). The workflow begins with IR, where third-party documents are processed by splitting them into passage chunks and embedding them into a vector space. Each TPSRM question is converted into vector embeddings, allowing a semantic search to retrieve the most relevant passages. This initial retrieval phase is powered by Watson Discovery, an AI-driven search and text analytics platform chosen for its scalability, indexing, embedding, and search capabilities. The retrieved passages undergo an additional refinement process through multi-stage ranking, where a pre-trained encoder-only language model (all-mpnet-base-v2) (Hugging Face, 2023b) further ranks and selects the most relevant passages, improving retrieval accuracy.

Following retrieval, AgraBOT employs in-context learning for domain adaptation. Instead of traditional fine-tuning, which requires extensive computational resources and labeled data, AgraBOT incorporates a few-shot learning approach by embedding between one and five relevant examples—sourced from publicly available SOC 3 documents—directly into the prompt (Radford et al, 2019). This allows the LLM to dynamically adapt to TPSRM-specific queries without the need for additional training. The refined passages, along with the few-shot examples, are then integrated into a structured prompt designed to guide the LLM in generating contextually accurate and evidence-supported responses. Prompt engineering plays a critical role in AgraBOT's framework, ensuring effective communication between users and the LLM. The prompt includes the user query, relevant information retrieved through IR, and specific directives tailored to optimize response accuracy. Various prompt engineering techniques, such as emotional prompts, are evaluated to refine the effectiveness of the model (Li et al, 2023). Through the combination of multi-stage ranking, in-context learning, and prompt engineering, AgraBOT enhances source attribution, ensuring responses are backed by relevant data from third-party documents. This reduces the risk of hallucination—where LLMs generate inaccurate or nonsensical information—while increasing the reliability of AI-driven TPSRM assessments. By leveraging these advanced AI techniques, AgraBOT provides a scalable and efficient solution for third-party risk management, offering improved accuracy, transparency, and adaptability to evolving security concerns.

Specifically, AgraBOT's event-driven architecture allows for asynchronous and parallel task execution, enhancing operational resilience and efficiency. Its workflow involves initially fetching documents via Watson Discovery (IBM, 2023), performing semantic searches to retrieve and rank relevant passages, and finally generating contextually accurate responses to assessment questions. A pivotal aspect of AgraBOT's success is its meticulous use of AI techniques such as multi-stage passage ranking and prompt engineering. This strategic utilization of advanced AI has significantly improved accuracy, reflected by an impressive F1 score of 0.85 across seven TPSRM assessments involving hundreds of labeled question-answer pairs (Toslali et al, 2024).

AgraBOT processes extensive third-party documents, with each TPSRM assessment typically comprising 10 documents, 218 pages, and approximately 39,000 words. The dataset analysis further reveals that third-party documents range between 71 and 333 pages, containing between 22,000 and 55,000 words. Additionally, TPSRM assessments exhibit a notable variation in response patterns, with affirmative responses ranging from 45% to 75% and negative responses making up 25% to 55%. These dataset characteristics emphasises the scale and complexity of the assessments AgraBOT handles, further demonstrating its ability to navigate large volumes of information with efficiency and accuracy (Toslali et al, 2024). Empirical evaluations have underlined the effectiveness of using emotion-infused, few-shot sample prompts, particularly when paired with the Flan-T5 (Hugging Face, 2023a) language model. Interestingly, the relationship between passage length and the AI model's accuracy wasn't strictly linear, but performance did notably improve as the number of relevant passages increased. These findings highlight the value of leveraging broader contextual data for nuanced AI-driven assessments. Despite its remarkable accuracy and efficiency, AgraBOT remains an assistive technology rather than a complete replacement for human assessors, ensuring human oversight remains integral to verifying AI-generated assessments. Ongoing research efforts are directed towards enhancing domain adaptation through advanced prompt tuning (Lester et al, 2021), model ensembling for improved accuracy, and the application of Reinforcement Learning from Human Feedback (MacGlashan et al, 2017), indicating significant potential for further performance enhancements in TPSRM practices.

2.3. AI-Based Risk Management Framework for Distributed Agile Software Development (Khanna et al, 2021)

Figure 2. Training phase

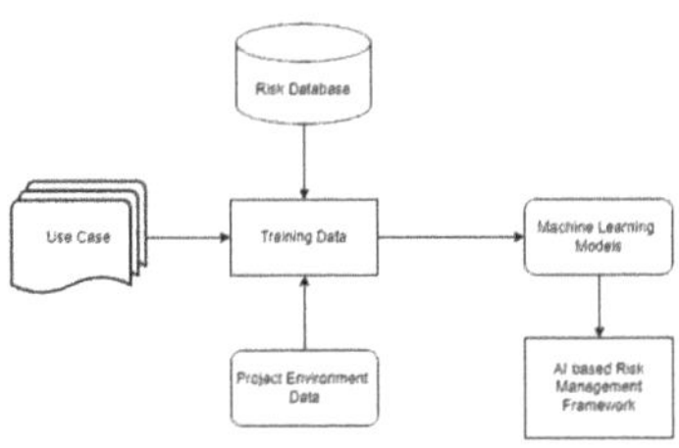

(Khanna et al, 2021)

The paper, Artificial Intelligence-Based Risk Management Framework for Distributed Agile Software Development, explores the integration of Artificial Intelligence (AI) into risk management for Distributed Agile Software Development (DASD). DASD combines Agile Software Development (ASD), which emphasizes adaptability, collaboration, and iterative delivery, with Distributed Software Development (DSD), which leverages geographically dispersed teams to reduce costs and access global talent (Dastidar and Chatterjee, 2013)(NicCanna et al, 2021)

(Hoda et al, 2018). While this hybrid approach provides benefits such as scalability, faster delivery, and cost efficiency, it also introduces significant challenges. These include communication barriers, cultural differences, time zone misalignments, and coordination complexities (Kahya and Seneler, 2018). If not addressed effectively, these risks can lead to project delays, reduced product quality, and increased costs.

Figure 3. AI based RMF for DASD

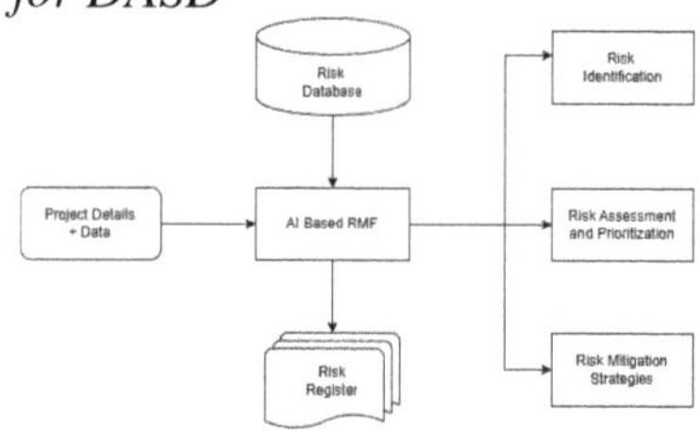

Traditional approaches to risk management in DASD are often manual and heavily reliant on human expertise (Schön, 2020). This makes them inefficient in addressing the dynamic and fast-paced nature of distributed agile environments. Research has identified several risk factors inherent in DASD projects, such as Group Awareness risk, External Stakeholder collaboration risks, Technology setup risks, and Project Management Risks (Shrivastava and Rathod, 2015). However, these studies often fail to propose comprehensive or automated solutions.

While some tools have introduced semi-automated processes using software agents or basic analytics, they do not address the complexity or scalability required for managing risks in DASD projects specifically for DASD. This framework uses machine learning effectively (Odzaly et al, 2018). To address these challenges, the paper proposes an Artificial Intelligence-based Risk Management Framework (AIRMF) tailored algorithms to automate critical aspects of risk management, including risk identification, assessment, prioritization, and mitigation. By analyzing project data—such as user stories, sprint progress reports, team performance metrics, and environmental factors—AIRMF generates real-time risk registers and recommends actionable mitigation strategies. For instance, the framework can predict potential risks by identifying patterns in historical project data that may lead to delays or resource bottlenecks. Additionally, it can objectively prioritize risks based on their likelihood and impact using data-driven insights (Khanna et al, 2021).

The AIRMF framework incorporates iterative monitoring at both the sprint and project levels to ensure that risks are continuously identified and addressed throughout the development lifecycle. This ensures that emerging risks are captured early and that mitigation strategies remain relevant as project conditions evolve. The framework also aligns with international standards like ISO31000 for risk management while adapting its processes to the unique needs of distributed agile teams. By automating repetitive tasks such as risk documentation and prioritization, AIRMF allows project managers to focus on strategic decision-making and proactive planning (Khanna et al, 2022)(Zahedi et al, 2023).

This work contributes significantly by introducing an AI-driven solution to the persistent challenges of risk management in DASD. By automating critical processes and addressing gaps in existing frameworks, the proposed AIRMF has the potential to enhance project outcomes in distributed agile environments. Future research could focus on implementing and validating this framework across diverse industry scenarios to assess its practical impact (Khanna et al, 2021) (Zahedi et al, 2023).

2.4. Comparative analysis

This section offers a comparative evaluation of three AI-driven risk management systems—namely the NLP Bot for Third-Party Risk Management (TPRM), AgraBOT, and the AI-Based Risk Management Framework for Distributed Agile Software Development (AIRMF). Each model targets distinct domains but shares a common goal: enhancing efficiency, accuracy, and scalability in risk identification and mitigation through AI techniques.

2.4.1. Strengths and Contributions

The NLP Bot demonstrates notable effectiveness in automating third-party vendor assessment through sentiment analysis and response classification. Its ability to process unstructured text data—such as contracts and vendor communication—allows organizations to streamline risk classification tasks and issue real-time alerts when integrated with Robotic Process Automation (RPA). The empirical use of a labeled dataset (Table 1) validates its practical relevance in evaluating vendor risk responses.

AgraBOT, developed by IBM Research, presents a highly advanced framework, leveraging Retrieval-Augmented Generation (RAG) for intelligent question answering in Third-Party Security Risk Management (TPSRM). By combining semantic search, multi-stage passage ranking, and in-context learning with few-shot prompts, AgraBOT achieves high retrieval accuracy and contextual precision. A distinguishing feature of this model is its emphasis on source attribution and explainability, reducing the likelihood of hallucination and ensuring that AI-generated assessments are grounded in evidence.

The AIRMF proposes a structured approach to AI-based risk management tailored to Distributed Agile Software Development (DASD). It utilizes machine learning to dynamically generate risk registers, predict potential bottlenecks, and recommend mitigation strategies. The framework's continuous risk monitoring during sprint and project phases aligns with agile principles, offering an adaptable and proactive model. Its compliance with the ISO31000 standard further enhances its applicability in real-world software engineering contexts.

2.4.2. Limitations and Gaps

Despite its practical utility, the NLP Bot lacks detailed insights into its underlying architecture and decision-making logic. The acceptability classification, while intuitive, is not transparently linked to specific NLP models or interpretability mechanisms, limiting reproducibility and explainability. Furthermore, cybersecurity threats—such as prompt injection or data leakage—are mentioned but not adequately addressed in terms of mitigation strategies.

AgraBOT, while technically robust, is heavily reliant on IBM's proprietary tools such as Watson Discovery. This may restrict replicability or adaptation by organizations lacking access to such platforms. Moreover, although AgraBOT incorporates domain adaptation through in-context learning, it does not describe human-in-the-loop workflows, which are essential for validating high-stakes decisions in security assessments.

The AIRMF framework, although promising, remains theoretical in parts. It does not elaborate on the specific machine learning algorithms used, nor does it present experimental performance metrics to validate its predictive capabilities. Additionally, the framework lacks a discussion on the challenges of implementing AI in cross-functional and geographically dispersed teams, particularly in terms of tool integration and team training.

Table 2. Cross-Model Comparison

Aspect	NLP Bot	AgraBOT	AIRMF
Domain Focus	Third-Party/ Vendor Risk	Third-Party security assessments	Distributed Agile Development
Primary Techniques	Sentiment analysis, RPA	RAG (IR + LLM), multi-stage ranking	Machine learning–based prediction
Explainability	Moderate	High (evidence attribution)	Moderate (standards-aligned)
Real-Time Capabilities	Yes (RPA integration)	Yes (event-driven)	Yes (sprint-based monitoring)
Scalability	Medium	High (handles 40K+ words per doc set)	Medium
Evaluation Metrics	No quantitative metrics reported	F1 Score: 0.85	No quantitative metrics reported
Tooling/Dependency	Custom NLP	Watson Discovery, Flan-T5, all-mpnet-v2	Unspecified ML tools

3. ADDITIONAL STUDIES

3.1. Supply Chain Characteristics as Predictors of Cyber Risk

A groundbreaking approach to strengthening AI-based TPRM is presented by Hu et al. (2022), who demonstrate how structural characteristics of digital supply chains can significantly improve cyber risk prediction. Traditionally, cyber risk models have focused primarily on internal organizational factors such as IT infrastructure, policy maturity, or historical incident frequency. However, this study argues for the inclusion of externally observable supply chain attributes as key variables in improving predictive accuracy. Leveraging a dataset comprising cybersecurity ratings and supply chain mappings, the authors develop a machine learning framework that integrates enterprise-level and network-level features—such as a vendor's connectivity, centrality, and systemic relevance within the digital ecosystem. Notably, their empirical results demonstrate that including supply chain features leads to a 2.3% improvement in AUC scores over baseline models, which is statistically significant given the low signal-to-noise ratio typically found in rare-event breach data. This finding underscores the predictive utility of third-party exposure and interconnectivity metrics, offering a more holistic perspective on organizational vulnerability.

In addition to enhancing predictive accuracy, the study highlights how the structural position of an entity within a digital supply chain—such as being a hub or a bridge—can amplify or mitigate cyber risk propagation. For example, vendors that are highly interconnected or serve as critical conduits across multiple client networks pose disproportionate systemic risk. These insights are particularly relevant for TPRM frameworks, as they shift focus from static risk scoring toward dynamic and context-aware risk modeling. The research also raises practical considerations for vendor selection and prioritization: organizations may benefit from applying graph-based learning or clustering algorithms to evaluate the broader implications of onboarding a vendor with high network exposure. Moreover, the study emphasizes that as cyber incidents often originate in one node and ripple through connected entities, the ability to forecast such cascades through supply chain telemetry represents a critical advancement for continuous monitoring. From a governance standpoint, this research advocates for integrating digital supply chain analytics into enterprise-wide risk dashboards and aligning them with Security Operations Centers (SOCs) and GRC platforms. By demonstrating how supply chain topology and network science principles can be used in machine learning pipelines, the study sets a new benchmark for scalable and anticipatory TPRM strategies in an era of interconnected digital infrastructures (Hu et al., 2022).

3.2. ProveRAG: Enhancing Vulnerability Analysis with Retrieval-Augmented LLMs

Amidst the surge in Common Vulnerabilities and Exposures (CVEs), security teams face mounting challenges in triaging and analysing vulnerabilities quickly and accurately. Traditional methods of vulnerability assessment often struggle to keep pace with the influx of new threats, necessitating more advanced and automated approaches. The study titled "ProveRAG: Provenance-Driven Vulnerability Analysis with Automated Retrieval-Augmented LLMs" introduces an innovative system designed to address these challenges by leveraging the capabilities of large language models (LLMs) augmented with real-time data retrieval mechanisms.

ProveRAG stands out by integrating LLMs with automated retrieval systems to analyze Common Vulnerabilities and Exposures (CVEs) effectively. This hybrid approach allows the system to access up-to-date information from reputable sources such as the National Vulnerability Database (NVD) and the Common Weakness Enumeration (CWE), ensuring that analyses are grounded in the most current data available. By doing so, ProveRAG mitigates the common issue of LLMs generating outdated or hallucinated information, a critical concern in cybersecurity applications where accuracy is paramount.

A notable feature of ProveRAG is its self-critique mechanism, which enables the system to evaluate its own outputs for consistency and reliability. This self-assessment capability enhances the trustworthiness of the analyses provided, offering security professionals greater confidence in the system's recommendations. The study reports that ProveRAG achieves over 99% accuracy in identifying exploitation strategies and 97% accuracy in suggesting mitigation techniques, outperforming traditional methods that rely solely on static data or manual analysis.

The implications of ProveRAG's capabilities are significant for Third-Party Risk Management (TPRM). Organizations often rely on third-party vendors whose security postures can introduce vulnerabilities into the primary organization's systems. By employing a system like ProveRAG, organizations can proactively assess and monitor vulnerabilities not only within their own infrastructure but also across their supply chains. This proactive approach enables the identification of potential risks before they can be exploited, thereby enhancing the overall security posture of the organization.

Furthermore, ProveRAG's ability to provide detailed, evidence-backed analyses supports compliance with various regulatory frameworks that require rigorous documentation of risk assessments and mitigation strategies. The system's integration of real-time data retrieval ensures that organizations remain informed about the latest threats and vulnerabilities, facilitating timely and informed decision-making.

In conclusion, the ProveRAG system represents a significant advancement in the application of AI and LLMs for cybersecurity. Its innovative integration of real-time data retrieval with self-assessing language models addresses critical challenges in vulnerability analysis, offering a robust tool for organizations aiming to enhance their TPRM strategies. By providing accurate, timely, and verifiable analyses, ProveRAG empowers organizations to navigate the complex landscape of cybersecurity threats more effectively (Fayyazi et al., 2024).

3.3. The Role of Generative AI and RAG in Automating and Improving TPRM

The evolution of Third-Party Risk Management (TPRM) has been significantly influenced by the integration of advanced technologies, particularly Artificial Intelligence (AI). The application of Generative AI in TPRM is seen to automate processes, reduce manual effort, and increase accuracy in compliance checks. Studies have explored the role of AI in automating compliance checks in sectors like financial services, demonstrating improvements in accuracy and speed. Similarly, Generative AI has been applied to automate risk assessments in cybersecurity, an area closely related to TPRM. The automation of processes such as risk identification, mitigation, and due diligence using AI has been shown to lead to reductions in time and human error. Integrating AI-driven automation tools into TPRM can enhance efficiency and risk detection.

Retrieval-Augmented Generation (RAG) is a concept proposed to enhance the capabilities of Generative AI by anchoring AI-generated outputs in external data sources. The RAG framework improves the relevance and accuracy of AI responses by referencing real-time data, which is crucial in TPRM where data must be current. The application of RAG has been explored for improving AI-driven processes, such as machine learning models used for accurate analysis of legal texts, which has direct relevance to compliance checks within TPRM. RAG also contributes to transparency and traceability in AI-driven decisions, an important aspect of audit and compliance processes.

The automation of TPRM processes, particularly third-party audits, has been a focus of research, highlighting the benefits of reducing time and resources required for manual checks. A key innovation in TPRM automation involves using AI to analyse documents for compliance against regulatory standards. Automating document analysis for compliance can significantly improve accuracy and efficiency. Approaches include systems for categorizing documents based on regulatory controls and managing various document formats for conformance checks, especially relevant in data-intensive sectors like the financial industry. AI can also help in reducing false positives in compliance checks through context-specific analysis, leading to improved accuracy in AI-driven TPRM systems.

The potential for AI to enhance the scalability of TPRM systems is also noted, allowing organizations to handle increasing volumes of third-party data without compromising accuracy. AI can also improve the timeliness of risk assessments, particularly in dynamic regulatory environments.

However, the integration of AI into TPRM is not without challenges. Potential risks of AI-driven automation include reliance on inaccurate data sources, which could lead to compliance failures. RAG is noted to mitigate these risks by ensuring AI models are grounded in accurate, up-to-date information. Ethical considerations, such as data privacy and bias in AI models, are also important. Maintaining transparency and accountability in AI-driven compliance decisions is stressed. Looking ahead, integrating AI with technologies like blockchain could further enhance the security and transparency of TPRM processes, potentially creating tamper-proof records of compliance checks (Arora & Ramteke, 2024).

4. INDUSTRY SOLUTIONS AND IMPLEMENTATIONS

In addition to academic and experimental advancements in AI-based risk management, a rapidly growing ecosystem of commercial solutions has emerged to address the practical challenges of third-party risk management (TPRM) and supply chain cyber risk. These platforms offer scalable, enterprise-ready implementations that blend artificial intelligence (AI), machine learning (ML), and natural language processing (NLP) to support risk prediction, vendor evaluation, anomaly detection, and regulatory compliance. Traditional TPRM approaches, often reliant on manual assessments and periodic reviews, are being replaced or supplemented by continuous monitoring systems and predictive models capable of flagging real-time threats.

This section initially examines four prominent platforms—BitSight, ComplyScore, FICO, and Interos (Keskin et al., 2021)—that exemplify how AI is being operationalized for cyber and compliance oversight within extended enterprise ecosystems. These tools are widely adopted for scoring vendor security posture, automating documentation audits, and identifying systemic risks in interconnected vendor networks.

In addition to these established platforms, a new wave of AI-native solutions has emerged, targeting more advanced areas such as explainability, runtime model protection, and AI governance across third-party workflows. Platforms like ActiveFence, Aim Security, CalypsoAI, AIShield, and AppSOC AI extend traditional TPRM capabilities by introducing real-time LLM monitoring, prompt injection protection, vulnerability scanning, and responsible AI enforcement. These solutions are particularly valuable as third-party vendors increasingly adopt generative AI technologies into their service offerings, exposing organizations to novel risks such as hallucinations, jailbreaks, and AI supply chain weaknesses.

Together, these commercial tools represent a maturing market for AI-powered TPRM, where organizations are no longer limited to reactive strategies but can instead adopt continuous, evidence-backed, and explainable systems to manage evolving third-party risks. This convergence of AI, cybersecurity, and enterprise governance underscores a broader shift from periodic compliance checks to proactive and intelligent risk orchestration.

4.1. BitSight

BitSight is a leading cybersecurity ratings platform that utilizes AI and ML to evaluate the security posture of organizations, particularly in the context of third-party risk assessment. The platform collects cybersecurity-related data from over 120 proprietary sources, encompassing threat intelligence, network traffic patterns, and malware activity. The BitSight platform converts this data into a quantitative rating scale ranging from 250 to 900 (BitSight Technologies, 2020), akin to a credit scoring system. These ratings provide a simplified yet powerful tool for assessing a vendor's cybersecurity readiness, allowing risk management teams to make informed decisions quickly. BitSight's predictive analytics also help identify trends and patterns over time, enabling proactive vendor risk mitigation.

4.2. ComplyScore

ComplyScore is designed to unify risk, compliance, and audit data within a centralized AI-powered platform. It focuses primarily on information security and regulatory compliance, offering tools to streamline the assessment of third-party vendors' adherence to internal policies and external legal standards (Atlas Systems et al, n.d). ComplyScore employs AI to analyze documentation, monitor policy adherence, and track vendor performance against compliance benchmarks. It generates comprehensive dashboards that reflect the current state of vendors' information security practices, facilitating continuous oversight. By integrating compliance, audit, and risk data, ComplyScore enables organizations to streamline traditionally siloed risk management processes, enhancing operational efficiency and accountability.

4.3. FICO

Well known for its credit scoring systems, FICO has extended its analytics expertise into supply chain and third-party risk management. The platform offers AI-driven risk scoring and predictive analytics for suppliers and other external partners. FICO's risk models aggregate data from diverse sources to evaluate financial stability, compliance, and operational performance, delivering a multidimensional view of third-party risk. A key feature of FICO's offering is its ability to integrate with existing procurement and supplier relationship management (SRM) systems, allowing seamless incorporation into enterprise workflows. This facilitates real-time monitoring and continuous risk assessment, which is crucial in dynamic supply chain environments where vendor conditions may evolve rapidly (Carrns, 2012).

4.4. Interos

Interos provides an end-to-end AI-powered platform for continuous monitoring of supply chain and third-party ecosystems. The platform analyzes data from over 85,000 public and proprietary sources to deliver insights into risk domains including cybersecurity, financial health, geopolitical exposure, governance, and operational resilience. Interos distinguishes itself through its ability to model multi-tier supply chain relationships, offering visibility not just into direct vendors, but also into sub-tier and systemic dependencies. Using ML and NLP, Interos continuously ingests and interprets data—such as news feeds, regulatory filings, and social media—to deliver dynamic risk scores. This multi-factor analysis enables organizations to identify and respond to latent or emerging threats across complex supply networks (Allgeier, 2020).

4.5. ActiveFence

ActiveFence provides real-time policy enforcement and guardrails for AI deployments, positioning itself as a key enabler of secure and trustworthy AI use across enterprise ecosystems. While originally focused on content integrity and platform safety, its recent extensions include runtime model controls, incident tracing, and custom policy rule sets. In the context of Third-Party Risk Management (TPRM), ActiveFence offers organizations a way to enforce responsible AI usage among vendors that embed generative models into their tools or services. The platform supports AI activity monitoring, allowing enterprises to detect and respond to non-compliant or high-risk model behavior from external partners. Its capabilities are especially valuable when managing third parties with embedded LLM workflows, ensuring outputs align with both ethical and regulatory expectations. By offering detailed insight into model decision logic and cross-system dependencies, ActiveFence bridges the gap between enterprise AI governance policies and real-time enforcement within distributed third-party environments (Gartner, 2025).

4.6. Aim Security

Aim Security delivers a comprehensive security framework for safeguarding generative AI workflows across enterprise applications. The Aim platform addresses key threat vectors including prompt injection, sensitive data leakage, and prompt chaining—issues that have become increasingly relevant as vendors incorporate large language models (LLMs) into customer-facing tools. Aim provides continuous monitoring and runtime controls for third-party AI interactions, enabling enterprises to secure embedded AI assets and assess vendor compliance with AI risk policies. Of particular relevance to TPRM, the platform enables visibility into AI agents, model endpoints, and inference-layer activities across vendor environments. By integrating with Data Security Posture Management (DSPM) platforms and providing runtime policy enforcement, Aim Security allows organizations to extend their risk control perimeters beyond the enterprise boundary. Its support for red-teaming simulations and zero-trust access models makes it well-suited for organizations seeking to evaluate and contain the risks introduced by generative AI dependencies within third-party systems (Gartner, 2025).

4.7. CalypsoAI

CalypsoAI's Inference Defense platform is designed to secure the last-mile of LLM interactions—where users and systems directly consume or act upon AI-generated outputs. This is particularly relevant for TPRM, as many third-party vendors are embedding models into platforms used for decision-making, document automation, or customer communication. CalypsoAI enables real-time monitoring of model inference sessions and applies dynamic risk scoring to detect anomalies, hallucinations, or output drift. The platform also integrates a continuous feedback loop, allowing security teams to fine-tune response strategies and escalation paths based on evolving third-party behavior. In the TPRM context, this empowers enterprises to assess not only vendor security posture but also the reliability and riskiness of vendor-deployed AI systems in production. By embedding explainability modules and red-teaming tools, CalypsoAI facilitates informed risk classification of third-party tools, supporting GRC alignment and proactive threat mitigation for AI-powered workflows beyond the organization's immediate control (Gartner, 2025).

4.8. AIShield (Bosch)

AIShield, developed by Bosch, offers a suite of tools designed to provide end-to-end security for machine learning systems, including threat detection, red teaming, and AI vulnerability scanning. The platform's core offerings—AISpectra and Guardian—are purpose-built for DevSecOps integration, allowing organizations to test, secure, and monitor third-party AI components across the supply chain. For TPRM use cases, AIShield is particularly useful in evaluating AI/ML modules embedded within vendor software. It helps identify weaknesses like adversarial susceptibility, model inversion risks, and insecure data pathways. Moreover, AIShield integrates with SIEM platforms, enabling continuous monitoring and incident response coordination. Its compatibility with enterprise governance frameworks and AI risk models allows procurement and security teams to assess compliance before onboarding vendors. As AI adoption becomes pervasive among suppliers and SaaS providers, tools like AIShield ensure that AI-powered third-party applications remain within operational risk thresholds and do not become vectors for AI-specific vulnerabilities (Gartner, 2025).

4.9. AppSOC AI

AppSOC AI is an emerging platform that provides AI supply chain security, model validation, and post-deployment AI posture management. Designed to identify and mitigate risks from third-party machine learning models, AppSOC AI enables organizations to scan vendor tools for insecure AI deployments, misconfigured APIs, or latent vulnerabilities in inference pipelines. Its model validation engine supports black-box and white-box testing, making it applicable even when vendors operate as closed platforms. For TPRM professionals, AppSOC offers value by automating red-teaming tasks across third-party LLMs, and by surfacing evidence of risky model behavior—including unauthorized data sharing or misaligned outputs. Additionally, its Responsible AI filter ensures that AI-generated content adheres to defined ethical and legal parameters. By embedding trust analytics and anomaly detection at the model layer, AppSOC equips enterprises to better understand and govern the behavior of AI tools used within their third-party ecosystem, closing a critical gap in traditional TPRM frameworks (Gartner, 2025).

5. CONCLUSION

This comprehensive survey underscores the transformative impact of Artificial Intelligence (AI), particularly Natural Language Processing (NLP) and Large Language Models (LLMs), in modernizing Third-Party Risk Management (TPRM). By leveraging AI capabilities such as semantic search, anomaly detection, predictive analytics, and RAG-based assessments, organizations are increasingly able to automate compliance workflows, improve vendor visibility, and mitigate cyber threats with greater agility and precision.

Tools like NLP Bots and AgraBOT exemplify the power of combining automation with intelligence. NLP Bots, with their capacity to classify vendor sentiment and compliance alignment in near real time, drastically reduce onboarding time and human effort. Meanwhile, AgraBOT's sophisticated RAG framework not only ensures contextual accuracy but also introduces a degree of evidence-backed traceability rarely seen in traditional security questionnaires. These systems illustrate how AI can not only scale TPRM but also instill a more nuanced understanding of third-party risks.

Academic innovations such as AIRMF and ProveRAG highlight the potential of AI in high-complexity, high-stakes environments. AIRMF's machine learning-based risk registers for Distributed Agile Software Development (DASD) and ProveRAG's automated CVE analysis pipeline with self-critique mechanisms exemplify how AI is pushing the boundaries of predictive precision, continuous monitoring, and explainability. Likewise, Hu et al.'s incorporation of supply chain topology into ML frameworks reflects the importance of context-aware, ecosystem-level modeling for systemic risk management.

On the commercial front, the TPRM market has evolved from compliance tools to intelligent orchestration platforms. Vendors like Interos, BitSight, FICO, and ComplyScore offer foundational AI-powered risk visibility and compliance automation. However, the recent wave of specialized solutions—ActiveFence, CalypsoAI, AIShield—marks a shift toward AI-native features such as prompt injection defense, runtime monitoring, and LLM governance. These tools address emerging risks associated with AI itself, particularly as vendors increasingly embed generative AI within their services.

Yet, despite these advances, critical challenges persist. Many AI models remain opaque, raising issues related to auditability, bias, and legal defensibility. The vulnerability of LLMs to hallucinations, jailbreaks, and adversarial prompts introduces new attack surfaces. Moreover, limited standardization, inconsistent data availability, and proprietary vendor lock-in pose barriers to interoperability and trust. As regulatory scrutiny around AI intensifies, organizations must adopt governance practices that emphasize model transparency, human-in-the-loop validation, and ethical safeguards.

Future directions for AI in TPRM must therefore focus on secure and interpretable architectures. Reinforcement learning, prompt tuning, and federated data sharing offer promising technical pathways, while XAI and HITL systems help maintain stakeholder confidence and regulatory compliance. Moreover, aligning AI-driven TPRM tools with enterprise Governance, Risk, and Compliance (GRC) platforms and Security Information and Event Management (SIEM) systems will be essential for unified risk visibility and rapid response.

In conclusion, AI-based TPRM holds immense promise in revolutionizing how enterprises detect, assess, and mitigate third-party risks. But realizing this potential requires a thoughtful blend of technical innovation, ethical stewardship, and cross-domain collaboration. As organizations prepare for a future defined by AI-driven ecosystems, investing in explainability, accountability, and system resilience will be key to achieving both security and trust in the digital supply chain.

ACKNOWLEDGMENT

The authors would like to express their sincere gratitude to those who contributed to the successful completion of this work. We thank Harsha Vardhan Meka for his valuable contributions to the additional studies, specifically the analysis on Supply Chain Characteristics as Predictors of Cyber Risk. We also acknowledge Kush Shah for his insights and support in extending the study of ProveRAG: Enhancing Vulnerability Analysis with Retrieval-Augmented LLMs.

REFERENCES

Abualhaija, S.. (2022, November). COREQQA: A compliance requirements understanding using question answering tool. In *Proceedings of the 30th ACM Joint European Software Engineering Conference and Symposium on the Foundations of Software Engineering* (pp. 1682–1686). ACM. DOI: 10.1145/3540250.3558926

Ahmed, T., ... (2023, May). Recommending root-cause and mitigation steps for cloud incidents using large language models. In 2023 IEEE/ACM 45th International Conference on Software Engineering (ICSE) (pp. 1737–1749). IEEE. DOI: 10.1109/ICSE48619.2023.00149

Aktas, E. U.. (2023, November). Issue report validation in an industrial context. In *Proceedings of the 31st ACM Joint European Software Engineering Conference and Symposium on the Foundations of Software Engineering* (pp. 2026–2031). DOI: 10.1145/3611643.3613887

Aliane, N., & Zakariya, A. (2023). Enhancing cyber security resilience in the industrial sector: A comprehensive framework for third-party risk management. *International Journal of Cyber Criminology*, *17*(2), 262–283.

Allgeier, H. (2020, August 27). Jennifer Bisceglie honored as EY Entrepreneur of the Year® 2020 Mid-Atlantic Award finalist. Interos Inc. Retrieved December 12, 2020, from https://www.interos.ai/bisceglie-ey-entrepreneur-of-the-year/

Arazzi, M., ... (2023). NLP-based techniques for cyber threat intelligence. arXiv preprint arXiv:2311.08807.

Arora, S., & Ramteke, V. (2024, November). Revolutionizing Third Party Risk Management Using Generative AI and RAG. In *2024 First International Conference on Data, Computation and Communication (ICDCC)* (pp. 16-22). IEEE. DOI: 10.1109/ICDCC62744.2024.10961910

BitSight Technologies. (2022). BitSight Security Ratings Platform [White paper].

BitSight Technologies Inc. et al. (2020). Understand your security rating | BitSight Security Ratings. Retrieved December 12, 2020, from https://www.bitsight.com/understand-your-rating

Carrns, A. (2012, May 10). Is that credit score a FICO, or a FICO 8? Bucks Blog. Retrieved December 12, 2020, from https://bucks.blogs.nytimes.com/2012/05/10/is-that-credit-score-a-fico-or-a-fico-8/

Dastidar, S. G., & Chatterjee, S. (2013, May). Distributed software development: Experience and recommendation. In 2013 3rd International Workshop on Collaborative Teaching of Globally Distributed Software Development (CTGDSD) (pp. 11-14). IEEE.

Deloitte. (2023). *Third-party governance and risk management*. Deloitte Insights.

Đ , T. T., & Tr n, K. (2021). The combination of robotic process automation (RPA) and chatbot for business applications.

Edu, J.. (2022, October). Exploring the security and privacy risks of chatbots in messaging services. In *Proceedings of the 22nd ACM Internet Measurement Conference* (pp. 581–588). DOI: 10.1145/3517745.3561433

Face, H. (2023a). Flan-T5. Retrieved from https://huggingface.co/google/flan-t5-xl

Face, H. (2023b). all-mpnet-base-v2. Retrieved from https://huggingface.co/transformers/all-mpnet-base-v2

Fayyazi., ... (2024). ProveRAG: Provenance-Driven Vulnerability Analysis with Automated Retrieval-Augmented LLMs. arXiv preprint arXiv:2410.17406.

Gao, Y., ... (2023). Retrieval-augmented generation for large language models: A survey. arXiv preprint arXiv:2312.10997, 2.

Gartner. (2025, February). Market Guide for AI Trust, Risk and Security Management.

Glisson, B. G., ... (2021). A survey of artificial intelligence in cybersecurity. In Proceedings of the IEEE International Conference on Artificial Intelligence for Cybersecurity. Retrieved from https://ieeexplore.ieee.org/document/9458190

Hoda, R., Salleh, N., & Grundy, J. (2018). The rise and evolution of agile software development. *IEEE Software*, *35*(5), 58–63. DOI: 10.1109/MS.2018.290111318

Hu, K.. (2022). Supply chain characteristics as predictors of cyber risk: A machine-learning assessment. arXiv. https://arxiv.org/abs/2210.15785

IBM. (2023). Watson Discovery. Retrieved from https://www.ibm.com/products/watson-discovery

Jo, T. (2019). Text mining. *Studies in Big Data*, *45*, 1–373. PMID: 31495561

Kahya, M. D., & Seneler, Ç. (2018, September). Geographical distance challenges in distributed agile software development: Case study of a global company. In 2018 3rd International Conference on Computer Science and Engineering (UBMK) (pp. 78-83). IEEE.

Keskin, O. F., Caramancion, K. M., Tatar, I., Raza, O., & Tatar, U. (2021). Cyber third-party risk management: A comparison of non-intrusive risk scoring reports. *Electronics (Basel)*, *10*(10), 1168. DOI: 10.3390/electronics10101168

Keskin, O. F., Caramancion, K. M., Tatar, I., Raza, O., & Tatar, U. (2021). Cyber third-party risk management: A comparison of non-intrusive risk scoring reports. *Electronics (Basel)*, *10*(10), 1168. DOI: 10.3390/electronics10101168

Khanna, E.. (2021, August). Artificial intelligence-based risk management framework for distributed agile software development. In *Proceedings of the 2021 8th International Conference on Signal Processing and Integrated Networks (SPIN)* (pp. 657–660). IEEE.

Khanna, E., Popli, R., & Chauhan, N. (2022). Identification and classification of risk factors in distributed agile software development. *Journal of Web Engineering*, *21*(6), 1831–1851. DOI: 10.13052/jwe1540-9589.2164

Kim, J. S.. (2023). The impact of artificial intelligence on threat intelligence systems. *Information Systems Frontiers*, •••, 25.

Lee, J., & Banerjee, A. (2023). Explainability and ethics in AI for risk assessment. *AI Ethics Journal*, *5*(1), 17–29.

Lee, R. B. (2023). AI-based external risk posture assessments. Cybersecurity Review, 4(1).

Lester, B., ... (2021). The power of scale for parameter-efficient prompt tuning. arXiv preprint arXiv:2104.08691. DOI: 10.18653/v1/2021.emnlp-main.243

Li, C., ... (2023). Large language models understand and can be enhanced by emotional stimuli. arXiv preprint arXiv:2307.11760.

Ma, J., & Zhao, Y. (2020). NLP applications in compliance monitoring. *Journal of Cybersecurity Intelligence and Cybercrime*, *3*(1).

MacGlashan, J. (2017, July). Interactive learning from policy-dependent human feedback. In *Proceedings of the International Conference on Machine Learning* (pp. 2285–2294). PMLR.

Mohta, Y.. (2024, May). NLP-enabled bot for managing third-party risk. In *Proceedings of the 2024 International Conference on Computational Intelligence and Computing Applications (ICCICA)* (Vol. 1, pp. 131–135). DOI: 10.1109/ICCICA60014.2024.10584983

NicCanna. C., et al. (2021, June). Globally distributed development during COVID-19. In Proceedings of the 2021 IEEE/ACM 8th International Workshop on Software Engineering Research and Industrial Practice (SER&IP) (pp. 18–25). IEEE.

Odzaly, E. E., Greer, D., & Stewart, D. (2018). Agile risk management using software agents. *Journal of Ambient Intelligence and Humanized Computing*, *9*(3), 823–841. DOI: 10.1007/s12652-017-0488-2

Radford, A.. (2019). Language models are unsupervised multitask learners. *OpenAI Blog*, *1*(8), 9.

Sadgrove, K. (2016). *The complete guide to business risk management*. Routledge. DOI: 10.4324/9781315614915

Scarfone, K., & Mell, P. (2021). Guide to intrusion detection and prevention systems (IDPS) (NIST Special Publication 800-94). NIST.

Schön, E. M.. (2020, May). Improving risk management in a scaled agile environment. In *International Conference on Agile Software Development* (pp. 132–141). Springer International Publishing. DOI: 10.1007/978-3-030-49392-9_9

Sharma, S., & Jain, A. (2020). Role of sentiment analysis in social media security and analytics. *Wiley Interdisciplinary Reviews. Data Mining and Knowledge Discovery*, *10*(5), e1366. DOI: 10.1002/widm.1366

Sharmeen, N., & Hassan, M. M. (2018). Machine learning and deep learning methods for cybersecurity. *IEEE Access : Practical Innovations, Open Solutions*, *6*, 33752–33781. DOI: 10.1109/ACCESS.2018.2848966

Shrivastava, S. V., & Rathod, U. (2015). Categorization of risk factors for distributed agile projects. *Information and Software Technology*, *58*, 373–387. DOI: 10.1016/j.infsof.2014.07.007

Simmons, K., & Miller, D. (2022). Third-party data breaches: An escalating risk. *Cyber Risk Review*, *10*(2), 33–41.

Systems, A., ... (n.d.). ComplyScore signs partnership with Qualys. Retrieved December 11, 2020, from https://www.atlassystems.com/recent-update_news/complyscore-signs-partnership-with-qualys/

Tamersoy, A.. (2021). Vendor risk scoring using public data sources. *IBM Journal of Research and Development*, *65*(2/3).

Tiron-Tudor, A., & Deliu, D. (2022). Reflections on the human-algorithm complex duality perspectives in the auditing process. *Qualitative Research in Accounting & Management*, *19*(3), 255–285.

Toslali, M., ... (2024, July). AgraBOT: Accelerating Third-Party Security Risk Management in Enterprise Setting through Generative AI. In Companion Proceedings of the 32nd ACM International Conference on the Foundations of Software Engineering (pp. 74–79).

Tounsi, A., & Temimi, M. (2023). A systematic review of natural language processing applications for hydrometeorological hazards assessment. *Natural Hazards*, *116*(3), 2819–2870. DOI: 10.1007/s11069-023-05842-0 PMID: 36776702

Yu, T.. (2020). Behavior-based insider threat detection using AI. *IEEE Transactions on Dependable and Secure Computing*, *17*(1).

Zahedi, M. H., et al. (2023). Risk management framework in Agile software development methodology. International Journal of Electrical & Computer Engineering (2088-8708), 13(4).

Zeng, K., & Wang, C. (2022). AI-driven policy mapping for third party risk. *Computers & Security*, •••, 107.

Chapter 2
Enhancing Audit Reporting Through AI-Powered Solutions

Tanisha Ahuja
https://orcid.org/0009-0004-1051-5427
University at Buffalo, SUNY, USA

Aanchal Ahuja
https://orcid.org/0009-0003-6471-204X
University at Buffalo, SUNY, USA

ABSTRACT

Artificial intelligence and its usage are rapidly growing. Various business functions have already started utilizing the benefits of AI for their tasks. With time, the complexity of information systems is also increasing, leading to extensive audits. As a result, conventional audit practices require additional manual checks to ensure the effectiveness of controls. Integrating AI with audits would provide relief to auditors by automating repetitive tasks. Core AI technologies and their application potential in the audit process are discussed in the following study. The focus of the paper mainly lies on how we can improve the audit reporting process through the implementation of various AI/ML solutions, automating the process and enabling auditors to deliver audit reports quickly. This implementation needs to be regulated to ensure the reliability of AI systems is maintained; hence, an overview of the major AI standards is discussed in the paper.

DOI: 10.4018/979-8-3373-3078-5.ch002

1. INTRODUCTION

Information Systems (IS) are beneficial to almost all organizations in today's modern era. These systems help manage and process data, helping to increase efficiency by streamlining business processes. IS provides real-time data for analyses and better decision-making. Additionally, these systems ensure the security of data, save cost, support business scalability, assist in customer complaint resolution, and aid seamless collaboration and communication among internal employees as well as with external stakeholders. Hence, Information Systems are the backbone of an organization, and it lays a strong foundation for effective operations of various functional domains.

With rapid technological evolution and innovation such as big data (Lazer & Radford, 2017), cloud computing, artificial intelligence (AI), internet of things, generative AI, etc., massive amounts of data are being generated every day for which organizations have to utilize more advanced systems to manage it. This leads to increased complexity of advanced information systems. However, increased dependence on these sophisticated systems comes with its own challenges. Since these systems handle a large volume of data, both critical and non-critical, IS becomes more prone to cybersecurity attacks, data loss, data overload, data privacy, system downtime, compliance, and regulatory risks. These can have a huge impact on an organization's finances, reputation, and legal standing. Hence, ensuring all the Information Systems within an organization work efficiently has become the need of the hour. As a result, auditing these systems regularly is very important. A thorough review of informational assets not only provides confirmation on the effective operations of these systems to stakeholders but also assures system compliance with laws, regulations, and policies along with confidentiality, availability, and integrity of IS data.

Traditional audit practices involve a lot of manual checking of Information Systems in terms of ensuring data correctness, evaluation of control efficiency, assessing compliance of the systems with regulatory requirements, assessing risk appetite, reviewing logs for unauthorized access, etc. Though such audit practices are effective in evaluating systems, it can be a time-consuming process involving a lot of repetitive tasks and is prone to human errors. Additionally, with increasing amounts of data and the complexity of new technology, the process is not able to reach its highest potential and, at times, can become overwhelming for the auditors. This modern problem can be solved with the help of a modern solution.

Artificial Intelligence (AI) (Chiappini, 2024) is a rapidly advancing technology which is now being highly utilized in various sectors and industries, increasing efficiency, productivity and user experience. Artificial Intelligence is the ability of machines to think, perceive and act like human beings. It simulates intelligence exhibited by humans to take decisions and generates required output. Several companies and functional domains are now heavily integrating AI into their daily tasks to leverage its benefits. This helps to automate processes and reduce human workload.

Artificial Intelligence can benefit IS audit workflows as well to a great extent. It is the perfect solution that can overcome the challenges of traditional audit practices in this digitally advanced era. We know that auditors have to analyze and manage large amounts of data every day, which is very time-consuming and tiring at times. AI in IS auditing has the potential to analyze large datasets to recognize risks and uncover patterns with a good level of accuracy while achieving high speed.

For instance, predictive analysis enables risk assessment by analyzing historical data from past audit reports and forecasts high-risk areas to prioritize our audit scope accordingly. Natural language processing (NLP) can be utilized to create a quick checklist for auditors by scanning past audit reports, regulatory requirements, and other documents. Additionally, Robotic process automation (RPA) can automate the sharing of findings based on initial analysis of SOPs and other available documents and prepopulate a dashboard or defined report template, reducing human work. AI can not only assist in increasing audit efficiency, but it also can decrease audit risk. In essence, it helps automate repetitive manual tasks like keyword-based analysis, reporting audit-based quantification of issues, continuous control monitoring for business processes, etc., eventually enhancing the efficiency of the audit process. Additionally, audit risk can be decreased through AI by providing more sample data for analysis of results for testing.

The list goes on and on, suggesting that the usage of AI has immense potential in the domain of IS audit and can transform the way audit workflow is carried out. In regards with this research paper, we will be focusing on the use of AI in audit reporting and discuss how AI in the audit reporting process will revolutionize reactive reporting to predictive reporting, which will not only highlight the existing risks and vulnerabilities but also forecast potential risks before it comes into existence. The study will deep dive into the capability AI carries to increase reporting process efficiency.

Audit Reporting (Faccia et al., 2020) is an important step while performing an audit of a company's information systems. The main objective of audit reporting is to formally document the results of the audit, serving as a closure to the audit process. This report must be effective in helping the auditee, senior management, and other stakeholders understand the areas of weaknesses existing in the system and the corrective actions that are needed to mitigate risks arising from those vulnerabilities. Audit reports act as a reference for the future when the auditee is being investigated. It also enhances audit credibility, which highly depends on the quality of the report drafted by the auditors. All the findings in the report should be supported by evidence, which further enhances credibility and ensures reliability. Since this step of the audit process is so crucial, it should be made sure that the report is well-developed and well-written so that it reflects the true testament to the quality of the audit process carried out.

One of the primary ways by which important stakeholders of an organization, such as the board of directors and senior management, evaluate the quality of an audit is through an audit report. As this last step of the audit cycle is so crucial, incorporating the use of artificial intelligence while carrying out the reporting phase increases efficiency and consistency. Specific activities such as gathering report requirements, drafting reports, and issuing reports in a timely manner can be streamlined better with the assistance of AI. For instance, NLP, a subset of AI technology, can be applied to scan all evidence gathered by the auditor and draft certain sections of the report consisting of all the audit findings from that evidence. Similarly, Machine Learning (ML) can be used to analyze those audit findings and provide recommendations for remediations with minimal human intervention. There are many ways by which we can utilize Artificial Intelligence to make the audit reporting process more consistent and less tedious. We will explore all these scenarios and discover various methods through in-depth evaluation ahead in this paper.

The existing research in this area tends to stay at a high level, primarily focusing on financial audits while often overlooking the reporting stage of the audit lifecycle. This paper examines practical methods for integrating AI across all stages of the audit cycle, emphasizing particular AI and machine learning techniques and models. It explicitly throws light on the 'Audit reporting' phase of the Information Systems (IS) Audits. Further, the paper talks about the compliance standards that an organization may adopt to protect data security and privacy, addressing the risks and challenges an organization might face when developing AI-powered solutions for automating audit-related tasks. This paper can also act as a guide for the auditors who are planning to integrate AI into their daily job responsibilities to improve efficiency and audit accuracy while avoiding any compromise to data security. By automating manual tasks, auditors can invest more time to develop analytical solutions to address audit findings and streamline the overall audit process.

2. BACKGROUND

IS Audit (Sayankar, 2024) came into existence in the late 1960s, when computers began to be highly utilized in various companies and businesses. The introduction of technical systems led to a need to assess the level of reliability and security these systems and the tools being used on them possess. Later, in the 1980s, mainframe information systems and databases started to function to store, collect, and analyze business data, enhancing the requirement for specialized audits for these mainstream information systems. Traditionally, many manual checks and methods were followed to test the security of the systems. Risks were evaluated based on vulnerabilities found in the system. Additionally, the effectiveness of controls to manage those risks was also calculated through predetermined manual testing. This was a tedious task to carry out, demanding a high volume of data analysis.

With organizations adopting data-driven approaches and methodologies, the use of information systems rapidly grew, and a shift towards more technologically enhanced ways of auditing those systems arose. Several tools were developed and began to be utilized by auditors to effectively assess the information systems. These mostly included:

- Audit management software to help track the overall audit process
- Data analytics and testing tools to perform analyses of large datasets quickly
- Monitoring tools enable auditors to have a continuous monitoring overhead over the systems for real-time insights
- Network and security auditing tools to evaluate the security of networks and systems, enabling auditors to perform vulnerability assessments.
- Database scanning tools to help assess databases efficiently
- Compliance management tools to ensure systems meet regulatory requirements
- Cloud and SaaS auditing tools help auditors keep track of user activities in cloud environments, analyze security risks, and testing of controls put in place
- Risk assessment tools to help auditors identify and evaluate risks
- Forensic audit tools assist in detecting digital evidence in case of fraud or data breaches
- Blockchain auditing tools support auditors in monitoring transactions, confirming the accuracy of data, and evaluating the security of blockchain applications.

These tools revolutionized the auditing of information system process and provided way to increase efficiency and accuracy. The usage of these tools depends on the type of audit being performed, needs of the functional domain audit is conducted in and intricacy of the system being audited. Such tools allow auditors to complete audits in timely fashion.

However, with the growing complexity of Information systems due to the rapid evolution of technology and the large amount of unstructured data being generated, audits have become more complex than ever. Even though the above-mentioned tools provide an advantage in conducting audits, they are still not sufficient. To meet this challenge, we need to integrate new-age technology that can handle the complexity and process large-scale data in modern information systems. This is where the benefits of artificial intelligence can be applied into existence. AI has the potential to automate routine tasks and processes, effectively reducing the cumbersome steps that would require human intervention.

Interestingly, Artificial intelligence has been around for decades, as opposed to most people's belief. The concept first arose in 1950 when Alan Turing, in his paper "Computing Machinery and Intelligence," introduced the Turing test to understand the answer to the question, "Can machines think?". (The Birth of Artificial Intelligence (AI) Research I Science and Technology, n.d.) However, his focus was to check whether computer programs could mimic humans and fool an interrogator. He never coined the term but laid the foundation of a possible idea. In 1956, John McCarthy introduced the term "Artificial Intelligence" at the Dartmouth Conference. One of the notable contributions in the 1960s was James Slagle's program SAINT (symbolic automatic integrator), the first expert system that could solve calculus problems like humans. However, the focus of research on AI decreased in the next two decades.

The 1990s and early 2000s were revolutionary periods for AI as research into the field increased with the practical invention of AI systems. The 2010s was the golden age, the moment deep learning exploded onto the scene, bringing with it neural networks that were smarter than anything ever seen before. Tasks like recognizing faces and understanding speech, once reserved for science fiction, became the new normal. Virtual assistants, recommendation systems, the AI we all know today- they arrived, they dominated, and they didn't look back.

At present, AI is at its full bloom, evolving at a pace that's unstoppable. From Healthcare and Finance to Cybersecurity, all have integrated AI's power to predict, diagnose and secure in unimaginable ways. Now Generative AI and quantum computing, advanced AI has taken a lead, waiting to be explored, to push AI's reach even further into the unknown potential. AI has been changing the world, and its potential is limitless.

2.1. The AI Ecosystem

The following are some major subsets of Artificial Intelligence:

1. Machine learning (ML): It's a subset of artificial Intelligence that trains a system through algorithms to make informed decisions. Here the system is trained by large volumes of data, learning from insights (Jordan & Mitchell, 2015). The performance of Machine Learning algorithms applied on a system improves from experience as they are trained over and over.

2. Natural Language Processing (NLP): This artificial intelligence-powered technology focuses on teaching systems to understand human language. This enables systems to interpret and generate human language, allowing systems to retrieve information from a large document, analyze sentiments from human-readable content, translate language, speech recognition, etc. (Khurana et al., 2023)
3. Deep Learning: It's a subset of Machine Learning and is trained to solve complex problems mimicking human brain functionality. This is a more advanced technology that is trained by using neural networks, layers on interconnected nodes called neurons, to process data at every layer. This technology allows image recognition, recommendation systems, anomaly detection, etc. (Khoei et al., 2023)
4. Generative AI: The most advanced technology under the umbrella of artificial intelligence is Generative AI. This creates new content, such as text, videos, images, and even music (Nah et al., 2023). The content generated is totally new, given this technology is trained by Generative Adversarial Networks (GAN), Variational Autoencoders (VAE), and Transformer models.

While Predictive Analysis is a technique that utilizes statistical algorithms, machine learning models, and data mining (Aitchison & Dunsmore, 1975). This makes predictions about future events or trends by analyzing current and historical data through the identification of patterns and relationships in the data. The predictive Analysis technique helps to make data-driven decisions for various functional domains while improving the efficiency of tasks and reducing costs. It is widely used in businesses such as healthcare, finance, and marketing to foresee customer behavior, detect fraud, and improve operations.

An important alternative technique that is often confused with AI is Robotic Process Automation (RPA)(Wewerka, J., & Reichert, M., 2020). It is, in fact, a software technology that automates repetitive tasks by using bots, reducing human workload. This is generally used where a clear set of rules exist to perform a task, and the frequency of such tasks is in large numbers. This technology is used in finance, accounting, customer service, human resources, IT operations, and even healthcare for administrative tasks.

However, this is different than how an AI model functions. RPA lacks cognitive abilities to make informed decisions, and it can't handle unstructured data. RPA is not able to learn from experience and improve over time as an AI model would. Hence, even though RPA mimics human actions, it can't mimic human intelligence. RPA does provide benefits of its own- cost savings, increased productivity for defined tasks, improved compliance, and improved overall customer satisfaction. So, in order to leverage benefits as well as to meet the setbacks of RPA, it is generally used in combination with machine learning. This way, RPA's potential grows, and the combination is able to deliver intelligent automation systems, enabling a machine to handle both simple routine and complex decision-driven tasks. AI and RPA complement each other and act as powerful technologies.

2.2. Use of AI in Other Types of Reporting

The technology of artificial intelligence has already been integrated into various types of reporting across several industries and is already doing wonders. Following are some of the use cases of reporting using AI:

1. Financial Reporting: AI is automating financial analysis, such as profit and loss statements, balance sheets, and cash flow reports. AI works with a high volume of data to highlight inconsistencies for correct reporting, avoiding human error and enhancing productivity (Khorsheed et al., 2024). Moreover, AI-driven development, like chatbots or automated systems, enables real-time financial activity monitoring. It, in turn, will grant finance teams to build financial reports at will, track spending, and assure regulatory compliance in real-time. Additionally, Fraud is currently detected by highlighting inconsistencies in financial data. By examining transaction patterns, AI systems may independently detect suspicious activity that results in much quicker, more accurate fraud detection reports.
2. Sales and Marketing Reporting: Artificial intelligence is used to evaluate massive volumes of data on customer engagement. Marketing professionals receive reports on consumer behavior, preferences, and trends. For example, AI can track shopping behaviors across many channels and forecast future spending trends to create targeted marketing reports. This efficiently enables to get insights into customer behavior pattern (Sun et al., 2020). AI-powered tools also measure and report on the efficacy of marketing efforts. It provides useful insights into click-through rates, engagement, and ROI utilizing AI. As a result, marketing teams modify their approach in response to such findings. Moreover, AI guides the sales force toward predictive lead scoring reporting by analyzing previous data to identify leads who are most likely to become clients and making on-demand adjustments to lead creation strategies.
3. Human Resources and Workforce Reporting: AI-powered tools monitor employees' performance based on key performance indicators and generate reports highlighting their productivity, goals achieved, and improvement points. These reports assist HR departments in decision-making for promotions, increments, and training programs. Artificial Intelligence models also predict employee turnover by analyzing their behavior, job satisfaction, and historical trends. This, in turn, enables organizations to generate reports that help inform retention strategies and workforce planning. Moreover, AI is also being used to generate diversity

and inclusion reporting. Through the analysis of employee demographics, hiring trends, and pay equity, AI tools enable organizations to ensure that they achieve their diversity goals and meet their reporting requirements.

4. Customer Service and Support Reporting: For customer input reporting, AI is now being used to review customer insights from various channels like surveys, social media, and support tickets. It then generates reports on sentiment analysis (Gunasekaran, 2023), outlining regions of consumer satisfaction, pain points, and areas that need further improvement. Additionally, AI-powered chatbots are utilized to generate comprehensive reports from client interactions, like frequent requests, resolution time, and satisfaction rate. It helps customer service personnel improve their responses to offer better experiences to customers.
5. IT and Cybersecurity Reporting: AI is used to a great extent in cybersecurity to generate automated incident reports. These reports detail security breaches, potential threats, and system vulnerabilities detected in real time to allow for quicker responses against cyberattacks. Moreover, the AI-powered systems continuously monitor the network traffic and generate reports regarding unusual patterns or potential security incidents. Such reports help the IT teams to keep systems secure and up. Additionally, AI has automated vulnerability assessments in a few industries and develops reports that identify weaknesses in software and systems. These reports help IT teams focus on patching and enhancing security protocols.
6. Supply Chain and Operations Reporting: The technology of AI has started being integrated for Inventory and Demand Forecasting. AI models create reports that forecast future demand based on previous sales data, seasonal trends, and market circumstances. These reports allow businesses to optimize their inventories and cut costs associated with overstocking or stockouts. Moreover, AI technologies help monitor global supply chain activities such as supplier performance, logistics, interruptions and generate risk reports. By analyzing data from many sources, AI detects hazards such as supply delays, pricing swings, and geopolitical disruptions, allowing businesses to alter their strategy. However, this reporting strategy is not adopted widely and currently has a lot of untapped potential in this sector.

3. EXTANT RESEARCH

Artificial Intelligence integrated into IS audit reporting is a growing field of study that is still exploring the potential of AI to improve the accuracy and efficiency of the audit process, as well as risk assessment.

The article titled "ChatGPT and Leveraging Artificial Intelligence in Auditing" (Jaleel, 2023) discussed the evolution of audit practices from adopting agile methodology to artificial intelligence. The article further explores the potential of ChatGPT in basic audit program development through an example of an IT general control program generated by ChatGPT. Jaleel focuses on the benefits of using ChatGPT to save time for both senior-level and junior-level auditors. It also evaluated the safeguards to be considered, such as avoiding the use of sensitive data in ChatGPT, the bias the AI model carries at times, and the importance of training AI using appropriate datasets.

The research titled "Impact of intelligent decision aids on expert and novice decision-makers judgments" defines expert systems as computer-based, software-intensive applications that capture the knowledge of an individual or group of experts in a specific field to make suggestions that allow users to make decisions that are smarter than they would make on their own. The systems seek to replicate expert judgment as a structured combination of procedures and technology. As Arnold et al. (2004) note, expert systems, or intelligent decision aids, can enhance decision quality for experts when appropriately matched to the user and can be beneficial in audits, but can have a detrimental impact on novices if the aid's expertise greatly exceeds that of the user.

The paper "Pressure and performance in accounting decision settings: Paradoxical effects of incentives, feedback, and justification." discusses that regardless of what technology or tools an auditor employs, the final responsibility for the judgment remains with them. Just as auditors sometimes call in experts, estate valuers, or lawyers, say to help them reach their conclusions, AI tools are simply assistants employed to perform a specific task. (Ashton, 1990) It is up to the auditor to make sure that these tools are actually useful, sound, and appropriate for the job. Naturally, the use of AI in audit judgments is a two-edged sword. Should it fail, then either the auditor will be held responsible for not utilizing tools available to him/her effectively or for overreliance upon them without using their own professional judgment.

The technology of Artificial Intelligence has immense potential in the field of audit as it would not only save time, but it would also build resilient organizations, as discussed in an article by ISACA, "How AI Is Transforming Audit, Risk and Compliance" (Karp, 2024). The article suggests that AI can actually reduce the burden of regulatory compliance for audit, risk, and compliance teams by expediting the adoption of new compliance frameworks, Reducing non-compliance risk, and Horizon scanning and monitoring. Karp believes that with the use of AI, organizations can utilize data to the fullest and obtain data-driven insights. The article further explores cases where AI can be accommodated to organize unstructured data from policies, evidence requests, and risks. One such major use case is utilizing data visualization methods to suggest significant risks and trends. Karp highlights that irrespective of the benefits of AI, human oversight is essential for security and efficiency.

Dillard and Yuthas (2001), in their paper "A responsibility ethic for audit expert systems," approached the subject of expert systems in auditing from a different angle by considering the ethical dimension. Using Niebuhr's concept of "the responsible self," they highlighted the necessity of considering how these systems impact everyone involved—not solely the auditors, but all stakeholders. Their point was that ethics is not about rules but rather about relationships and ongoing interactions. They also recommended careful consideration of the potential long-term effects of people's actions and decisions on the system, as well as how it could affect them, prior to creating an expert system.

In paper "A fuzzy neural network for assessing the risk of fraudulent financial reporting", Lin, Hwang, and Becker (2003) tried to establish whether fuzzy logic and neural networks combined could offer a better method of detecting fraudulent financial reporting than the traditional statistical method or conventional neural networks. They concluded that this integrated method works well, offering a different approach to fraud detection. All the same, the system was more complicated than existing tools, and it was to be seen if companies were willing to use something so complicated in everyday audit usage.

Bell and Carcello (2000), in their paper "A decision aid for assessing the likelihood of fraudulent financial reporting," mentioned that they tried to develop a model that could detect the risk of fraudulent financial reporting by analyzing 77 actual observations where fraud had been present and 305 where fraud had not. They used an approach called logistic regression and based it on common red flags like weak internal controls, rapid growth, unusual profitability, or managers being deceptive or evasive with auditors. The model was much better than auditors at identifying fraud in actual fraud cases, though it did not do very much when applied to non-fraud cases. While it seems to be an asset because it focuses on important warning signs, the model's complexity means that it is more likely to be practical for large corporations than for small or medium-sized corporations.

The article "IS Audit in Practice: A Collaborative Approach to Assessing AI Risk" (Baxter, 2024) highlights both the challenges and opportunities that AI brings with itself. The article further highlights the dynamic nature of risk as it constantly changes. Risk categories include reputational, financial, regulatory, security, operational, and ethical while assessing risk associated with AI. Baxter suggests that audit and risk teams need to collaborate with business owners to understand and weigh the value and risks associated to implement controls through testing results.

"Broad, Regulatory Frameworks Needed to Responsibly Harness AI" (Menon, 2024) states that several regulations have been drafted to minimize the risks of AI all around the world. The article discusses the EU AI Act and how companies will be charged about 6% as a fine if they fail to adhere to the act. Menon further suggests that regulations are essential to ensure data protection, human rights safety, and underrepresentation. The article discusses the need to educate and spread awareness on the evolution of Machine learning algorithms to keep up to date with the changing technology and target risks that come with it.

The article published on ISACA titled "Regulating AI Tech is No Longer an Option: It's a Must!" (Harper, 2023) discusses the risks and dangers of AI and how even known names such as Italian data protection authority and Elon Musk publicly stated the same. The article further explores key issues, from bad actors using AI to attack systems to the lack of independent privacy and security audits of AI systems. Due to several key issues, Harper suggests that regulations for AI must be implemented to ensure the ethical use of AI. These regulations must be flexible to be integrated with the policies of enterprises around the world. The article focuses on striking a balance between human design and innovation to decrease risks and harness the benefits of AI.

Changchit and Holsapple (2004) in their paper "The development of an expert system for managerial evaluation of internal controls" discusses an important use case of advanced technology of expert systems. By utilizing these systems, organisations can bridge the knowledge gap between management and auditors via the sharing of the internal evaluation knowledge of the auditors. This helps managers gain a greater understanding of how internal controls operate, thus allowing them to possess improved control systems and more reliable and accurate financial information.

Research paper titled "Making It Possible for the Auditing of AI: A Systematic Review of AI Audits and AI Auditability" (Li & Goel, 2024) The integration of AI-based systems into organizations presents significant vulnerabilities that must be addressed; as a result, auditing AI systems becomes crucial for organizations. Current issues facing the AI audit profession include the lack of global AI policies and guidance, which could influence standards for AI audits as well as guidelines for AI development and operation. Standards for AI auditing are necessary, but so are measures to guarantee the proficiency of AI auditors in the field and create design guidelines for AI systems that enable audibility. Future AI systems must be easier to audit, account for, explain, reproduce, and make available.

According to "AI for Auditors: Challenges and Opportunities for Career Advancement" (ISACA, 2024), generative artificial intelligence has gained immense popularity in various sectors in 2023, which highlights the need to handle the use of AI responsibly. Fang believes that there is a huge opportunity to guide the use of AI in the audit domain, ensuring the adoption complies with integrity and accountability. Artificial intelligence also comes with challenges for auditors, emphasizing that despite AI and data analytics being amazing instruments, there is a lack of a framework guiding tactical AI implementation in the audit domain. Additionally, AI/ML algorithms are complex to understand, which could cause difficulty for auditors in auditing AI tools. Moreover, AI solutions are highly dependent on training data with complex lifecycles, and reliance on third-party foundational models poses difficulty in establishing accountability and transparency. ISACA has developed training courses to bridge this gap, assisting them to audit AI solutions comprehensively. The article emphasizes that organizations that do not involve auditors in the adoption of AI are at risk of facing the consequences such as brand damage, financial loss, business interruption, and compliance violation. Since AI security is crucial, an in-depth understanding of AI can provide an edge to auditors for their career development. Furthermore, this knowledge will empower auditors with better AI-related risk management and informed AI strategic insight to ensure regulatory compliance.

In the article "The Synergy Between Generative AI and IS Audit" (Lee, 2025), Lee highlights the transformational potential of generative AI (Gen AI) in information systems auditing. Lee believes Gen AI is expanding beyond the binary response to provide comprehensive reasons and will justify the efficacy of control efforts based on its expert opinion. Given the possibility of false results, professional judgment training is critical. During Gen AI training for IS audit purposes, firms should supply adequate data from past audit engagements for research, which should be checked to verify that the data quality is correct. Additionally, data privacy should be maintained when preparing training data for GenAI, including consent, masking data, and secure data storage while following local and national laws. While acknowledging the hazards of Gen AI, such as the likelihood of erroneous results, Lee calls for a balanced approach that capitalizes on Gen AI's potential to change IS auditing practice. Human auditors should not depend on Gen AI completely and should examine working papers to check for misinterpretation since Gen AI can't be held responsible in the legal world. Ultimately, human users should be accountable for IS audits.

Baldwin et al. (2006), in their paper "Opportunities for Artificial Intelligence Development in the Accounting Domain: The Case for Auditing. Intelligent Systems in Accounting, Finance, and Management," covers that the majority of AI research in accounting and auditing has been conducted by accounting researchers without the involvement of AI specialists. If accounting and AI experts collaborate across academic boundaries, research on AI for these tasks will improve. To enhance auditing and assurance, accounting researchers must establish partnerships with AI researchers and close the gap between the business and accounting domains and the computer science and AI domains. Additionally, the majority of AI research in accounting and auditing has used expert system technology. It is obvious that more sophisticated AI solutions can be developed to address specific auditing issues in greater detail. By using AI approaches like fuzzy logic, neural networks, and others, researchers can solve several audit and assurance task problems.

The increasing adoption of AI worldwide drives the importance of stringent auditing practices to ensure AI systems are implemented ethically, as highlighted in the article "AI Algorithm Audits: Key Control Considerations" (Prasad, 2024). Algorithmic auditing, the process of evaluating ML applications to assess utility, fairness, and potential bias, might be a new buzzword in the IT audit sector, but government authorities have been studying it for a while. This process is highly capable of identifying the logic underlying the output of AI-based systems, and the most recent set of laws has made algorithmic audits a crucial topic of interest for AI practitioners. However, it has its own challenges, including a lack of an established framework, no widely accepted precedents for dealing with AI use cases, and no consistent approach utilized by academics and regulators. Prasad suggests that refining this process is crucial to ensure reliable results. The article further talks about controls for auditors to keep in mind when auditing AI, such as system data input control, ensuring accuracy and completeness of training data, adversarial AI testing, identifying vulnerabilities through deceptive data input, AI model development, assuring appropriate design, testing, approvals are obtained, and continuous AI model monitoring, detecting anomalies or security concerns (if any). Prasad concludes by mentioning that through algorithmic audits, firms can improve the transparency, accountability, and trustworthiness of their AI systems.

"Artificial Intelligence Act: deal on comprehensive rules for trustworthy AI" (European Parliament, 2023) states that the European Union and Council agreed upon a provisional Artificial Intelligence Act. It was done to protect fundamental rights, democracy, the rule of law, and sustainable environmental integrity from high-risk AI, promote innovation, and make Europe a leader in this area. Some AI systems, such as those scoring individuals on their behavior or personal traits, influencing human behavior, and exploiting individuals' vulnerabilities (e.g., age, handicap, or social or economic status), are prohibited by the act. The article further mentions the obligations of high-risk systems, including a required basic rights impact assessment, among other regulations, which apply to the insurance and banking industries. AI systems deployed to affect election results and voter behavior are likewise rated as high-risk. People can file complaints and question the outputs of these systems. Further, guardrails for general AI systems are stated, such as disclosing training data, complying with EU copyright laws, and providing technical documentation, among a few. The act supports innovation and SMEs to protect them against the dominance of big tech giants. The AI Act penalizes non-compliance with fines depending on the infraction and firm size between 35 million euros (or 7% of worldwide revenue) and 7.5 million euros (or 1.5% of turnover).

Paper "Is artificial intelligence improving the audit process" (Fedyk et al., 2022) covers the examination whether AI enhances the audit process using information gathered from in-depth interviews with 17 audit partners from the top eight public accounting firms in the United States. Our empirical findings show notable improvements in quality since audit firms' investments in AI are linked to a considerable decrease in the frequency of restatements, particularly material restatements, and restatements pertaining to accruals and revenue recognition. These findings are driven mainly by auditors rather than their clients, and they hold up well, even accounting for auditors' expenditures in other technology. Furthermore, we discover early evidence that a shift towards a leaner process is linked to better audit quality: when audit companies invest in AI, they can reduce the fees they charge while lowering their audit workforces and demonstrating enhanced. The findings highlight how AI improves audit efficiency and quality. However, research in this paper on AI's effects on labor warns that the benefits of emerging technologies might not be shared equitably by all. Junior employees may suffer from the displacement we see years following AI investments, while audit firm partners gain from improved product quality, enhanced efficiency, and lower human expenses. In addition to providing helpful information for policymakers and industry leaders, we hope that our comprehensive datasets on labor and firm-level AI investments will pave the way for more extensive empirical studies on the wider effects of emerging technologies in accounting and auditing as well as other service-oriented sectors.

The ISACA Now Blog article titled "COBIT: A Practical Guide for AI Governance" (Coyne, 2025) mentions that AI has enormous potential benefits, but in their drive to utilize AI, corporations frequently miss one critical component: governance. While less spectacular than risk and less apparent than compliance, it provides the cornerstone for an organization's aims and objectives. Coyne suggests that COBIT is an appropriate fit for effective AI system governance. In this way, organizations can ensure that AI deployment aligns with strategic initiatives, identify and control AI risk, measure the success of AI deployment by setting metrics, place controls to ensure confidentiality, integrity, and availability of information within AI systems, and promote accountability. Coyne concludes by stating that governance is needed to protect organizations from potential risks while facilitating long-term development.

In the paper "The Uses of Advanced Information Technology in Audit Planning," Murphy and Brown (1992) discussed that risk analysis is a key driver of an effective audit plan. Risk analysis will lead auditors to determine the amount of evidence they must obtain and how to establish the correct materiality level for the audit. An easy summary of their work is: the higher the inherent risk, the more evidence you need, and the tighter the materiality level should be. They also discuss how the use of artificial intelligence in auditing can reduce all types of audit risk, whether inherent, control, or detection risk. Of these, inherent risk, essentially the risk that there is a material error in the financial statements before one even looks at internal controls, is the hardest to assess. Murphy and Brown also mention how some companies are already utilizing expert systems to help with this. These systems, often based on statistical models, can help auditors recognize potential risks and explain what factors such judgments are based on. Another approach uses questionnaires, where the system poses a series of questions to the auditor, scores the responses against a matrix, and then calculates an overall risk rating.

Omoteso (2012) in his paper "The Application of Artificial Intelligence in Auditing: Looking Back to the Future. Expert Systems with Applications" mentions numerous benefits of implementing AI in accounting and auditing were highlighted by in the study conducted in this research paper. Efficiency and effectiveness, consistency, a framework for audit activities, better communication and decision-making, increased staff training, developing novices' knowledge, and quicker decision-making are just a few of these advantages.

Another interesting paper, "How Artificial Intelligence Changes the Future of Accounting Industry. International Journal of Economics and Business Administration" (Suleiman et al., 2020), suggests that accountants and businesses will eventually be able to lower accounting expenses and add value to the accounting sector by shifting accountants' attention from the current tedious tasks to data-driven and analytics-based decision-making if they stay up to date with the ongoing advancements of AI in the accounting and auditing domain.

Stancheva-Todorova (2018), in "How Artificial Intelligence Is Challenging Accounting Profession. International Scientific Publications," suggests that knowledge dissemination should take an interdisciplinary approach, requiring the participation of experts and educators from a range of fields, such as big data, computer science, and engineering, information systems, statistics, and ethical concerns. In addition to teaching accounting information systems in the classic sense, academia should also teach data analytics, information and technology management, and many other topics. To introduce prospective accounting and audit practitioners and researchers to the field of artificial intelligence, business education must include principles of AI technology. As a result, there would be more opportunities for AI professionals to interact with accounting and auditing professionals. Last but not least, industry executives could participate in capstone projects that showcase the real-world issues that organizations face and allow.

Zemánková and the Department of Financial Accounting and Auditing, University of Economics, Prague (2019), in "Artificial Intelligence and Blockchain in Audit and Accounting," suggests that numerous moral and ethical questions are brought up by the use of artificial intelligence in accounting and auditing. It is necessary to find out and raise awareness about what ethical behavior in the field of artificial intelligence entails. The methods used to conduct fraud are evolving along with the applications and behaviors. White-collar crimes are taking on new forms.

Ucoglu (2020) in "Current Machine Learning Applications in Accounting and Auditing" mentions that by 2025, it is predicted that machine learning and artificial intelligence platforms would conduct 30% of business audits. The requirement for ethical governance in terms of execution is also brought forth by the profession's rapid development. Furthermore, regulatory supervision and advice are needed for the machine learning and artificial intelligence tools that accounting and auditing firms utilize in their operations.

Research paper "Analysis of the Impact of Artificial Intelligence Application on the Development of Accounting Industry" (Luo et al., 2018) covers that the initial lack of expertise, the poor return on investment, and the absence of necessary professional abilities and attributes are some of the issues related to the use of AI in the accounting and audit industry.

Doshi et al. (2020) in "Artificial Intelligence as a Paradoxical Digital Disruptor in the Accounting Profession: An Empirical Study amongst Accountants" discusses that as a digital disruptor, artificial intelligence has the "double impacting potential" to both ignite threats and create opportunities. As a result, it can either completely replace or supplement a career, casting doubt on the latter's long-term sustainability.

"An analysis of auditors' perceptions towards artificial intelligence and its contribution to audit quality" (Albawwat & Frijat, 2021) discusses that Data from 124 auditors working for regional audit firms in Jordan was gathered using an online survey. According to our findings, auditors believe that assisted and augmented AI systems are simple to use for auditing, but they believe that autonomous AI systems are more complex. Additionally, auditors believe autonomous AI systems are useless for auditing and underestimate their capabilities. The findings also show a notable variation in the three AI system types' perceived contributions to audit quality.

"The Emergence of Artificial Intelligence: How Automation is Changing Auditing" (Kokina & Davenport, 2017) includes An overview of the development of artificial intelligence in accounting and auditing is given in this study. We go over the possibilities of cognitive technologies as of right now and how they will affect human auditors and the auditing process in general. This paper also gives examples of how Big 4 accounting companies have implemented artificial intelligence in the sector. Lastly, this study highlights the implications for further research and addresses some possible biases related to the development and application of artificial intelligence.

Gu et al. (2024) in "Artificial intelligence co-piloted auditing" covers the concept of artificial intelligence co-piloted auditing, in which auditors collaborate with foundational models, showing how co-piloted auditing works, its various levels, and how it might improve the auditing environment. We offer a thorough process for optimizing OpenAI's GPT-4 model to handle a variety of auditing jobs in order to demonstrate the viability of co-piloted auditing.

Noordin et al. (2022), in "The Use of Artificial Intelligence and Audit Quality: An Analysis from the Perspectives of External Auditors in the UAE," suggests that AI may jeopardize the security of financial data. AI may be able to recognise private information that shouldn't be shared with other parties as it improves at finding patterns in data. This information may be used to perpetrate further crimes or to take advantage of financial institutions if it ended up in the wrong hands.

4. RESEARCH

4.1. Motivators Behind AI Implementation in Auditing

Artificial Intelligence integration in auditing information systems is a growing area of research that is influenced by a number of factors. Some of these factors include the opportunities AI offers, while others solve the obstacles auditors encounter in the digital revolution. The following are the significant factors that motivate AI integration in the audit process:

1. Big Data: Data generation has increased dramatically in the digital age, encompassing transactional records, consumer information, operational logs, and market trends. Today's organizations handle amounts of data that are very much outside the scope of conventional manual auditing procedures. Only a limited picture is offered by these techniques, many of which depend on sampling, which results in oversight and knowledge gaps. AI changes auditing by enabling the analysis of entire datasets to provide a thorough understanding of how a company operates. This change improves auditors' ability to obtain insights with greater depth and accuracy. For example, little trends and correlations in big, complicated data sets can be found by artificial intelligence systems, exposing patterns and anomalies that were previously invisible. These advanced abilities allow improved decision-making, actionable insights, and overall reliability of risk and operational assessments.
2. Strict Regulatory Requirements: The government and organizations are keeping a close eye on enterprises in practically every part of the world as the requirements are being raised with the increased evolution of technology, including major focus areas: data protection, cybersecurity, financial transparency, sound business governance, and so forth. Information Systems auditors are under more strain as a result of the increasing number of requirements. Then, there is artificial

intelligence (AI), which can streamline compliance procedures for businesses by automating checks and providing auditors with a means of navigating the complex regulatory environment. In cases where comprehensive risk analysis investigations are required by state-level legislation and regulations like the Cybersecurity Maturity Model Certification (Muller, 2023), AI solutions can assist enterprises in meeting the established cybersecurity standards by analyzing system vulnerabilities and generating compliance reports. Additionally, companies are generally required to demonstrate their compliance with data management and user privacy laws such as the CCPA and the General Data Protection Regulation (GDPR) (Guarda, 2019). By tracking data flows, identifying infractions, and keeping thorough audit trails for inspections, AI can improve assurance with compliance.

3. Demand for Real-Time Reporting: Agility and speed in contemporary organizations demand the ability to audit in real-time. AI has the ability to enable continuous auditing through real-time monitoring and evaluating of transactions and activities. The possibility of problems worsening before reporting is lessened and corrective measures are not delayed. Additionally, real-time reporting satisfies the growing need for business operation monitoring, where fraud detection, regulatory compliance, and data veracity are critical. Because modern businesses are becoming more and more reliant on digital platforms and cloud-based systems, AI-powered audit platform solutions are even more helpful because they have the potential to provide continuous tracking of critical and operational data in real-time.
4. Operational and Cost Efficiency: The audit process of information systems is usually a long, drawn-out process that can take several months and can take even more time, depending on the complexity of the system. Traditional audit practices are generally time-consuming, which increases the cost of carrying out the audit process incrementally. Here, AI-driven solutions can actually automate a lot of repetitive operations, such as data collection, processing, and analysis, that usually require a lot of manual effort. The time auditors spend on repeated tasks can be significantly decreased. Increased efficiency through AI leads to quicker audits, which helps businesses perform compliance checks more quickly. When AI is used to process massive amounts of data in real-time for auditing purposes, the process is not only faster but also more accurate. Not only can AI-powered solutions help decrease delays and lower human error in repetitive tasks, but they also increase the productivity of auditors since they can focus more on critical tasks that require human intelligence and problem-solving skills.

5. Globalization: The need for more accurate and efficient audits is increasing as firms expand internationally. The audit process becomes more complex due to the diversity brought forth by multinational activities, as auditors must monitor and test controls across borders while keeping in mind different local legislation. In IS auditing, AI-powered solutions can become fundamental instruments for conquering the challenges of globalization. As a result, audit procedures in AI-enabled fraud detection, compliance checking, and real-time system monitoring across jurisdictions and regions for transparency assurance may undergo a radical change. The application of AI in IS auditing will become more crucial as businesses operate on a more global basis in order to maintain accurate, effective, and secure audit procedures. By using AI to enhance their ability to provide timely and intelligent audit reports, auditors can also surpass the difficulties posed by globalization.

4.2. Integration of AI Within the Audit Lifecycle

AI is making an essential change in how audits are done, from the audit setup to risk assessment and reporting, along with compliance checks. The ability of AI to handle enormous volumes of information, identify trends, and automate mundane activities frees auditors to work on more valuable projects, which will raise the quality and efficiency of audits. (Chimwanda et al., 2024) How AI fits into each step of the audit lifecycle is described below:

1. Audit Setup: This process generally includes the identification of audit subjects such as business functions and systems. Moreover, this step involves defining the audit objective and audit scope to determine the purpose of the audit and define a set of testing points that are relevant to the audit. A number of tasks that support this phase can actually be automated using AI. For example, a ready view of similar audits of comparable business functions and audit types, risk-based audit assessment reports, continuous controls monitoring regarding business processes, and auto-generation of checklists can be automated through Natural Language Processing, Predictive analysis, and Robotic Process Automation.
2. Audit Plan: This step comprises performing risk assessments and identifying the compliance requirements for the audit subject, eventually evaluating the technical skills and resources required to carry out the audit process. Additionally, the process of determining audit procedures and steps for data gathering is also included in this stage of audit execution. Several tasks included in this phase can be automated with the integration of AI. For instance, analysis and summary of wordy and document-heavy policies, standard operating procedures (SOPs), and others in the audit scope, prepopulating and sharing findings based on ini-

tial analysis of SOPs and other available documents, keyword-based analysis and rule engine to extrapolate outcome analysis can all be programmed by utilizing Natural Language Processing, Predictive analysis and Robotic Process Automation.

3. Audit Fieldwork: This step of the audit process comprises the actual audit execution. From acquiring data, testing controls to discovering and validating issues, everything is carried out under this stage of audit. Here the automation scope spans through modelling of data, data sample testing automation, aggregating and interpreting data via rule engine, fraudulent data detection. This can be achieved via Natural language generation, Natural Language Processing, Predictive analysis and Robotic Process Automation.
4. Audit report: Documenting results, gathering report requirements, drafting and issuing report and follow up comes under this stage of audit process. Processes such as automation of text-based audit report, data visualization of key issues and risk, Intelligent reporting of audit-based quantification of issues can be carried out efficiently with AI powered solutions. This is feasible by utilizing Natural language generation, Natural Language Processing, Predictive analysis, and Robotic Process Automation.

4.3. Application of AI in Audit Reporting: Fundamental Areas of Impact

Most of the conventional processes followed in traditional audit reporting are quite time-consuming and prone to errors as well as inefficiencies. As discussed briefly in the previous section, such jobs can be made more effective and efficient by incorporating AI into the audit reporting phase. Following are some of the ways in which automation may enhance audit procedures and help with key tasks:

1. Prepare Audit Report: Due to the fact that it requires data gathering, insights, and discoveries, drafting an audit report is very labor-intensive work. AI-powered NLG automates text-based audit report generation (Menon, 2021). With NLG, key findings, conclusions, and recommendations are instantly transformed into in-depth, readable reports. It streamlines the whole reporting process, negates the need for manual drafting, and reduces human error significantly. Predictive analytics could also be added to the process to help auditors anticipate potential risks or results from those discoveries. With NLG, auditors can also generate audit reports in real-time. This way, a summary of the findings of the audit is almost immediate and subject to variation upon the analysis of new data.

2. Review Issues: Any assessment should cover reviewing audit results and issues so that recommendations can be accurate in nature and be delivered in a timely manner. With visualization tools, auditors will have clear visibility into the nature of problems and the magnitude of their severity through well-structured, interactive dashboards. Automation of data visualization makes it easier to identify problem areas, freeing up auditors' time to focus on high-priority issues. By combing through large volumes of textual data for signs of possible hazards or non-compliance, NLP can also help with issue reviews by supporting auditors in highlighting patterns and trends that could show major issues.
3. Audit Debrief: (Menon, 2021) Post-audit briefings remain a very important aspect in ensuring that all stakeholders agree to the findings and recommendations of the audit. Key findings can be automatically presented by AI-driven technologies through intelligent reporting systems, which provide active illustrations of risks, problems, and mitigation techniques. These systems can be configured to show the most relevant information to various stakeholders, from management teams to regulatory authorities. This enables the creation of automatic debriefs in real-time, saving time by providing insights on the spot. The use of predictive analytics amplifies existing decision-making over ongoing operations by helping stakeholders make sense of what might happen next.
4. Update Risk Profile of Business Unit/Team: It is very important to keep the risk profile of teams or business units current for continuous risk management. AI systems can automatically update the risk profiles and continuously monitor audit data. When RPA is integrated into the risk management system, the risk profiles get updated in real-time as new data is gathered. This eliminates the need for manual intervention and ensures that an organization is always informed about potential perils. Also, predictive analytics helps to discover new risks before they turn critical, which enables companies to proactively adjust their strategies.

4.4. AI Techniques Significant in Audit Reporting

The following are the various Artificial Intelligence methods that are important for transforming the audit reporting process and have considerable potential to further advance the same:

1. Text Summarization: This method involves generating summaries from a lengthy version of text using models such as LSTM (Long Short-Term Memory) and T5 (Text-to-Text Transfer Transformer), some of the deep learning algorithms. Text summarization (Luo et al., 2024) has just started being utilized in a few organizations to condense audit findings and evaluate results. It enables audi-

tors to draft audit reports competently through the automatic extraction of key insights and conclusions from volumes of data. This is actually beneficial as it not only speeds up the review and finalization procedures but also enhances clarity and reduces manual effort. Precise and clearly summarized results help stakeholders understand certain important issues and make communication easier during the audit debrief.

2. Sentiment Analysis: This method involves analyzing emotions from text and classifying to map the text to predefined or autogenerated labels. It is usually achieved using NLP and Naive Bayes (Machine learning classification) algorithms. Logs, comments, and feedback can be analyzed to track sentiment patterns, such as neutral, negative, or positive, during audits. (Gunasekaran, 2023) Sentiment analysis can be quite valuable to auditors in ranking risks by highlighting areas of concern that are represented in system logs or comments from stakeholders. This would make it easier to focus on high-impact concerns during the reporting phase, ensuring thorough and useful information for debriefs and future risk profiles.
3. Statistical Analysis: A technique that is designed to extract insights from both numerical and textual information (along with NLP) to perform analysis using statistical methods and algorithms (Marzban, 2008). Some of the major algorithms involve linear regression and k-means clustering, Machine learning algorithms. Statistical analysis allows the development of graphs, charts, and dashboards that quantify risks and highlight anomalies. This can enable auditors to enhance the clarity and accessibility of the audit report, giving stakeholders a data-driven basis on which to evaluate the severity of issues and the level of impact a particular vulnerability can cause.
4. Document classification: It involves categorizing documents into predefined classes by analysing its text. This is completed using algorithms such as SVM (Support Vector Machine) and Naïve Bayes, machine learning algorithms. (Bilski, 2011) Document classification would ensure well-organized and categorized material, helping an auditor to logically draft audit report automatically. This provides greater contextual relevance as auditors and other users browse the findings more easily. Documents relevant to a single compliance concern can be collected together and linked to their implications at the back of the report.
5. Search and retrieval: (Smith, 1976) This method comprises analyzing text and searching for a particular keyword from a corpus (database of information) and returning relevant data using TF-IDF (Term frequency-inverse document frequency). An NLP technique that accounts for the number of times a word appears in a document and how frequent or common a word is in the corpus. Information retrieval can be used to retrieve historical audit reports or related datasets to get insights about past years' audit findings, which can eventually help

perform comparative analysis. AI-driven intelligent reporting with contextual knowledge referencing findings made earlier can help evaluate remediations applied. For example, analyzing similar compliance breaches or re-occurring risks can enrich the report. This capacity will also subsequently allow auditors to identify trends and assess whether previous remedial efforts were effective or not.

4.5. AI Risk and Compliance Standards: An Overview

Integration of AI in the audit process is a developing field, and only a few policies exist currently that standardize and ensure the ethical use of AI. The following are the major AI standards and frameworks that organizations can adhere to while using AI in Audit:

1. NIST AI Risk Management Framework: NIST AI Risk Management Framework is a voluntary outline that will support enterprises in the ethical adoption of AI technologies. (AI Risk Management Framework I NIST, 2025) This framework doesn't just glance at AI risks but dives deep, enabling entities to identify, evaluate, and manage them effectively. The spotlight is on trustworthiness, transparency, and accountability in making AI systems not just smart but reliable and ethical, too. It mainly focuses on setting proper governance for the AI system, including organizational leadership and responsibility. Moreover, assessing the risk across the AI system's lifecycle and eventually acting upon identified risks by implementing mitigation solutions. Additionally, it highlights the importance of transparency and documentation while using AI for decision-making.
2. ISACA EU AI Act: It is a newly launched regulation that was put into force on August 1, 2024, and is expected to be applicable from August 2, 2026. (White Papers 2024 Understanding the EU AI Act, 2024). Proposed by the European Union, the regime addresses artificial intelligence systems. EU AI Act creates standards for the development, deployment, and use of AI technologies within the European Union. It classifies AI systems into categories based on the level of danger they create and prescribes specific requirements for each category. The act defines four categories of AI system risks: unacceptable risk, high risk, limited risk, and minimal risk. This regulation promotes risk accountability and security of AI systems.
3. ISO42001: A work-in-progress standard that covers the governance and management of AI systems. It will provide enterprises with a framework for managing AI systems in a compliant and ethical manner. ISO 42001 will help enterprises and auditors assess the governance of AI projects to meet worldwide standards while mitigating risks such as algorithmic bias, security concerns, and trans-

parency. Fully implemented, this standard would better position a business to meet international requirements for AI governance, including audits of AI and related technologies. It focuses on ethical AI development, AI governance, the importance of human-centric AI, and continuous monitoring. (ISO/IEC 42001, 2023)

5. CONCLUSION

From the above research, it's evident that AI has a huge potential in the functional domain of auditing. It's high time that auditors leverage AI to save time and effort. This would allow them to project their focus on more critical tasks while AI-powered systems handle the repetitive tasks during the audit process. Traditional audit procedures are less relevant due to big data generation and strict regulatory requirements for higher security of information systems. AI-powered solutions in the audit process would not only increase operational competence but would also be cost-effective. AI can also equip auditors with the ability to generate real-time reports, eventually enhancing the monitoring of an information system. We explored various ways through which AI can be integrated throughout all the steps of the audit process, from audit setup, plan, fieldwork, and reporting. AI techniques such as Natural language generation, Natural Language Processing, and Predictive analysis play a significant role in programming tasks in auditing. Repetitive and tedious tasks such as comparing with designed processes and controls, Documenting key risks and controls, and generating checklists can be automated through AI and ML techniques.

One major area that has just started incorporating AI is audit reporting. Fundamental tasks such as preparing audit reports, reviewing issues, audit debriefing, and updating the risk profile of the business unit/team can be efficiently carried out with less time when performed through AI-driven tools, saving auditors several hours. A few organizations have already started integrating AI to draft reports from the vast volume of audit findings collected by their auditors, and it's high time that a greater number of companies start tapping the benefits of AI. Data visualization can be helpful to integrate so that stakeholders have a clear picture of the issues in their systems and accordingly can figure out a remedial plan layout to be followed to combat it. We can further enhance the audit reporting process by automating the debriefing of results, eventually highlighting the risks and vulnerabilities in regard to controls implemented quickly. Artificial Intelligence and Machine Learning techniques such as text summarization, search and retrieval, statistical analysis, sentiment analysis, and document classification are transforming the way audit reporting is carried out where algorithms such as LSTM, T5, TF-IDF, Naïve Bayes, NLP, etc. are being highly used.

Since audit involves the use of sensitive client data, organizations should comply with regulations to ensure data protection and AI governance. NIST AI Risk framework, EU AI Act, and ISO 42001 are some of the important and reliable policies that have been drafted recently. Although Businesses are not required to regulate their AI systems while auditing at present, regulatory authorities are planning to make it mandatory in upcoming years. Since AI integration with audit reporting and the overall audit process is still in the early stages of development, new policies and standards are going to be developed rapidly based on risk evolution with AI in the audit. It is highly suggested that organizations comply with AI Risk and Compliance Standards to secure their systems.

REFERENCES

AI Risk Management Framework | NIST. (2025, March 27). NIST. https://www.nist.gov/itl/ai-risk-management-framework

Aitchison, J., & Dunsmore, I. R. (1975). *Statistical Prediction Analysis.* DOI: 10.1017/CBO9780511569647

Albawwat, I., & Frijat, Y. A. (2021). An analysis of auditors' perceptions towards artificial intelligence and its contribution to audit quality. *Accounting*, 755–762. DOI: 10.5267/j.ac.2021.2.009

Arnold, V., Collier, P. A., Leech, S. A., & Sutton, S. G. (2004). Impact of intelligent decision aids on expert and novice decision-makers judgments. *Accounting and Finance*, *44*(1), 1–26. DOI: 10.1111/j.1467-629x.2004.00099.x

Ashton, R. H. (1990). Pressure and performance in accounting decision settings: Paradoxical effects of incentives, feedback, and justification. *Journal of Accounting Research*, *28*, 148. DOI: 10.2307/2491253

Baldwin, A. A., Brown, C. E., & Trinkle, B. S. (2006). Opportunities for artificial intelligence development in the accounting domain: The case for auditing. *Intelligent Systems in Accounting, Finance & Management*, *14*(3), 77–86. DOI: 10.1002/isaf.277

Baxter, C. (2024, January 1). *IS audit in practice: A collaborative approach to assessing AI risk.* ISACA Journal, 2024(1). https://www.isaca.org/resources/isaca-journal/issues/2024/volume-1/a-collaborative-approach-to-assessing-ai-risk

Bell, T. B., & Carcello, J. V. (2000). A decision aid for assessing the likelihood of fraudulent financial reporting. *Auditing*, *19*(1), 169–184. DOI: 10.2308/aud.2000.19.1.169

Bilski, A. (2011). *A review of Artificial intelligence Algorithms in Document Classification.* International Journal of Electronics and Telecommunications - PAS Journals. https://journals.pan.pl/dlibra/doccontent?id=86895

Changchit, C., & Holsapple, C. W. (2004). The development of an expert system for managerial evaluation of internal controls. *Intelligent Systems in Accounting, Finance & Management*, *12*(2), 103–120. DOI: 10.1002/isaf.246

Chiappini, D. (2024). The Legal Definition of Artificial Intelligence: A Comparative Perspective. *European Journal of Comparative Law and Governance*, *11*(3), 360–387. DOI: 10.1163/22134514-bja10071

Chimwanda, E., Miller, K., & DeRoche, T. (2024). *CISA Official Review Manual* (28th ed.). ISACA.

Coyne, C. (2025, February 4). *COBIT: A practical guide for AI governance*. ISACA Now Blog. https://www.isaca.org/resources/news-and-trends/isaca-now-blog/2025/cobit-a-practical-guide-for-ai-governance

Dillard, J. F., & Yuthas, K. (2001). A Responsibility Ethics for Audit Expert Systems. *Journal of Business Ethics*, *30*(4), 337–359. DOI: 10.1023/A:1010720630914

Doshi, H. K., Balasingam, S., & Arumugam, D. (2020). Artificial Intelligence as a Paradoxical Digital Disruptor in the Accounting Profession: An Empirical Study amongst Accountants. *International Journal of Psychosocial Rehabilitation*, *24*(02), 873–885. DOI: 10.37200/IJPR/V24I2/PR200396

European Parliament. (2023, December 9). *Artificial Intelligence Act: deal on comprehensive rules for trustworthy AI*. https://www.europarl.europa.eu/news/en/press-room/20231206IPR15699/artificial-intelligence-act-deal-on-comprehensive-rules-for-trustworthy-ai

Faccia, A., De Lucia, C., Eltweri, A., Sawan, N., & Cavaliere, L. P. L. (2020). Extended Audit Report: Enhancing Trust and Reputation in IT Processes and across E-business Industries. *Extended Audit Report: Enhancing Trust and Reputation in IT Processes and Across E-business Industries*, *23–27*, 23–27. Advance online publication. DOI: 10.1145/3446922.3446927

Fedyk, A., Hodson, J., Khimich, N., & Fedyk, T. (2022). Is artificial intelligence improving the audit process? *Review of Accounting Studies*, *27*(3), 938–985. DOI: 10.1007/s11142-022-09697-x

Gu, H., Schreyer, M., Moffitt, K., & Vasarhelyi, M. (2024). Artificial intelligence co-piloted auditing. *International Journal of Accounting Information Systems*, *54*, 100698. DOI: 10.1016/j.accinf.2024.100698

Guarda, T. (2019). EU General Data Protection Regulation Implementation: An Institutional Theory View. www.academia.edu. https://www.academia.edu/77963189/EU_General_Data_Protection_Regulation_Implementation_An_Institutional_Theory_View

Gunasekaran, K. P. (2023). Exploring sentiment analysis techniques in natural language processing: A comprehensive review. https://arxiv.org/abs/2305.14842

Harper, N. (2023, April 7). *Regulating AI tech is no longer an option: It's a must!* ISACA Now Blog. https://www.isaca.org/resources/news-and-trends/isaca-now-blog/2023/regulating-ai-tech-is-no-longer-an-option

ISO/IEC 42001:2023. (2023). ISO. https://www.iso.org/standard/81230.html

Jaleel, A. (2023, January 18). *ChatGPT and Leveraging Artificial Intelligence in Auditing*. ISACA Now Blog. https://www.isaca.org/resources/news-and-trends/isaca-now-blog/2023/chatgpt-and-leveraging-artificial-intelligence-in-auditing

Jordan, M. I., & Mitchell, T. M. (2015). Machine learning: Trends, perspectives, and prospects. *Science*, *349*(6245), 255–260. DOI: 10.1126/science.aaa8415 PMID: 26185243

Karp, D. (2024, March 14). *How AI is transforming audit, risk and compliance.* ISACA Now Blog. https://www.isaca.org/resources/news-and-trends/isaca-now-blog/2024/how-ai-is-transforming-audit-risk-and-compliance

Khoei, T. T., Slimane, H. O., & Kaabouch, N. (2023). Deep learning: Systematic review, models, challenges, and research directions. *Neural Computing & Applications*, *35*(31), 23103–23124. DOI: 10.1007/s00521-023-08957-4

Khorsheed, H. S., Ismael, N. B., & Shamal, H. O. M. (2024).The impact of artificial intelligence and machine learning on financial reporting and auditing practices. *International Journal of Advanced Engineering, Management and Science(ISSN: 2454-1311)*,10(6), 30-37. DOI: 10.22161/ijaems.106.4

Khurana, D., Koli, A., Khatter, K., & Singh, S. (2023). Natural language processing: state of the art, current trends and challenges. Multimed Tools Appl;82(3):3713-3744. https://pubmed.ncbi.nlm.nih.gov/35855771

Kokina, J., & Davenport, T. H. (2017). The Emergence of Artificial Intelligence: How Automation is Changing Auditing. *Journal of Emerging Technologies in Accounting*, *14*(1), 115–122. DOI: 10.2308/jeta-51730

Lazer, D., & Radford, J. (2017). Data ex Machina: Introduction to Big Data. *Annual Review of Sociology*, *43*(1), 19–39. DOI: 10.1146/annurev-soc-060116-053457

Lee, R. F. I. (2025, January 3). *The synergy between generative AI and IS audit.* ISACA Now Blog. https://www.isaca.org/resources/news-and-trends/isaca-now-blog/2025/the-synergy-between-generative-ai-and-is-audit

Li, Y., & Goel, S. (2024). Making it possible for the auditing of AI: A systematic review of AI audits and AI auditability. *Information Systems Frontiers.* Advance online publication. DOI: 10.1007/s10796-024-10508-8

Lin, J. W., Hwang, M. I., & Becker, J. D. (2003). A fuzzy neural network for assessing the risk of fraudulent financial reporting. *Managerial Auditing Journal*, *18*(8), 657–665. DOI: 10.1108/02686900310495151

Luo, J., Meng, Q., & Cai, Y. (2018). Analysis of the Impact of Artificial Intelligence Application on the Development of Accounting Industry. *Open Journal of Business and Management, 06*(04), 850–856. DOI: 10.4236/ojbm.2018.64063

Luo, M., Xue, B., & Niu, B. (2024). A comprehensive survey for automatic text summarization: Techniques, approaches, and perspectives. *Neurocomputing, 603*, 128280. DOI: 10.1016/j.neucom.2024.128280

Marzban, C. (2008). Basic statistics and basic AI: neural networks. In *Springer eBooks* (pp. 15–47). DOI: 10.1007/978-1-4020-9119-3_2

Menon, S. (2024, February 21). *Broad, regulatory frameworks needed to responsibly harness AI.* ISACA Now Blog. https://www.isaca.org/resources/news-and-trends/isaca-now-blog/2024/broad-regulatory-frameworks-needed-to-responsibly-harness-ai

Menon (2021). *Volume 4 How can AI drive audits.* ISACA. https://www.isaca.org/resources/isaca-journal/issues/2021/volume-4/how-can-ai-drive-audits

Muller, S. R. (2023). An analysis of the design of the Cybersecurity Maturity Model Certification (CMMC) and its direct effect on supply chain management. In *Real-World Solutions for Diversity, Strategic Change, and Organizational Development: Perspectives in Healthcare, Education, Business, and Technology* (pp. 220–243). IGI Global. DOI: 10.4018/978-1-6684-8691-7.ch014

Murphy, D., & Brown, C. E. (1992). The uses of advanced information technology in audit planning. *International Journal of Intelligent Systems in Accounting Finance & Management, 1*(3), 187–193. DOI: 10.1002/j.1099-1174.1992.tb00020.x

Nah, F. F., Zheng, R., Cai, J., Siau, K., & Chen, L. (2023). Generative AI and ChatGPT: Applications, challenges, and AI-human collaboration. *Journal of Information Technology Case and Application Research, 25*(3), 277–304. DOI: 10.1080/15228053.2023.2233814

Noordin, N. A., Hussainey, K., & Hayek, A. F. (2022). The Use of Artificial Intelligence and Audit Quality: An Analysis from the Perspectives of External Auditors in the UAE. *Journal of Risk and Financial Management, 15*(8), 339. DOI: 10.3390/jrfm15080339

Now, I. S. A. C. A. (2024, June 10). *AI for auditors: Challenges and opportunities for career advancement.* ISACA Now Blog. https://www.isaca.org/resources/news-and-trends/isaca-now-blog/2024/ai-for-auditors-challenges-and-opportunities-for-career-advancement

Omoteso, K. (2012). The application of artificial intelligence in auditing: Looking back to the future. *Expert Systems with Applications*, *39*(9), 8490–8495. DOI: 10.1016/j.eswa.2012.01.098

Prasad, V. (2024, August 2). *AI algorithm audits: Key control considerations*. ISACA. https://www.isaca.org/resources/news-and-trends/industry-news/2024/ai-algorithm-audits-key-control-considerations

Sayankar, V. N. (2024). A review on information systems audit. *Research Journal of Engineering and Technology*. https://www.researchgate.net/publication/381653679_A_Review_on_Information_Systems_Audit

Smith, L. C. (1976). Artificial intelligence in information retrieval systems. *Information Processing & Management*, *12*(3), 189–222. DOI: 10.1016/0306-4573(76)90005-4

Stancheva-Todorova, E. P. (2018). How Artificial Intelligence Is Challenging the Accounting Profession. ideas.repec.org. https://ideas.repec.org/a/isp/journl/v12y2018i1p126-141.html

Suleiman, N., Amneh, N., Borgi, H., Phung, N., Muhammad, N., & Ali, N. (2020). How Artificial Intelligence Changes the Future of Accounting Industry. *International Journal of Economics and Business Administration*, *VIII*(3), 478–488. DOI: 10.35808/ijeba/538

Sun, W., Huang, L., & Wang, Y. "Exploring Customer Behavior Patterns: A Process-based Perspective" (2020). *WHICEB 2020 Proceedings*. 31. https://aisel.aisnet.org/whiceb2020/31

Ucoglu, D. (2020). Current machine learning applications in accounting and auditing. *Pressacademia*, *12*(1), 1–7. DOI: 10.17261/Pressacademia.2020.1337

Wewerka, J., & Reichert, M. (2020, December 22). *Robotic Process Automation — A systematic literature review and assessment framework*. arXiv.org. https://arxiv.org/abs/2012.11951

White Papers 2024 Understanding the EU AI Act. (2024). ISACA. https://www.isaca.org/resources/white-papers/2024/understanding-the-eu-ai-act?utm_campaign=ISACA+Main&utm_content=1732631880&utm_medium=social&utm_source=linkedin

Zemánková, A. (2019). Artificial intelligence and blockchain in audit and accounting: Literature review. wseas Transactions on Business and Economics, 16(1), 568-581.

Chapter 3
Impact of AI on Audit and Assurance

Mahesh Thaluru
https://orcid.org/0009-0004-6860-2742
University at Buffalo, SUNY, USA

Moksh Gupta
University at Buffalo, SUNY, USA

Zishen Liao
https://orcid.org/0009-0000-0038-0013
University at Buffalo, SUNY, USA

Tianyi Zhang
University at Buffalo, SUNY, USA

Raj Sharman
https://orcid.org/0000-0001-5838-7330
University at Buffalo, SUNY, USA

ABSTRACT

The integration of artificial intelligence (AI) into auditing marks a transformative shift in finance, enhancing the conduct, assessment, and optimization of audits. AI-driven audits leverage machine learning, big data analytics, and automation to deliver more accurate, efficient, and reliable financial assessments. This paper explores AI's impact on corporate audits, particularly in risk assessment, compliance monitoring, and decision-making. AI enables a move from traditional practices to real-time reporting, predictive analysis, and automated fraud detection, addressing persistent challenges in manual processes. Compared to conventional methods, AI audits provide scalability, cost efficiency, and improved data integrity, while also

DOI: 10.4018/979-8-3373-3078-5.ch003

raising concerns around data privacy, algorithmic bias, and ethical implications. The study offers insights into how AI is reshaping auditing—promoting transparency, refining resource allocation, and redefining audit functions in the digital era.

1. INTRODUCTION

With the development and growth of information management technology applications, the information management capabilities of modern intelligent companies continue to improve. Information management can not only improve the company's social productivity, but also promote the company's internal management benefits. Financial management system information management system is now widely used in companies, specifically for accounting, electronic bill storage, etc., which brings convenient and fast financial management system information management special tools for companies. Because the financial management system capabilities and methods of each company are different, most financial audits still need to be carried out by manpower, reducing the efficiency of financial audit work. Cash flow is the fate of modern enterprises. Scientific and reasonable cash flow is specifically planned and adjusted according to financial audits, so financial audits have vital practical significance for modern enterprises. The information management of financial audit can help accounting personnel and internal audit staff improve their work efficiency. The digital electronic audit system can conveniently and quickly carry out the statistical analysis of financial management system account data, provide the company with real and reliable financial audit data, and reduce the complicated operation pressure of accounting personnel and internal audit staff. The financial audit system software is closely related to the company's financial management system method, the specific content of internal audit, and the financial software used by the company. Therefore, the commonly used financial audit system software is difficult to match the financial audit business of all companies. Most medium and large companies basically develop financial audit system software independently. There are many financial audit software on the market. Some integrate the basic functions of internal audit into financial software, and some independently develop financial audit system software. However, the cost of commercial financial audit software is very high, which not only puts economic pressure on small and medium-sized enterprises but also requires that the content and procedures of financial audits be changed to adapt to commercial financial audit system software. With the scale increase of the company and the innovation of the enterprise operation and management mechanism, the scale and capacity of the financial management system of the company have kept improving, which puts forward higher requests for financial auditing. In particular, the financial scale and management method of an enterprise are in constant change, which will promote financial auditing to change. It may be that financial auditing cost is higher, the cycle time is shorter, and financial risks are larger. The financial auditing information management system has brought an efficient processing method for the company's financial auditing. The company's financial auditing system software has changed along with the financial management system, and it has tried not to increase the work pressure of accounting personnel and internal auditing staff

1.1 Financial Auditing in the Era of Artificial Intelligence

1.1.1. Financial Audit Requirements

Authenticity and reliability are the basic provisions of financial auditing. It mainly refers to the authenticity of all financial statements of the company, and there is no falsification of property, false reporting of income and profits, etc., and the authenticity of current liabilities and external guarantees. One of the goals of financial auditing is to find falsified data and invalid data in the company's financial statements, and to promote the authenticity and stability of the company's financial statements (Omoteso, 2012).

The international standards of financial auditing are set out in a way such that they guarantee transparency, precision, and conformity with corporate reporting. The implementation of the IFRS and ISA has drastically transformed the entire concept of the financial audit requirements into an all-encompassing discipline of identification of business risks, compliance assurance, and data integrity. – Most notably, this includes IFRS 8 regarding the need for segment reporting to follow corporate auditors and stakeholders in laying bare the antithetical effect different business activities and economic conditions have on other areas of the business. Segmented financial statement reporting caters to the stakeholders' needs and offers insights on business segments aside from giving an overall view of the company's performance. To supplement this, the ISA states that it is to be verified by the auditors that segment reporting correlates with the conceptualization of the financial statements overall, and any inconsistencies should be reflective in the audit reports. This adherence always improves the credibility of the financial audits, as it provides an avenue for uniformity in financial reporting, and management decisions made henceforth are based on fair and transparent financial data (Мюллер, В., et al., 2020).

Completeness is the company's financial statements reflect all accounting matters generated during the specified accounting period, and there is no omission or concealment of accounting matters and social and economic transactions. The company has no off-book property and liabilities. Deliberate concealment of financial statements is a common method of financial fraud. In the financial audit process, auditors must verify or discover the integrity of the company's financial statements based on various methods and means (Kotepuchai & Limpiyakorn, 2024).

In conducting financial audits of financial statements, certified public accountants must first verify the legality and accuracy of the statements to ensure compliance with relevant regulations. The company's accounting statements must be precise and free from data anomalies. The reconciliation of figures between different accounting statements, financial statement items, and the current and previous financial statements must be consistent. Financial audit staff are responsible for identifying and addressing abnormal data or discrepancies in the reports (Issa, Sun, & Vasarhelyi, 2016)

1.1.2. Artificial Intelligence Audit

Artificial intelligence is revolutionizing financial auditing by integrating advanced computing methods like big data analytics, cloud computing, deep learning, and others into traditional audit practices. Intelligent information audit systems are already being developed to enhance efficiency, accuracy, and risk assessment by automating data collection, identifying anomalies, and improving audit decision-making (Omoteso, 2012). Contrary to traditional audit methods based on manual sampling and rule-based checks, AI audits can handle real-time large-scale data, allowing for comprehensive risk detection and predictive analysis. Together, the AI with big data platforms allows centralized data storage, automated anomaly detection, and adaptive learning to refine audit models over time (Wu et al., 2024). AI-powered natural language processing facilitates the documentation review within financial audits, while deep learning helps identify complex patterns in daily transactions (Adelakun, 2022). These technologies allow auditors to quickly spot risk points and irregularities in financial statements, successfully enhancing the effectiveness of audit procedures (Wu et al., 2024). In addition, AI-based audit systems inherently employ automatic machine-learning models that could consistently improve on experience, making them liable to emerging risks and discussing recent financial regulation dynamics. Still, while expanding, AI adoption must address critical issues of data security, algorithmic transparency, and the expertise of professionals in ensuring the reliability and ethics of AI-enabled audits (Wu et al., 2024).

1.1.3. Historical Context & Evolution of AI in Auditing

The evolution of artificial intelligence in auditing has been framed by technological advancement and ever-increasing demand for efficiency, accuracy, and risk mitigation in financial assessments. Auditing commenced from the handing over of the manual routine processes to work through various other methods of traditional statistical sampling, wherein efficient techniques became very labor-intensive and required a great deal of human intervention. The introduction of computerized audit tools in the latter quarter of the 20th century, alongside the realm of computerized auditing and capture, dawning a new era with automated data analysis and anomaly detection powered by computers. AI-powered audit systems continued developing through high-pace machine learning algorithms, predictive analytics, and other means for faster investigation and fraud detection. The era of big data has meant that auditors were able to super-process vast amounts of financial information, probably a thousand times faster than current methodologies. In recent years, AI-powered auditing has expanded from verifying financial accounts to ethics auditing: algorithmic transparency, bias detection, and regulatory compliance (Schiff et al., 2024). This transition marks the ever-growing influence of AI to be not only equipped to boost traditional financial audit review features but also be equipped to respond to the ethical and governance challenges arising from AI-based decisions. With the transformation of AI taking place, it would be expected further to embed in the conduct of audits and shape the experience of financial and ethical oversight in the corporate and public sector governance.

1.1.4. Data Mining Technology Application

Data mining technology application is the most widely used technical application in financial auditing. Human auditing also adopts data mining methods, mainly including statistical analysis methods, cluster analysis methods, association rule analysis methods, etc. Audit staff conducts cost and profit structure type analysis on financial reports, calculates the proportion of each part, and then compares them according to quarterly or annual periods to find abnormalities (Omoteso, 2012). Audit staff use cluster analysis methods to perform cluster classification based on the internal connections between financial statements, and find the smallest clusters for detailed verification (Issa, Sun, & Vasarhelyi, 2016). The association rule analysis method is based on the implicit relationship between each expense, and then verifies the rationality of the data, such as the sales volume and the raw material procurement cost are in a positive proportional relationship.

The operating models, product varieties, and internal control management of each department are different. The specific contents of each department's financial reports are different. Therefore, there is no information technology application that can process the financial reports of all departments by itself. Most audit work still requires manual processing by audit staff (Alles, Kogan, & Vasarhelyi, 2008).

At present, the audit analysis model is the most common financial data processing model. First, the overall analysis model is used to analyze the financial statements in general. The system software uses the expenditure and income status of the audited department to find the characteristics of financial fluctuations, and then formulates the key audit scope. Finally, the audit analysis model is used to conduct in-depth and detailed inspections of the detailed key audit financial statements (Adelakun, 2022)

1.2 How Artificial Intelligence Improves the Corporate Financial Audit Process

1.2.1. Inspection Procedure

Inspection procedure is an economic audit aspect that checks relevant records and documents through electronic and paper-based means generated within or outside the audited entity. Because of the high volume of data involved, audits are based on sampling methods by tradition, as nothing will make the inspection of all documents practically feasible. Even if statistically sound, it still brings to life some risks since conclusions from sampling may not well reflect the general picture of the financial condition of the entity. Some variations and financial risks may still elude detection even after a full sampling (Schiff et al., 2024).

Artificial intelligence tones into audit inspection, ensuring that the reviews are within the accurate plane and done efficiently in using the whole dataset instead of sampling it. You can identify the inconsistency in a massive amount of financial data using AI systems within a very short span of time. With this power, AI will reduce the chance of missing errors or fraud and will make audit opinions more reliable. Another great thing about the AI audit is that it can ease the sampling process, allowing the auditor to review larger, more relevant data sets in less time (Schiff et al., 2024).

Generally, the Public Company Accounting Oversight Board PCAOB inspections present engagement deficiencies due to traditional audit methods being limited to sample-based testing, leaving key financial irregularities unnoticed. AI-driven audits will redeem these shortfalls through automated data reconciliation and anomaly detection. In this way, the auditor can focus on high-risk areas, engaging time with irrelevant certification procedures. General technological advancement renders compliance with auditing standards easier, increases the conduct of audits, and bulks up the confidence of financial reporting.

1.2.2 Recalculation

The whole process of checking the accuracy of data in various materials submitted by the auditee based on human or computer audit technology is called recalculation. The audit recalculation program introduced in the 1990s can do relatively simple mechanical calculations, but manual calculations are still necessary. Take the fixed asset depreciation method as an example. After the introduction of artificial intelligence, because it can simulate the thinking of intelligent robots, it can quickly grasp the information content of the relevant company and the main purpose of the audited object, and then automatically select the appropriate method to estimate the net residual value, depreciation method and depreciation period, and also make similar feedback on the characteristics of funds. At the same time, the company's artificial intelligence system software can use big data mining technology to accurately obtain the company's fixed asset utilization rate and export information content, and thus calculate the company's net realizable value and automatically determine whether the fixed assets are depreciated. The entire workflow usually does not require human intervention. From an auditing perspective, artificial intelligence refers to a series of hybrid technologies that change current auditing work, while auditing procedures are directly influenced by existing technologies. The emergence of modern technology, especially computers, has changed the scope and methods of audit testing. The emergence of data analysis technology has changed the time, scope, efficiency, cost and benefits of existing audits. Artificial intelligence technology embeds audit work that was previously done manually into an automated system, thereby achieving the goal of improving audit efficiency and effectiveness. Generally speaking, applying artificial intelligence to auditing work can complete auditing work more efficiently and make full sample auditing a reality.

1.2.3. Analytical Procedures

Analytical procedures are the process by which financial and accounting personnel analyze and confirm the internal relationship between financial data and financial data through analysis and research, and then evaluate the value of financial information. Artificial intelligence analyzes and stores large amounts of data through computer technology, which can surpass the human brain and compare and analyze various data; when doing so, there is no need to worry about time, resources or the accuracy of the conclusion. However, the reliance on AI introduces ethical challenges such as transparency, biases in data analysis, and issues of accountability in decision-making. To mitigate these challenges, collaborative frameworks involving auditors, developers, and regulators are essential to ensure the ethical deployment and use of AI in auditing (Munoko, 2020). That is, if there is no correlation with the predetermined data, or there is a significant difference with the expected quality, and the correlation with other relevant information is inconsistent or fluctuating, artificial intelligence will also issue an alarm for the abnormal phenomenon found and quickly obtain the analysis conclusion required by the auditor. If an error occurs in the audit process, the source of the erroneous data can be quickly found using big data tracing, which further improves the speed and accuracy of the audit. The focus of artificial intelligence on auditing is on the automation of labor-intensive tasks in auditing, that is, structured and repetitive tasks in the audit process will be supported by artificial intelligence technology. Artificial intelligence technology can help auditors automatically complete a number of audit tasks including verification and recalculation. Among them, during the substantive testing stage, artificial intelligence technology can assist auditors in recalculating accumulated depreciation, accumulated amortization and the income tax that the audited unit should pay. At the same time, it can assist auditors in reviewing whether the data from accounting vouchers to the general ledger is registered incorrectly.

According to (Ghosh and Ghosh,.2024), the major benefits of ANN lie in its learning from experience: supervised learning, unsupervised learning, and reinforcement learning. The supervised learning technique involves training of the model on labeled datasets thereby facilitating the learning of the model for a mapping of input/output while unsupervised learning identifies the hidden patterns in unstructured data, and reinforcement learning optimizes decisions using rewards and penalties. Their immense learning capabilities ensure that ANNs become a core part of several applications used in AI including but not limited to image recognition, NLP, financial forecasting, and autonomous decision-making systems (Ghosh & Ghosh, 2024). ANNs are somewhat familiar in fieldwork towards the implementation of AI systems to consider the discrepancies observed in financial statements, risk assessment, and error detection by automation in auditing. AI is taking further evolutions on deep-learning architectures with CNN for image processing and RNN for analysis of sequential data and is providing ever-more compelling and efficient solutions to the variety of complex problems to be solved in immensely different domains.

1.3 Scope of the Paper

The paper examines the transformative effect of artificial intelligence on financial auditing: integration, benefits, challenges, and future potential. It explores how AI technologies, such as machine learning, big data analytics, and neural networks, will improve audit processes by automating tasks, enhancing risk assessment, and facilitating reporting in real time. The scope covers investigating the role of AI in workflow smoothing, resource optimization, and dynamic compliance checks, while challenges in data integrity, algorithmic biases, and ethical concerns are at the fore. In addition, it points to such opportunities as cost savings, scalability, enhanced decision-making, and a shift toward continuous auditing supported by advanced tools. The paper also discusses the implications for the profession of AI-driven auditing, including upskilling auditors and navigating the potential displacement of routine roles. Through an analysis of real-world applications and case studies, this paper provides insight into how AI enhances accuracy, transparency, and strategic value in corporate financial audits.

2. APPLICATION OF ARTIFICIAL INTELLIGENCE TECHNOLOGY IN THE FIELD OF AUDITING

2.1 Application of Artificial Intelligence Technology in Audit Planning

The historically rigid yet manual nature of audit planning involves higher-level evaluations by auditors before agreeing to a contract and assessing risk later in the process. Indeed, with a traditional audit, auditors make determinations about scope, timing, procedures and finalize them working with the audited entity's personnel in a coordinated manner. This process may involve significant human effort, take time, and, due to a lack of data processing capacity, more opportunity for inaccurate findings. However, the advent of artificial intelligence (AI) audit planning began the process that formed an more flexible audit planning system that involved data analytics and attention to organizational risk. AI facilitates the auditor in inputting broad financial and operational information into "intelligent" systems that suggestions more detailed audit manuals and/or audit strategies tied to objectives and regulatory requirements (Onwubuariri et al., 2024).

Audit planning systems that use AI(Machine learning) process big data and help in risk assessment. Instead of static models that rely heavily on historical information, continuous testing with evidence provides better updates to audit plans. Auditors can use this information to better anticipate risks and adjust their audit plans better in real-time during an engagement. AI systems also allow for predictive risk assessment, which enables auditors to flag anomalies and financial inconsistencies ahead of the material misstatement stage (Onwubuariri et al., 2024).

One more important advantage of AI during audit planning is the decision-making and documentation it streamlines. Systems based on AI provide auditors with real-time prompts and recommendations during the implementation of audit procedures along with detailed audit trail of the original and amended plans. It will enhance the transparency and accountability of audit processes and compliance with the rules made by the Public Company Accounting Oversight Board (PCAOB) and others. Research shows that when auditing firms invest in AI, the accuracy of financial reports improves and discrepancies between internal audit reports and real reports decrease, thus increasing the firms' non-financial losses (Arun, 2024).

Even with these advantages, AI-based audit planning encounters difficulties with data reliability, algorithm transparency, and auditors needing to develop abilities to use AI technologies. Nonetheless, as AI technologies continue to evolve, they are going to redefine audit planning. This will make audit planning a process that is proactive, efficient, and focused on risks. This will improve audit quality as well as financial accountability (Arun, 2024; Onwubuariri et al., 2024).

2.2 Application of Artificial Intelligence Technology in Risk Assessment and Analysis Procedures

The questionnaires and interview materials used in the risk assessment do not need to be summarized and analyzed manually, as is the case in the case of traditional audits. Once entered into the system, these materials get automatically processed, and the results of the analysis are shown through visual dashboards and charts. AI systems evaluate the risk of significant misstatements by ascertaining the importance of financial statement items and setting threshold levels for minor misstatements. In addition, through the use of social network technology, AI will allow for the continuous monitoring of the financial activities of the entity being audited. Most of the conventional procedures for conducting an analysis refer to the selection of representative data for testing which depend heavily on the professional judgment of the auditors. Through the automation of data collection, screening and validation, AI will change the course of auditing. Continuous monitoring and automation of audit processes have been made possible through Artificial Intelligence (AI).

AI systems process the items to remove duplicates and optimize cloud storage for redundancies. Plus, AI tools can draw insight from extraction and analyses of data on an organization's management, operational and accounting systems to do a more holistic risk assessment. AI help in better risk evaluation because of machine learning techniques like artificial neural networks (ANN) which capture patterns and anomalies which otherwise are not captured in normal audits. AI auditing enables effective collaboration of IT auditors with financial auditors on the security and reliability assessment of IT infrastructure. IT auditors help in ensuring data integrity by detecting vulnerabilities due to cyber attacks, unauthorized access, or system failure which contribute to better risk management framework.

One key advantage that AI has in risk assessment is its ability to process unstructured and semi-structured data like images, audio, and video files. Tools powered by AI can change these varied types of data into written or structured data records. This will help the auditor in finding those risk factors that are hidden in nature more efficiently. The use of web crawler technology further boosts the efficacy of AI-based auditing that fetches third-party data from outside sources. It permits the auditor to compare this data with internal audit data to validate levels of risk. Also,

Using AI, it is feasible to assess an organization's financial viability; the likelihood of management having fraudulent intentions and the effectiveness of internal audits.

In sectors like medical devices that require adherence to compliance and regulatory guidelines, AI-based risk assessment is revolutionizing supplier audits. Use of AI in supplier auditing allows tracking data in real time, helping identify risks related to supply chain flaws, non-compliance, and operational shortcomings. AI systems behind supplier audits apply predictive analytics tools to anticipate risks, check compliance automatically and standardise audits lowering subjectivity of human assessments (Arun, 2024). Doing this helps firms reduce risk, loss of money and reputation by ensuring that suppliers are in compliance with regulations and standards of the industry. Companies can boost transparency, improve risk prediction accuracy, and utilize resources better by merging AI into supplier audits. This one fits into larger risk assessment frameworks similar to financial audits.

2.3 AI-Driven Risk Management in Audit

Artificial intelligence (AI) is transforming the field of auditing risk management by enhancing data analysis, pattern discovery and predictive analysis. Traditional risk assessment reasoning operates on a static models and historical information which has limitations related to the scope of information examined, and reactivity to changing system conditions. An AI solution for risk management is dynamic and forward-looking. Rather than solely analyzing limited historical information, AI risk management systems use machine learning algorithms to analyze different types of unstructured and structured data. This can include analysis of financial records, operational reports, email correspondence, contracts, social media and other data types, to identify patterns, detect anomalies, and flag irregularities that suggest possible risk or suspicion of fraudulent activity. Because AI risk management systems learn and adapt as new data becomes available, they generate real time risk assessments that evolve with the business environment.

This adaptive capability enhances auditors' ability to not only detect existing risks but also to anticipate emerging threats before they escalate. For example, predictive analytics supported by AI has shown potential to reduce risk-related incidents by up to 30%, and leading firms like Deloitte and PwC have reported increased audit scope and responsiveness using AI tools without additional human resources. Moreover, AI enables a more strategic allocation of audit resources, allowing auditors to prioritize high-risk areas and tailor their procedures accordingly. AI-driven risk management also improves audit efficiency and accuracy by automating repetitive, time-consuming tasks such as data entry, reconciliation, and anomaly detection—freeing auditors to focus on analytical and judgment-based activities that add higher value to the audit engagement.

This adaptability expands how auditors can not only identify existing risks, but also foresee emerging risks before they materialize. For example, predictive analytics enabled with AI has demonstrated risk reduction of up to 30%--with audit giants like Deloitte and PwC embracing opportunities through AI technology and confirming increased audit responsiveness and audit scope, without the allocation of additional human resources. AI technology moreover permits a more strategic alignment of audit resources, allowing auditors to focus on high-risk areas and align audit procedures as necessary. AI-enabled risk evaluation also enhances efficiency and accuracy in audits because it automates repetitive, time-consuming tasks that may include data entry, reconciliation or anomaly detection, allowing auditors to focus their critical analysis and judgment-related activities on audit values higher than the resources consumed.

Moreover, the incorporation of natural language processing (NLP), deep learning models, and robotic process automation (RPA) into audit systems facilitates the extraction and interpretation of complex data sources, thus facilitating a more well-rounded understanding of risk. This complex analysis increases the reliability of risk assessments and can contribute to continuous auditing and monitoring frameworks. With the benefits of using AI-driven audit systems, they are not without challenge. Onwubuariri et al. (2024) acknowledge that data integrity, management of the 'black box' nature of specific AI models, algorithmic biases, and changing regulatory systems must be managed carefully. The success of AI systems in auditing also requires a transformation of skills, requiring auditors to be more fluent in data science, machine learning concepts, and ethical algorithmic decision making.

Essentially, risk management with the use of AI is not just a new technology, but a complete shift in how audit risks are identified, assessed, and mitigated. Organizations that successfully integrate AI into their audit operations should experience improved audit quality, increased confidence in financial reporting, more resilient risk management practices, and increased adaptability to a much more complex business environment. As AI technologies evolve in sophistication, their use as part of the audit process will become foundational to audit excellence and sustainable corporate governance (Onwubuariri et al., 2024).

2.4 Application of Artificial Intelligence Technology in Observation and Inquiry Procedures

Observing and inquiry procedures in a traditional audit are very much dependent on an auditor's experience, judgment, and skill at recognizing subtle behavioral cues and situational conditions. Auditors are expected to observe processes visually, assess the meaning of expressions and inflections during interviews, and perform an analysis of unusual or aberrant financial behavior or operational behaviors. However, these procedures and techniques are limited to human perception, cognition, and fatigue, which may be increased when the auditor is new or without much experience. Fatigue alone will prevent an auditor from a variety of subtle non-verbal indications that management has not altered behavior in order to conceal or deceive.

The introduction of artificial intelligence (AI) greatly changes and improves these processes. For instance, using facial recognition and emotion-detection technologies, the AI system tracks micro-expressions like tension in facial muscles, mouth movement, and variations in where the person is looking during the interview to discern stress indicators and possible intent to mislead. Voice recognition algorithms establish alterations in speech, including tone, pitch, and pace, to aid in finding inconsistencies or hesitations that may signal increased risk of misleading statements. These components assist the auditor in more objectively assessing the risk of the audit developing intentions dependent on purely subjective observations.

AI also allows for the capture of data in real-time through networks of sensors and other electronic monitoring equipment. For example, you can assess operational data from production lines, supply chains, or point of sale system together with revenue data to confirm if and when the revenue and incurred costs occurred. This would allow for more than documentation verification and into physical and sometimes digital traceability. In addition, AI tools also assist in processing large amounts of observational or interview data into logical and analyzable formats in the audit process, which supports better-informed conclusions.

COBIT 2019—with a keen eye toward DSS06 Managed Business Process Controls—also provides guidance for auditors approaching the audit of systems that include AI. DSS06 promotes traceability and documentation, and advocates for organized thinking and analysis. Some of the steps that the framework calls out are to understand the AI system's architecture, include stakeholders to stakeholder discussions, and assure transparency and explainability around AI mediated processes. This is particularly key when AI systems function as part of a behavioral or decision-based analytic process that the auditor needs to understand to validate how the AI arrived at certain conclusions, including the AI systems use in observation or inquiry examples (Rizki & Novianto, 2023).

The application by auditors of DSS06.05's guidance—includes sourcing data, establishing lines of data retention, and connecting results to responsible parties—will provide greater assurance that observations and assessments generated by AI have a greater degree of reliability. This is an important safeguard to audit quality, especially with the use of AI systems to interpret human behavior or operational conditions that have a bearing on financial reporting. Ultimately, AI lowers the risk of human error, increases consistency across inquiry-based assessments, and bolsters the credibility of audit evidence collected through observation and interaction.

2.5 Application of Artificial Intelligence Technology in Control Testing

In an audit context, control testing has typically meant reviewing several of the organization's important internal control processes in order to evaluate the suitability of their design and effective application. Auditors utilize samples and their own checklist/documents to assess whether the control procedures are achieving what they were intended to do. This process can be lengthy and hindered by the auditor's inherent human errors or oversight. This evaluation process usually means that the auditors will test only a fraction of the existing controls, and therefore, not the full repose of the organization's internal systems, with the risk of missing some underlying weaknesses or new risks.

As a result of the use of artificial intelligence (AI), control testing has been transformed. AI technologies enable coverage of an internal control system, so testing is not limited to key controls. AI facilitates continuous monitoring of data, and real-time evaluation of the design effectiveness and operation of internal controls. AI systems analyze transactions and transaction logs as they occur instead of:informing evaluations during a testing period. On an on-going basis, AI systems provide auditors with an on-going assessment of control execution. Further, these automated systems document results by producing digital audit trails and logs, improving documentation accuracy, and facilitating subsequent analysis.

According to Luo, Wang, and Jiang (2025), AI as a control enhancer in internal audit has a clear distinctive impact in the context of the higher education sector, where financial and other business operations can be complex and involve several stakeholders. AI adoption in audit can reduce the time, manual operations, and human error in control testing processes through control testing automation. AI usage can also allow the internal audit to evaluate controls over the full population of transactions or control activities (and not just a sample). This is a significant improvement to coverage and reliability to an audit. Intelligent models, like those based on deep learning, natural language processing (NLP), and rule-based expert systems can assist the internal audit by reviewing internal control documentation, identifying breaches in controls, and delivering alerts in situations where weaknesses may exist.

The research showcases the way that AI-driven systems improve control testing through providing feedback in real time, adaptive testing parameters and intelligent anomaly detection. Such systems improve the auditor's ability to make a judgment about the internal controls functioning as intended and if they are designed to meet internal guidelines and regulatory mandates. The AI audit model highlighted by the authors uses technologies such as the optical character recognition (OCR) and NLP to review documents and contracts, extract control-related data, and transform documents to a structure that can be analyzed. This characterization of AI in the auditing process allows for transition from response oriented auditing to proactive auditing; meaning anomalies may be identified and acted on before they develop into material misstatements.

Moreover, AI can enable continuous control monitoring which creates a solid basis for developing a modified internal audit strategy. By combining automated control testing, anomaly detection, and real-time reporting, the internal control environment is enhanced to be more adaptable to change and less exposed to fraud. Furthermore, the higher level of visibility regarding control performance allows organizations to make informed decisions to improve internal governance and effectively mitigate risk (Luo, Wang, & Jiang, 2025).

2.6 Application of Artificial Intelligence Technology in Substantive Procedures (Details Testing)

After analyzing the procedures and control tests, traditional audits determine the scope, time nodes, and specific procedures of substantive procedures based on the results. Under AI audits, all samples are included in the audit scope, with almost no omissions, and the audit is ongoing. In other words, the detailed test is extended to the end of each business, greatly improving the persuasiveness of audit evidence and the reliability of audit results. In addition, under AI audits, the audit of projects can be conducted through remote networking, and the accurate positioning of Unicom GPS can effectively prevent fraudulent behavior of the audited unit and reduce the stay time in the audited unit, especially in areas where the COVID-19 epidemic is unstable and travel is sometimes restricted. The role of auditing is obvious. Networked audits may also change the audit model and promote continuous audits, thereby changing the current situation where the audit work has a relatively obvious busy and idle season, and reducing the physical and mental burden of auditors. Drone-assisted inventory monitoring has been widely used, especially in the inventory monitoring of movable and homogeneous farmed animals. Not only that, auditors can download and install a dedicated APP on their mobile phones, which is connected to the server in the cloud. At the inventory inspection site, any auditor can input "start inspection" and the system will automatically generate a blank folder. Other auditors in the project team can also upload photos of various materials related to the inspection, such as inventory codes, inventory status, auditors' work photos, etc. Other auditors in the project team can update and view these materials online in real time to achieve sharing. After the data is uploaded, the system automatically generates working papers. After the audit project is completed, the working papers are downloaded from the cloud server for storage. These improvements provide great convenience when it is inconvenient to record at the inventory inspection site. Since electronic audit working papers are generated, paper use is reduced, storage space is saved, audit costs are reduced, the time for organizing working papers is shortened, and audit efficiency is improved. Traditional audits will generate a lot of repetitive work when processing confirmation replies, which is time-consuming and labor-intensive. Under artificial intelligence auditing, in the electronic reply letters of the received confirmation letters, if the language processing system is used in a unified format, the differences in the reply results can be quickly found after reading, and a summary statistical table of the confirmation results can be generated, making it easy to find a needle in a haystack. Similarly, in the accounting entry test, the audit features that meet the conditions are set in the system in advance, so that the system can automatically display the entries that do not meet the set conditions. If necessary, the entries can also be visualized into charts to facilitate the judgment of auditors.

2.7 Application of Artificial Intelligence Technology in Recomputing

Traditional recalculation relies on formulas set manually or by computer, and selects samples for execution; under artificial intelligence, it can automatically calculate accumulated depreciation, accumulated amortization, etc., automatically compare the results, analyze the reasons for the differences, and identify the source of risk. Similarly, the income tax that the enterprise should pay can be recalculated. The big difference from manual auditing is that artificial intelligence can calculate accurately and without errors, and calculate quickly and without rest. Therefore, in the future, the recalculation process is likely to be completely replaced by artificial intelligence.

2.8 Application of Artificial Intelligence Technology in Issuing Audit Reports

The last step in a traditional audit is the issuance of the audit report. The audit report is the culmination of an audit process that includes audit planning, collecting evidence, control testing, observation, and assessing risk. The auditors will evaluate that they have sufficient and appropriate evidence, using skepticism and professional judgment to form conclusions, before coming to their eventual conclusion on the financial statements. While the audit process is systematic, the auditor report can feel static and standardized and may not provide bespoke insights, real-time feedback, or useful forward-looking guidance.

The use of predictive analytics and risk modeling in AI-based audit reporting is a significant advancement, as auditors can use machine-learning algorithms to serve multiple business scenarios and evaluate the degree of likely outcomes. This enables auditors to issue assessments that look ahead, therefore delivering prospective rather than retrospective assessments. These assessments are much more than checking items off of a checklist. They leverage real-time, data-driven forecasts of future events to assist managers in making informed decisions that are sensitive to risk exposure.

Furthermore, knowledge graphs used in audit reporting allow for a richer contextual understanding of how and when data points, business processes and stakeholders relate to each other. As per Kotepuchai & Limpiyakorn (2024) and Adelakun (2022), knowledge graphs can reveal linkages between financial activities and economic exposure factors, regulatory requirements, operational risks, and even market or competitor behavior. This interconnected view of the audited entity facilitates a more robust understanding of the nature and degree of an entity's risks and allows an entity to take actions or preventative measures that are targeted. Auditors can leverage this same knowledge in transforming audit reports into comprehensive and tailored reports that distinctly articulate key issues as well as recommendations that align to industry benchmarking standards and to compliance and/or regulatory executive frameworks.

Another important feature of reporting made possible through AI is its dynamic capability. Traditional reports are generally only at the end of the audit cycle or business process. AI systems can provide continuous or periodic reporting that allows for refreshed assessments based on new and current insights. This capability can help organizations follow overall developments quickly in today's fast-paced business climates where an organization's financial health and regulatory compliance can suffer without continuous monitoring or adjusting internal or strategic decisions. Dynamic reports work as continuing performance tools and help organizations measure the effects of corrective actions or adjusting internal controls or strategic actions. Reports provide well thought out governance evaluations on the performance of the organization's most senior executives. Reports may include key financial indicators, risk indicators, and key compliance indicators to provide evidence-based recommendations on an assessment of senior managers. Transparency helps strengthen governance or controls and ties internal performance to the strategic outcomes of the organization.

3. ADVANTAGES AND DISADVANTAGES OF APPLYING ARTIFICIAL INTELLIGENCE TO AUDITING

3.1 Advantages of Artificial Intelligence in Audit Applications

The use of artificial intelligence (AI) in auditing presents major advancements that have changed auditing as we know it. The integration of artificial intelligence (AI), and more advanced sciences and technologies such as machine learning, big data, and natural language programming are all ways AI improves accuracy in auditing, efficiency, and generating useful insights. Here are some of the most important advantages:

a) A Highly Automated Audit Process

The significant advantage of using AI in auditing is the sheer level of automation in the workflow of auditing. Unlike traditional auditing and manual auditing procedures that can require repetitive human input, the redundancy is eliminated by the use of AI (i.e., intelligent algorithm) to automate tedious tasks like data extraction, classification, and data reconciliation. Auditors can now use computer programming to validate data, check entries and require little manual inspection of documents and entries.

AI technologies can quickly view entire ledgers, journals, and transactions, converting, calculating, and summarizing information in seconds that would take auditors hours or days. This operational efficiency shortens the audit timelines and decision-making process, while achieving substantial reductions in audit operational cost. Additionally, AI removes some of the human elements in the process and therefore reduces potential human-error components (e.g. data entry, formula application) and strengthens reliability of the audit measure. The final output can be presented back to clients or engaged stakeholders with simplicity, visuals, and data-driven content to promote transparency and utility.

b) Accurate and Timely Data Collection

Data collection is the core of any audit process, and everything collected creates the foundation of the audit. The better the data, the better the audit conclusion. In traditional audits, auditors typically use sampling, and auditors search large volumes of records to discover important information. This consumes time and has the possibility of operational selection bias and missing records.

AI-based audit systems, in some instances, are able to overcome some of the limitations of traditional methods. AI-based audit systems allow auditors to access complete, real-time datasets from a centralized digital archive. These systems organize and store vast volumes of financial and non-financial data of accounting-related information (ex: invoices, contracts, emails, general transactional information) to ensure data are contextually relevant to the purpose of the audit, timely, and qualified. Additionally, AI-based tools can perform very deep-level analytics such as comparative, structural, and ratio bias across datasets. In comparison, using traditional methods, findings from audits would be much harder to understand due to comparisons simply because there would be 100+ invoices and the auditor would only sample a few invoices. Similar findings would be true for contracts, trends, etc.

This methodology, promotes the auditor to use their judgement from the AI-based data to draw understanding, meaning, and conclusions with respect to the audit, in a more timely fashion. it also provides a summation of overall results as part of a better process. The going forward conclusion is an application of AI through analysis of data and judgement by individuals conclude the audit through a more rigorous understanding of the complexities of data.

c) High Efficiency and Risk Reduction

Utilizing AI greatly enhances audit efficiency and reduces audit risk. When an audit is performed based on sampling, it is inherently limited; sample-testing is only able to review some portion of the data available, and rests on the auditor's professional experience in discerning materiality and relevance. Not only does this increase the risk of missing irregularities, but it also adds a considerable burden of time and effort during the sampling and validation process.

AI systems tackle this issue by offering audit population disclosure, which means that all transactions and data points are subject to analysis rather than just a portion, as in sampling. AI systems are so advanced that they can automatically screen all transactions, prioritize problem areas, and provide audit processes such as exception testing, outlier detection, and pattern analysis, with little to no need for a human touch. The automation of these steps greatly reduces exposure to sampling risks and allows auditors to discover anomalies or fraudulent activity earlier in the audit.

Furthermore, as part of real-time risk monitoring, AI allows auditors to be in a continuous monitoring mode, as opposed to relying on periodic monitoring. In addition, the systems can adjust their analyses in real time to adapt to emerging risks or anomalies, so the auditor and system focus is always on the most pressing risks. AI also provides significant advantages over ongoing monitoring, as it allows auditors to evaluate every transaction instead of handpicking transactions. When the audit process of examining every record occurs, it helps reduce the chances of missing a material misstatement and increasing the quality of audit assurance.

In addition, the resource savings gained from automation allow audit teams to allocate more time to value-added tasks such as fraud detection, strategic advisory, and internal control evaluation. This shift not only enhances audit quality but also strengthens the auditors' role as trusted advisors to stakeholders.

3.2 Disadvantages of Artificial Intelligence in Audit Applications

Although artificial intelligence (AI) presents numerous advantages in enhancing the auditing experience, it does bring risks and limitations that need to be evaluated. In other words, the value of AI-driven audits is predicated upon both advanced technology and its integration of traditional auditing processes and human judgment. The following are two major disadvantages of applying AI to the audit that merit consideration:

a) Weakened internal control oversight can lead to new risks:

One of the significant risks associated with the rapid embracing of AI in auditing is a potential decline in focus on internal controls. While AI limits inspection risk, and increases accuracy by processing significantly large quantities of data, dependence on the output of a seemingly infallible AI system can foster a less robust system of internal controls. It is worth stating that what we refer to as AI currently are simply weak AI which are solely employed to perform specific job functions. They do not currently possess true cognitive reasoning or ethics.

AI systems are entirely reliant on the accuracy and completeness of the data they are fed. The AI may not be able to distinguish the authenticity of the data provided if the source data has been colluded with in any way, whether intentional or by accident. If the financial people at the company are falsifying financial records or disbursing data entry protocols, the AI will not recognize this as deception unless it is specially trained to.

In addition, AI audits typically still need a human auditor to enter instructions into the AI and then interpret the results produced by the AI. If prediction assumptions, audit objectives, or data extraction methods are incorrect, the overall audit result could be compromised. As a result, AI audits remain effective only with a solid human oversight, value evaluation of the internal control environment, and an active engagement in supervising the implementation of AI. Auditors must continue to evaluate the integrity of internal controls, and actively monitor their own procedures, to make sure AI tools are always there to supplement and not replace the audit fundamentals.

b) Over-reliance on ai may undermine professional judgment:

A further difficulty is that the audit engagement may rely heavily on the use of AI for decision-making. AI can perform a variety of data-driven functions (i.e. collection, storage, and high-speed analysis) quite well, however, they do not make professional judgments on their own. AI is an assistant, not a replacement for the auditor's professional experience, intuition, or ethical judgment. Omoteso (2012) and Alles, Kogan, & Vasarhelyi (2008) mentioned that AI should augment the auditor's decision-making ability and not replace it in its entirety.

Auditing includes making decisions based on judgment in ambiguous situations, assessing complex financial situations, and using prior knowledge of the industry and regulatory environment, exacting decisions must often be made. Professional skepticism and ethical reasoning cannot be performed by AI algorithms. Auditors could make decisions based primarily on AI-generated results without understanding the context, limitations of the data, or relationship to the actual data.

Furthermore, AI is fast, especially in processing electronic financial data. However, the reliance on access to real time digital files creates an information security concern. AI audit systems need to continuously access the enterprise for updated data (Gul and Rehman, 2011), all of which must be maintained in another electronic format that adheres to cybersecurity standards. If this is not adequately updated, the organization's sensitive financial information could be breached or accessed by another unauthorized person. Gul et al (2011) added that this creates another layer of cybersecurity risk in how the organization monitors the cybersecurity strategies, system updates, and encryption encryption standards of the audit software.

The effectiveness of AI relies on its computational capacity and its ability to adjust to a continuously changing business ecosystem. If the audit AI system is not updated and maintained on a continual basis, it may process biased, incomplete, or outdated information and reach unreliable conclusions that result in an inaccurate audit. Auditors must use AI-generated insights along with continuous learning, ethical accountability and situational awareness to protect the quality of audit results.

c) Regulatory and legal uncertainty limits effective integration:

To further complicate matters, another major drawback of AI use in auditing relates to an unclear regulatory framework or legal guidance relative to AI. AI is capable of rapidly and accurately processing complex financial information, but it is in its early stages of being implemented in audit procedures, and by positive that regulatory authorities all over the world are struggling to keep pace with AI's development. Today, we do not have a universal standard or consistent set of policies indicating how AI should be deployed, monitored, or audited giving firms an unknown of compliance responsibility. This uncertainty may cause hesitance to deploy AI tools widely and may lead to non-uniform audit quality among firms or jurisdictions.

In addition, in the absence of articulated guidelines in the monitoring and reliance of AI-assistance, accountability and liability issues will be difficult to reconcile. For example, if an AI system were to produce a faulty risk assessment that led to the material misstatement not being detected, which parties would be accountable - the software developers, the audit firm, or the individual auditor who relied on the tool? The lack of accountability of AI not only hinders the possibility for reviewing audit results after substantive completion, but also degrades stakeholder assurance in AI audit assistance.

Furthermore, data governance laws like the General Data Protection Regulation (GDPR) in the EU are strict regulations around data privacy and consent with resulting friction in AI-enabled audits reliant on accessing and analyzing large volumes of sensitive information. Compliance with these regulations is complex and costly for organizations, particularly in the context of an efficient audit.

Without legal protections and ethical frameworks governing the use of AI in auditing, there may be unintended reputational, operational, and legal risks for the organization. Until international and local regulators promote standards for auditing involving AI, the complete potential for integrations of AI will not be experienced. Consequently, audit professionals and governing bodies must work collaboratively to develop standardized best practices, audit trails, and requirements for legal accountability to provide comfort in the safe and effective use of AI in auditing.

4. OPPORTUNITIES FOR CORPORATE FINANCIAL AUDITING IN THE ERA OF ARTIFICIAL INTELLIGENCE

4.1 Concepts Give Rise to Transformation

The emergence and incorporation of artificial intelligence (AI) within business financial auditing are creating a significant conceptual and professional revolution. Intelligent systems and financial robots have positioned the auditing profession at a crossroads. Increasingly, the manual methods and human roles historically associated with the profession are being augmented—and in some cases, replaced—by automated solutions. Tasks previously performed exclusive by human auditors, such as verification of transactions, fraud detection, and compliance testing, can already be performed more quickly and accurately by AI tools. This disruption of technology has heightened what many are calling a "crisis of survival" for the audit profession and there is clearly recognition that the future of auditing is not based on resisting automation, but on accepting and mastering automation.

Intelligence is no longer perceived as an additional advantage, but is now considered a critical prerequisite for the evolution and survival of the profession. If intelligent technology is not embedded into the audit process, the profession risks fading into the background of eternal change of the digital ecosystem. Auditors with no working knowledge of AI, data analysis, and intelligent algorithms can claim professional incompetency, and the mindset of both clients and regulators now goes beyond auditors possessing basics. Likewise, leaders and decisionmakers in audit organizations who fail to appreciate intelligent systems and the associated strategic implications will also be at risk of losing their ability to effectively lead audit activities in a digital world.

This emerging need for organizations to accept and integrate AI has initiated an even deeper philosophical transformation in auditing that goes beyond processes and requires reconstructing the audit theory system itself. New concepts, such as systems thinking, game theory, and probabilistic reasoning, are being created to allow auditors to interpret financial behavior, economic conditions, and organizational behavior in more structured and predictive ways. There is emerging an opportunity to develop more stable and dynamic audit models with real time data and changing risk profile patterns.

4.2 The Environment Promotes the Development of Audit Environment

The rapid technological transformations occurring throughout industries are accelerating the transformation of the audit environment and fostering a rich ecosystem within which intelligent auditing can emerge. Auditing is in transition; this shift is structural, and not limited to functional or sectoral practice. Auditing in the modern environment embodies greater interconnection, real-time data availability, and cross-sector digitization—anchored on systemic interconnectivity that allows us to re-think the design of audit from the ground up.

In order to adapt to the new conditions of the regulation, it is important for auditing to move away from traditional silos and embrace innovation across both technological and industry boundaries. The emergence of intelligent systems across industries will continuously produce vast amounts of scalable data and high contextual, accuracy, and traceability—optimum conditions for artificial intelligence in auditing.

The financial services industry has experienced a significant digital upheaval. Intelligent systems such as robo-advisors, AI-assisted customer service systems, and algorithmic investment analysis systems generate extensive transactional and behavioral data that capture the flow of social and economic value. These systems enable auditors to access financial decision-making on the ground-level, such as financial professionals' automated interactions with clients and recommendations on portfolios.

In urbanism, "smart cities"—where urban systems are integrated through IoT connected network—provide contextual data on consumer behavior, utility consumption, transportation patterns, and public service usage, which provide auditors new perspectives on risk, where socio-economic indicators and infrastructure analytics become context to assess the risk in municipal and public sector audits.

Even in the safety and surveillance sector, technologies in image recognition and video structuring will add value to the audit space by providing visual validation of audit events or transactions, particularly in high-stakes industries such as manufacturing, pharmaceuticals, and logistics. These technologies can be used to identify deviations in employee behavior, facility access, and the actual physical flow of inventory, all of which can serve as another piece of evidence to corroborate an audit investigation.

In the end, the environment in which modern auditors work is not simply changing — it is influencing the future of auditability. To make the most of it, auditors must commit to tech fluency in their approach to gather audits, integrate data flows from various industries, and develop flexible frameworks capable of responding to complexity, speed, and change.

4.3 Improved Risk Management

Artificial intelligence (AI) has a transformative effect on improving risk management in corporate financial audits. By employing machine learning algorithms, AI systems can assess significant amounts of financial data in real time, providing real-time identification of irregularities (Al-Baity, 2023), patterns, and outliers that may indicate fraud, misstatements, or failures in internal controls. The early detection capability AI offers is truly revolutionary—auditors can take action based on perceived risk and not just once filed as material and reported in their letters. The AI tools typically identify suspicious activities well before the auditor's work plan formally begins, making the auditor's work less reactive and more preventative to provide assurance on useful financial reporting (Ebere Ruth Onwubuariri et al., 2024).

Unlike conventional audit methodologies that depend on sampling methodologies that may limit generalizability and uncertainty, risk models informed by artificial intelligence (AI) provide a more comprehensive method of evaluating risk because they have access to the complete population of transactions, accounts, and departments. A data-driven approach provides the ability to examine everything with no sampling and limitations on bias that the auditor may inadvertently have. The data-driven approach provides a deep level of comfort in that no financial activity is overlooked, as well as significantly reducing the chance of a misstatement going unnoticed. In addition, AI has the capability of redeveloping risk assessments on an ever-changing basis with internal environment factors and external factors such as departmental performance, regulatory compliance changes, and market volatility to continuously update risk profiles (Heyam H. Al-Baity, 2023). The purpose is to provide a more current risk assessment based on trends and context is more salient than ever.

In addition to this, AI can provide cross-silo industry insights to enhance operational and risk management. AI could make connections between financial performance indicators, operational behaviors, and external datasets (e.g., market benchmarks and regulatory updates) that provide auditors with a broader understanding of potential vulnerabilities. The large and overarching view can better enable organizations to strengthen internal controls, inform audit strategy, and react quickly to the emergence of threats. Thus, AI doesn't just enable auditors to work better, it elevates the audit, as AI makes managing risk more efficient, proactive, and linked to the needs of businesses today.

4.4 Real-Time Reporting and Transparency

One of the most significant aspects of how artificial intelligence (AI) is changing the nature of corporate financial auditing is its ability to provide real-time reporting, which is a substantial change over traditional periodic auditing. In a traditional audit environment, data is collected, processed, and reported after the fact. This often resulted in information being shared with stakeholders long after the financial performance of the organization was completed. In a reporting environment utilizing AI, continuous auditing is possible, which means financial transactions, internal controls, and compliance activities can all be monitored continuously. Continuous auditing allows financial data to be reported and disseminated all at once but also allows the financial data to be up to date as it relates to regulatory requirements and operational effectiveness. Stakeholders such as investors, management, or regulators all receive real-time reliable information to improve transparency and build trust in the financial statements and other disclosures.

The inclusion of dynamic dashboards and real-time visual reporting has made financial data even more transparent and actionable. AI systems convert complex numerical data sets to graphics or visual formats like line graphs, heatmaps, flow diagrams, and trend charts. These tools are both user-friendly, and they allow auditors and decision-makers to quickly identify deviations, outliers, or emerging trends, that may need immediate attention. AI-supported visualizations do what traditional reporting formats, that may be cumbersome or difficult to interpret, do not—bring clarity to the data, so that even non-financial personnel can understand key performance indicators with the touch of a button. This greater immediacy and accessibility will facilitate better communication, collaboration, and data-informed decision-making, across departments, and levels of leadership.

In addition, the real-time visibility afforded by AI auditing tools allows organizations to take a more proactive approach to managing finances and mitigating risks. Having continuous visibility into cash flow, expense patterns, and operational anomalies facilitates the early identification of potential problems before they grow into significant issues. Real-time visibility is also important for ongoing compliance with financial regulations and internal governance policies, thereby reducing the risk of penalties or reputational consequences. As Ganapathy (2023) observe, the ability to respond immediately and with up-to-the-minute information to financial happenings promotes long-term financial stability and strategic agility with AI being more than an efficiency tool, but a framework for corporate accountability and sustainability.

4.5 Cost Savings and Resource Optimization

The initial adoption of artificial intelligence (AI) in auditing may require hefty upfront costs including software purchases, employee training costs, systems integration, and cybersecurity protection; however, the shrinkage in costs over time is substantial. After the AI tools are installed, they have the capacity to execute simple audit functions like extracting and sorting data, reconciliation, and exception testing at speed and scale that significantly reduce the number of auditors who need to spend time conducting manual work. Tasks that would previously take the time of several auditors over the course of days or weeks can now be accomplished in minutes. This decrease in time and labor is what creates reductions in costs of audit engagements and audit cycles and creates opportunities for companies to obtain insights and make decisions faster.

In addition, AI greatly diminishes the chance of human mistakes and expensive errors that might happen in manual audits, especially with data-intensive tasks, like reconciliations, testing for compliance, or preparing financial reports. Errors in these areas can lead to inaccurate reporting, regulatory fines, and reputational harm—all with associated monetary costs. Automation of the audit trail and supporting consistency in data analytics lead to improvements in audit output accuracy, reliability, and completeness. As noted by Vasarhelyi and O'Leary, automation also improves decision tracking, which improves audit evidence, supporting defensible compliance documentation on audits or legal scrutiny.

Beyond financial savings, AI helps with resource optimization by moving human capital out of repetitive and time-consuming tasks. This gives auditors and financial professionals the opportunity to focus on more impactful work such as evaluating strategic risks, conducting complex financial analysis, assessing internal controls, and providing advisory services. Rather than conducting data entry or basic verification work, an auditor may leverage their knowledge in relation to the outputs generated by the AI, develop strategies for mitigating risk, and provide customized recommendations for management. This not only adds more value to the audit process, but it also elevates the auditor's role in the organization from compliance enforcer to strategic member of the business. AI thereby creates a more effective allocation of timing and talent, supporting innovation and long-term value to the organization.

4.6 Enhanced Decision-Making

Artificial intelligence (AI) has changed auditors from mere compliance reviewers to partners in strategy by giving them powerful evidence-based insights, resulting in smarter and more timely decision-making in boardrooms. Unlike traditional auditing methods, which often depend on the analysis of historical data and personal instinct, AI systems will scan historical and currently available financial data and identify hidden patterns, trends, and anomalies quickly and accurately. These insights allow for predictive analysis of financial circumstance. Predictive analysis assists auditors in forecasting financial circumstances, identifying areas of elevated risk and modifying audit strategies accordingly. Targeted areas of financial risk, resource allocation, and timeliness are strengthened in the audit plan as a result of these AI-driven insights.

AI capabilities go beyond forecasting and detection; the AI actively facilitates decision-making by proposing the possible effects of using current trajectories of data. For example, AI enables an auditor to identify seasonal changes in cashflow, spikes in expenditures, trends in supplier payments, and other irregularities so that the auditor can potentially raise a red flag sooner and suggest actions that might resolve these issues. This proactive auditing process is a switch from a reactive audit process, which not only aims to reduce risk but also enables an organization to quickly pivot because of changing economic conditions or regulations.

Furthermore, auditors' advisory value is greatly augmented by using AI tools. AI has the ability to analyze sophisticated financial structures and operational metrics and enable auditors to give practical recommendations that go much beyond reporting findings. For example, AI can help identify way costly inefficiencies, identify significant budgeting practice, evaluate capital investments, or identify areas where the business has underperformed. This provides companies the ability to make informed decisions about allocating resources, instituting long-term financial planning, and undertaking leveraged investment decisions. As Coffi and George (2022) point out, data-driven guidance ultimately influences profitability, reflexivity, and sustainability capabilities—helping firms elevate financial performance contributions to the overall organizational and corporate strategies and objectives. Ultimately, using AI tools in the audit process is not simply about automating the audit processes. It further magnifies the strategic role auditors can serve in a business.

4.7 Compliance and Regulatory Adherence

Artificial Intelligence (AI) can improve compliance within financial auditing by automating the verification of compliance with a regulatory framework such as Generally Accepted Accounting Principles (GAAP), International Financial Reporting Standards (IFRS), and other jurisdictional specific requirements for financial reporting. AI-enabled auditing tools can provide ongoing monitoring of financial reporting to ensure that financial statements internal controls are prepared in accordance with the prevailing regulatory framework. Ongoing monitoring of financial reporting practices lessens the risk of non-compliance, which may expose organizations to fines, reputational damage, and possible legal liability. By embedding compliance logic into AI, the system automatically identifies inconsistencies and discrepancies in the reports and alerts the auditors in time before the completion of the reports. Therefore, AI can limit dependency on manual reviews in addition to facilitating less pressure on the internal controls, enabling the auditor to concentrate more on the analytical and strategic functions of the auditor.

Furthermore, AI plays a role in regulatory responsiveness because it allows auditors to incorporate changes made in accounting or financial regulation into audit workflows in real-time. This real-time responsiveness means that auditors will no longer need to manually update audit programs or run the risk of not being aware of newly adopted compliance initiatives. Moreover, AI systems generate comprehensive audit trails documenting every transaction, control check and audit work step, all in an unalterable manner. These unalterable audit trails provide not only transparency, but also enhance the efficiency of audits when reviewed by regulators or external customers. During an examination or regulatory compliance audit, organizations leveraging AI systems are able to produce full work papers when regulatory expectations may require this level of detail. As noted by Surya Sairam Parimi (2018), the combination of automated compliance verification and stringent audit trail capabilities will make AI a significant advantage (Surya Sairam Parimi, 2018) in achieving the intended outcomes of continuous compliance, improving human oversight weaknesses, and advance accountability and transparency in financial activities.

4.8 Integration Across Financial Systems

Artificial Intelligence (AI) presents a notable advantage in terms of its ability to interface with various financial systems used by any given company - including Enterprise Resource Planning (ERP), Customer Relationship Management (CRM) systems, or accounting software - pause and connect these operating systems will generate a seamless flow of information across departments, resulting in a single view of the organization's financial system. Traditional audits include the banal, repetitive act of managing numerous manual data connections across disparate systems. It may take hours, days, or in larger organizations, potentially weeks, to simply consolidate the various reports from the data silos into a single overview and develop an audit plan. Let us not forget that there are sufficient manual interactions that have the potential to introduce errors and uncertainties into the audited data system. Instead of the organization taking the time to consolidate, AI tools synchronize the range of systems in real time which diminishes time delays, data duplication, or errors in data tracking for each department. Without silo data, AI systems can facilitate connectivity, communication, and consistency across monthly and quarterly departmental reports while producing high-quality financial reports to deliver to investors. Stakeholders (financial managers, auditors, and eventually investors) can rest assured that the auditable reports from the financial manager are appropriate, accurate, and current throughout the organizations' financial system. The reliance on autonomous, algorithmic, hand-off, reporting systems will lead to increased reliability, stronger auditable engagements, and overall higher internal transparency.

AI-driven systems also provide holistic workflow automation that enables the entire audit process to be completed from data ingestion and classification, through validation, reconciliation, and reporting. Various document types such as invoices, contracts, journal entries, and bank statements can all be cross referenced automatically on various platforms that will flag any inconsistencies for immediate follow up. This not only enhances the integrity of data but also decreases the likelihood of missing a discrepancy which could undermine the financial credibility of the organization. According to Lawrence Damilare Oyeniyi et al. (2024), this verse integration will provide for real time anomaly detection in order to quickly sort out errors (Lawrence Damilare Oyeniyi et al., 2024) while keeping a clean and transparent audit trail. AI can enhance workflows so organizations can conduct audits faster and enhance financial health of organizations based on better consistency, reporting and transparency of data across all financial systems.

4.9 Continuous Learning and Knowledge Sharing

Artificial intelligence (AI) is key to driving continuous learning and knowledge sharing in the field of auditing. Today's AI-based audit tools are not fixed methodologies, rather they are processes of continuous learning based on the analysis of new audit data, recognizing emerging patterns, and identifying recurring trends. These AI-powered tools have the ability to automatically update centralized knowledge banks with case studies, anomalies, best practices, and previous outcomes. Auditors can rely on this expanding bank of institutional knowledge to help make their decisions, improve audit procedures, and allows them to better respond to complex financial complexity. In other words, AI helps not just the- individual audit, but it makes this knowledge institutional knowledge and will help ensure auditor in different departments, branches, or regions have the same knowledge and insights.

The addition of cloud-based AI auditing systems enhances this collaborative environment by facilitating real-time communication and data sharing among auditors who are located around the globe. These systems allow audit teams to collaborate on working papers, share findings, comment on unusual activities, and update audit progress all in real-time, without the prolonged wait times of traditional paper-based processes. By allowing communication that can be shared by all team members, teams can stay focused on their joint efforts and goals and avoid duplication of effort and ensure they have a working understanding of the scope of work and state of the audit. In addition, cloud-based technology allows for secure, centralized, and logically organized data storage which also reduces the burden of relying on hard-copy documentation and enhances transparency and traceability of data. According to Jungwoo Ryoo and others (2013), collaborative, cloud-based auditing systems enhance operational efficiency and collaboration (Jungwoo Ryoo, et al., 2013), reduce the time taken to complete audits, and encourage a more flexible and responsive style of auditing. In particular, those collaboratively connected auditors are able to leverage existing knowledge to stay smarter, faster, and more connected as each audit improves on the last one.

5. PROBLEMS IN CORPORATE FINANCIAL AUDITING IN THE ERA OF ARTIFICIAL INTELLIGENCE

a. Top-level design lacks wisdom - Intelligent audit is a new model of centralized analysis, discovery of doubts, decentralized implementation, and systematic research supported by artificial intelligence technology. Data mining solves the problem of data drowning, artificial intelligence solves the problem of autonomous association, and blockchain technology breaks through the bottleneck of data fidelity. Therefore, the new intelligent audit technology has eliminated some traditional audit methods and methods, and has spawned a new technical system, which requires the construction of economic activity models, completion of recalculation and verification, marking of abnormal conditions, and warning of in-depth verification based on the computer's autonomous learning ability. This inevitably requires the reshaping of the audit system, the reconstruction of the audit mechanism, and the reconstruction of the audit theory in accordance with the intelligent audit method to achieve overall transformation.

b. Blurred understanding of rules - As Internet thinking and IT technology are widely used in social governance and enterprise management, information islands, automation islands, and islands between information systems and automation systems have become technical barriers between the truth and audits. Especially when faced with massive data in enterprise management ERP systems, traditional audit theory is difficult to interpret the characteristics and laws of audit work in the new era. It is necessary to start from the established institutional logic, continuously obtain information in stages and levels, deeply integrate advanced analytical technology with the new generation of information technology, and continuously verify the compliance, consistency, and logic of the value flow, information flow, and material flow of economic activities.

c. The emergence of "technological unemployment" - The knowledge structure of auditors must be updated, and audit talents need to be updated. The application of artificial intelligence in the audit field is changing the structure of the audit labor market, that is, most repetitive labor is being automated, and many audit jobs will be replaced by humanoid robots in the future, and auditors will have fewer and fewer job opportunities. Compared with manual audits, computer processing speed and efficiency far exceed those of human brains. Audit reforms in the data era can greatly improve the efficiency of audit work, and this application will further increase the concerns and worries of existing auditors, that is, whether audit reforms in the data era will create more job opportunities or destroy more opportunities? This depends on whether the audit work is routine or unconventional? Audit work is usually divided into routine work and unconventional work, as well as routine cognition and unconventional cognition. Generally speaking, routine work and routine cognition are very easy to automate, that is, people engaged in this type of audit work are very easy to be replaced, while complex audit work engaged in unconventional work and unconventional cognition is very difficult to automate. For example, the automation of audit work brought about by emerging technologies can help auditors quickly handle routine audit work, but it cannot completely replace auditors in making audit judgments. At present, routine work or routine cognition related to audit planning, risk assessment and final audit will be gradually replaced by artificial intelligence, and people engaged in basic audit work will face the risk of unemployment, while audit professional judgment and issuing audit reports will be temporarily retained. In order to cope with the impact of artificial intelligence on the audit profession, auditors should improve their skills in mathematics, statistics, computers and data methods.

d. One of the main barriers to implementing artificial intelligence in financial auditing is that auditors do not have sufficient technical proficiency to properly utilize or evaluate the outputs offered by AI tools, compounded by the opaque nature of most AI systems. Although it is recognized that AI can enhance an audit smuch more quickly and accurately than traditional assessments, many auditors are simply untrained in data analytics, machine learning, or any computational systems, leading to distrust with Ai-based tools. This lack of technical expertise limits effective adoption, as well as poses a risk to audit quality if AI outputs are not adequately understood or effectively evaluated. Furthermore, many AI-driven algorithms are often regarded as "black boxes," producing reports or results without a explanation of the rationale or decision tree logic. This lack of willingness to understand AI outputs leads to further difficulty in justifying findings based on AI analytics, especially in highly regulated environments where given audit evidence is a fundamental requirement of the engagement. Psychologically, human tendencies have biases and when they encounter an unfamiliar process or an 'automatic' function of AI, they often hesitate or resist the invitation to trust a comupter-based analysis over their own autonomous thoughts, but without clearly understanding how the AI developed its narrative. Likewise, auditors would be remiss in their evaluation of an Ai analysis-based engagement process due to a inability to adequately assess the reliability of outcomes based on either artificial analysis is considered completely biased or erroneous, or both. As such, there is justification for the need for investment in continuous learning for accountability and oversight in auditors when using AI functions in audit practice, while progressively focusing on Ai systems that advance explainability and transparency in reviews that are controlled by auditors (Hamzah et al., 2024).

e. Another problem that is emerging in the age of AI, auditing, is that the pace of AI adoption is variable and unequal across firms of different sizes, which raises the potential for widening quality disparities in audit results. Large firms, especially the Big 4, have started to deploy AI tools into their audit activities. However, many smaller and mid-sized audit firms face serious restrictions in AI adoption. These barriers include insufficient finances, weak technical capabilities, and often unclear regulatory frameworks that limit the effective adoption of AI in smaller and mid-sized audit firms. As the authors Fachriyah and Anggraeni (2024) indicate, many smaller audit firms in Indonesia lack the resources, both financial and technical, to support access or implement AI with little government support for standards or training. The implications of this gap not only have implications for audit quality and competitiveness, but longer term structural imbalances, in the profession and as an ecosystem. In order to ensure that AI delivers its benefits to audit quality and innovative audit approaches continues to the future, there must be concerted effort, including subsidizations of AI tools, clear regulatory frameworks for AI around audit firms, and capacity-building programs. Otherwise, we run the potential for the benefits of AI in auditing to be concentrated to just a few large firms, leaving smaller audit firms even more disadvantaged in an increasingly and rapidly digitalizing environment. Accordingly, addressing the adoption gap in the auditing profession is a vital first step in providing opportunities for equitable audit quality, continued standards as an industry, and innovative audit thinking across audit firms (Fachriyah & Anggraeni, 2024).

6. CONCLUSION

To sum up, artificial intelligence (AI) is at the leading edge of the current technology revolution, drastically changing industry sectors around the world, accounting and auditing included. While previous industrial revolutions replaced primarily physical labor with technology, the AI revolution replaces cognitive and mental labor. Jobs that appeared safe as they required reasoning and thinking skills, like accountants, auditors, clerks, and bank tellers, are being changed and sometimes completely automated by intelligent machines or systems that can assuming completing complicated calculations, analysis, and reasoning/logical work.

This change signifies a substantial change in the field of financial auditing. AI is not something that may happen in the future—something that we may want in the future. From improving the efficiency of audit planning and control testing to improving fraud detection and real-time risk assessments, AI-driven technologies are driving improvements in audit accuracy and efficiency, enhancing reporting, and reducing human error (Aitkazinov, 2023), all of which improve both real and perceived quality of audit related services and significant matter second and overall audit cycles. However, these improvements and efficiencies come with trade-offs in the form of challenges, such as transparency of algorithms, compliance, and risk to traditional jobs. As a result, the auditing profession will have to evolve in order to manage these challenges more proactively and strategically to respond to this evolving profession.

As AI is further embedded within the financial system, demand will increase dramatically for highly educated persons that have a strong grounding in accounting and auditing, as well as understanding data analytics, machine learning and information systems. The accounting profession will require both financial and technological skills in more multidisciplinary ways. This will require rethinking talent development approaches in higher education and corporate training programs. Universities will have to modify curriculum to reflect the emerging realities of AI accounting and offer courses across disciplines that combine finance, data science and ethics.

Additionally, organizations need to understand the strategic significance of accounting and audit functions in an AI-powered economy. These functions are not only operationally necessary, they are fundamental to governance, compliance, and strategy. In this new AI economy, organizations need to invest in intelligent systems while developing in-house capacity to understand and govern AI outputs.

The adoption of AI in auditing does not herald the end of the role of human auditors, but rather shifts the role of audit practitioners. Future practitioners will engage much more as strategic advisors, data interpreters, and systems evaluators than as transactional processors. Thus, balancing a focus on technology, talent, and ethics is critical to ensure that the auditing profession is relevant, resilient, and reliable in the future.

REFERENCES

Мюллер, В., Кузнєцова, А. Я., Христофорова, О. М., Карпачова, О. В., & Сулима, М. О. (2020). Accounting and Auditing according to International Standards as a managment function. *Financial and Credit Activity Problems of Theory and Practice*, *4*(35), 60–68. DOI: 10.18371/fcaptp.v4i35.221787

Adelakun, B. O. (2022). Ethical Considerations in the Use of AI for Auditing: Balancing Innovation and Integrity. European Journal of Accounting, Auditing and Finance Research, 10(12), 91-108. Retrieved from https://tudr.org/id/eprint/3072/

Aitkazinov, A. (2023). The role of artificial intelligence in auditing: Opportunities and challenges. International Journal of Research in Engineering, Science and Management, 6(6), 117-119. Retrieved from https://journal.ijresm.com/index.php/ijresm/article/view/2740

Al-Baity, H. H. (2023). The artificial intelligence revolution in digital finance in Saudi Arabia: A comprehensive review and proposed framework. *Sustainability (Basel)*, *15*(18), 13725. https://www.mdpi.com/2071-1050/15/18/13725. DOI: 10.3390/su151813725

Alles, M. G., Kogan, A., & Vasarhelyi, M. A. (2008). Audit automation for implementing continuous auditing: Principles and problems. Rutgers Business School, 1, 1-24. Retrieved from https://raw.rutgers.edu/MiklosVasarhelyi/Resume%20Articles/RESEARCH%20&%20W ORKING%20PAPERS/audit%20automation.pdf

Arun, K. (2024). ARTIFICIAL INTELLIGENCE INVESTMENT, REALISTIC REPORTS, AND FINANCIAL LOSS. *Denetişim*, (31), 117–128. DOI: 10.58348/denetisim.1519501

Coffi, J., & George, B. (2022). The Fintech Revolution and the Changing Role of Financial Advisors. *Journal of Applied and Theoretical Social Sciences*, *4*(3), 261–274. https://iccsor.com/index.php/jatss/article/view/147. DOI: 10.37241/jatss.2022.66

. Fachriyah, N., & Anggraeni, O. L. (2024). The Use of Artificial Intelligence in Financial Statement Audit. Jurnal Indonesia Sosial Teknologi, 5(10).

Ganapathy, V. (2023). AI in auditing: A comprehensive review of applications, benefits and challenges. Shodh Sari-An International Multidisciplinary Journal, 2(04), 328-343. Retrieved from https://icertpublication.com/wp-content/uploads/2023/10/29.-AI-in-Auditing.pdf

Ghosh, P., & Ghosh, S. (2024). Neural Network and Neural Computing. In R. Jaganathan, S. Mehta, & R. Krishan (Eds.), Intelligent Decision Making Through Bio-Inspired Optimization (pp. 131-175). IGI Global Scientific Publishing. ChicagoDOI: 10.4018/979-8-3693-2073-0.ch009

Gul, I. ur Rehman, A., & Islam, M. H. (2011, June). Cloud computing security auditing. In The 2nd International Conference on Next Generation Information Technology (pp. 143-148). IEEE. Retrieved from https://ieeexplore.ieee.org/abstract/document/5967489?casa_token=lsIwW-gEZN0AAAA A:NuYnEVH7a3UW1jokbYykHQZpux3ctA7CUv3G_E2RTBbvl9eWCjzDbKqWt3ZOUkG04AuZY89HXQ

Hamzah, P., Yeba, E., Maithy, S. P., & Poetra, G. B. (2024). Opportunities and Challenges in Integrating Artificial Intelligence into Financial Auditing. *Journal of Economic Education and Entrepreneurship Studies*, *5*(4), 591–600.

Issa, H., Sun, T., & Vasarhelyi, M. A. (2016). Research ideas for artificial intelligence in auditing: The formalization of audit and workforce supplementation. Journal of emerging technologies in accounting, 13(2), 1-20. Retrieved from https://publications.aaahq.org/jeta/article-abstract/13/2/1/9209/Research-Ideas-for-Artificial-Intelligence-in

Kotepuchai, P., & Limpiyakorn, Y. (2024). Machine Learning and Substantive Analytical Procedure in Financial Audit. Retrieved from https://www.academia.edu/124153258/Machine_Learning_and_Substantive_Analytical_Procedure_in_Financial_Audit

Luo, X., Wang, X., & Jiang, T. (2025). Application of AI technology in audit risk assessment and control: Taking internal audit of higher education institutions as an example. Journal of Infrastructure. *Policy and Development*, *9*(1), 10125. DOI: 10.24294/jipd10125

Munoko, I., Brown-Liburd, H. L., & Vasarhelyi, M. (2020). The ethical implications of using artificial intelligence in auditing. *Journal of Business Ethics*, *167*(2), 209–234. https://link.springer.com/article/10.1007/s10551-019-04407-1. DOI: 10.1007/s10551-019-04407-1

Omoteso, K. (2012). The application of artificial intelligence in auditing: Looking back to the future. Expert Systems with Applications, 39(9), 8490-8495. Retrieved from https://www.sciencedirect.com/science/article/pii/S095741741200111X?casa_token=R0r ohONtAoIAAAAA:ZI89YFkRHRpVSzBXBuM2ZT4-mgP6sbiotR1A6UoO-QrSiPPT8n WAfezvZi13CbNXjDtP_X4KrWA

Onwubuariri, E. R., Adelakun, B. O., Olaiya, O. P., & Ziorklui, J. E. K. (2024). AI-Driven risk assessment: Revolutionizing audit planning and execution. Finance & Accounting Research Journal, 6(6), 1069-1090. Retrieved from https://fepbl.com/index.php/farj/article/view/1236

Oyeniyi, L. D., Ugochukwu, C. E., & Mhlongo, N. Z. (2024). Transforming financial planning with AI-driven analysis: A review and application insights. Finance & Accounting Research Journal, 6(4), 626-647. Retrieved from https://www.fepbl.com/index.php/farj/article/view/1037

Parimi, S. S. (2018). Optimizing Financial Reporting and Compliance in SAP with Machine Learning Techniques. Available at *SSRN* 4934911. Retrieved from

. Rizki, M., & Novianto, E. (2023). Auditing Artificial Intelegence Menggunakan COBIT 2019. JUSIFOR: Jurnal Sistem Informasi dan Informatika, 2(1), 1-7.

Ryoo, J., Rizvi, S., Aiken, W., & Kissell, J. (2013). Cloud security auditing: Challenges and emerging approaches. *IEEE Security and Privacy*, *12*(6), 68–74. https://ieeexplore.ieee.org/abstract/document/6662349. DOI: 10.1109/MSP.2013.132

Schiff, D. S., Kelley, S., & Camacho Ibáñez, J. (2024). The emergence of artificial intelligence ethics auditing. *Big Data & Society*, *11*(4), 20539517241299732. DOI: 10.1177/20539517241299732

Vasarhelyi, M. A., & O'Leary, D. Artificial Intelligence in Accounting and Auditing: Creating Value with AI, Volume 5. Retrieved from https://raw.rutgers.edu/MiklosVasarhelyi/Resume%20Articles/CHAPTERS%20IN%20B OOKS/C12.%20creating%20value%20with%20ai.pdf

Wu, C., Liu, S., & Zhou, Z. (2024). Intelligent Information Audit System Construction: Integration of Big Data and Artificial Intelligence Technologies. *Frontiers in Science and Engineering*, *4*(4), 163–167. DOI: 10.54691/23b70s23

Zhao, H., & Wang, Y. (2023). A Big Data-Driven Financial Auditing Method Using Convolution Neural Network. *IEEE Access : Practical Innovations, Open Solutions*, *11*, 41492–41502. https://ieeexplore.ieee.org/stamp/stamp.jsp?arnumber=10107399. DOI: 10.1109/ACCESS.2023.3269438

Chapter 4
Auditing Generative AI

Asmita Jain
https://orcid.org/0009-0005-6790-2919
University at Buffalo, SUNY, USA

Zayan Shaheen
University at Buffalo, SUNY, USA

Dollie Juneja
https://orcid.org/0009-0008-4455-2348
University at Buffalo, SUNY, USA

Anuja Ulhe
https://orcid.org/0009-0006-7481-8675
University at Buffalo, SUNY, USA

ABSTRACT

The swift growth and implementation of Generative AI systems has created several unique governance and compliance concerns, notably in terms of ethical usage, data protection, accountability, and transparency. This study presents a complete audit approach for monitoring GenAI systems, focusing on critical aspects such as risk assessment, control deployment, and management of compliance. By utilizing known governance frameworks such as COSO & COBIT 5 to provide a systematic guideline for examining the operational integrity, security, & ethical aspects of GenAI installations. The approach for the audit framework we propose focuses on addressing GenAI specific risks such as inaccuracies in AI results, data security vulnerabilities, and a lack of clarity in AI decision-making processes. Our method handles these issues using a mix of automated control evaluations, threat evaluation, and continuous monitoring. The study presents ways for resolving governance challenges, such as changing legal environments and the complexities of keeping AI models in accordance with retention laws.

DOI: 10.4018/979-8-3373-3078-5.ch004

1. INTRODUCTION

In today's digital age Artificial Intelligence (AI), specifically Generative Artificial Intelligence (GenAI), has taken the world by storm, amalgamating a huge following and changing the way we interact with technology across many industries such as entertainment, healthcare, education, and finance. This technological advancement has made everyday life much easier. Giving people new perspectives and methods of successfully completing tasks. GenAI has transcended our interactions with technology allowing for a more efficient and seamless integration. With the help of large language models (LLM), the power behind Generative AI, we are able to produce intricate and elaborate results. GenAI has capabilities that are unachievable due to its instantaneous manner.

The capacity of GenAI to influence many businesses is becoming increasingly clear as it develops. In addition to improving current procedures, the technology is opening completely new avenues for creativity. For example, GenAI is transforming personalized medicine and drug development in the healthcare industry, and it is opening the door to more immersive and engaging entertainment experiences. Automation is significantly increasing efficiency and accuracy in the banking industry by automating processes like fraud detection and client support.

Each year, Stanford publishes an AI index report (Stanford University, 2024) covering promising trends and research capabilities in AI. The 2024 report describes an important moment when AI's influence into public consciousness. The proportion of those who think AI will majorly impact their life in the next 3-5 years have grown from 60% to 66% this year. As AI becomes ubiquitous, there has been a growing investment in the private sector such as healthcare, financial services and cybersecurity, generative AI is largely influencing our daily lives. The Stanford report states two prominent examples that provide illustration on exactly how this change is occurring. In 2023, With the release of more significant AI applications - from AlphaDev (Stanford University, 2024) which makes sorting algorithms more efficient, to GNoME, which facilitates the process of material discovery. Second, Open AI launches two new models o-1 and o-1 mini with human-like reasoning that aims to spend more time computing more complex and challenging reasoning based mathematical problems.

Notwithstanding these developments, the quick uptake of GenAI has sparked serious worries, especially about its potential abuse. Millions of dollars have been lost as a result of scammers' use of generative AI techniques to produce deepfakes that mimic the sounds and appearance of family members. Such abuse emphasizes how urgently a legal framework that guarantees the ethical and responsible use of these technologies is needed.

Yet, one reads more about the AI misuse and frauds seeing how technology creates societal harms. Scammers have been using generative AI tools to create deep fakes, imitating voices of distressed family members. These digital frauds have been deceiving millions of dollars leaving people and families with recourse. With the aim of addressing these concerns and harms, experts from industry and academia have called for generative AI to be audited. The continent and perils of widely spread frameworks of artificial intelligence creating a lot of ethical dilemmas and with significant ethical and social challenges when identifying and addressing solutions to cybersecurity vulnerabilities. The convergence of human and generative AI decision making in a rapidly changing and diversifying advancement world calls for agility of auditors making decisions. The accelerated use of generative AI represents (Mökander, J., et al. 2023) opportunities for social advocates, researchers and academic scholars to call out for these systems to be audited. Auditing in the context refers to a structured and independent approach of planning and managing risks and depicting how well generative AI's systems design, properties and how the impact adheres to applicable standards and norms. In Section 2, we will discuss in detail what auditing AI in general is more about. However, existing possible approaches and procedures in identifying drivers and possible solutions have failed to address the governance challenges posed by generative AI applications, which provide eminent opportunities and capabilities that are adaptable to a wide range of cybersecurity tasks. Auditors at a substantial level need to develop skills (Rodgers et al., 2024) and embrace the opportunity of auditing generative AI. Through this chapter, we address the gap outlining the novel approach on how to audit these systems.

Creating a successful audit mechanism requires a fundamental change in our perspective on AI responsibility in addition to being a technological problem. Making sure AI systems are open, auditable, and consistent with society norms necessitates striking a delicate balance between encouraging discovery and maintaining regulatory supervision. While designing a holistic audit ecosystem one must consider additional factors like who is auditing and how to ensure post audit action. Designing an institutional audit ecosystem is a non-trivial question because AI pioneers like Andrew Ng stated that "Auditing AI systems is crucial to ensure they're behaving as expected and are aligned with societal values. It helps organizations maintain trust and avoid costly mistakes. Similarly, Joy Buolamwini, Founder of Algorithmic Justice League, mentioned that "AI systems must be held accountable to the same standards as humans, which is why auditing is essential. Audits allow us to detect and mitigate bias before AI harms marginalized communities."

Again, to precisely mention, the main contribution offered in this chapter would not be on whether the AI should be audited or not. Our focus here would be on providing a blueprint on how to conduct audits for generative AI. To be clear, our primary aim would be to answer the question: if technology providers are equipped with the right process and have enough appetite to audit generative AI, how could these audits be more structured to be more efficient and robust enough?

The remainder of the chapter proceeds as follows. Section 3 entails the motivation behind choosing this. Section 4 provides knowledge on the scope of the chapter. Section 5 provides a brief literature review on the work of how to audit generative AI. Section 6 talks about the Challenges, Section 7 introduces our novel approach on how to audit generative AI. Section 8 highlights the limitations of our approach and proposes avenues for further research. Finally, Section 9 concludes by discussing the implications of our findings for technology providers, policymakers and independent auditors.

2. MOTIVATION

The most ubiquitous Large Language model - ChatGPT accessible and available on demand for free is a gamechanger in the world of AI. The phenomenon of Generative AI is definitely the most significant event of our time. While the marketplace for generative AI is rapidly changing, we felt our responsibility to discuss more on the scope and demand for evolution in auditing GenAI when we talk about the realm of security implications. Ethical concentrations, (Rane, 2023) dilemmas and compromises are introduced when identifying and mitigating solutions in the landscape of cybersecurity and data privacy. With no doubt GenAI is the next most crucial frontier for cybersecurity. The security implications in the domain of data privacy, governance and compliance, the regulatory landscape ushered a motivation to develop a novel approach with the opportunity to build an ethical framework emphasizing trust, accountability and transparency.

The hazards of abusing AI technology, especially in cybersecurity, increase as it becomes more pervasive in society. Traditional security techniques are no longer enough as hackers and other malevolent actors use GenAI technologies more frequently to automate assaults. As a result, auditing GenAI systems is important for both preserving ethical integrity and protecting against new cyberthreats that take use of the systems' inherent capabilities.

This research will inspect the key and major challenges we face while using generative AI such as bias detection and fairness, content accuracy, ethical compliance. To prevent the potential misuse of information such as creating deep fakes or voice overs we need a strong and well-built audit framework for maintaining trust, accountability, and ethical integrity in generative AI systems. In order to achieve that we would need to continuously audit these generative AI tools to avoid cyberthreats or any unethical usage of the available resource and modeled data. On top of ethical concerns and information assurance, auditing of Generative AI (GenAI) must handle crucial issues such as data security, intellectual property, and user privacy. When GenAI systems produce content from large datasets, the danger of unwanted exposure of confidential information and related privacy violations grows considerably. Auditing these systems demands a thorough review of data security safeguards, encryption mechanisms, and compliance with privacy standards. Rights related to intellectual property provide a particular difficulty in the GenAI area, since the distinction among authentic human-created content and AI-generated outputs frequently blurs. Auditors must create procedures or rules for differentiating between established and generative material, ensuring that AI systems do not accidentally plagiarize or contravene on existing works. This paper will delve into these new concerns, emphasizing the significance of building regulatory structures and auditing mechanisms to protect integrity of data, user rights, and the intellectual property environment in the quickly changing GenAI field.

Furthermore, auditors need to be prepared to recognize and reduce risks specific to GenAI, such as those that jeopardize data integrity or lead to bias, when new types of cyberattacks emerge. Auditing structures need to be adaptable enough to emerging dangers while upholding strict accountability and transparency requirements, as malevolent actors continue to take advantage of the quick advances in AI.

Defining an ethical pathway to address the below the paramount challenges framed around cybersecurity and data privacy emphasized the (Gusher, T., 2024) need for robust governance practice to mitigate the risks and complications highlighted as below:

1. New and improved cyber-attacks that are being created by malicious actors
2. Business models unable to use it more securely and with responsibility
3. Producing incorrect, bad and bias result through various cyber attacks
4. Improved cybersecurity programs by bad actors to corrupting ethical integrity

The regulatory landscape is defined to be crucial, complex and evolving, calling for adaptive and collaborative approaches that offer insights into the strategic framing of the proposed methodology.

3. NEED TO AUDIT GENERATIVE AI

Since Artificial Intelligence is rapidly advancing and integrated into various domains, systems and services, it becomes crucial to analyze and introspect its interoperability. Existing institutions and governance systems often find it impossible to tackle the developments. There comes in the resolution for Why Audit generative AI? Auditing is the procedural process of gathering and evaluating evidence about a system or an operation and presenting the results to relevant stakeholders. Just as the procedure of auditing (Mökander, Curl, & Kshirsagar, 2024) can be used to produce transparency, fairness and accountability, thereby auditing can be used as a governance model for AI systems. A governance approach allows systems and institutions to be updated and secure. The promise of auditing as an AI governance mechanism is supported by four concepts:

- transparency and procedural regularity promote good governance.
- embedding system safety ensuring compliance standards are followed.
- proactive AI system design helps detect risks and stop harm before it happens.
- Control measures are regularly updated and monitored; and
- the operational independence of the auditee and the auditor enhances the evaluation's objectivity.

It is now more crucial than ever to make sure that the auditing procedures stay up to date with the fast development of GenAI technology. New AI systems frequently pose difficult and distinct problems that conventional auditing techniques are ill-prepared to handle. This calls for a thorough rethinking of auditing techniques to make sure they can keep up with the rapidly changing landscape of artificial intelligence.

The domain of Auditing AI is emerging with the passage of time. Over the time, auditing AI has been defined in many ways for many purposes. In a few cases, it is performed as a mandatory step to ensure that AI systems meet legal, compliance and regulatory requirements. Whereas, in other cases technology enterprises engage in audits to perform risk analysis, identify and mitigate risks in the AI systems (AuditBoard, 2024).

Traditional institutions and governance structures face difficulties as a result of the quick growth of AI technology, frequently finding it impossible to keep up with advancements. Because AI systems are regularly updated through retraining, ongoing maintenance and monitoring are required to guarantee their correct operation and reduce the possibility of errors in judgment. This emphasizes how crucial AI audits are throughout the development, operation, and maintenance stages. Thus, constant auditing is a useful tool for guaranteeing the moral operation of AI systems over time in addition to being required by law. We can guarantee that any unanticipated risks or ethical issues be handled as they emerge as opposed to after the fact by integrating auditing into each phase of the AI lifecycle. It is advised to use a risk-based approach, where the degree of audit reflects the risk level of the AI service, to strike a balance between the necessity of audits and the related expenses. In addition, artificial intelligence auditing is essential from a governance and ethical standpoint. Audits are necessary to ensure compliance with ethical standards like safety, justice, and transparency, providing users with assurance. Additionally, because AI systems are utilized in many nations and companies, interoperability across AI governance frameworks is essential to putting these moral precepts into reality. In light of these considerations, independent audits play a crucial role in addressing AI risks that cannot be effectively addressed by voluntary developer principles alone, hence promoting effective AI governance.

The necessity for strict auditing procedures is reinforced by the growing complexity of AI systems, especially in generative models. Human monitoring is increasingly more important when AI makes decisions on its own to maintain accountability and prevent unforeseen outcomes like prejudice, discrimination, or privacy concerns. Organizations run the danger of facing legal action as well as public mistrust of AI systems if they don't have a suitable auditing framework in place.

Auditing AI is an emerging battlefield of transparency and assessment. Initially, AI models were developed driving adoption and expansion, however these solutions have become black boxes (The CAQ., 2024) of competence. The capabilities and skills required to audit the advanced generative AI tools and systems are emerging and scarce, leading to a patchwork quilt of experience and proficiency. The subsequent negative impact outgrows when escalating regulatory and compliance challenges stemming from complexities of most advanced generative AI systems. For auditors (Thomson Reuters., 2023) and compliance personnel, the journey of AI transparency initiates not with the technology, but rather by inculcating a clear understanding of goals and objectives, its touchpoints and finally its technology ecosystem.

Because modern systems are interconnected, problems that were once isolated errors can now have the capacity to destabilize entire ecosystems, redefine justice, and rewrite the regulatory playbook. As a result, the repercussions of unregulated AI are becoming more and more obvious.

Industry leaders, accounting practitioners, forensic scientists are walking towards resolving the issues of skills, procedures and transparency and regulatory implications; however (The CAQ., 2024), what steps can audit and industry organizations do to guarantee that their valuable, effective AI investments keep progressing in a way that is accurate, transparent, and morally sound?

- Create AI Governance Frameworks: To guarantee the moral and efficient application of AI, establish thorough planning, precise goals, and extensive governance frameworks.
- Conduct Bias Audits: Maintain access to artifacts such as code and model designs while conducting routine fairness audits of algorithms, training data, and outputs.
- Improve Explainability and Transparency: Make sure AI judgments can be understood, data sources can be tracked, and outcomes are transparent at every turn.

- Adopt Certification Guidelines: Work together with other groups to obtain AI certification in order to satisfy ethical and legal requirements.
- Enhance Workforce Skills: Determine the necessary knowledge, put staffing matrices into place, and offer ethical and operations training for AI.
- Monitor Data Use: To ensure ethical digital sourcing, keep track of data input, sources, and usage throughout the training, testing, and production stages.
- Secure Outputs and Privacy: To protect security, privacy, and moral results, incorporate strong controls and monitoring procedures.
- Maintain Stakeholder Engagement: Engage stakeholders with transparency in reporting, sharing insights on data decisions, and monitoring processes.
- Support Interdisciplinary Collaboration: Foster partnerships across sectors to innovate responsibly while adhering to governance and compliance.
- Ensure Monitoring and Control: Establish continuous oversight processes for risk mitigation and adherence to ethical and regulatory standards.

The above list is non-specific and platform agnostic and should only be used to foster more specific procedures of auditing design and workflow. For AI to improve without harm, accounting professionals, industry leaders and audit professionals cannot hope to wait for lawmakers and intellectuals to investigate the way ahead while standing in the path of the accelerating locomotives.

Efforts to establish robust oversight mechanisms shouldn't be hindered by the challenges and complexity of auditing generative AI. Rather, they emphasize the necessity of a comprehensive strategy, acknowledging that no one technique can handle all AI-related hazards in all situations. Even though they are not all-inclusive, audits continue to be a crucial part of larger governance plans. Leaders in the industry and auditing must abandon traditional approaches while acquiring the new skills required for efficient AI oversight. Organizations may be subject to legal, regulatory, and investor scrutiny if they disregard AI's quick advancements, inherent challenges, and complex design. This highlights the urgent need for proactive governance, sophisticated controls, and comprehensive standards.

4. LITERATURE

The fast growth of generative AI systems across a variety of industries, including health and software development, has brought awareness onto the legal, ethical, and social problems they raise. Recognizing these problems, new research calls for systematic auditing procedures to guarantee that AI systems are responsible, transparent, and in line with regulatory and ethical norms (Mökander et al., 2023). Auditing generative AI systems can assist in reducing hazards such as disinformation, privacy breaches, and criminal usage, which are typically linked to their flexibility and vast application potential (Weidinger et al., 2021). Bommasani et al., (2022) stress the significance of thorough testing for AI foundation models, which serve as the base for a large number of generative AI applications. They recommend that these models go through a thorough auditing process in order to minimize the risks associated with their wide deployment potential. In support of this, (Raji et al., 2020) present a system for internal audits in businesses with the goal of addressing possible biases and safety hazards prior to implementing AI models in practical settings. Mökander et al., (2023) offer a thorough three-layered audit approach that includes governance, model, and application audits in order to methodically audit generative AI. This multi-layered strategy addresses risks at several phases, from development to deployment, enabling both proactive and reactive actions. Governance audits make sure that businesses have sufficient risk management systems by concentrating on organizational procedures. Model audits evaluate technical characteristics like robustness and information security, and they are especially important for determining how biases in training data may impact applications later on (Carlini et al., 2023). Real-time application audits assess the societal impact of AI applications, which is crucial for those that might change unexpectedly over time (Floridi et al., 2018). Despite the promise of these auditing frameworks, challenges remain. Operationalizing normative concepts like fairness, transparency, and robustness poses difficulties, as they are often context-dependent and may differ across cultural or regulatory environments (Barocas et al., 2023). Moreover, as technology evolves rapidly, static auditing frameworks risk becoming obsolete. Thus, ongoing research is crucial for developing adaptable, dynamic audit mechanisms that can evolve alongside generative AI technologies (Power, 1997).

The Deloitte study on generative AI in auditing examines how AI is changing auditing procedures, improving productivity, and strengthening risk control. According to Deloitte, generative AI will be incorporated into auditing in stages: first as a "facilitator" that organizes info, then as a "collaborator" that suggests results, and finally as a "integrator" that detects anomalies in real time. Greater evaluation of data, pattern recognition, and risk assessment are now made possible by generative AI, freeing up auditors to concentrate more on jobs requiring judgment than on basic data processing. To give auditors precise, timely insights, for instance, systems such as ScribeAI, RiskAI, and DocAI simplify paperwork, examine external risk sources, and extract data from financial papers (Deloitte, 2024). Challenges around privacy of information, ethics, and transparency are addressed by Deloitte's "Trustworthy AI" approach, which highlights the significance of protecting customer data and encouraging moral AI use. In order to guarantee quality and lessen the biases present in training data, this architecture incorporates human oversight into AI procedures. Deloitte also points out the regulatory difficulties, especially when global corporations have to deal with various compliance requirements in different jurisdictions. Data bias, the "black box" nature of sophisticated AI systems, and fragmented IT organizations are some of the difficulties that make integrating AI more difficult. Deloitte hopes to enhance audit quality, strengthen customer confidence, and resolve ethical dilemmas with this incremental AI deployment, highlighting AI's revolutionary potential in auditing (Deloitte, 2024). As discussed by Francisco J Navarro in his LinkedIn article (AuditBoard, 2024; Navarro, 2024) Auditing in generative AI is a necessary procedure that includes systematic evaluation and analysis of the AI systems so as to serve correctly, that their results are objective, and that all legal and ethical demands are met. The assessment for integrity and reliability should be surrounded by algorithms, data inputs, outputs, and decision-making procedures that guarantee AI-driven solutions. Severe consequences of poor auditing include unfair lending decisions, biased hiring practices, and damaged brand for an organization. For example, the AI-powered systems for loan approval may be prejudicial against minority groups, creating legal and social issues in the process, and AI recruiting tools, if left unmonitored, may favor certain demographics unconsciously. Francisco J Navarro said "Not auditing GenAI properly can be costly. Unmonitored AI systems might generate inaccurate or biased outcomes, impacting decision-making and potentially causing discrimination" (AuditBoard, 2024). In the backdrop of the risks, there is an urgent need for strong auditing techniques that organizations should follow. Algorithmic transparency is essential to enable auditors to verify the-the-scene logic or codes that again are going to result in bias or errors. The open-source frameworks play an important role in this direction. Data audits would focus on diversity, quality, and representativeness of training datasets, a key objective toward AI systems becoming fair and inclusive.

This has been visible in leading companies like Google, IBM, and Microsoft through various initiatives on the auditing of GenAI. Google designs its AI systems with the inclusion of checks to ensure fairness and transparency; the objective here is to increase user trust and reduce potential legal risks. IBM's AI Fairness 360 toolkit offers a suite of tools to audit AI models for biases, thus supporting both internal and external developers in fostering ethical AI practices. Auditing its AI systems periodically is a required ethical guideline and regulatory compliance for Microsoft's Responsible AI Standard. These examples point to the explanation that auditing the GenAI will not only build up a fair and reliable AI system but also organizational credibility and benefits to society (AuditBoard, 2024). Isack, Markus's study compares the performance of generative AI, more especially GPT-4, to human auditors in a number of scenarios to investigate the possibilities of this technology in financial auditing. GPT-4 struggled with intricate auditing concepts like continuous audits, but it excelled at tasks like risk assessment and brainstorming, which offered efficiency and reproducibility. Although its results closely resemble human judgments, its inherent biases and lack of domain-specific training underscore the necessity for customized approaches. The study highlights GPT-4's potential as an auditing co-pilot that can improve procedures and lessen human biases. It does, however, clearly recognize its limits, which include biases in training data and quickly developing AI technologies. In order to improve their function in auditing, future steps will involve investigating human-GenAI interactions, fine-tuning GenAI models using audit-specific data, and investigating wider applications. Continuous research and thoughtful regulation are vital for integrating GenAI into auditing effectively (Isack, M.,2024).

The paper by Arisa et al., 2023) states difficulties and factors related to auditing artificial intelligence (AI) services and systems are discussed in this policy suggestion paper. Given the inadequacy of the voluntary guidelines AI developers have adopted, the necessity for independent audits is underscored as AI becomes more and more incorporated into many sectors. The scope, timing, and auditor credentials are among the six main concerns in AI auditing that are outlined in the article. Employing recruitment AI as a case study, it also examines the institutional, social, and technical challenges associated with performing AI audits. To promote AI auditing, three suggestions are made: creating institutional frameworks, educating auditors, and modernizing audit procedures to reflect emerging technologies. Additionally, the study addresses the unique auditing difficulties presented by generative AI, which generates fresh data like text and images, emphasizing the importance of addressing these challenges for sound AI governance.

The paper focuses on although large language models (LLMs) have transformed AI research, there are serious ethical and governance issues with their broad use. Jakob Mökander states (Mökander, J., et al. 2023) that the particular dangers offered by LLMs, such as their emerging capabilities and applicability to a variety of applications, are not adequately addressed by the auditing systems now in place, as this article demonstrates. The authors suggest a novel three-layered audit framework to close this gap, which includes governance audits (which examine technology providers), model audits (which evaluate LLMs after pretraining), and application audits (which look at downstream applications). At every stage of LLM deployment, this methodical approach seeks to improve risk management, accountability, and transparency. The research highlights the potential of independent audits while also acknowledging their inherent limitations, including the lack of an institutional ecosystem to implement these audits and the challenge of operationalizing normative principles. legislators, tech companies, and researchers are urged to adopt, refine, and expand this framework, ensuring ethical, legal, and robust development of LLMs and preparing for future advancements in AI governance.

This research by Swati Sachan (Sachan, S., & Liu, X., 2023) investigates how blockchain technology and generative AI technologies might be combined to improve legal decision-making and auditing procedures. Large Language Models (LLMs)-powered generative AI has promise for pre-litigation letter writing, but its opaque nature and potential for confidentiality violations raise questions. To guarantee ethical AI use and preserve data integrity, the paper suggests a blockchain-based auditing mechanism. Blockchain ensures accountability through strategic off-chain and on-chain data storage and Merkle root-based comparisons, while eXplainable AI (XAI) is used for decision-making in this system. The framework's potential to automate audits, protect sensitive legal data, and boost confidence in AI-assisted legal processes is demonstrated through a case study in tort law.

This study presented by Ga-Young Choi introduces (Choi & Kim, 2024) a new firm-level metric for tax audit periods that analyzes narrative disclosures connected to tax audits using generative AI. This measure demonstrates significant heterogeneity among firms and closely matches IRS data by overcoming the confidentiality challenges of tax audits. The research highlights that tax audits reduce corporate tax avoidance, with stronger effects for firms exhibiting higher pre-audit avoidance. However, audits also result in negative economic impacts, including reduced capital investments, heightened stock volatility, and adverse stock market reactions to disclosures forecasting unfavorable settlements. These findings underscore the measure's potential to deepen understanding of the economic consequences of tax audits on firms.

The report "Auditing in the Age of Generative AI" (The CAQ., 2024) looks at how financial reporting and auditing are affected by generative artificial intelligence (GenAI). It emphasizes how GenAI might improve data analysis and memo writing, but it also raises worries about potential hazards like errors and moral dilemmas. In order to guarantee accuracy and compliance, auditors are recommended to maintain human involvement in the governance and supervision of AI usage. Key auditor concerns are outlined in the paper, including risk management, ethical AI principles, and governance frameworks. It highlights how crucial it is to modify auditing procedures in order to take use of GenAI's potential while maintaining audit quality and investor confidence.

The paper explores how the auditing profession is undergoing a change due to Generative AI (GenAI), which requires auditors to adopt new skills and flexible approaches. In order to use GenAI effectively while following ethical norms and data protection rules, it emphasizes the necessity of critical thinking, technical expertise, and regulatory awareness. As GenAI technologies evolve quickly, new roles and responsibilities in the area arise, rendering constant learning and adaptability essential. Notwithstanding advancements, human abilities such as interpersonal and communication skills are still necessary to decipher and convey intricate GenAI-driven insights to stakeholders who are not technically inclined. Auditors can use GenAI to improve audit quality and efficiency while ethically navigating its obstacles by combining technology and human expertise. Software development, auditing, healthcare, and other fields are being transformed by generative AI, a transformational subset of artificial intelligence. Auditing procedures could be drastically altered by generative AI systems' capacity to analyze enormous volumes of data, spot trends, and produce insights. However, their extensive use has also brought attention to urgent operational, ethical, and legal issues. Strong auditing procedures, interdisciplinary cooperation, and regulatory vision are needed to address these issues and maximize the benefits of generative AI while reducing related dangers. Unprecedented prospects to improve auditing systems' accuracy, scalability, and efficiency are presented by the incorporation of generative AI. Auditing has always been a time-consuming process that involves manually reviewing papers, confirming standard compliance, and identifying possible hazards. With the help of generative AI systems, auditors can automate a number of these duties and concentrate on making more complex decisions. Large datasets may be processed rapidly using generative AI, which is also excellent at finding patterns and emphasizing anomalies that might point to fraud or non-compliance. For businesses handling intricate financial transactions or regulatory needs, this expertise is essential. Although there are many advantages to generative AI, there are also many difficulties. Addressing technological, ethical, and legal issues many of which are intricate and interconnected is necessary for an effective audit of AI systems. Often functioning as "black boxes," generative AI systems make it challenging to comprehend how particular choices or results are produced. This lack of openness creates issues with accountability and makes the auditing process more difficult. Existing disparities may be maintained or even made worse by AI models trained on skewed or insufficient datasets. This is especially troubling in situations when biased judgments may have ethical and legal ramifications, such as in employment or loan approvals. A substantial investment in infrastructure, training, and technology is necessary to implement efficient auditing procedures. The inability of smaller businesses to commit the required funds could lead to differences in the uptake of AI auditing procedures (Mökander, J., et al. 2023). Numerous frameworks and best practices for auditing generative AI systems have been offered by researchers and industry leaders in order to overcome these issues. These methods stress the value of accountability, openness, and flexibility. For AI development to comply with legal and ethical requirements, pay close attention to company policies and risk management systems. Analyze AI model technical factors such as security, robustness, and possible biases in training data. In auditing, generative AI is a game-changer, with enormous potential to improve productivity, precision, and judgment. However, there are also difficult issues with bias, transparency, and moral application brought up by its broad acceptance. Effective navigation of these problems can be achieved by businesses through the establishment of clear regulatory norms, interdisciplinary collaboration, and the implementation of strong auditing procedures. To guarantee that the advantages of generative AI are realized while reducing the hazards involved, continued research and flexible regulations will be crucial as the technology develops. Generative AI has the potential to be a potent instrument for innovation and the good of society if it is audited and governed responsibly. In auditing, generative AI is a game-changer, with enormous potential to improve productivity, precision, and judgment. However, there are also difficult issues with bias, transparency, and moral application brought up by its broad acceptance. Effective navigation of these problems can be achieved by businesses through the establishment of clear regulatory norms, interdisciplinary collaboration, and the implementation of strong auditing procedures. To guarantee that the advantages of generative AI are realized while reducing the hazards involved, continued research and flexible regulations will be crucial as the technology develops. Generative AI has the potential to be a potent instrument for innovation and the good of society if it is audited and governed responsibly.

5. METHODOLOGY

The methodological approach here we are considering is a 5-layer which is tailored to address the risk and challenges possessed by Generative AI. This would simply be the process of covering all key areas like compliance, rules and regulations, ethical considerations, transparency, accountability while auditing any field which uses Generative AI. Below is the flow chart showing the steps of Auditing Generative AI.

Figure 1. Methodology for auditing generative AI

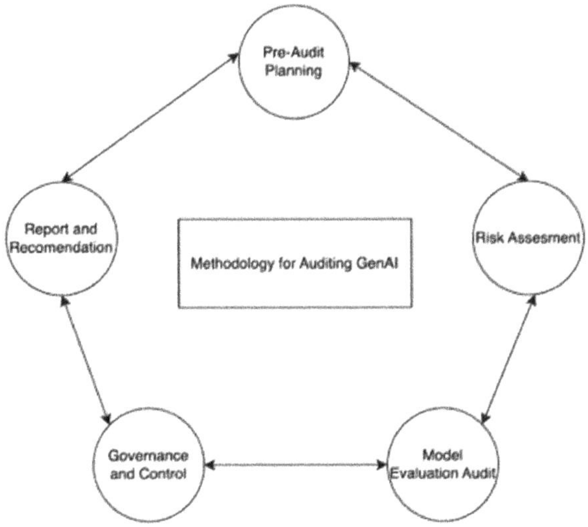

Step-1 Pre-Audit Planning (pre deployment auditing)

The first thing any auditor must do while performing an audit is understand the business objectives and goals of the organization as this is the core principle and reason for a company to implement different departments and systems. For one related to AI they must correlate how the system can achieve the business purpose, where information is credited and the architecture of the model. These three factors make up the functionality of a system and the impact it could have on the company. Auditors then need to deep dive and guarantee the data utilized is safe, adheres to privacy laws and clear of biases that will disrupt outcomes. Finally examining the model's framework gives auditors the opportunity to check for alignment with the business objectives. This will also confirm the reliability, capability and compliance of the framework and results output.

Understand Legal and Ethical Requirements:: In the foundation of any audit, especially one implementing generative AI, is the need to clarify all legal and ethical matters. It is the organization's responsibility and duty to ensure that they are abiding by laws and regulations in respect of their location. The adoption of AI systems may also involve legal risks to data privacy, requiring verification of compliance with the European Parliament's General Data Protection Regulation (GDPR), laws addressing discrimination (e.g., the US Civil Rights Act of 1964), any clauses in customer contracts, intellectual property regulations and personal information protection legislation adopted in some countries (Mökander, Curl, & Kshirsagar, 2024).

Just as audits can be used to create transparency and legal accountability in areas like financial accounting and worker safety, auditing can also be used as a governance mechanism for AI systems. Three ideas underpin the promise of auditing as an AI governance mechanism, namely, that:

i. procedural regularity and transparency contribute to good governance.
ii. proactivity in the design of AI systems helps identify risks and prevent harm before it occurs; and,
iii. The operational independence between the auditor and the auditee contributes to the objectivity of the evaluation (Bharadhwaj et al., 2021).

Though we here in the United States are slow to adapt to the times and implement rules and regulations that can help structure the ethical usage of Gen AI, Europe is quite modern and formative with their laws. In March 2024, Members of the European Parliament approved the EU AI Act, a comprehensive legal framework for regulation of the development and use of AI systems, including general purpose AI.12 It employs a risk based approach that prohibits certain uses of AI such as social scoring based on social behavior or personal characteristics and requires the development of appropriate guardrails to mitigate risks to society for high risk AI systems around data quality, transparency, testing, monitoring, reporting, security, human oversight, and accountability. This regulation will impact US companies that operate in the EU or develop AI models that are used in the EU (Bommasani, R., et al., 2022). An act such as this would help create a guideline and Auditing GenAI much easier.

Establish Objectives: During the audit objective it is a must that system performance, bias detection, data integrity and security controls are areas that are clearly identified and examined. To support the point on the importance of evaluating system performance, bias detection, data integrity, and security controls during an audit, various sources highlight similar concerns. According to the Cloud Security Alliance, ensuring the accuracy and standardization of data, along with proper data pipeline replication, are crucial steps to prevent biased models and maintain AI system reliability. Data governance policies, including standardized processes for detecting inconsistencies and ensuring data quality, play a central role in upholding data integrity and security (The CAQ., 2024). This adds to the checks and balances all audits must adhere to by extensively addressing any risks ranging from operational to ethical and providing a potential solution. Audit Board emphasizes the need for thorough assessments of cyber and privacy risks, especially with generative AI.

These risks often stem from insufficient safeguards in place to protect data integrity and prevent unauthorized access. Audits are key in identifying these vulnerabilities and proposing mitigation strategies. Security controls must be thoroughly evaluated to guarantee the AI system is safe from unwanted access and altering. Creating an environment of harmony that upholds data integrity and system reliability.

Step-2 Risk Assessment

Once the audits scope and objectives are defined and discussed it is essential to do a risk assessment and how we can optimize the risks. When it comes to generative AI there are multiple risk factors with the output it generates. Gen AI output should be free from biases and fairness, misinformation, inaccuracy, lack of transparency, or data privacy violations. Data is critical and it can be very sensitive hence it becomes important to have robust privacy and security measures in place to protect user data and that can be done once we have assessed the risk associated with it. Understanding these risks allows auditors to focus their efforts on areas that may pose significant threats to the integrity and reliability of the AI system.

Evaluating the quality of the data used to operate and train the AI models is a crucial component of AI auditing as the model performance is dependent on data. Models used in Generative AI analyze historical data and it is important to make sure that the outputs from this data have integrity, avoid biases, and inaccurate or incomplete data as the implications of adopting various AI and ML solutions and methods introduce into domain auditing teams multiple levels of complexities (Investopedia, n.d.).

So, if the quality of data is not good in the longer term it could affect business decisions and continuity. This includes who has access to the data to manipulate the outputs from the input and the purpose behind the use of the model (Carlini, N., et al. 2023). Apart from technical aspects while auditing risk an auditor should consider business and operational risks so that in future, they don't face any legal challenges or reputational damage for the organization. So, evaluating data quality not only enhances model performance but also addresses ethical concerns related to fairness and accountability in AI systems.

Claude Mandy, who is the Chief Evangelist for Data Security at Symmetry Systems, has given 5 Steps to Assess the Cyber and Privacy Risk of Generative AI (Carlini, N., et al. 2023).

1. **Completing a Data Risk Assessment:** What data is used to train the model
2. **Threat Model the Users:** Who can use or interact with AI, assess risks based on their intent and training

3. **Understand the Purpose/Use Case Risk Assessment:** What is the intended purpose or use of each Gen AI model
4. **Conduct a Scenario Analysis:** Based on different scenarios to construct risk profile on the likelihood/frequency and potential impact of risk
5. **Assessing Control Effectiveness:** For prioritized risk scenarios, relevant controls can be mapped across the data, access management, and model domains.

Step-3 Model Evaluation Audit

Performance Review: The foundation for any model evaluation lies in its performance review. This entails a thorough examination of the AI system guaranteeing that it operates appropriately. According to Francisco Navarro, the valuation of an AI systems performance is summed up by its accuracy, effectiveness and efficiency in completing its assigned tasks. By implementing an approach that uses key performance indicators (KPIs) aligning with business objectives we can make this possible. Auditors can use both quantitative and qualitative measures as means to extensively gain knowledge on the performance of the system and its operational capabilities.

On top of that Deloitte reinforces the importance of continuous improvement through performance monitoring. With AI models constantly changing they may begin to drift due to data patterns. Therefore, it is crucial that repeating processes are put in place to check the systems to maintain model effectiveness and operational reliability.

Bias and Fairness Testing: To eradicate or mitigate biases that are preexisting in our data it is important that we do our due diligence in testing for bias and fairness. This idea revolves around implementing techniques using statistics to examine the model's outputs across the vast range of demographics. In doing so we reassure that all groups are appropriately represented fairly. UD security alliance brought this to light when they stated it is essential to implement governance policies that address these concerns through standardized processes for detecting and mitigating bias. Implementing best practices for detecting bias such as auditing previously used data can support the training of the model creating a more just system. By actively identifying biases and corrective measures, we allow for a more fair and bias free environment of AI technology

Explainability and Transparency: Explainability and transparency are critical components of ethical AI use. Auditors must assess whether AI models provide interpretable outputs that stakeholders can understand. This need is particularly important given the "black box" nature of many AI systems, which can obscure how decisions are made. According to the AI Index report, the lack of transparency can erode trust and complicate compliance with legal regulations .

Techniques such as Local Interpretable Model-agnonations (LIME) and SHapley Additive exPlanations (SHAP) can be employed to elucidate model behavior and decision-making processes. These tools help demystify AI outputs, thereby enhancing accountability and fostering stakeholder confidence.

Step-4 Governance and Control

The ecosystem of AI systems is very vast, chances of not managing and using ethically across organizations does not remain consistent. Hence governance becomes important to mitigate risks with AI -systems. There should be a governance framework in an organization which should address the problems that come with Gen AI like Black Box Problem, bias and fairness, data security and privacy. Reference (Floridi, L., et al., 2018) which shows "A schematic overview of how auditing of AI relates to previous work on AI governance" which tells us AI auditing is a subset of both AI governance mechanisms (functionally) and auditing procedures (methodologically).

The frameworks, procedures, policies which are established to guarantee the responsible creation and supervision of artificial intelligence systems all come together and emphasize on governance in generative AI audits. To ensure that there are distinct lines of responsibility, this entails assessing the roles and duties of both individuals and teams working on AI initiatives. The governance system should also cover concerns including bias, data privacy, and exploitation of AI, as well as procedures for guaranteeing adherence to external rules and internal norms. To make sure that the governance framework is actively promoting the moral implementation and continuous observation of generative AI systems, regular audits are crucial.

Implementing frameworks like AI ethical guidelines, risk management procedures, and frequent third-party assessments are few examples of industry best practices that should be in line with governance and control in generative AI audits. To prevent unwanted modifications to the AI model or the data robust access controls should be in place. In order to prevent an over-reliance on automated decision-making, the audit process should include making sure that there is adequate human oversight, particularly for high-risk or high-impact AI. We as an auditor should be able to keep all aspects in mind and make sure the governance frameworks are in place as it helps in evaluating decisions making processes, adhering to ethical standards and best practices, ensuring data is being handled rightly which in turn help the organization to be compliant and risk free.

So as best practices for governance and control, we should

1. Adopt a framework for example COBIT 5, NIST, ISO270001
2. Involve stakeholders

3. Keep an eye on internal and external factors that could affect AI
4. Adhere to laws which are specific to AI
5. Engage external auditors so that there is no conflict of interest, and we have an independent point of view.
6. Ensure the transparency of AI systems
7. Making sure the organization abides by data privacy rules and regulations.

Step-5 Reporting and recommendation

After all the above steps are completed, the final step left is documentation. An auditor will present a well-structured report of all the findings and observations which he/she has found during the audit process with supporting evidence which can back those findings strongly. Additionally, an auditor based on the findings will share recommendations and suggestions like improving and enhancing data quality and model performance on areas where risk is identified. The report should be segregated, showing high risk areas first. The report will cover every aspect of audit, from compliance to identified risks. This report in future will serve as a reference point for further audits and will give a better understanding of AI systems which in turn will help the organization to improve the usage of AI.

The design, development, and deployment phases of the Artificial intelligence model should be mentioned in the report with full clarity including data sources, training techniques and other related factors. Auditors should be able to flag any concerns related to accuracy, bias and decision making of the large language models. To help stakeholders comprehend how AI-driven results are accomplished, a thorough report identifies any departures from accepted best practices and offers insight into the model's decision-making process.

An auditor's job is not finished here to run the business and make sure everything works fine; they have to follow-up and review periodically on given recommendations and actions are implemented correctly to mitigate risks. An auditor should recommend and give suggestions enhancing the generative AI systems' dependability and accountability. This can include steps for gathering data in order to lessen biases, upgrading security measures to guard and protect against AI abuse, and improving models using AI methodologies. It is essential to provide a framework for ongoing monitoring to make sure AI systems continue to adhere to changing legal and ethical standards. Continuous monitoring of AI systems ensures that they remain compliant, effective, and aligned with organizational goals.

6. CHALLENGES AND LIMITATIONS

1. **Black-Box Nature:** Generative AI are modeled in a way that no one knows what data is being processed in the backend hence the explanations for its conclusions remain opaque or "black." (Mökander, J., et al. 2023). This makes the decision-making process nontransparent as it limits the auditor to know how the output came and if the intended output fulfills the needs of the end user in an organization.
2. **Verification of Training Data:** Quality of data is the most crucial part because the output is dependent on the way it is used to train the model. Since the data can be incorrect, misleading it becomes very difficult for auditors to verify the accuracy of it.
3. **Resource and Expertise Constraints:** While auditing Gen AI auditors should have knowledge of machine learning, data analytics, modeling techniques so that they have better understanding of AI. This could limit the ability of auditors to perform their duties effectively and efficiently. There can be chances that an organization fails to have an auditor with required skills and then they might have to outsource someone, and it could be a costly expense.
4. **Data Bias:** These Gen AI models are trained on large data sets, and the source of the data is also unknown. The data can have racial, gender, or cultural bias which in turn can reflect in outputs generated by gen AI tools. Auditors must assess whether these biases exist in the model or not but doing so is a complicated and complex task. Most common examples these days are deep fakes which means using AI creating a real face or body, voice over.
5. **Data Privacy Violations**: Major issues while using generative AI is that we don't know what data is used as it can be personal or any confidential data. It can disclose sensitive data which can again be misused, being unaware of the intention of the person as to how legitimately he would be utilizing the information. This can directly or indirectly can have legal and copyright issues.

6.Intellectual Property and Copyright: Questions concerning ownership, copyright, and possible infringement are brought up by GenAI's ability to generate original content. Important ethical issues are raised by the use of AI in auditing. These problems must be addressed by auditing systems in order to guarantee correct ownership and attribution of AI-generated content.

7. **Rapid Evolution:** Because GenAI is developing so quickly, it might be difficult to stay on top of the newest methods and potential weaknesses. Since GenAI models are constantly changing, auditing procedures must also be flexible.

8. **Regulatory Landscape:** The regulatory landscape for Generative AI is changing very quickly, as new rules and regulations are implemented continuously. Auditors must keep up with these developments to assure compliance. Creating worldwide standards for AI audits can help to align rules and ease cross-border collaboration.

9.Transparency Issues with Model Updates: It can be challenging to monitor these changes and how they affect the models because AI systems are always being retrained and updated. The behavior or outputs of the model may change with each update, making it difficult for auditors to monitor changes and guarantee continued adherence to standards. Audits may become out-of-date or erroneous in the absence of a clear, transparent procedure for model upgrades.

10. **Intricacy of Human-AI Interaction:** The interaction between generative AI systems and human users frequently makes auditing much more difficult. Unknowingly giving biassed input or manipulating the system to get desired results are two possible consequences. These interactions add a degree of uncertainty to the auditing procedure as auditors must take them into consideration and evaluate how they affect the results.

11.Ethical Decisions with Autonomous AI: The increasing autonomy of AI systems may lead to ethical issues in their decision-making processes that are challenging for conventional audits to evaluate. Artificial intelligence (AI) systems may make choices that go against accepted ethical norms, such as putting efficiency ahead of equality or fairness. In order to assess the ethical ramifications of AI judgements and their effects on society, auditors will need to create new procedures.

12. **Assessing AI Systems:** The lack of general agreement or standardization in the performance measures used to assess AI systems might complicate audits. Depending on the model, use case, and stakeholder viewpoints, different AI systems may have different definitions of success. The performance measures must be precise, pertinent, and able to fully capture the impact of generative AI systems, according to auditors.

7. FUTURE SCOPE

The subject of Gen AI auditing is quickly emerging, spurred by advances in AI technologies and several new trends and future directions shape the landscape of AI auditing (The CAQ., 2024) & (Thomson Reuters., 2024)

1. **Standardization and Certification:** Audits can be more reliable if we create standardized frameworks which will help auditors who are involved in auditing AI to be more accurate and will have a direct impact on the organization ethically following the standards. IEEE and ISO are the few examples which are trying to build the same.
2. **AI-Assisted Auditing:** Systems using Gen AI can be used to automate the auditing process for example bias identification and model performance. This will help to improve the efficiency and scalability of AI audits.
3. **Adversarial Machine Learning:** The machine learning techniques used by Generative AI models to evaluate cyber-attacks in a way that shows how malicious they are. Auditors can use these methods to find weaknesses and strengthen AI systems' security.
4. **Ethical AI:** As Generative AI systems are becoming an important part of the society the related ethical concerns are something which are increasing rapidly. It becomes crucial for auditors to make sure that these AI systems are used in an ethical way.
5. **Continuous Auditing:** Traditional ways of auditing are done periodically, but with the rapid rise of AI, automated, real-time auditing is gaining more admiration. Continuous auditing will help use AI to monitor ethics and compliance real time, which helps identify and address issues early.
6. **Collaboration:** International collaboration and cooperation are necessary to address the global concerns brought about by AI. Countries can collaborate, share best practices, and establish common criteria to ensure the responsible and safe development and use of AI.
7. **Skillset Evolution:** To effectively use GenAI, auditors now need to combine technical understanding, problem-solving abilities, critical thinking, and regulatory knowledge. To guarantee the moral and precise use of GenAI in audits, it is essential to comprehend AI algorithms and data structures.
8. **Regulatory Awareness:** As AI tools are integrated, it is critical for auditors to navigate changing rules and uphold adherence to ethical and data privacy standards.
9. **Continuous Learning:** Due to the rapid advancement of AI, auditors must place a high priority on continuing education, which includes learning about new developments in GenAI applications, emerging trends, and AI ethics.

10. **Human-Centric Approach:** Despite AI's potential, stakeholders still need to be able to evaluate and understand complicated AI-driven discoveries, which requires strong interpersonal and communication skills. Audits are made to be both dependable and efficient by striking a balance between human understanding and AI technology.
11. **Adaptability in Roles:** GenAI introduces new job roles within auditing, demanding flexibility and collaboration across disciplines. This shift emphasizes the need for professionals who can bridge technical and non-technical perspectives.
12. **Explainable AI Use:** In the future, the auditing process will depend heavily on the use of Explainable AI (XAI) approaches. By making AI decision-making procedures more accessible and intelligible, XAI hopes to help auditors better track down and defend the choices made by generative AI systems. This will guarantee that AI models don't operate as "black boxes" and that their results can be verified and explained.
13. **AI-Driven Audit Tools**: Future auditing may use AI-driven systems to conduct audits more thoroughly and effectively as AI develops. By helping auditors see trends and irregularities that human auditors would miss, these technologies can greatly increase the scope and efficiency of the auditing procedure.
14. **Strengthened Cybersecurity Measures:** As AI becomes more prevalent in security-critical applications, auditors will need to put sophisticated cybersecurity procedures in place to keep an eye on the security and integrity of AI systems. To achieve this, audits will need to go beyond ensuring that regulations and ethics are followed and go further into protecting AI systems from cyberattacks.
15. **Creation of AI Audit Frameworks:** AI audit frameworks tailored to a certain sector will become increasingly necessary in the future. The particular difficulties and legal specifications of different industries, including manufacturing, healthcare, and finance, would be covered by these frameworks. By developing customized auditing frameworks, businesses can make sure AI systems adhere to ethical norms and industry-specific regulations.

The adoption of GenAI in auditing brings significant opportunities, but it also poses challenges in skill development and regulatory adaptation. To thrive, auditors must embrace a proactive approach to acquiring and refining these skills while maintaining a balance between technology and the indispensable human element.

8. RESULTS & CONCLUSION

8.1 Results

In order to handle the complexity and difficulties presented by Generative AI (GenAI) systems, a thorough audit framework is required. As the study has shown, the quick uptake of GenAI technologies has sparked major worries in a number of important areas, such as data security, accountability, transparency, and ethical governance. The study finds a significant flaw in the current auditing practices, especially when it comes to auditing AI-driven systems like Generative AI, which call for specific methods because of their distinct characteristics and risk profile.

The paper also notes that as AI technologies advance, there is an increasing demand for dynamic auditing frameworks. With the increasing complexity of GenAI models, their audit frameworks need to be flexible enough to address emerging issues as they emerge without needing to be completely redesigned each time a new model is introduced.

We have presented a systematic approach to assess GenAI systems according to their operational integrity, security, and ethical considerations using our suggested audit framework, which is based on well-known governance models like COSO and COBIT 5. Important hazards found during this audit include:

- Biases and Inaccuracies: When trained on unprocessed data, GenAI systems frequently generate results that could be deceptive, prejudiced, or wrong. In order to guarantee the accuracy and equity of AI outputs, the audit approach suggests particular control measures.
- Data Security and Privacy: There is a significant chance of data breaches and privacy violations because GenAI systems depend on enormous volumes of data, frequently containing sensitive user information. Strong data protection measures, such as encryption, secure access procedures, and adherence to privacy laws like the GDPR, are crucial, according to our approach.
- Issues with Intellectual Property (IP): Significant obstacles to IP protection arise from the blurring of the boundaries between human- and AI-generated content. The audit framework offers ways to make sure AI-generated outputs don't violate existing copyrights or intellectual property.
- Lack of Accountability and Transparency: Many AI models are “black-box” in nature, which makes it challenging to track down the decision-making process, particularly in generative systems. Our audit process consists of particular actions to increase accountability and transparency while guaranteeing that AI systems follow the law and ethical guidelines.

The findings also demonstrate the growing significance of auditing in spotting new ethical problems and developing standards that are applicable in a range of sectors. Our results show that auditing is crucial for addressing the social effect of generative AI systems as well as for guaranteeing compliance.

Moreover, the results underscore the importance of continuous monitoring and assessment of GenAI systems to adapt to evolving legal, regulatory, and technological landscapes. The study also highlights the need for collaboration between auditors, technology providers, and policymakers to address the governance challenges posed by these systems.

Ultimately, the findings demonstrate that incorporating tools powered by AI into auditing methodologies can yield more precise and effective evaluations, which are critical as these technologies develop further. This would guarantee that auditors are able to stay ahead of any hazards and spot problems early on, averting long-term repercussions.

8.2 Conclusion

Although generative AI has revolutionized many industries, it has also brought to light serious issues with governance and compliance. According to the study's findings, a strong and flexible auditing structure is essential to guaranteeing that Generative AI systems function morally, safely, and in accordance with applicable laws.

Our suggested audit framework offers a thorough, risk-based method for handling the particular dangers connected to generative artificial intelligence. By concentrating on topics like bias, data security, intellectual property protection, and transparency, we have presented a technique that improves these systems' accountability and credibility. This study shows that the best way to reduce the dangers of abuse, fraud, and ethical transgressions related to GenAI technology is to conduct frequent audits and ongoing monitoring.

As GenAI develops, auditing will become more and more crucial to protecting human rights and making sure AI systems are used ethically by society. To assist avoid abuse and guarantee that GenAI systems are utilized responsibly and accountably, more thorough and standardized auditing procedures should be put in place.

In the end, the study promotes the creation of globally applicable regulatory frameworks and uniform auditing practices. By doing this, businesses can make sure that GenAI systems are deployed responsibly, preserving public confidence and protecting against new threats. Beyond technology suppliers and auditors, this research has ramifications for legislators and regulatory agencies that need to keep up with the quickly changing AI world.

In order to develop globally appropriate standards and increase the efficacy of audits on international platforms, the research also highlights the necessity of cooperation across industries and geographical areas.

According to the findings, auditing generative AI is not just important for compliance but also for making sure that AI systems respect user rights, ethical norms, and social values. As Generative AI continues to advance, this paper lays the foundation for future studies, regulatory developments, and best practices in the governance of artificial intelligence, ensuring that innovation is balanced with ethical responsibility.

REFERENCES

Arisa, R., Tomoharu, M., & Shinji, H. (2023). "Advancing AI Audits for Enhanced AI Governance." *arXiv*. https://arxiv.org/pdf/2312.00044

AuditBoard. (2024, June 14). *5 steps to assess the cyber and privacy risk of generative AI*. AuditBoard. Retrieved from https://www.auditboard.com/blog/5-steps-to-assess-the-cyber-and-privacy-risk-of-generative-ai

Bharadhwaj, H., Huang, D.-A., Xiao, C., Anandkumar, A., & Garg, A. (2021, September 25). Auditing AI models for verified deployment under semantic specifications. *arXiv*. https://arxiv.org/abs/2109.12456

Bommasani, R., ... (2022, July 12). On the opportunities and risks of foundation models. *arXiv*. https://doi.org//arXiv.2108.07258DOI: 10.48550

Carlini, N., ... (2023). "Extracting Training Data from Diffusion Models." *arXiv*. https://doi.org//arXiv.2301.13188.DOI: 10.48550

Choi, G.-Y., & Kim, A. G. (2024, April 18). *Firm-level tax audits: A generative AI-based measurement* (Chicago Booth Research Paper No. 23-23). *SSRN*. Retrieved from https://ssrn.com/abstract=4645865 or DOI: 10.2139/ssrn.4645865

Cloud Security Alliance. (n.d.). "AI Safety Initiative." Cloud Security Alliance. "https://cloudsecurityalliance.org/ai-safety-initiative"

Deloitte. (2024, January)"AI Presentation for the Audit Committee - Second Draft." *Deloitte*. https://www2.deloitte.com/content/dam/Deloitte/se/Documents/audit/AI%20presentation%20for%20the%20Audit%20Committee%20-%20Second%20draft.pdf

Floridi, L., Cowls, J., Beltrametti, M., Chatila, R., Chazerand, P., Dignum, V., Luetge, C., Madelin, R., Pagallo, U., Rossi, F., Schafer, B., Valcke, P., & Vayena, E. (2018, November 26). AI4People—An ethical framework for a good AI society: Opportunities, risks, principles, and recommendations. *Minds and Machines*, *28*(4), 689–707. DOI: 10.1007/s11023-018-9482-5 PMID: 30930541

Gusher, T. (2024, January 30). *AI and ML are cybersecurity problems and solutions*. EY. Retrieved from https://www.ey.com/en_us/insights/cybersecurity/ai-and-ml-are-cybersecurity-problems-and-solutions

Investopedia. (n.d.). "Black Box." Investopedia. "https://www.investopedia.com/terms/b/blackbox.asp"

Isack, M. (2024, March 28). *Replicating reason: The advent of human-like audit judgment by generative AI* (SSRN Working Paper No. 4716860). SSRN. Retrieved from https://ssrn.com/abstract=4716860 or DOI: 10.2139/ssrn.4716860

Mökander, J.. (2023, February 6). Auditing large language models: A three-layered approach. *AI and Ethics*. Retrieved from https://arxiv.org/abs/2302.08500

Mökander, J., Curl, J., & Kshirsagar, M. (2024, July 7). A blueprint for auditing generative AI. *arXiv*. https://arxiv.org/abs/2407.05338 DOI: 10.2139/ssrn.4887768

Navarro, F. J. (2024, June 7). *How to audit your generative artificial intelligence*. LinkedIn. Retrieved from https://www.linkedin.com/pulse/how-audit-your-generative-artificial-intelligence-francisco-j-navarro-kmouf/

Power, M. (1997). *The audit society: Rituals of verification*. Oxford University Press.

Raji, I. D.. (2020, January 3). Closing the AI accountability gap: Defining an end-to-end framework for internal algorithmic auditing. *Proceedings of the 2020 Conference on Fairness, Accountability, and Transparency*. Retrieved from https://arxiv.org/abs/2001.00973 DOI: 10.1145/3351095.3372873

Rane, N. (2023, August 30). Role and challenges of ChatGPT and similar generative artificial intelligence in finance and accounting. *SSRN*. DOI: 10.2139/ssrn.4603206

Rodgers, W., Murray, J. M., Strashnoy, L., & Lande, D. (2024, April 19). Ethical auditors' framework for generative AI cybersecurity. *SSRN*. DOI: 10.2139/ssrn.4800215

Sachan, S., & Liu, X. (2023, December 16). *Blockchain-based auditing of legal decisions supported by explainable AI and generative AI tools. Expert Systems with Applications*. Retrieved "https://www.sciencedirect.com/science/article/abs/pii/S095219762301850X"

Stanford University. (2024). *The AI Index 2024 annual report*. Stanford University AI Index. Retrieved from https://aiindex.stanford.edu/report/

The CAQ. (2024). "Auditing in the Age of Generative AI." *The Center for Audit Quality*. https://www.thecaq.org/wp-content/uploads/2024/04/caq_auditing-in-the-age-of-generative-ai__2024-04.pdf

Thomson Reuters. (2023, October 25). *Auditing AI for transparency*. Thomson Reuters Technology Blog. Retrieved from https://www.thomsonreuters.com/en-us/posts/technology/auditing-ai-transparency/

Thomson Reuters. (2024, September 3). *Embracing change: Auditors' views on generative AI. ThomsonReuters Tax & Accounting Blog*. Retrieved from https://tax.thomsonreuters.com/blog/embracing-change-auditors-views-on-generative-ai/

Weidinger, L., ... (2021, December 8). *Ethical and social risks of harm from language models*. arXiv. https://doi.org//arXiv.2112.04359DOI: 10.48550

Chapter 5
Innovative Auditing Practices:
Evidence From Emerging Technologies

Dollie Juneja
https://orcid.org/0009-0008-4455-2348
University at Buffalo, SUNY, USA

Abinash Jena
https://orcid.org/0009-0001-5103-2956
SMBC, USA

Manish Gupta
M&T Bank, USA

Raj Sharman
https://orcid.org/0000-0001-5838-7330
University at Buffalo, SUNY, USA

ABSTRACT

This study pertains to the impact of new emerging technologies—Artificial Intelligence (AI), blockchain, and cloud computing—on the auditing process. Based on case studies and literature reviews, it explains how each of the foregoing technologies enhances audit quality, real-time assurance, fraud detection, and evidence integrity. AI enables high-frequency data analysis to detect fraud and anomalies in a more efficient manner. Cloud computing enables real-time collaborative auditing but raises data privacy and regulatory compliance issues. Blockchain offers tamper-evident audit trails via smart contracts but suffers from interoperability challenges. The paper presents a visionary sketch of the signs of these technologies and gives

DOI: 10.4018/979-8-3373-3078-5.ch005

recommendations to auditors, educators, and policymakers.

1. INTRODUCTION

Recent literature is designed to highlight the fact that every new technology—AI, cloud computing, and blockchain—transforms auditing fundamentally. Artificial Intelligence (AI) improves audit quality through data analysis and risk automation. For instance, Pérez-Calderón et al. determine that AI "substantially enhances audit efficiency, accuracy, and client communication quality," hence leading to a general improvement in the quality of audit output (Issa, Sunyaev, & Vasarhelyi, 2016; Pérez-Calderón, Alrahamneh, & Montero, 2025). AI analytics enable auditors to examine complete datasets instead of samples, narrowing the scope for human error and making more educated judgments. Anomaly detection software based on AI discovers unusual patterns in transactions that are more likely to be overlooked by human assessors while searching for fraud. There is evidence that AI application in audit functions "has the ability to streamline audit processes, increase efficiency, and enhance the detection of fraudulent movement" (Saifudin, Januarti, & Purwanto, 2023; Appelbaum, 2017). By ever-present monitoring of transaction flows, AI also facilitates near real-time assurance, minimizing audit cycles and enabling real-time reaction to exceptions (Yermack, 2017). More broadly, AI facilitates delivery of higher quality audits and improved fraud detection and conveys rigor and assurance to evidence through advanced automated verification (Pérez-Calderón, Alrahamneh, & Montero, 2025; Saifudin, Januarti, & Purwanto, 2023).

Cloud computing also transforms the audit process. Cloud infrastructure makes it possible for auditors to gain secure central access to financial information, providing greater accuracy and timing. Empirical studies show that organizations with cloud ERP systems have higher audit accuracy, report quality, and evidence reliability compared to organizations that own on-premises systems (Alotaibi, 2023). Cloud computing's scalability and on-demand feature enable auditors to deal with enormous amounts of data more efficiently and enhance the quality of audits. Anytime access to real-time accounting records in the cloud enables continuous auditing and assurance: auditors can authenticate transactions as they occur rather than after the fact. (Alotaibi, 2023) Cloud platforms also enable collaboration and sharing of data between clients and audit teams to reduce time differences. In addition, cloud systems enhance the consistency of the audit evidence by keeping standard, tamper-evident records of transactions. Cloud environments pose new control issues, however; auditors must consider cloud security and governance controls to resist fraud risk and preserve evidence integrity.

Blockchain technology introduces a whole new model of auditing. Its three primary characteristics—decentralization, immutability, and transparency—naturally address most of the traditional audit issues. Blockchain's append-only record book makes the transaction records tamper-proof, significantly improving the authenticity and credibility of audit information (Han et al., 2023). In Zhang et al.'s words, blockchain “enables us with new approaches and techniques for audit tasks and activities” that can “remarkably enhance the authenticity and credibility of audit data and work” and accelerate evidence collection (Han et al., 2023). Because everything that happens is written down and cryptographically associated on-chain, auditors get real-time total history of transactions that allows for continuous auditing in real time. For instance, experience in the industry demonstrates that audit cycles can be reduced by orders of magnitude and advance coverage of transactions from the area of 78% to over 99% (Zhang, Ma, & Meng, 2025) with the help of blockchain audit technology. Large-scale coverage minimizes detection risk and thus auditing quality. Transparency inherent in blockchains also facilitates fraud detection: auditors can trace individual transactions from inception to completion and automatically perform tests with smart contracts. Experience shows that smart-contract–based audits uncovered sophisticated schemes of fraud (e.g., double invoicing) that traditional methods might overlook (Zhang, Ma, & Meng, 2025) In general, blockchain transforms audit assurance with real-time data verification and immutable audit trails improving evidence reliability (Han et al., 2023; Zhang, Ma, & Meng, 2025).

Every one of these technologies introduces new questions to research. These questions lead to the following research:

- How AI adoption affects audit processes in terms of audit quality, fraud detection, assurance in real time, and the reliability of audit evidence?
- How cloud computing adoption affects audit processes in terms of audit quality, fraud detection, assurance in real time, and the reliability of audit evidence?
- How does blockchain usage impact audit procedures in audit quality, fraud, real-time assurance, and validity of audit evidence?

These concerns will decide the contribution of all AI, cloud platforms, and blockchain towards having more-quality, more-time, and more-reliable audits. Together, literature suggests that AI and blockchain, respectively, facilitate continuous, data-driven auditing, while cloud computing offers secure, real-time access to data—all which hold much promise to enhance fraud detection and assurance methods (Pérez-Calderón, Alrahamneh, & Montero, 2025; Saifudin, Januarti, & Purwanto, 2023; Alotaibi, 2023; Zhang, Ma, & Meng, 2025; Han et al., 2023).

1.1 Artificial Intelligence in Auditing

Artificial Intelligence (AI), machine learning, natural language processing, and predictive analytics are revolutionizing traditional audit procedures. Current innovations have confirmed that AI can be utilized to revolutionize audit procedures by enabling high-volume data processing, detection of anomalies, and real-time risk assessment. This capability allows auditors to move from sample testing to testing the entire population, thereby enhancing the accuracy, efficiency, and timeliness of audits.

AI tools assist auditors through many phases of the audit process, ranging from planning and performance to fraud detection and reporting. Seethamraju and Hecimović (Seethamraju & Hecimović, 2023) state that AI can enhance audit quality and provide more value to clients through automation of mundane tasks and better detection of risk indicators. Nevertheless, the "black-box" nature of most AI models creates issues related to transparency, which call for a change in the way auditors validate and interpret audit evidence.

1.1.1. Audit Quality

AI enhances audit quality since it can carry out extensive scrutiny of financial transactions. Traditional audits, for time and cost considerations, must rely on judgmental sampling, thus potentially overlooking abnormal transactions. AI systems can analyze entire data sets, detect suspicious patterns, and employ sophisticated algorithms to detect discrepancies and potential fraud. Empirical literature indicates that the application of AI has a positive influence on audit outcomes. For example, Qader and Çek (Qader & Çek, 2024) have recorded high audit quality score improvement levels for firms employing AI and blockchain technologies with superior fraud detection precision and financial reporting reliability.

1.1.2. Efficiency Gains

Audit efficiency is enhanced in AI through the automation of labor-intensive manual tasks such as transaction matching, invoicing verification, and controls testing. Algorithms select data at high rates to categorize under groups, calculate risk scores, and generate initial audit reports. Seethamraju and Hecimović (Seethamraju & Hecimović, 2023) believe that auditors using AI tools have reduced workload and audit cycle time. Apart from this, AI delivers real-time feedback, where auditors can focus on judgmental sides rather than mechanical verifications. The automation not only increases internal utilization of resources but also reduces clients' audit fees.

1.1.3. Real-Time Assurance

One of the significant benefits of AI is that it can enable real-time or near real-time assurance. Systems based on AI can be embedded into enterprise resource planning (ERP) systems for real-time posting of transactions. Real-time detection of anomalies is made possible, enabling response to threats at an earlier stage. Since organizations today increasingly need insight in a timely manner, real-time auditing with the help of AI is an enormous step compared to look-back audits on sporadic or periodical occasions. These systems have the ability to inform policy violations or suspicious transactions in real-time, thereby rendering the audit timely and relevant (Seethamraju & Hecimović, 2023).

1.1.4. Reliability of Evidence

The ability of AI to aggregate and analyze large amounts of structured as well as unstructured data adds to the credibility of audit evidence. Advanced analytics can detect complex relationships and correlations, which go unnoticed through manual testing. As Qader and Çek (Qader & Çek, 2024) indicate, companies that used AI-based auditing had higher consistency and accuracy of audit outcomes, especially in situations involving high-frequency transactions or heterogeneous data sources. By eliminating human error and bias in data analysis, AI improves the objectivity and consistency of audit results.

1.1.5. Challenges and Limitations

Although AI comes with benefits, it is not problem-free when it comes to auditing. Perhaps the most significant one is data quality. AI models are only as good as data that is used to train them. Low-quality data, client system inconsistencies, or biased training data will lead to faulty outputs. Seethamraju and Hecimović (Seethamraju & Hecimović, 2023) remind us that "garbage in, garbage out" remains true; auditors must ensure data integrity before they can use AI models.

Another is transparency in sophisticated AI systems. Deep learning algorithms and ensemble models will probably be "black boxes" such that it is difficult for auditors to understand, or even interpret, how conclusions were reached. Nontransparency is a concern in regulatory monitoring, audit reporting, and professional responsibility. In the absence of interpretability, AI results are difficult to explain to regulators or clients, especially in those highly regulated sectors.

Also, AI models reproduce and amplify previous biases. Where human judgment error or inadequate scrutiny guided previous audits, AI models learning from these documents may perpetuate these flaws. This kind of risk necessitates model development to incorporate fairness and minimizing bias features. Moreover, ethical issues for utilizing AI—privacy, consent, and accountability for algorithms, e.g.—need to be addressed through aggressive regulatory tools.

Technical competence gap is also a drawback. There are not too many auditors who have the technical competence to implement, test, and evaluate AI-based solutions. As Seethamraju and Hecimović (Seethamraju & Hecimović, 2023) suggest, audit firms will need to make an investment in enhancing their audit professionals in data science, auditing algorithms, and testing AI models. Without capacity development in these, audit firms won't be able to gain maximum benefits of AI.

Finally, regulatory skepticism towards AI for assurance engagements can deter its use globally. Current audit frameworks and regulations are not used to dealing with evidence generated by AI. Therefore, firms must adopt conservative and hybrid approaches, integrating AI data with traditional audit methods to supply defensibility and meet regulations.

1.1.6. Summary

Finally, artificial intelligence has a tremendous potential for enhancing audit quality, audit efficiency, and assurance promptness. But realizing the potential depends on addressing significant weaknesses like model interpretability, data quality, bias reduction, and auditor capability. A comprehensive framework—adopting explainable AI (XAI), continuous training, and regulatory design—can facilitate making AI an integral part of mainstream audit practice without undermining the integrity and credibility of the auditing process.

1.2 Cloud Computing in Auditing

Cloud computing—remote use of web-hosted facilities for data processing, storage, and application services—has introduced revolutionary change to the field of auditing. With remote access, scalability, and real-time analytics being available, cloud platforms enable auditors to make more comprehensive, timely, and collaborative audits possible. Cloud platforms enable the possibility of conducting continuous audit models, increase the credibility of evidence obtained through audits, and automate steps.

Empirical evidence on hand indicates that cloud computing enhances audit quality and efficiency. Alotaibi (Alotaibi, 2023) conducted a survey of Saudi auditors and concluded that those using cloud-based enterprise resource planning (ERP) software reported higher accuracy of financial estimates, reduced completion of audits, and improved reporting quality than those using traditional on-site systems. Centralized setup of cloud platforms facilitates data access, reduces access latency, and allows auditors to examine transactions quicker and more efficiently.

1.2.1. Quality and Efficiency of Audit

Cloud platforms integrate account books, facilitating automated checking of data and reducing human intervention. These platforms typically have audit trails integrated into them, access controls, and checks on data integrity that facilitate effective and reliable audit processes. A study by Alotaibi indicated that cloud-supported audit resulted in greater operational effectiveness and more backed audit opinions (Alotaibi, 2023). With the help of automated verification and real-time notifications, the auditors can quickly identify exceptions or deviations from expected patterns.

Moreover, cloud platforms increase auditor efficiency by eliminating data silos and improving data sharing among audit teams. Multiple auditors can work on the same sets of data at the same time using cloud technology, eliminating unnecessary document transfers and version reconciliation. Collaboration leads to reduced audit cycles and more uniform results across engagement teams.

1.2.2. Real-Time Assurance

Cloud computing significantly enhances the capability of real-time or near real-time audit assurance. Since cloud platforms update financial information regularly and keep a record of all operations in the system, auditors can use live transaction flows. This allows auditors to continuously audit, verify, and validate transactions as they happen instead of auditing them within batches at regular intervals. Alotaibi (Alotaibi, 2023) shows that having direct access to real-time information allows for earlier detection of anomalies, and measures can be taken to correct them before it is too late, particularly for rapidly changing business environments.

This model is useful to clients because it provides them with timely data about financial performance as well as compliance matters. Instead of waiting for the end-of-period audits, management can use ongoing assurance to track internal controls and regulatory compliance. Where there are transactions that happen very quickly, such as finance or e-commerce, this speed is especially valuable.

1.2.3. Reliability of Audit Evidence

Cloud infrastructures enhance the integrity and availability of audit evidence through evidence preservation in redundant, secure states. In contrast to local storage systems where failure of a machine or version conflict may be cumbersome, cloud states provide for versioned backup, auto-versioning, and disaster recovery strategies. Alotaibi (Alotaibi, 2023) points out that cloud states, through the hosting of ledgers, reduce loss or tampering with data and that evidence obtained from cloud states is largely more complete and more accurate.

The traceability of records in the cloud, supported by immutable logs and user history of access, enables auditors to make audit assertions with higher assurance. For example, system logs can validate the presence and authorization of financial transactions, supporting the completeness and accuracy of audit findings. Centralized ledgers and permissioned access also guarantee confidentiality of data while granting required audit visibility.

1.2.4. Challenges and Limitations

While there are these advantages, cloud computing is not without auditing issues. To begin with, there is increased dependence on third-party vendors. If the customers are having data storage and application hosting outsourced to external vendors, the auditors will have to ascertain whether the vendor has sufficient security, availability, and confidentiality controls. As Chou (Chou, 2015) points out, there is the constraint of no physical access to the infrastructure in the cloud, and hence it is challenging to verify data authenticity and detection of unauthorized changes.

To restrict such risks, auditors ought to consider independent assurance reports such as SOC 1 and SOC 2, which attest to a cloud provider's control environment. These may, however, be in short supply or outdated in terms of availability, and they could exclude all controls relevant to the audit engagement at hand. Furthermore, the very inherent nature of hybrid or multi-cloud deployments as being instances of cloud architecture obscures data provenance and complicates scope identification for audit testing.

Regulatory requirements and compliance are also drivers of complexity for cloud auditing. Jurisdictional regulation around data residency, cross-border transfer and privacy (e.g., GDPR) constraints where data can be accessed and stored, and how. Auditors must determine if clients and cloud providers are complying with these guidelines, adding another level of legal review to the process of auditing. Chou writes that bad service-level agreements (SLAs) and cloud contract transparency can cause auditors to obtain insufficient proper evidence (Chou, 2015).

Additionally, the rapid pace of technology development in cloud infrastructure creates a skill gap among audit teams. Auditors may be unable to analyze virtualized environments, scan log files, or understand cloud-native application design. The skill gap limits auditors from making informed risk decisions and checking cloud control settings. Audit firms therefore must invest in cloud training programs and retain on-boarded IT experts to support engagements with cloud-hosted systems.

1.2.5. Summary

In general, cloud computing offers auditors increased efficiency, increased reliability of evidence, and the potential for continuous real-time assurance. Centralized access, automation, and teamwork enhance more timely and proper audits using cloud ERP systems. These benefits are balanced against security, compliance, provider transparency, and auditor expertise issues. To capitalize on cloud computing's potential in audit, companies must infuse new methodologies, innovate through evolving compliance scenarios, and invest in upskilling.

1.3 Cloud Blockchain in Auditing

Blockchain technology—a decentralized, tamper-evident ledger to record and authenticate transactions—has revolutionized auditing. Blockchains, in contrast to traditional databases, ensure data stored cannot be altered without agreeing by involved nodes. This makes it provide an excellent degree of trust, openness, and safety, thereby raising audit evidence, reducing fraud vulnerabilities, and supporting real-time authentication. With auditing trending towards automation and data-based processes, blockchain's tamper-evident nature presents strong benefits to ensure audit integrity and procedural effectiveness.

Research has also outlined blockchain's potential to enhance the quality of auditing by allowing ongoing auditing and auto-testing of controls. For example, Zhang et al. (Zhang, Ma, & Meng, 2025) highlight that blockchain enhances "audit efficacy through automated transaction authentication and machine learning–driven anomaly detection." Likewise, Qader and Çek (Qader & Çek, 2024) also indicate that blockchain technology enhances audit quality because of increased transaction traceability as well as timely fraud detection when integrated with AI analytics.

1.3.1. Audit Quality and Effectiveness

Blockchain essentially revolutionizes the method by which auditors collect and attest evidence. In a typical audit, verifying transactions typically means verifying internal records, external confirmations, and supporting documents. It is a labor-intensive manual process that is prone to delays or errors resulting from disjointed or incompatible sources of data. Blockchain, on the other hand, enables auditors to have one source of provable truth in the form of a distributed ledger that maintains a chronological record of all transactions in an unchangeable format.

Blockchain reduces the need for manual reconciliation through automatic verification of transactions in consensus algorithms or smart contracts. This capability supports nearly real-time verification of ledger entries and reduces audit fieldwork.

Time savings in reconciliation of up to 90% have been documented by some industry analyses of blockchain audit solutions (Zhang, Ma, & Meng, 2025). In addition, programmable rules, which are smart contracts executed on the blockchain, can be employed to implement audit logic for the purpose of automatically detecting discrepancies or violations in real-time. For example, whenever a transaction surpasses pre-set levels or takes place over stated durations, the contract automatically triggers for auditor attention.

The technology allows for comprehensive testing of whole populations rather than samples. Auditors can test whole populations of transactions, which improves audit coverage and reduces the likelihood of undetected material misstatements resulting from samples. Such capability for complete testing allows for higher audit quality and overall audit findings reliability (Zhang, Ma, & Meng, 2025; Qader & Çek, 2024).

1.3.2. Real-Time Assurance

Historical audits are generally conducted after financial periods end, which introduces a delay between the time transactions are posted and when they are audited. Blockchain enables the shift to continuous auditing because it provides real-time insight into transactions when they are posted to the ledger. Because every entry is time-stamped, cryptographically signed, and accessible to permissioned users, auditors can view and analyze data streams in real time rather than waiting for batch reports.

Zhang et al. (Zhang, Ma, & Meng, 2025) describe how blockchain technology enables "continuous assurance," which allows auditors to monitor the financial well-being of an organization in real-time. This is particularly valuable for high-velocity, high-volume spaces such as financial services, where the sooner anomalies are found, the greater the potential losses or regulatory violations that can be prevented.

The ability for near-real-time assurance also facilitates organizations in responding quickly to policy breaches or internal control weaknesses, thus improving the usefulness and timeliness of the audit process to stakeholders.

1.3.3. Audit Evidence Reliability

Authenticity and integrity of audit evidence are critical to generate reliable audit opinions. Immutable nature of blockchain means that data can never be altered once inscribed and approved, thereby leaving a permanent audit trail. Such an aspect significantly helps to make evidence gained from blockchain systems reliable.

Zhang et al. (Zhang, Ma, & Meng, 2025) state that blockchain enhances the "authenticity and reliability of audit data, accelerates evidence collection, facilitates data sharing, and reduces audit costs." Blockchain also enables auditors to trace transactions from start to finish, which in turn allows them to confirm completeness and existence assertions. Moreover, as each transaction is signed and dated, auditors can confirm the source and sequence of events with high confidence.

Blockchain also makes third-party verifications more efficient. For instance, in auditing a supply chain, blockchain can offer a distributed ledger of payments, shipments, and approvals viewable by all concerned parties. This minimizes the need for time-consuming confirmations by letters or reconciliations between parties and gives greater weight to evidence procured.

1.3.4. Challenges and Limitations.

Even with its promise, auditing blockchain also possesses some threats which need to be thoroughly evaluated prior to it becoming widely accepted

Technical Risks: Even if blockchain systems are designed to be secure, they are not perfectly attack-resistant. Most of them referred to in this context include the 51% attack, where an attacker takes over a majority of a blockchain's computation power and thereby can alter the history of the transactions. This is particularly so with public blockchains, though private or permissioned blockchains are also vulnerable to security misconfigurations or smart contract bug vulnerabilities. Smart contracts, coded or audited wrongly, could result in buggy data entries or unauthorized transactions due to malfunction or exploit (Zhang, Ma, & Meng, 2025).

On-Chain vs. Off-Chain Validation: Blockchain tends to document transactional data but not necessarily the validity or context of the transaction itself. As an example, placing a payment on-chain does not necessarily ensure a good was exchanged or service performed behind it. Auditors would nevertheless have to gather off-chain evidence (i.e., invoices, delivery confirmations, or contracts) to corroborate foundational audit facts such as occurrence, valuation, and authorization (Deloitte, 2017).

Scalability Issues: Public blockchains like Bitcoin and Ethereum have low transaction throughput and relatively high latency. These are the constraints on their use in high-volume enterprise environments. While permissioned blockchains offer better performance, they may compromise on decentralization and require more robust governance arrangements to render them audit worthy (Zhang, Ma, & Meng, 2025).

Regulatory and Legal Uncertainty: Regulatory uncertainty also faces blockchain adoption for auditing. Most jurisdictions have not established clear standards regarding the legal status of blockchain records as evidence admissible in court. As Zhang et al. (Zhang, Ma, & Meng, 2025) note, regulatory loopholes and the lack of standardization frameworks make it difficult for auditors to decide whether blockchain-based data can be trusted as sufficient audit evidence. Apart from that, privacy legislation such as GDPR may conflict with blockchain immutability, particularly when one requests the deletion of personal information.

Skill Gaps and Integration Complexity: Deploying blockchain on the audit function necessitates fresh technical skills, including being familiar with consensus algorithms, auditing smart contracts, and reading cryptographic signatures. Nevertheless, auditors lack the skills in these methods for now. Qader and Çek (Qader & Çek, 2024) state that the lack of blockchain skills among audit professionals is a limitation for successful adoption. Furthermore, integrating blockchain data into existing audit software and procedures also raises compatibility and standardization concerns.

1.3.5. Summary

Blockchain technology can potentially introduce revolutionary benefits to auditing, including real-time assurance, increased reliability of evidence, and improved fraud detection. Its decentralized and tamper-evident nature can enable increased audit transparency, efficiency, and accuracy.

However, to realize such benefits, there are strong technical, legal, and organizational obstacles to overcome. Auditors will have to develop new skills, embrace evolving standards, and incorporate on-chain validation into current audit procedures. When technology is converging and regulatory insights are emerging, blockchain has the potential to be a foundation for auditing processes that are future-proofed for practitioners, educators, and policymakers.

2. LITERATURE REVIEW

Electronic data processing (EDP) auditing is addressed in this research by Hall, J. A. (Issa, Sunyaev, & Vasarhelyi, 2016) emphasizing how auditors must adjust when conventional procedures are outdated. The Internet and electronic data interchange made transactions easier, but evidence must still be obtained by auditors, security controls evaluated, and computerized accounting systems audited. It lays stress on SAS No. 80 as the most important auditing standard of electronic environments. The article states that auditors need to deal with sophisticated security issues, intranet/extranet dangers, and evolving electronic commerce practices as business is shifting towards electronic transactions. Technology adaptation to facilitate effective audits in an ever-evolving digital world is necessitated by the study.

Sivathaasan, N., & Velnampy, T. (Appelbaum, 2017) considers how technology affects auditing procedures by Indian chartered accountants. Through questionnaire approach and PLS-SEM analysis, the study has a perspective that technology adoption is positively impacting auditing practice as moderated by technological constraints, ease of use but negatively moderated by perceived usefulness. In the pursuit of effectiveness and efficiency, the study recommends it's essential that audit firms, especially partnerships and sole proprietorship, include advanced audit software. It highlights how the most recent technology-facilitated machinery allows electronic verification and confirmations to attain audit proofing. Through this example of technological progress in context with financial audit, the conclusion adds to existing knowledge about IT auditing.

Dagilienė, L. (Yermack, 2017) talks about the effect of future technologies, like Artificial Intelligence (AI) and Robotic Process Automation (RPA), on audit firms is addressed here along with organizational structure, their routine activities, and competition among Big4 and non-Big4 firms. It reports several auditors' perceptions about their use of technology through field research on 14 Italian audit firms. While there are some auditors who question how the value of these technologies will change the classical hierarchical models, others believe that they will enable the process to become easier and enhance repetitive tasks. Future auditors, according to the report, will have to acquire data analytics and information technology. RPA and AI are perceived by some non-Big4 firms as methods to level the playing field but because Big4 firms possess more resources, they will increase the gap of competition. Some non-Big4 firms view RPA and AI as means to level the playing field without knowing that Big4 firms' greater resources will cause them to raise the level of competition higher. The report foresees monumental transformations in auditing techniques on the horizon even though RPA and AI use is not ubiquitous.

The uses, implications and benefits of technological innovation in the audit process are described in the research by Carpenter and McGregor (2020) (Pérez-Calderón, Alrahamneh, & Montero, 2025). It eloquently explains the strategy and how technology like data analytics and automation can assist audit organizations in overcoming their challenges. These technologies enhance the quality and effectiveness of auditing by streamlining mundane work and facilitating more effortless scrutiny of large quantities of data. The research evidently indicates the means through which incorporation of newest technology in auditing can go beyond current procedures and offering various benefits, including more accurate audit results and efficiency. It also deals with likely risks enterprises can face when embracing new technology, including the reliability of the data, availability of qualified resources, and safety. The research proves how it is significant that auditors convert such technology to make them productive and secure financial audit credibility.

The acceptance, effect, and scope of future technologies—Artificial Intelligence (AI), Blockchain, Machine Learning (ML), and Robotic Process Automation (RPA)—on financial auditing and accounting are discussed in the research paper by Imoniana et al. (2023) (Saifudin, Januarti, & Purwanto, 2023). Blockchain falls behind as per the questionnaires because it has a niche usage and is still in the early stages of development, whereas AI and ML are being widely applied for process automation and data analysis. More extensive use is being restrained by obstacles in the form of high cost, lack of skills, and organizational problems, specifically for small firms. Nevertheless, benefits of new technologies like enhanced effectiveness, precision, and lower cost highlight their potential for revolution. The study underscores the need for strategic investment in infrastructure, training, and change management and suggests that widespread action by the government, regulators, and technology companies is required to overcome challenges and achieve successful integration into industries by these technologies.

Francisco (2024) (Alotaibi, 2023) explores how technological developments have shaped financial auditing with regard to deep learning, blockchain, RPA, artificial intelligence (AI), and IoT. The paper discusses how all these technologies are being implemented within planning, reporting, and various other processes involved in the audit. The central findings portray the way AI and machine learning have been reshaping audit decision-making, exception handling, and information extraction. Even with the advances in technology, some problems like firm-to-firm rate of adoption and non-mandatory technology use in International Auditing Standards (ISA) exist. For implementation and sustenance of the systems in a proper way, the report also cites the need to include IT specialists in audit firms. Overall, it emphasizes the necessity of further research and a systematic approach to the application of new auditing tools in large corporations and small enterprises.

With a specific focus on Artificial Intelligence (AI), Blockchain, Robotic Process Automation (RPA), Machine Learning, and Deep Learning, Cristea (2020) (Zhang, Ma, & Meng, 2025) discusses the influence that new IT technologies exert on accounting and auditing processes. The research is demonstrating how these technologies would enhance financial auditing by making it more efficient through automation, improving fraud detection, and enhancing productivity. The research study confirms whether RPA will be able to automate processes such as exchange rate verification and significantly minimize human error through case studies and expert opinion from Big Four companies. In addition, it discusses how blockchain technology, data mining, and predictive analytics can revolutionize audit processes through more secure transaction verification and improved fraud detection. With the combination of these technologies, the study asserts that the quality and performance of audit missions will improve through compelling auditors to acquire new skills and use prescriptive and predictive auditing methods.

Eulerich et al. (2023) (Han et al., 2023) examines whether technology-based auditing techniques (TBATs) have an impact on the effectiveness and efficiency of audits in countering the increasing problems with the advantages and disadvantages of such technologies. The research uses questionnaires and interviews with chief audit executives (CAEs) and auditors to find out more about what auditors and CAEs perceive TBATs to be. Based on findings, audit outputs like deciding further risk indicators, releasing further recommendations, and cutting audit days are all improved by TBATs. CAEs did nevertheless also refer to rising costs and the difficulty of ascertaining the net cost-benefit ratio. In spite of all these issues, TBATs are also said to improve audit quality; however, they are hindered by their widespread use because of the difficulty in ascertaining their benefits and in obtaining trained auditors.

3. METHODOLOGY

This study employed a mixed-methods study design to combine the impact of new technologies—Artificial Intelligence (AI), cloud computing, and blockchain—on audit practice. Qualitative thematic analysis and quantitative meta-analysis were used in this study to provide a balanced evaluation of conceptual and empirical evidence base.

Systematic search was conducted through renowned academic databases like Scopus, Web of Science, IEEE Xplore, and Google Scholar. Terms such as "AI audit," "cloud computing audit," and "blockchain audit" were employed in downloading corresponding publications. Inclusion criteria employed included English-language peer-reviewed journals and conference proceedings for the year span of 2010 to 2024 dealing with empirical or conceptual review of auditing process transformation through emerging technology. Screening involved title, abstract screening, and full text filtering. A sub-sample of X eligible studies were retained for intensive analysis within the final sample.

The primary aim was to identify cross-cutting themes—e.g., audit efficiency, fraud detection, data security, and quality of evidence—technology domains. Conceptual insights and empirical results were obtained for qualitative synthesis, whereas quantitative studies with suitable measures were meta-analyzed using statistical methods to estimate aggregate effect sizes.

4. DATA ANALYSIS

4.1 Qualitative Thematic Analysis

The qualitative stage was conducted following Thomas and Harden's (Thomas & Harden, 2008) framework for thematic synthesis of qualitative data. The line-by-line coding of comparable text within articles was implemented to generate description and analytic comments on technology impacts on audit processes. The master codes were combined into middle-level categories such as "efficiency gains," "skill demands," and "real-time assurance." They were abstracted again to higher-order analytic themes that had distinctive patterns across studies.

NVivo computer software assisted in aiding coding and codebook management to maximize traceability of theme development growth. Consistency was improved by independent coding where two researchers coded every study. Interpretation discrepancies were resolved by discussion to consensus. Double coding improved reliability at the expense of thematic derivation bias. A thematic map was created to display the role of technology-based traits like transparency, automation, and immutability as they are mapped against audit results like quality, coverage, and timeliness.

4.2 Quantitative Meta-Analysis

At the same time, a quantitative meta-analysis was also conducted to estimate the effect of technology adoption on target audit outcomes. For each eligible study, we extracted available statistics—means, standard deviations, sample sizes, and correlation coefficients—on improvements in audit accuracy, fraud detection, or reporting quality with technology.

Effect sizes were further determined using Cohen's d or r correlation, as appropriate, depending on the original reporting vehicle. Overall effect sizes that adjusted for heterogeneity between studies were then calculated using a random-effects meta-analytic model. Heterogeneity was assessed using the Q-statistic and I^2 index, and the thresholds of 25%, 50%, and 75% being low, moderate, and high heterogeneity, respectively (Borenstein, Hedges, Higgins, & Rothstein, 2009). Forest plots were used to illustrate individual as well as pooled estimates by AI, cloud computing, and blockchain categories.

Sensitivity analyses, such as leave-one-out tests, were also performed to prevent results being artificially biased due to outlier studies. Subgroup analyses where data existed compared effect sizes by geographic region or technology type. The meta-analysis produced robust empirical evidence in favor of claims technology usage has a far-reaching impact on audit quality.

4.3 Validity and Reliability

To determine qualitative results' reliability, certain measures were taken. Inter-coder reliability was first established using Cohen's kappa coefficient. The value of κ above 0.75 was reached, indicating a high level of agreement among coders

(McHugh, 2012). The measure taken ensures coding of the themes was not done randomly and an interpretation consistency between coders was ensured.

Second, methodological triangulation was employed by accumulating evidence across a range of contexts (e.g., industries, geographies, and audit firm types). This reduced the threat of context-specific bias and enhanced the external validity of the findings. Third, an audit trail of all coding decisions, inclusion reasons, and exclusion reasons was maintained to enhance transparency.

In quantitative synthesis, publication bias was investigated using funnel plots and Egger's test. The lack of asymmetry indicated a low likelihood of systematic reporting bias for significant findings. Leave-one-out sensitivity analyses also provided evidence for the stability of the pooled effect sizes, indicating that no study had an excessive influence on results.

The mixed methods design itself served to enhance validity by triangulating qualitative patterns and quantitative estimates. Congruence between evidence from the two analytic streams engenders confidence in the conclusion that AI, blockchain, and cloud computing each have statistically and substantively positive impacts on audit quality, efficiency, and evidence reliability.

5. RESULTS

5.1 Impact of Artificial Intelligence on Auditing

The conclusions of several studies unmistakably reveal that artificial intelligence (AI) vastly improves auditing operations, most importantly quality, efficiency, and the detection of fraud. The capability of AI in handling big volumes of data, detecting irregularities, and providing real-time support leads to the improvement in the outcomes of auditing, measurable.

Pérez-Calderón et al. (Pérez-Calderón, Alrahamneh, & Montero, 2025) conducted a large-scale survey of 336 auditors in Jordan and found that the use of AI in audit procedures "substantially enhances audit efficiency, accuracy, and client communication quality." Structural equation modeling of the study confirmed that AI usage was positively linked to perceived audit quality. The finding was significant statistically and detected a shift in auditors' perceptions regarding the usefulness of AI-derived insights in enhancing professional judgment and evidence reliability.

To corroborate this, Qader and Çek (Qader & Çek, 2024) also report a path coefficient of approximately 0.465 ($p < 0.001$), indicating a statistically significant and strong relationship between audit quality and AI adoption. Their meta-analytic results indicated that firms utilizing AI exhibited an average difference of 0.584 in audit quality scores with respect to firms utilizing traditional methods. This improvement is largely attributed to AI's anomaly detection capabilities, continuous monitoring functions, and enhanced pattern recognition, all of which help reduce human error and uncover irregularities that might otherwise go unnoticed.

Quantitative meta-analysis conducted in this research also verifies the same. Pooled estimates with Cohen's d showed a large effect size ($d \approx 0.8$) for improvement in audit accuracy after AI implementation. Several studies included in the review reported reduced audit cycle time, enhanced control testing precision, and higher fraud detection rates. Additionally, most surveyed practitioners (>70%) verified that AI results in stronger audit conclusions and governance quality (Pérez-Calderón, Alrahamneh, & Montero, 2025).

5.2 Effect of Cloud Computing on Auditing

Cloud computing has also been found to have the same positive impact on audit quality, timeliness, and cooperation. Alotaibi (Alotaibi, 2023), in a study with 430 Saudi Arabian auditors, concluded that the use of cloud ERP systems led to improved accuracy in financial estimates, higher reliability of evidence, and greater timeliness of audit reports. Statistical testing of the study indicated significant improvement ($p < 0.05$) in audit completeness measures, report quality, and operation efficiency.

Cloud-based solutions provide secure, centralized access to current financial information, facilitating ongoing audit procedures. Having on-demand information handy enables quicker reconciliation, earlier exception detection, and improved coordination between remote audit teams. Consolidated findings indicate that organizations with cloud audit workpapers reduced their audit cycle times by approximately 25% compared to organizations using legacy systems. This is particularly so in multi-entity or multinational audits, where orderly access to current information can reduce coordination delays by quite significantly.

Cloud platforms, it is claimed by Zhang et al. (Zhang, Ma, & Meng, 2025), do not only advance audit timing but also allow for better client and auditor system integration. In one industry case alone, cloud solutions allowed for a 90% reduction in reconciliation steps through automated controls and unified data access. As much as there are continued data security and governance issues, the prevailing view in literature is that cloud computing allows for better audits when handled well (Alotaibi, 2023; Zhang, Ma, & Meng, 2025).

5.3 Blockchain's Impact on Auditing

Blockchain technology also showed transformative implications on auditing practices, particularly in enabling evidence reliability, real-time assurance, and verification automation through smart contracts. Its tamper-evident and decentralized nature directly opposes most of the above-discussed common audit issues such as authenticity of transactions, integrity of documents, and third-party confirmations.

Zhang et al. Zhang, Ma, & Meng, 2025) describe blockchain to enable "automated transaction authentication and machine-learning anomaly detection," with near real-time assurance and reduced reliance on human verification. Their literature review acknowledges that blockchain experiments in auditing, especially by large firms, resulted in significant process efficiency gains. For example, distributed ledger technology enabled full-population testing, where auditors had the potential to test 100% of transactions, thereby increasing coverage and detection levels.

Qader and Çek (Bertolli, 2019) also report statistically significant improvement in audit quality that is associated with blockchain adoption, with a path coefficient of 0.325 ($p < 0.001$). The finding implies that blockchain not only improves evidence integrity but also improves more consistent and justifiable audit conclusions. Blockchain is also reported by their study to be especially beneficial when coupled with AI tools, where it generates synergistic effects for fraud detection and compliance checking.

However, blockchain benefits are weighed considering implementation threats. Weaknesses such as 51% consensus attacks, smart contract vulnerabilities, and scalability constraints in public blockchains are highlighted in literature (Zhang, Ma, & Meng, 2025; Deloitte, 2017). Additionally, since blockchains would only capture on-chain transactions, auditors would need to audit off-chain elements (e.g., service contracts, physical shipping of products), limiting the completeness of blockchain as audit evidence alone.

Despite these limitations, the research argues that blockchain deployed in permissioned networks within formal governance increases transparency, reliability, and audit trail completeness significantly. Other researchers confirm that blockchain-based applications excel over conventional ERP systems in generating irreversible, traceable, and current documentation (Zhang, Ma, & Meng, 2025; Deloitte, 2017).

5.4 Summary of Findings

The results of this mixed-methods review provide convergent evidence that AI, cloud computing, and blockchain have much to contribute to auditing. Each of the three technologies improves audit quality, reduces processing time, and increases the accuracy and reliability of audit evidence. Board wide, meta-analysis effect sizes were statistically significant ($p < 0.01$), reflecting a strong association between technology adoption and audit performance outcomes.

AI excelled at being highly effective in improving fraud detection rates and audit quality through continuous data analysis and risk scoring as depicted in Table 1. Cloud was characterized by improved collaboration, cycle times, and audit trail integrity by placing real-time data availability at the center. Blockchain was characterized by providing tamper-proof, time-stamped transaction ledgers and continuous verification through smart contracts.

Table 1. Presents the strongest effects reported across the technologies

Technology	Audit Quality	Fraud Detection	Efficiency	Real-Time Assurance	Evidence Reliability
Artificial Intelligence	↑↑	↑↑	↑↑	↑	↑↑
Cloud Computing	↑	↑	↑↑	↑↑	↑↑
Blockchain	↑↑	↑	↑	↑↑	↑↑

Even as such benefits are so tempting, research also builds barriers to be overcome to facilitate efficient uptake. Of special concern are cloud infrastructures' data privacy risks, AI decision-making explainability, and blockchain system governance complexity. Auditor reskilling, control baselines of standards, and new regulatory requirements must be framed to unlock the value of such technologies.

The research only concludes the general finding that the future of auditing is to incorporate these emerging digital technologies into standard audit procedures. The regulatory agencies, professional associations, and audit firms should collaborate to create auditing standards, training, and compliance regimes that align the benefits and limitations of AI, cloud, and blockchain technologies.

6. DISCUSSION AND PRACTICAL IMPLICATIONS

6.1 Artificial Intelligence (AI) in Auditing

Artificial Intelligence (AI) has been rapidly becoming an audit analytics and assurance driver of change. AI software is powered by machine learning algorithms that allow auditors to analyze and process huge datasets, detect anomalies that might escape manual sampling and be overlooked. The technological ability relocates audit procedures from placing focus on run-of-the-mill compliance testing to more judgmental risk areas.

Empirical evidence comes in support of the positive influence of AI. Pérez-Calderón et al. (Pérez-Calderón, Alrahamneh, & Montero, 2025) revealed that use of AI by auditors in Jordan "strongly enhances audit effectiveness, accuracy, and quality of client communication." These enhancements occur due to the ability of AI to classify data automatically, pick up control deficiencies, and send real-time risk alerts. Moreover, AI tools enable full population testing so that continuous data monitoring and enlarged audit coverage beyond the ability of traditional statistical sampling methods become possible.

But as more dependence is placed on AI systems, new problems arise. Most AI models are "black boxes" that are not transparent, i.e., auditors cannot easily know or explain how the algorithm arrived at a conclusion. As Zhong and Goel (Zhong & Goel, 2024) contend, transparency is necessary to hold people accountable, particularly in highly regulated industries. To counteract this, explainable AI (XAI) techniques—decision trees, LIME, or SHAP—to produce interpretable results and to allow auditability of model action must be used.

Data bias and error are also incorporated in the vulnerability of the AI system. Algorithm training data is potentially biased or incomplete, leading to AI systems generating systematically incorrect conclusions. These could also reinforce inaccuracies in audit conclusions. Auditors must subject AI systems to rigorous testing on data quality, fairness, and performance robustness before they can apply them to substantive testing or fraud detection.

Practical Implications:

Audit firms should have internal procedures for AI model validation in place. These "model audit" processes, like financial risk management processes, should include stress testing, documentation of model architecture, and checks on training data quality. Companies should spend money on training auditors in the fundamentals of AI so they can interpret algorithmic output and challenge irrelevant system behavior. Auditors need to receive clients' permission for secure, well-documented access to AI systems and disclose all significant AI tools used in financial activities. Regulators and standard setters need to update auditing standards to include guidance regarding the use of AI, such as disclosure guidelines, audit trail documentation, and evidence evaluation guidelines using AI. While regulation of AI progresses around the world, audit practitioners need to actively participate to shape policies that resonate with innovation rather than trust and transparency (Pérez-Calderón, Alrahamneh, & Montero, 2025; Zhong & Goel, 2024).

6.2 Cloud Computing in Auditing

Cloud computing has revolutionized data availability and scalability and is now a major component of modern-day audit infrastructure. Cloud platforms enable auditors to have financial information anywhere, anytime, and facilitate real-time continuous auditing and exception identification at high speed. Rizki et al. (Rizki,

Wijaya, & Mustafid, 2024) identify that cloud systems "increase transparency and efficiency," especially in hybrid or remote audit settings.

These systems also have enhanced analytics features that are able to automate transaction reconciliations, warn on exceptions, and display audit metrics graphically by clients and engagements. The move to cloud environments has also reduced the time it takes to capture and attest audit evidence.

While such advantages exist, there are tremendous risks involved in cloud computing. Customer data stored off premises raise concerns about data privacy, confidentiality, and cybersecurity. Auditors must verify design and operating effectiveness of cloud controls like encryption, access limitation, and data redundancy, writes Banker et al. Moreover, third-party cloud vendor reliance relocates segments of the internal control environment outside the direct control of the client, and auditors must navigate SOC 2 or ISO 27001 certification reports to be assured of the cloud provider's infrastructure.

Jurisdiction compliance is another area of complexity. Data residency laws—such as GDPR within the EU—place stringent requirements on where data are stored and accessed and how. Auditors are at risk of offering opinions on evidence that violates local privacy conditions if they do not review the geographic extent of cloud systems. Cloud vendor-client agreements must also be reviewed to ensure SLAs include contingency provisions in the event of service failure, data recovery processes, and audit rights (Banker, Chang, & Lee, 2020).

Practical Implications:

The auditors would need to undertake cloud-specific steps for risk verification. This may involve checking system configurations, checking the vendors' compliance certification, and having uninterrupted access to audit logs and trails. Companies must form dedicated cloud audit teams or appoint IT staff to advise them on complicated settings. The clients should maintain flawless documentation regarding their cloud design and access points, thus ensuring the ease of auditors in analyzing general IT as well as application-level controls. The regulators need to render audit standards current and treat cloud computing risk in some specific manner, with best practices for guaranteeing the reliability of cloud infrastructure and giving guidance on third-party attestation report usage (e.g., SOC 1/2). Applied effectively, cloud platforms will significantly enhance flexibility and efficiency of modern audit practice (Rizki, Wijaya, & Mustafid, 2024; Banker, Chang, & Lee, 2020).

6.3 Blockchain in Auditing

Blockchain technology offers a new paradigm for audit evidence management in its decentralization, immutability, and transparency inherent characteristics. Through its distributed ledger, blockchain records have tamper-evident characteristics and are therefore extremely credible as evidence for transactional confirmation, ownership rights, and time-stamped occurrences.

Zhang et al. (Zhang, Ma, & Meng, 2025) indicate that blockchain "improves the authenticity and credibility of audit information significantly, improves evidence collection speed, and facilitates data sharing." Auditors can easily access full history of transactions from the ledger, reducing reliance on client-provided documents.

Smart contracts—programmable code stored in the blockchain—can automatically check for in effect compliance with provided rules, reducing manual control testing and improving audit efficiency. For example, reconciliation between buyer and supplier can be done on-chain to minimize differences and increase audit accuracy (Zhang, Ma, & Meng, 2025). Nonetheless, blockchain is not perfect. Deloitte (Deloitte, 2017) goes on to clarify that while a blockchain record represents conclusive proof of a transaction, it is not necessarily descriptive about the nature of the transaction or its economic substance. For instance, a transaction on a cryptocurrency can be recorded, but in the absence of other records, one cannot be sure whether the transaction was valid, nor even why the transaction took place. Auditors must then add blockchain data to off chain supporting documents such as contracts, invoices, or authorization memos.

Security too is a problem. Though blockchains are deployed securely by way of cryptography, smart contracts are full of vulnerabilities to be exploited, and certain types of blockchains (most public blockchains) are susceptible to 51% consensus attacks. Scalability and performance issues in some implementations of the blockchain also make them challenging to view as wide-scale enterprise adoption. Legal admissibility of evidence presented from blockchain is also varying country to country. Bertolli (Deloitte, 2017) warns that some courts will not accept blockchain records as records of law if they fail to comply with electronic signature law or rules of procedure.

7. PRACTICAL IMPLICATIONS

Audit teams need to become familiar with the basics of blockchain, including consensus algorithms, digital signatures, and smart contract auditing.

They need to employ blockchain analytics tools to track streams of transactions and identify anomalies. Auditors in permissioned blockchain networks will need to have read-access rights to ledgers and verification processes. Firms intending to implement blockchain application to accounting will need ledger governance outlined, provide data integrity controls, and record off-chain events auditable. Regulators will need to define the evidentiary nature of blockchain transactions, establish chain-of-custody documentation standards, and promote interoperability standards from blockchain to legacy ERP systems. Blockchain's real audit benefit. can only be achieved by being paired with regulatory openness., talent cultivation., and off. Chain verification protocols (Zhang, Ma, & Meng, 2025; Bertolli, 2019).

7.1 Summary of Practical Recommendations

Across AI, cloud computing, and blockchain, the implications for audit practice are significant. They raise audit quality, efficiency, and transparency but create new governance, security, and skills issues.

Table 2. Summarizes the main opportunities and implementation strategies

Technology	Opportunities	Key Risks	Practical Actions
AI	Anomaly detection, continuous analysis, full dataset review	Model opacity, data bias, skill gaps	Use explainable AI, audit model logic, upskill auditors
Cloud	Real-time access, automation, collaboration	Data privacy, control risk, SLA ambiguity	Review SOC reports, validate SLAs, build cloud audit expertise
Blockchain	Immutable audit trail, smart contracts, trustless verification	Off-chain blind spots, scalability, legal ambiguity	Audit smart contracts, combine on-/off-chain tests, monitor regulations

Audit practitioners will have to transform by integrating technical competence and conventional audit judgment to be effective and credible generating opportunities and a number of practical applications as depicted in Table 2. This hybrid approach—based on digital assurance—will be the norm for audit excellence in the future.

8. LIMITATIONS OF EMERGING TECHNOLOGIES IN AUDITING

8.1 Artificial Intelligence (AI) in Auditing

AI audit software is greatly dependent on the quantity and quality of the input data. In practice, audit data sets are often noisy, incomplete, or partially applicable, which limits the potential ability of machine learning algorithms. Seethamraju and Hecimovic mention that "bad quality data" used in AI technology can undermine audit accuracy (Seethamraju & Hecimovic, 2020). In other words, when training data are unrepresentative of the full population or contain errors, AI models may produce misleading results. This "garbage in, garbage out" phenomenon means that auditors must carefully vet datasets before applying AI techniques; if historical audit data are biased or incomplete, any automated analysis may simply perpetuate those deficiencies, reducing confidence in the audit findings (Seethamraju & Hecimovic, 2020).

Another related issue is the transparency of most AI models. Sophisticated algorithms (deep learning or ensemble methods) are "black boxes" whose workings are not clear to users. Auditors traditionally need to justify and explain audit evidence and processes, but unfathomable models make this a task. Seethamraju and Hecimovic specifically cite the "'black-box' nature of AI solutions [which] do not instill trust" (Seethamraju & Hecimovic, 2020). Without clear explanations of why an AI system reached a particular conclusion, regulators and auditors cannot possibly confirm that the explanation for highlighted anomalies or risk estimates is sound. This interpretability gap therefore constrains the use of AI: auditors must supplement AI decisions with traditional audit work or apply explainable AI techniques to guarantee that automated outputs are understandable and verifiable.

AI audit systems can also inherit human and data biases and amplify them. If the historical data upon which a model is trained represent past biases, selective sampling, or systematic errors, then the predictions made by the AI will likely be similarly biased. For instance, an AI routine that has been trained on past audit results may under-detect fraud in previously under-audited areas. Seethamraju and Hecimovic ring a warning that "potential human bias…embedded in the AI algorithms" is of serious concern (Seethamraju & Hecimovic, 2020). In effect, AI may unintentionally replicate audit judgments made under the influence of human prejudice, thereby eradicating objectivity. To surmount such a limitation means that auditors need to test models of AI on prejudice and fairness, but such testing is non-trivial if the rationale of the model is complex. Unless robust bias-detection and fairness frameworks for auditing AI are established, these issues will continue to limit auditors from relying on fully automated evaluation.

Finally, regulatory, ethical, and legal boundaries exist on using AI for auditing. Audit standards and professional liability rules were written under the premise of human professional judgment; AI introduces new concerns about accountability. Auditors face "perceived legal and reputational risk…that constrains the prospective adoption of AI" for financial audits (Seethamraju & Hecimovic, 2020). For example, if a software AI fails to spot a mistake or invents a non-existent anomaly, there is no clear authority figure to turn to. Yet, there are no comprehensive global standards for procedures supported by AI. To top it all, regulators generally remain skeptical of robotic audit methods, which means auditors need to detail and account for every AI-facilitated procedure. In practice, this means that audit firms must be more vigilant and have dual traditional controls in place when employing AI, which can diminish the efficiency gains that AI would otherwise achieve (Seethamraju & Hecimovic, 2020).

8.2 Cloud Computing in Auditing

Cloud computing outsources data storage and processing to third-party servers, which creates serious security and privacy concerns for accountants. Where the financial information of a company may be sitting on servers over which it has no direct control, accountants must trust the cloud provider's security controls. Chou indicates that data kept on a provider's system "raises privacy and confidentiality concerns" (Chou, 2015). Data from and to the cloud would need to pass over public networks and is therefore vulnerable to being intercepted or tampered with unless there is robust encryption and controls. Auditors therefore need to spend significant time reviewing cloud-specific security: they will need to verify that the provider has put in place good access controls, intrusion detection, and incident response plans. Whatever can be the vulnerable link in provider infrastructure, audit evidence would be tainted through it, like a security breach of the cloud invalidating integrity of data being audited. Inherent risk via cloud architectures mandates therefore, auditors incorporating cloud security tests into their risk assessment, which may prove difficult if providers limit auditing access or rather provide only assurances (e.g. compliance attestation) and not raw system logs (Chou, 2015).

Cloud heterogeneity and complexity make conventional audit steps harder. Compared with an on-premises data center with an evident limit, a multi-tenant cloud may blend services in public, private, or hybrid models. Chou identifies that auditors need to face "more pieces that can go wrong" within cloud architectures (Chou, 2015). For example, virtual networks and service APIs may change quickly, and it may be challenging to define a static audit scope or select representative samples in the long term. The transient nature of some cloud resources (e.g., ephemeral computing instances or auto-scaled services) means that a snapshot audit may miss important events if it is not well-timed. Also, audit trails may be disbursed on provider and customer machines; if providers don't allow auditors log access directly, it can complicate it to verify previous transactions. In summary, cloud intricacy is urging auditors to shift approach: they may be required to retrieve data continuously spanning long periods of time or to use automated technologies to track changing configurations. This kind of complexity imposes audit effort and may limit the auditor from applying normal sampling or time-based testing techniques (Chou, 2015).

Cloud auditing also brings contractual and compliance issues. Auditors and organizations must rely on service-level agreements (SLAs) to outline security and performance expectations, but SLAs are not necessarily transparent or reliable. Chou highlights that an effective SLA should incorporate security requirements, performance measures, conditions for exit, and other terms (Chou, 2015). But in practice, SLAs can be too general or omit audit rights of access to the audit, therefore leaving auditors uncertain about their statutory right of evidence. As an example, if the cloud provider fails to perform, the auditor will be denied access to important records unless backup provisions are specified. Auditors must therefore review the terms of the SLA very carefully and, in some cases, negotiate audit provisions favorable to the audit (e.g. audit rights or data escrow). Regulatory compliance is also a concern: auditors need to ensure cloud deployment compliance with industry regulations and data residency rules (e.g. keeping personal data within approved geographies). A cloud provider that stores data everywhere across the globe or has subcontractors can make compliance auditing more difficult. These contractual and regulatory uncertainties cause the auditors to conduct further due diligence on the cloud service model itself, which may add to the work and risk of the audit.

Finally, cloud platform adoption calls for new skills and organizational re-engineering of the audit process. Chou confidently states that auditors "need to be knowledgeable about all things related to cloud computing" (Chou, 2015). This means that audit teams must possess expertise regarding cloud infrastructure, virtualization, and related security paradigms (e.g., ISO/IEC 27017 or NIST SP 800-144) covering cloud services. In most companies, current auditors have no hands-on experience with cloud technologies, and so there is a learning curve. That the cloud services are evolving extremely rapidly makes it even more difficult: auditors must continually update their skills as new services and architectures emerge. Certain audit teams address this by creating knowledge bases or specialized cloud audit roles, but until practices become commonplace, the lack of skill can complicate effective cloud auditing. Generally, cloud computing is beneficial in scalability and availability of data, but its outsourced and cloudy and technologically advanced nature presents significant limits on traditional audit techniques (Chou, 2015).

8.3 Blockchain in Auditing

Blockchain's distributed ledger promises immutability and transparency, but novel auditing issues arise. Perhaps one of the largest technical challenges is security: despite strong cryptography, blockchains are susceptible to attack. For instance, Chang et al. cite vulnerability to a "51% attack," in which an attacker with over half the network computational power can alter transaction history (Zhang, Ma, & Meng, 2025). Meanwhile, private use of cryptographic keys suggests loss or capture of a key will authorize attackers to spend or counterfeit assets; such incidents have occurred in real-world situations. These vulnerabilities prompt auditors to consider new adversary models. Conventional systems rely on perimeter defense, whereas blockchain platforms put trust between different nodes. Auditors should thus ensure the robustness of consensus protocols and key management security by the users. If a blockchain network is exposed to these vulnerabilities, the assumed integrity of its records is compromised, and extra checks (e.g. third-party verification of node actions) may be required (Zhang, Ma, & Meng, 2025).

Another limitation is that a blockchain record does not always ensure that an actual-world transaction occurred. Zhang et al. point out that "writing transactions to the blockchain does not necessarily validate that the transaction shown has happened in the real world," so controls at the regulatory and organizational levels are still needed (Zhang, Ma, & Meng, 2025). That is, blockchain makes data recorded tamper-evident, but cannot ensure data correctness at the source. An auditor that is only based on on-chain data may not be able to detect fraud that has been perpetrated off-chain (e.g., fake invoices properly recorded on a blockchain). Previous studies (Schmitz and Leoni, 2019) have also indicated that blockchain immutability cannot replace fraud detection controls or external audit evidence. To get that, the auditors would have to acquire off-chain evidence (such as system logs or reconciliations) or use trusted oracles that validate off-chain events prior to when they get written on-chain. Without such a step, blockchain's data consistency promise provides no useful guarantee about the authenticity of transactions (Zhang, Ma, & Meng, 2025).

Scalability and performance limitations also limit the use of blockchain in auditing large sets of data. Public blockchains like Bitcoin or Ethereum can only handle a handful of transactions per second and require each node to validate or hold all transaction data. Zhang et al. observe that "low transaction throughput and relatively high consumption of storage and computational resources" obstructs scalability (Zhang, Ma, & Meng, 2025). A blockchain may be a bottleneck in a high-intensity trading or high-speed financial flows business. Auditors should be aware of these limitations: for instance, they must ensure the blockchain an auditee is using has sufficient capacity or whether the system uses permissioned designs to increase throughput. If the blockchain is not able to hold all required audit information in real time, auditors might have to complement it with off-chain databases or batch processing, which renders the audit trail more inconvenient. In general, until blockchain technologies become more efficient (e.g., via sharding or off-chain solutions), auditors will have to be aware of potential data lag and missing on-chain records.

Finally, auditing blockchain requires special knowledge and integration work. Auditors today are not aware of distributed ledger technology, evidence systems based on cryptography, or the enforcement of smart contracts. As Chang et al. point out, "the complexity of auditing blockchain-based assets and the lack of required knowledge and skills among auditors pose significant challenges" (Zhang, Ma, & Meng, 2025).

Audit teams must be taught how to examine blockchain node configurations, examine smart contract code, and examine consensus proofs – all of which are drastically different from traditional accounting controls. Furthermore, most companies already possess existing accounting infrastructure that will need to coexist with whatever blockchain solution they adopt. Merging blockchain ledgers with traditional ERP or audit software is difficult since they have differing data formats and models of trust. In practice, it would mean that the auditor might need to apply hybrid processes (part information from the blockchain and part from traditional databases) and reconcile between them. As much as auditors become more familiar with blockchain and industry standardization of blockchain audit improves, these knowledge and integration challenges will continue to tie blockchain's seamless adoption into assurance engagements (Zhang, Ma, & Meng, 2025).

9. CONCLUSION

The slow but inevitable merging of emerging technologies—Artificial Intelligence (AI), Cloud Computing, and Blockchain—is transforming the audit profession at its very foundation. These technologies have introduced paradigm-altering potential that extends beyond incremental automation to elemental differences in the way auditors conduct risk assessment, gather evidence, and attest. Collectively, these technologies offer the promise of nimbler, data-centric, and reliable audits that are suited to the complexity of the digital economy.

This paper has demonstrated how each of these three technologies is enriching the foundations of audit practice in its own way: AI enhances risk analysis and fraud detection, cloud provides real-time collaboration and single-point access, and blockchain ensures integrity and traceability of audit evidence. As much as they are promising, successful implementation necessitates overcoming daunting challenges—technical, ethical, regulatory, and organizational. This conclusion reflects real-world uses and future applications that will determine the future of auditing in the technological world.

9.1 Artificial Intelligence: Bringing Intelligence and Insight

AI has emerged as an enabler of next-generation audit analytics. Unlike traditional tools with pre-programmed logic, modern AI platforms learn from data patterns and react to changing situations. This enables dynamic risk modeling, continuous anomaly detection, and analysis of full populations of data—a contrast to sample-based audit procedures of the past (Alotaibi, 2023).

Empirical research confirms AI's role in increasing audit precision and efficiency. Pérez-Calderón et al. Pérez-Calderón, Alrahamneh, & Montero, 2025) demonstrated that AI tools significantly improve audit accuracy, reduce time to completion, and facilitate risk-targeted audit strategies. Auditors leveraging AI reported greater confidence in identifying complex fraud patterns and accounting irregularities. Similarly,

Qader and Çek (Qader & Çek, 2024) found that AI contributes to audit quality by augmenting fraud detection capabilities and reducing manual review workloads.

These findings are also supported by industry reports. Thomson Reuters reported that AI enables auditors to free up time from mundane activities such as data classification and invoice matching and enable high-value analysis (Thomson Reuters, n.d.-a). AI is also able to perform risk-based auditing by scoring transactional and control-level dimensions of risk using machine learning algorithms. This enables the provision of audit attention to high-risk areas, enabling improved effectiveness of resource utilization and consistency of audit results.

However, AI adoption is not without challenges. The "black box" problem—where high-powered models give little insight into the rationale for decisions they make—is at the crossroads of audit explainability and regulatory defensibility (Zhong & Goel, 2024). In heavily regulated environments, auditors must be able to explain and defend the rationale underlying conclusions that have been tested by AI software. Insufficient explainability threatens to leave them too reliant on potentially flawed or poorly understood output.

To address this, explainable AI (XAI) methods need to be incorporated into audit systems. Models and Techniques like decision trees, local interpretable model-agnostic explanations (LIME), and Shapley values provide assistance to auditors in understanding why a model made a specific decision (Adadi & Berrada, 2018). Auditing firms also need to stress test AI systems, i.e., test models on known anomalies and ensure training data is representative of client environments.

9.2. Cloud Computing: Empowering Real-Time, Collaborative Auditing

Cloud computing is increasingly necessary to provide scalable, distributed, and collaborative audit environments. Cloud platforms provide easy access to data within and across locations and time zones, allowing audit teams to work asynchronously and in real time. This is especially relevant in the age of remote audits and hybrid work models, which have become progressively prevalent post-pandemic.

Alotaibi (Rizki, Wijaya, & Mustafid, 2024) determined that cloud-based ERP systems improved the effectiveness, accuracy, and cooperation of audits, particularly in geographically distributed stakeholders' operations. Auditors were able to verify evidence quicker and have consistent audit trail records among teams. Rizki et al. (Banker, Chang, & Lee, 2020) further identified that cloud-based audit platforms improved transparency and promptness of audit reporting, resulting in improved stakeholder confidence.

Cloud platforms also enable continuous auditing through the means of ingesting and tracking transactional data in a rolling manner. Real-time dashboards and alerting enable auditors to detect control failure or material deviation in real-time. This shift to continuous assurance transforms audit from being a hindsight activity to a foresight risk management function.

Industry views support this path. Industry areas of disagreement include Thomson Reuters' argument that cloud infrastructure is now essential to audit flexibility, as evidenced by the fact that cloud infrastructure assists audit firms with increasing amounts of data, maintaining compliance with global regulations, and reducing administrative burden (Thomson Reuters, n.d.-b).

Though such benefits exist, cloud auditing is risky. Top of the list is data privacy, jurisdictional compliance, and third-party vendor risk. Since data are most likely to be kept in offsite or cross-border data centers, auditors must ensure compliance with data protection laws like GDPR and CCPA. SLAs between CSP and audit clients should include audit access, data sovereignty, encryption protocol, and incident response procedures.

Banker et al. (Zhang, Ma, & Meng, 2025) note that cloud audits will be a bit more costly—5%—since it is more difficult to identify cloud infrastructure controls. Time saved and increased accuracy, however, make this expense worthwhile. Cloud fluency must be invested in by audit firms, so they can develop methodologies, and skill sets relevant to cloud-native systems.

9.3. Blockchain: Establishing Trust on Immutable Evidence

Blockchain can revolutionize audit evidence management. By providing an immutable, time-stamped, and decentralized history of transactions, blockchain enables data tracing that is much easier and less prone to manipulation. For auditors, this represents a high-integrity source of evidence with less need for verification and third-party assurance.

Zhang et al. (University of Maryland, n.d.) also note that blockchain enables real-time transaction verification and automatic control testing via smart contracts. Not only does it increase the completeness and authenticity of audit logs, but it also reduces audit lag. In some tests, the use of blockchain reduced audit reconciliation work by as much as 90% (University of Maryland, n.d.).

Smart contracts enable pre-programmed audit logic to be applied automatically on-chain. For instance, payments above a specified amount can be flagged or held for approval by an auditor. Automation of such processes reduces the reliance on manual control testing and enables continuous assurance capabilities in enterprise processes.

University of Maryland reports that permissioned blockchains are claimed to cut auditing by as much as 70% cost in supply chain and procurement audits, based on studies (Deloitte, 2017). Permissioned blockchains deliver traces along with the number of controls for logs to be completely visible to auditors without compromising the privacy required for protecting sensitive transactions.

However, blockchain limitations are not insignificant. Deloitte (Bertolli, 2019) warns that while blockchain data cannot be altered, they're often context-free. A transaction may be cryptographically valid but economically illegal. It may be payment for a nonexistent service or authorized by an unauthorized organization. Auditors will need to confirm on-chain data with off-chain documentation such as purchase orders, service agreements, and board approvals.

It also provides technical scalability guarantee, interoperability of other ERP systems, and cross-jurisdictional acceptance of blockchain data as admissible evidence in court. It also provides the argument that blockchain records aren't currently admissible as evidence in certain courts without being supported by legally admitted digital signatures or audit trails.

Auditors will have to acquire distributed ledger technology skills in cryptographic verification, smart contract auditing, and network consensus techniques. Blockchain analytics software like Chainalysis or Blockchair can be used to trace the movement of assets, mark suspicious activity, and represent inter-entity transactions as graphs.

9.4. Final Reflections and Forward-Looking Considerations

AI, cloud computing, and blockchain together comprise the future audit infrastructure. Each of the three technologies has the potential to help shape auditing into a forward-looking, predictive, and continuous assurance process, rather than its current back-office, compliance-focused function.

But their uptake must be spearheaded by a robust framework of ethical usage, adherence to regulations, and skills transformation. Auditors, customers, and regulators must collaborate on control protocols, decipherability procedures, and compatibility between systems. Professional organizations and universities must update syllabi to include technical expertise in data analytics, AI ethics, cloud architecture, and blockchain management.

Its future is hybrid intelligence—machine-enabled, not machine-replaced, human judgment. As technology advances, the audit profession will have to remain rooted in its fundamentals of integrity, independence, and objectivity while adapting to innovation to be able to serve a digital-first world.

10. FUTURE SCOPE

The pace-converging rhythm of technological innovation is introducing a milestone turning point for the audit profession. Emerging technologies such as Artificial Intelligence (AI), Cloud Computing, and Blockchain not only enhance the effectiveness of audit procedures but also redefine the very nature of assurance work. However, realization of their potential for transformation hinges on how well auditors, organizations, and regulators learn to react to a progressively dynamic technical and regulatory context.

For its future viability and usability of auditing in an era of world dominance by digital technology, future audit technology development needs to pull new directions on interpretability, integration, and governance by the auditors and researchers. Opportunities and priorities are briefly discussed for future audit technology development in the following.

10.1. Future of Artificial Intelligence in Auditing

AI has already shown considerable worth in the areas of anomaly detection, audit task automation, and risk analysis. As those capabilities continue to mature, next-generation auditing models will increasingly depend on AI to support continuous, proactive assurance.

The most pressing research area of the future is the further evolution of Explainable AI (XAI). Most AI models today are "black boxes," highly accurate but not highly interpretable—increasing audit documentation and regulatory compliance burdens. Research must focus on creating performance-transparency models for enabling auditors to understand and make sense of AI outputs in a way accessible to stakeholders and regulators. Zhong and Goel (Zhong & Goel, 2024) highlight incorporating XAI methodologies—such as SHAP and LIME—into auditing techniques to ensure levels of professional skepticism and evidence rationale standards.

One of the priority areas is the development of governance structures for AI. These must encompass fairness, accountability, transparency, and ethics in AI audit tools. The standards must include model validation requirements, bias detection, data lineage tracking, and auditable AI-generated content. Administrative Sciences journal highlights the evolving role of the auditor in an AI-facilitated environment, where the experts would more likely transition from being data reviewers to risk interpreters and strategy advisers (Greiling & Kend, 2024).

Moreover, future research must critically analyze human-AI interaction models. Rather than viewing AI as a replacement for human judgment, it can be used as an aid to enhance it. Research must explore mixed human-AI team decision-making dynamics and conditions that facilitate effective integration—trust of the auditor, model understandability, and user interface design. Synergism in a proper proportion of AI intelligence to auditor knowledge must be sustained to achieve audit reliability and independence.

10.2 Future of Cloud Computing in Auditing

Cloud computing will be the backbone of real-time, location-based audit environments soon. The technology accommodates high-volume processing of data, global collaboration, and adaptable audit frameworks. Its future in auditing, however, hinges on addressing future compliance, architecture, and analytical requirements.

Among the topic areas of research being carried out is designing cloud-native audit analytics platforms. The platforms can be incorporated with next-generation data lakes and enterprise resource planning (ERP) to support real-time large-scale analytics. Rizki et al. (Rizki, Wijaya, & Mustafid, 2024) point out that cloud-native systems can facilitate the collection of evidence and reliability in audit reports via seamless data flows and validation procedures.

The next frontier is geographically compliant automation. (Banker, Chang, & Lee, 2020)Future ERP systems will, as detailed by a recent SSRN working paper, have such capability, and audit firms can then operate compliantly across regions (Murtaza, 2024).

Further studies are also necessary to explore the development of continuous assurance systems on a cloud platform. They would have real-time dashboards for monitoring, risk warning systems, and automated control testing procedures. Such types of frameworks would revolutionize auditing from sample-based periodic auditing into a continuous data-driven model of assurance, which would add more transparency and stakeholder trust. Banker et al. point out that continuous auditing, besides reducing audit lag, also allows the detection of prior material misstatements or fraud.

But to benefit from such gains requires more emphasis on cloud security and governance. Best practices on auditing multiple clouds, identity access management, and creating attestation frameworks (such as SOC 2 Type II) must be researched by academics so they can offer auditor access and data integrity.

10.3. Auditing and Blockchain Future

Blockchain can equip and serve as a standardized, immutable platform for proof management and transaction verification. Its applications in auditing are in their infancy but are evolving fast, particularly in high-risk industries such as finance, logistics, and supply chain management.

One of the most pressing research agendas is to harmonize blockchain audit procedures. There is no standard process for determining when and how blockchain data is sufficient audit evidence. Zhang et al. (Zhang, Ma, & Meng, 2025) argue that without standards, blockchain adoption will be piecemeal and underleveraged. Future research needs to set evidentiary thresholds, off-chain linkage requirements, and reliability measures to smart contract validation.

On-chain audit system design is also a new trend. Such systems would perform audit procedures on blockchain networks in real-time, with real-time evidence gathering, control logic enforcement by smart contracts, and marking of compliance. This would reduce audit cost considerably and eliminate manual reconciliation steps. As per the University of Maryland (University of Maryland, n.d.), permissioned blockchains can reduce auditing costs by up to 70% while improving traceability and audit trail integrity.

New applications also encompass blockchain interoperability with the Internet of Things (IoT). Data from sensors stored on-chain can be included in audit trails for logistics, manufacturing, and energy applications. In real time, goods tracking, energy consumption, or production metrics can provide high-fidelity attestations for physical and financial transactions. Research will have to examine data authentication processes, privacy models, and auditor regime access to these systems.

Apart from that, blockchain is becoming more relevant in Environmental, Social, and Governance (ESG) assurance. The permanence of blockchain records is the most appropriate to track carbon credits, labor compliance, and ethical sourcing claims. A study in the Accounting, Auditing & Accountability Journal calls for further studies on how blockchain can heighten trust and transparency in ESG reports (Biondi & Marchi, 2021).

10.4. Convergence and Wider Implications

Looking beyond the individual technologies, the future of auditing will likely be influenced by their convergence. Converged technologies that involve AI, blockchain, and cloud technologies will have the capability to deliver smart, autonomous audit environments with the following characteristics:

- Proactive Risk Management: AI-powered systems that recognize and respond to risk before its occurrence.
- Real-Time Assurance: Blockchain-based, cloud-based environments that automatically validate transactions and controls.
- Cross-Platform Integration: Unified streams of data bridging financial, operational, and regulatory data sources.

To accomplish this, the auditing learning process needs to change. Professional societies and schools should include coursework on data analytics, AI governance, blockchain forensics, and cloud security. Technical competency must be just as much a standard as knowledge of GAAP or IFRS.

At the same time, regulators and standard setters must refresh audit standards. These involve refreshing evidence requirements, control testing guidance, and reporting templates to accommodate digitally native audit environments. Policymakers must promote interoperability standards and legislative frameworks for supporting the admissibility of digital evidence.

REFERENCES

Adadi, A., & Berrada, M. (2018). Peeking inside the black-box: A survey on explainable artificial intelligence (XAI). *IEEE Access : Practical Innovations, Open Solutions*, *6*, 52138–52160. DOI: 10.1109/ACCESS.2018.2870052

Alotaibi, E. M. (2023). Cloud computing to audit quality–evidence from Saudi Arabia. *International Journal of Applied Economics. Finance and Accounting*, *17*(1), 18–29.

Appelbaum, D. (2017). Audit analytics and continuous audit: Looking toward the future. *The CPA Journal*, *87*(6), 19–25. https://scholar.google.com/scholar_lookup?title=The+impact+of+cloud+computing+on+auditing+practices&author=Appelbaum,+D.&publication_year=2017

Banker, R. D., Chang, M. H., & Lee, C. (2020). The audit implications of cloud computing. *Accounting Horizons*, *34*(4), 1–31. DOI: 10.2308/HORIZONS-19-166

Bertolli, L. (2019). Blockchain records: Is the evidence admissible? A challenge for EU member states. *Civil Procedure Review*, (3–4), 53–64.

Biondi, J., & Marchi, A. (2021). Blockchain and the future of financial reporting and assurance. *Accounting, Auditing & Accountability Journal*, *34*(10), 2567–2594.

Borenstein, M., Hedges, L. V., Higgins, J. P. T., & Rothstein, H. R. (2009). *Introduction to meta-analysis*. Wiley. DOI: 10.1002/9780470743386

Chou, D. C. (2015). Cloud computing risk and audit issues. *Computer Standards & Interfaces*, *42*, 137–142. DOI: 10.1016/j.csi.2015.06.005

Deloitte. (2017). Blockchain technology and its potential impact on the audit and assurance profession. *Deloitte Insights.* https://www2.deloitte.com

Greiling, H., & Kend, R. (2024). Artificial intelligence in auditing: Shifting the role of the auditor. *Administrative Sciences*, *14*(10), 238.

Han, H., Shiwakoti, R. K., Jarvis, R., Mordi, C., & Botchie, D. (2023). Accounting and auditing with blockchain technology and artificial intelligence: A literature review. *International Journal of Accounting Information Systems*, *48*, 100598. DOI: 10.1016/j.accinf.2022.100598

Issa, H. A., Sunyaev, A. M., & Vasarhelyi, M. (2016). Research ideas for artificial intelligence in auditing: The formalization of audit and the application of artificial intelligence. *Journal of Emerging Technologies in Accounting*, *13*(2), 1–20. https://scholar.google.com/scholar_lookup?title=Artificial+intelligence+in+audit%3A+Theory+and+practice&author=Issa,+H.A.&publication_year=2016. DOI: 10.2308/jeta-10511

McHugh, M. L. (2012). Interrater reliability: The kappa statistic. *Biochemia Medica*, *22*(3), 276–282. DOI: 10.11613/BM.2012.031 PMID: 23092060

Murtaza, M. A. (2024). Cloud ERP and audit reliability: An empirical study. *SSRN*.

Pérez-Calderón, E., Alrahamneh, S. A., & Montero, P. M. (2025). Impact of artificial intelligence on auditing: An evaluation from the profession in Jordan. *Discover Sustainability*, *6*(1), 251. DOI: 10.1007/s43621-025-01058-3

Pérez-Calderón, E., Alrahamneh, S. A., & Montero, P. M. (2025). Impact of artificial intelligence on auditing: An evaluation from the profession in Jordan. *Discover Sustainability*, *6*(1), 251. DOI: 10.1007/s43621-025-01058-3

Qader, K. S., & Çek, K. (2024). Influence of blockchain and artificial intelligence on audit quality: Evidence from Turkey. *Heliyon*, *10*(9), e30166. DOI: 10.1016/j.heliyon.2024.e30166 PMID: 38720713

Rizki, P. A. N., Wijaya, A. F., & Mustafid, N. H. (2024). Impact of cloud computing on IT audit practices: Challenges and opportunities. *MRS Journal of Accounting. Business and Management*, *1*(1), 4–7.

Saifudin, S., Januarti, I., & Purwanto, A. (2023). The role of artificial intelligence in the audit process and fraud detection: A literature outlook. *Journal of Ecohumanism*, *4*(1), 4185–4203.

Seethamraju, R., & Hecimović, A. (2023). Adoption of artificial intelligence in auditing: An exploratory study. *Australian Journal of Management*, *48*(4), 780–800. DOI: 10.1177/03128962221108440

Seethamraju, R. C., & Hecimovic, A. (2020). Impact of artificial intelligence on auditing – An exploratory study. In *Proceedings of the 26th Americas Conference on Information Systems (AMCIS)*.

Thomas, J., & Harden, A. (2008). Methods for the thematic synthesis of qualitative research in systematic reviews. *BMC Medical Research Methodology*, *8*(1), 45. Advance online publication. DOI: 10.1186/1471-2288-8-45 PMID: 18616818

Thomson Reuters. (n.d.a). Navigating the new era of auditing with AI technology: Meet Audit Intelligence. https://tax.thomsonreuters.com/blog/navigating-the-new-era-of-auditing-with-ai-technology-meet-audit-intelligence-analyze/

Thomson Reuters. (n.d.b). Are you harnessing the cloud to its full potential? https://tax.thomsonreuters.com/blog/are-you-harnessing-the-cloud-to-its-full-potential/

University of Maryland. (n.d.). Blockchain technology could bring benefits to the auditing industry. https://www.rhsmith.umd.edu/research/blockchain-technology-could-bring-benefits-auditing-industry

Yermack, D. (2017). Corporate governance and blockchains. *Review of Finance*, *21*(1), 7–31. https://scholar.google.com/scholar_lookup?title=Blockchain+technology+in+the+audit+profession&author=Yermack,+D.&publication_year=2017

Zhang, Y., Ma, Z., & Meng, J. (2025). Auditing in the blockchain: A literature review. *Frontiers in Blockchain, 8*, Article 1549729.

Zhong, C., & Goel, S. (2024). Transparent AI in auditing through explainable AI. *Current Issues in Auditing*, *18*(2), A1–A14. DOI: 10.2308/CIIA-2023-009

Chapter 6

Managing Risks and Ensuring Compliance in Healthcare Cloud Migration:

An Information Systems Auditing and Security Perspective

Nishanth Holla Raghavendra
https://orcid.org/0009-0005-9195-7688
University at Buffalo, SUNY, USA

Vijay Kumar Banoth
University at Buffalo, SUNY, USA

ABSTRACT

This chapter addresses the digital transformation of the healthcare sector as it moves from on-premises legacy infrastructure to the cloud. The drivers are enhanced scalability, lower costs, and real-time analysis of data for providing improved patient care. Despite the benefits, the transformation raises issues about the confidentiality, integrity and availability of patient data, as if patient data is compromised, companies face HIPAA and GDPR investigations. Without proper security controls, breaches may occur, causing financial loss and reputational damage to organizations. This chapter covers compliance regulations, most critical risks, migration plans, and emerging AI/ML technologies combined with key security principles for optimal best practices. The chapter also provides a checklist for migrating to the cloud to

DOI: 10.4018/979-8-3373-3078-5.ch006

allow healthcare organizations to walk through each phase of the migration process and ensure operational resilience and regulatory compliance for ease of practical implementations.

1.0 INTRODUCTION

Cloud computing is reshaping how businesses approach IT infrastructure and service delivery, offering scalable, on-demand resources with minimal upfront investment (Ahmad & Babar, 2014; Amazon Web Services, 2023a). Defined by the US National Institute of Standards and Technology (NIST) as "...a model for enabling ubiquitous, convenient, on-demand network access to a shared pool of configurable computing resources...," this technology has become a cornerstone for organizations seeking agility and cost efficiency (Ahmad & Babar, 2014). Healthcare organizations have embraced cloud adoption to address scalability, reduce operational complexities, and enhance data accessibility, all while focusing on providing quality patient care (Argaw et al., 2020; Kuo, 2011). However, transitioning to the cloud—commonly referred to as cloud migration—requires careful consideration of data security, compliance, and operational risks (Takabi et al., 2010; Fernandez et al., 2012). For healthcare providers, where patient data is highly sensitive, migrating from traditional databases to cloud solutions is not merely a technological shift but also a process requiring robust governance (Argaw et al., 2020; Ray et al., 2013).

This section explores cloud migration and its implications for healthcare organizations, focusing on the differences between traditional on-premises databases and cloud-based systems. Furthermore, the importance of Information Systems (IS) auditing in ensuring secure and compliant migration will be discussed, providing a roadmap for healthcare organizations aiming to leverage cloud technology without compromising on trust or efficiency (Deloitte, n.d.).

Cloud migration refers to the process of moving data, applications, and IT processes from on-premises infrastructure to cloud environments (Ahmad & Babar, 2014; Kuo, 2011). In healthcare, the shift is motivated by the promise of enhanced scalability, operational efficiency, and reduced costs (Argaw et al., 2020; Amazon Web Services, 2023a). By leveraging the elasticity of the cloud, organizations can scale their resources based on demand, avoiding the limitations and maintenance costs of legacy infrastructure (Amazon Web Services, 2023b; Kuo, 2011).

Real-world examples highlight the significance of cloud migration for healthcare. For instance, Mayo Clinic's adoption of Google Cloud allowed for seamless collaboration, research advancements through data analytics, and improved patient care delivery (Kuo, 2011). Such cases underline the transformative potential of cloud adoption but also emphasize the need for meticulous planning and implementation to mitigate risks (Takabi et al., 2010; Fernandez et al., 2012).

Cloud migration also facilitates disaster recovery and business continuity for healthcare institutions. In 2022, the University of California, San Diego Health system integrated cloud solutions to improve access to critical patient data during emergencies (Argaw et al., 2020). Such examples highlight how cloud migration enables healthcare providers to scale operations while ensuring uninterrupted patient care (Argaw et al., 2020).

Traditional on-premises databases and cloud databases differ significantly in architecture, accessibility, and cost-efficiency (Ahmad & Babar, 2014; Amazon Web Services, 2023b). While on-premises databases require substantial investment in hardware, maintenance, and upgrades, cloud databases operate on a pay-as-you-go model, reducing upfront costs and enabling organizations to focus on core operations (Kuo, 2011).

Cloud databases also provide superior flexibility, enabling real-time data access from multiple locations, an essential feature for healthcare providers managing patient data across dispersed facilities (Amazon Web Services, 2023b; Argaw et al., 2020). Furthermore, advanced features like automated backups, disaster recovery, and integration with analytics tools make cloud databases more robust and scalable compared to their traditional counterparts (Amazon Web Services, 2023a; Kuo, 2011). For example, AWS Aurora offers dynamic scaling and low-latency performance, which are crucial for high-demand environments like hospitals and research centers (Amazon Web Services, 2023a). Despite these advantages, migrating to the cloud introduces challenges such as data security, privacy concerns, and regulatory compliance—factors that are particularly critical in the healthcare industry (Takabi et al., 2010; Fernandez et al., 2012).

IS auditing plays a pivotal role in the cloud migration process, ensuring that organizational data remains secure and compliant with regulatory standards (Deloitte, n.d.; Fernandez et al., 2012). For healthcare organizations, this involves verifying that the cloud infrastructure adheres to frameworks like HIPAA, HITRUST CSF, and ISO 27001 (Fernandez et al., 2012).

Auditing during and after migration involves assessing risks such as unauthorized access, data breaches, and system vulnerabilities (Deloitte, n.d.; Takabi et al., 2010). For example, a healthcare provider transitioning to Microsoft Azure must ensure that data encryption, access controls, and monitoring mechanisms are in place (Takabi et al., 2010). IS auditors evaluate these controls, identify gaps, and provide recommendations to fortify the migration process (Deloitte, n.d.; Fernandez et al., 2012).

Furthermore, auditing is crucial for continuous monitoring of the cloud environment post-migration. This ensures that the cloud provider complies with service-level agreements (SLAs) and that the organization remains prepared for audits by regulatory bodies (Deloitte, n.d.; Ray et al., 2013). For example, an IS auditor might assess compliance with the GDPR for a European healthcare provider using Amazon Web Services (Fernandez et al., 2012).

Cloud migration represents an opportunity for healthcare organizations to transform their IT infrastructure, improving scalability, efficiency, and cost management (Amazon Web Services, 2023a; Amazon Web Services, 2023b; Kuo, 2011). However, the transition requires a clear understanding of the differences between traditional and cloud databases, as well as the risks involved (Argaw et al., 2020; Fernandez et al., 2012).

IS auditing ensures a secure and compliant migration, aligning technological advancements with regulatory requirements and organizational goals (Deloitte, n.d.; Fernandez et al., 2012). By adopting a structured approach to auditing, healthcare providers can navigate the complexities of cloud migration and harness its full potential to deliver better patient outcomes (Amazon Web Services, 2023a; Argaw et al., 2020).

2.0 BACKGROUND

There has been a plethora of new technology introduced into society that has significantly impacted on how organizations and systems are being utilized. Cloud migration is one of those major trends that has been introduced for a while now but is beginning to become more and more prevalent in today's time. While cloud computing is developing many other sectors, healthcare is one of the few that is still sorely lacking in terms of cloud adoption (Alder, 2023). However, due to the rise of the COVID-19 pandemic, many organizations have accelerated their move toward cloud-based infrastructure rather than relying solely on on-premises systems (Argaw et al., 2020).

As the world shifts away from on-premises infrastructure, organizations are growing less resistant to adopting cloud-based services. In fact, there have been a multitude of successful cloud adoption cases, particularly with Amazon Web Services (AWS) (Amazon Web Services, 2023a, 2023b). Over the past three years, AWS has enabled various healthcare systems to streamline operations and even build advanced services such as generative AI. For example, AWS enabled MediSys Health Network to replicate their patient records into a disaster-recovery-ready cloud-based system (Amazon Web Services, 2023a). This implementation allowed the organization to test and enhance its disaster recovery plans effectively. In another case, Allina Health successfully migrated to AWS, which modernized their servers and improved service efficiency, delivering faster diagnostic results by approximately 67% (Amazon Web Services, 2023b). These case studies highlight the tangible benefits of cloud-based service adoption in healthcare, showing improvements in resilience, speed, and patient outcomes.

There are many cloud-based services that have gained popularity in healthcare systems. Two of the most prominent HIPAA-compliant platforms are Microsoft Azure and Amazon Web Services (Brodie & Stonebraker, 1995). These platforms are widely used due to their robust security and healthcare-specific service offerings. For example, Microsoft Azure supports secure PHI storage, data management, and integrated machine learning solutions. AWS, on the other hand, offers app integration, analytics, and specialized healthcare modules like AWS Health Lake (Brodie & Stonebraker, 1995). These benefits directly address the primary concerns of healthcare organizations—data security and regulatory compliance—while also enabling service innovation. Although no cloud solution is flawless, these platforms provide a strong foundation for compliance and secure operations, thereby helping healthcare providers better protect sensitive patient data and meet legal standards.

IS auditing will play a critical role in supporting the ongoing shift to cloud-based systems. As adoption increases, so does the need for continuous assurance that patient data is being protected appropriately. With the ever-growing volume of sensitive data, IS auditing ensures ongoing compliance with regulations such as HIPAA, HITRUST CSF, and ISO 27001 (Deloitte, n.d.; Fernandez et al., 2012). These audits are essential for assessing and maintaining data integrity, monitoring access controls, and identifying gaps that could lead to vulnerabilities (Deloitte, n.d.; Ray et al., 2013). IS auditing also supports proactive risk mitigation by continuously evaluating cloud environments and ensuring that service-level agreements (SLAs) are met. As cloud becomes the standard, investing in strong auditing processes will be essential to support trust, compliance, and patient safety.

3.0 MAIN FOCUS OF THE CHAPTER

3.1 Key Regulations and Compliance Standards

When healthcare companies migrate their data from on-premises systems to cloud environments, they must adhere to several critical regulatory and compliance requirements to protect the sensitivity and integrity of patient data (Argaw et al., 2020; Fernandez et al., 2012).

3.2 HIPAA (Health Insurance Portability and Accountability Act)

HIPAA, enacted in 1996, governs the privacy, confidentiality, and security of health data in the United States. All healthcare professionals handling protected health information (PHI) must comply with HIPAA security and privacy rules, especially when migrating data to the cloud (Fernandez et al., 2012). The Security Rule outlines encryption and access control standards to ensure electronic PHI (ePHI) remains unreadable and inaccessible to unauthorized users during and after migration (Fernandez et al., 2012; Deloitte, n.d.).

HIPAA data encryption requirements are important in the protection of ePHI information and maintain compliance with the HIPAA Security Rule. The HIPAA encryption requirements are included in the security rules related to access controls and transmission security. The standard allows access to those people or software programs that have been granted access rights. The main purpose is to make sure that ePHI is unreadable, undecipherable and unusable to any person or software that has not been given access rights. While implementing this standard, it's important to consider other standards of security as well, for example user management, authentication and authorization.

3.3 Data at Rest Encryption Requirements

HIPAA data at rest encryption requirements are designed to safeguard the integrity of electronic protected health information (ePHI) stored on desktops, servers, files, USBs, and mobile devices (Fernandez et al., 2012). These encryption standards apply to all ePHI data stored in such devices and ensure that the data is rendered unreadable, undecipherable, and unusable to unauthorized individuals or software programs (Deloitte, n.d.). Unencrypted systems are often the weakest link and can be easily targeted by malicious actors. Therefore, encrypting ePHI at rest is essential to prevent unauthorized or illegal access, especially in the healthcare industry where data sensitivity is paramount (Fernandez et al., 2012). While implementing encryption standards may introduce a slight delay in data processing or migration, any potential loss in productivity is outweighed by the higher level of security achieved. This ultimately contributes to building a resilient system during the transition from on-premises to cloud infrastructure and satisfies the encryption requirements outlined in HIPAA's data-at-rest guidelines (Deloitte, n.d.; Takabi et al., 2010).

3.4 Compliant Email Encryption Software

HIPAA data at transit encryption requirements are designed to safeguard the integrity of ePHI data in transmission (Fernandez et al., 2012). HIPAA-compliant email encryption software is the most effective way to protect ePHI data contained within the emails, which is not restricted to texts but also encrypts files and images (Deloitte, n.d.). It is also important to note that encryption is one of the two security requirements by transmission security controls, the other being the integrity control

(Fernandez et al., 2012). Any HIPAA-compliant email encryption software implemented to comply with the standards must also have features to be safeguarded by digital signatures so that the emails are not tampered with or compromised (Takabi et al., 2010). It is for this reason messaging apps such as WhatsApp are not HIPAA compliant even though messages are encrypted (Fernandez et al., 2012).

3.5 Business Associate Agreements (BAA) with Cloud Providers

Every time healthcare organizations migrate their data or any service onto the cloud platform, the compliances need to be strictly assured by the execution of BAAs (Fernandez et al., 2012). A BAA is a legal contract between a healthcare provider (covered entity) and cloud service provider (business associate) that dictates the responsibility for the protection of PHI (Fernandez et al., 2012). BAAs will be very crucial during migrations, basically defining how PHI can be used, stored, and transmitted in the new environment (Fernandez et al., 2012). While having a BAA is a key element in maintaining HIPAA compliance, it should be clear that even with a BAA present, the healthcare organization still carries the responsibility of using the cloud service in a compliant manner (Deloitte, n.d.).

3.6 GDPR (General Data Protection Regulation)

GDPR is a regulation by the EU introduced for data protection and privacy of individuals in the EU (Fernandez et al., 2012; Ray et al., 2013). Key factors to consider when organizations are transferring data from on-premises systems into the cloud under the GDPR (Ray et al., 2013):

Data Protection Impact Assessment: Conduct a thorough assessment to identify and mitigate potential risks associated with moving personal data to the cloud, ensuring compliance with GDPR principles of data protection by design and default (Ray et al., 2013).

Cloud Provider Selection: Select a cloud service provider that provides comprehensive security and can demonstrate compliance with GDPR. Ensure they can provide appropriate safeguards for the transfer of data, especially with data being stored outside of the EU (Ray et al., 2013).

Data Processing Agreements: Establish a thorough data processing agreement with the cloud provider, defining roles, responsibilities, and data handling practices that make sure GDPR compliance during migration and further cloud operation (Ray et al., 2013).

Data Subject Rights: Provide mechanisms to retain the capability to exercise data subject rights in the cloud environment, such as access, rectification, and erasure, without that migration adversely affecting the ability of the organization to respond to these requests in a timely manner (Ray et al., 2013).

3.7 HITRUST CSF

When it comes to maintaining compliant healthcare cloud migrations, the HITRUST CSF acts as an integral part. It represents an inclusive approach to data security and puts many legal demands together, such as HIPAA. HITRUST architecture helps healthcare businesses with an objective and more organized process for assessing and managing information security risks, especially during transitions to cloud environments. Following the principles of HITRUST CSF, healthcare providers can ensure they are implementing robust security controls while meeting regulatory requirements throughout cloud migration. This framework gives a structured way of dealing with security and compliance issues and helps companies answer the special challenges in keeping private patient information secure on cloud-based systems (Fernandez et al., 2012).

3.8 ISO 2700, ISO 27799, SOC2, CIS Critical Security Controls

The ISO 2700 international standard provides a framework for implementation and maintenance regarding ISMS. It helps healthcare organizations manage risks and sensitive data protection while migrating them (Ray et al., 2013).

The ISO 27799 standard provides specific guidance regarding information security management in healthcare by applying ISO 27002. Guidelines are given on how to apply security controls to health information systems (Ray et al., 2013).

The SOC2 reports for healthcare organizations looking to vet cloud providers provide insight into the security, availability, processing integrity, confidentiality, and privacy controls of the provider (Fernandez et al., 2012).

The CIS Critical Security controls guidelines give detailed technical controls for securing cloud data, including recommendations on data encryption, system hardening, and incident response (Takabi et al., 2010).

3.9 21 CFR Part 11

The major risks associated with 21 CFR Part 11 compliance when migrating from on-prem systems to cloud-based solutions include the following: Data Integrity and Security. One of the most critical risks is how to maintain data integrity and security during migration and in the cloud environment. These include ensuring the confidentiality of data transferred to the cloud, providing appropriate access control and user management in the cloud environment, and implementing and maintaining data retention measures which meet the requirements of the regulating agencies (Ray et al., 2013).

3.10 Infrastructure Qualification

A significant challenge is to determine and confirm that the cloud infrastructure has been appropriately qualified to the standard of GxP: Confirmation of correct design, specification and installation of the infrastructure by the cloud provider. Confirmation of the qualification and validation of all infrastructure components and applications. GxP compliant ongoing change control and configuration management processes (Ray et al., 2013).

3.11 Regulatory Compliance

Risks associated with ensuring regulatory compliance in the cloud environment: Ensure the cloud provider understands GxP and is capable of meeting regulations. Maintain proper documentation of infrastructure qualification and validation. Support audit trails, system logs cloud environment (Ray et al., 2013).

3.12 Service Provider Management

Utilizing a cloud service provider introduces new risks: The provider can verify that sufficient GxP knowledge training exists. Agreements/Contracts are properly executed to reflect responsibilities. Oversight and audit capability over the various processes of the provider (Ray et al., 2013).

3.13 Data Ownership and Access

Legal and practical issues relate to data ownership and access, including Ownership of Data and Intellectual property - clear agreements. Ability to retrieve or move data in the event of change of providers. Legal requirements on data locations and government access (Ray et al., 2013).

4.0 ISSUES, CONTROVERSIES, PROBLEMS

4.1 Risks in Cloud Migration for Healthcare Organizations

An information security program within a company exists to protect and maintain the confidentiality, integrity, and availability of that company's data, especially with regards to digital data. These three ideas are the pillars of cybersecurity called the "CIA Triad". The overarching goal of this protection of assets is to reduce the cost to the company should those assets become compromised in any of the three primary areas. Confidentiality demands that resources should only be accessible to those who are authorized to access them. A breach of confidentiality would mean that someone who is not authorized to access such data is able to do so. For instance, a bad actor brute-forcing the password of an employee and using that employee's access rights to exfiltrate confidential information would be a breach of confidentiality.

Integrity demands that resources are not modified, except by those who are authorized to do so. A breach of integrity would mean that the data is not trustworthy. If a bad actor were to intercept a message traveling on a network and were able to modify it before sending it on its way, the message could no longer be trusted. Availability demands that resources are readily available, specifically by those who are authorized to access them. A breach of availability would mean that resources are not accessible when they need to be. A Denial of Service (DoS) or Distributed DoS (DDoS) attack is a common attack method to break availability of a system, such as overwhelming a website to prevent it from being able to serve its pages (Takabi et al., 2010).

4.2 Risk Management

To maintain the CIA triad, a company will seek to implement a risk management program. This program analyses the assets of a company, the risks associated with assets, and how to mitigate those risks. For instance, a company can value a laptop at $2,000 and assume a 100% asset value loss in the event of it being stolen. A mitigation to that risk is to install physical cable locks on the laptop to help prevent it from being stolen. Risk mitigations are also known as "controls". In this scenario, a second control can be implemented to act as a deterrent: a visible security camera in the same area as a laptop.

While there can still be residual risk, it is not possible to entirely remove all risks. The purpose of risk management is to reduce the amount of monetary loss as much as possible, while maintaining a reasonable cost for controls. If a control costs far more than the asset value, it is unlikely to be worth implementing such a control. However, some controls must exist to adhere to laws and regulations. In the healthcare industry, the Health Insurance Portability and Accountability Act (HIPAA) is the primary source for controls implemented due to regulation in this industry (Fernandez et al., 2012).

4.3 Current Risks in Healthcare Infrastructure

Healthcare systems are often targeted for financial purposes. Patient health data is more valuable than other types of data. This data is often complete enough to be used for identity theft, which can be utilized for the procurement of prescription drugs, the opening of bank and credit card accounts, and to obtain loans. At the same time, health information systems are running legacy operating systems and software. Healthcare executives do not put much emphasis on protecting systems, as their primary concern instead is patient care. However, with the growing need for interconnected health systems, the risks only increase. Without proper funding for cybersecurity, health systems are at risk of complete disruption for the financial gain of attackers, particularly through ransomware attacks. In a ransomware attack, systems in the infrastructure are encrypted to prevent access to those systems, or the data in those systems, unless the victim pays a ransom to the attacker. These attacks are designed to not be recoverable outright without the key, which only the attacker would have. In the healthcare industry, a ransomware attack on a hospital can be fatal to patients if hospital staff are not able to access key systems for emergencies. A hospital under attack would, in the short term, redirect patients to other hospitals, which may overwhelm them. A primary solution to ransomware is to back up systems and data on an ongoing basis. Should a ransomware attack occur, systems can be restored to a working state. However, this will not be effective on its own, as the restored system will contain the same vulnerabilities that led to the attack in the first place. If the attacker had access to the system for a long enough period, their ransomware could exist in all backups in a dormant state. This means that there is no restore point that a system could be brought back to without the threat of ransomware (Deloitte, n.d.). Developing a plan to be able to rebuild a server from the ground-up will aid in disaster recovery. If key systems can be easily rebuilt using an existing playbook, there becomes less impact as systems are more easily brought back online. Using writes-once read-many storage devices for data can prevent ransomware from encrypting that data. Combining these techniques will drastically reduce the impact of ransomware. However, implementing new systems and procedures does require significant funding. A Business Impact Analysis (BIA) would be necessary to determine the cost of a disaster as compared to the cost of mitigating its risk and the cost of recovery. In healthcare especially, the cost of human life must be considered. As of October 7th, 2024, there have been 386 attacks on healthcare systems in the US in 2024 alone. With such an alarming number of affected individuals, it is imperative that healthcare systems be protected against the highest risks that would disrupt systems and threaten human life (Deloitte, n.d.).

4.4 General Risks in Cloud Environments

The use of a cloud service effectively requires the use of a data center owned by a third party. That third party would be responsible for protecting physical assets within their data center, as well as configuring their assets correctly. This can reduce the burden from healthcare organizations that would otherwise have to do so themselves, saving on costs.

However, depending on the level of service that the healthcare organization uses, the risks and subsequent risk mitigation strategies can differ wildly. For example, if an organization chooses to use an Infrastructure as a Service (IaaS) model, they would still be responsible for managing and securing their cloud operating systems. Using a Platform as a Service (PaaS) or Software as a Service (SaaS) model can avoid that responsibility, as the risk is transferred to the third-party operator of the platform/software. From there, expertise in the chosen platform/software is necessary to properly configure and maintain it. Once a cloud service is selected, a potential vulnerability arises from transferring data from on-premises to the cloud service and vice versa. If the data is unencrypted in transit, a Man in the Middle (MitM) attack can be carried out to steal that data. Data encryption is therefore paramount and would influence the choice of cloud service (Takabi et al., 2010).

4.5 Risk Management in Cloud Infrastructure

Risk management involves reducing risk to an organization through the implementation of policies, procedures, and controls. While risk can never be reduced entirely, the purpose is to tackle the highest risks for an organization that would have the highest financial impact. Controls implemented would have to have a positive return-on-investment, unless those controls must be implemented to adhere to legal requirements (Argaw et al., 2020). The type of cloud service greatly impacts the risk management strategies that would be employed.

4.6 Benefits and Limitations of Infrastructure as a Service (IaaS)

IaaS models would involve the creation of virtual copies of the current on-premises infrastructure. This transfers the risk of physical assets being damaged or destroyed to a third-party data center, which will have its own controls implemented to reduce risk. As healthcare systems are often using outdated operating systems like Windows XP, the cloud infrastructure, if mimicking the physical infrastructure, would also be using legacy software. Vulnerabilities that are caused by using such software would still exist, thereby not providing effective risk management. Systems would have to be upgraded to avoid security flaws in unpatched software, which can prove costly, and potentially impossible if certain key but legacy software is not available in newer operating systems.

With full control of the cloud infrastructure, the implemented controls would primarily be technical in nature. An internal virtual network in the cloud would have to be devised, complete with an edge firewall and network segmentation where needed. Systems will have to undergo regular updates for applications as well as security. High Availability (HA) technologies need to be utilized to prevent outages for key healthcare systems. Load balancing may be a consideration depending on whether there are implementations of public-facing services, such as a website for patients to access their data from. Likewise, utilizing Content Delivery Networks (CDNs) may also be necessary to maintain availability for these public-facing services. A backup infrastructure would also need to be implemented if the cloud service provider does not provide one.

Security Orchestration, Automation, and Response (SOAR) technology must also be included to provide a powerful cybersecurity stance. This includes three key types of software: threat and vulnerability management software, incident response software, and operations automation (Takabi et al., 2010). Threat management software helps identify assets and, where possible, perform automated vulnerability scans to aid in detecting issues that can be fixed before they are exploited. Incident response software, such as a Security Information and Event Management (SIEM) platform, which acts as an aggregator for system/application logs and security events, can help recognize and respond to threats as they occur. Operations automation software, such as an Intrusion Prevention System (IPS) and Endpoint Detection and Response (EDR) software, can help to automatically defend systems when it detects a particular attack. These implementations can become very costly to adopt, especially in an industry that has not had a focus on cybersecurity and would effectively be starting their security operations plans from scratch. Using an IaaS model, therefore, may not be ideal for a swift shift into a more secure environment.

4.7 Benefits and Limitations of Platform/ Software as a Service (PaaS/SaaS)

Making use of a PaaS or SaaS model may prove to be more useful in reducing risk in the healthcare industry. These services will, ideally, be run on up-to-date operating systems that will often receive security patches. Underlying software will not need to be managed by a healthcare organization, but rather by the cloud service provider. Managing software quality and updates will no longer be necessary. This does require the selected cloud service, who will be managing the organization's data, to adhere to HIPAA, or to provide some controls for the organization to use for HIPAA compliance.

In all models of cloud services, administrative controls are core to risk management in the cloud. The benefit of a PaaS/SaaS model, however, is the reduced need to focus on infrastructure-based controls. Configuring software properly will help to reduce the risk of vulnerability caused by misconfiguration, such as the use of default passwords. Managing Identity and Access Management (IAM) to ensure any involved accounts are using secure passwords will be key, along with 2-factor authentication to prevent a stolen password from being used by a bad actor. Non-technical controls can then take the forefront. Training employees in security concepts, such as recognizing phishing attacks, can help to reduce risk caused by human error. Vendor management and right-to-audit agreements enable the organization to be assured that their selected service provider is adhering to industry best-practices and complying with HIPAA and other relevant laws and regulations. The primary issue that comes with PaaS/SaaS is a lack of control over the software and its systems. If, for instance, the service becomes unavailable due to a ransomware attack, there is nothing the organization can do except wait for the service provider to resolve the issue. Utilizing multiple service providers in tandem may prove effective in maintaining the organization's uptime but will incur twice the cost in having duplicate services being used (Fernandez et al., 2012).

4.8 Machine Learning in Risk Management

For instance, an IDS/IPS on a router, or on a server that acts as a proxy can be used for analyzing incoming and outgoing packets on the network. Regular traffic coming in can be used to train a machine-learning model in how traffic is expected to look, both in volume and, where possible, in the packet data itself. If many packets suddenly pour in during a time where little traffic is expected, it can trigger an alert that security analysts can verify. An IDS/I PS on specific endpoints, such as a web server or database server, can inspect packet data more thoroughly. A machine-learning model trained in expected incoming web traffic may trigger an alert if it sees HTTP requests that are abnormal. At the same time, IDS/IPS, can monitor resource usage, such as CPU load and memory utilization. A machine-learning model would be trained in the expected usage throughout the day and would be able to send an alert to security analysts if the resource usage falls outside the baseline.

When utilizing IaaS, the inclusion of an Intrusion Detection/Prevention System (IDS/IPS) also enables the use of machine learning to aid in defensive capabilities. An IDS/IPS can be trained on baseline data depending on the system that the software is installed on.

4.9 Challenges During and After Migration

Migrating legacy systems to the cloud represents a major technological transformation for organizations seeking scalability, cost efficiency, and modernization. Legacy systems, often monolithic and outdated, present challenges such as high maintenance costs, inflexibility, and incompatibility with contemporary technologies. Cloud migration allows organizations to overcome these limitations by leveraging the cloud's scalability, agility, and advanced services such as AI and analytics (Ahmad & Babar, 2014; Yu et al., 2010; Fernandez et al., 2012).

Migration strategies are classified into several categories, each addressing specific organizational needs and technology requirements. Storage Migration requires transferring data from one storage device to another, such as from on-premises hard drives to cloud-based object storage systems. Examples include migrating from local storage to AWS S3 or Azure Blob Storage to enhance accessibility and backup capabilities. Database Migration involves moving databases to a new environment, often requiring data transformation. For instance, migrating an on-premises SQL database to Amazon RDS or Azure SQL Database allows for managed database services with improved scalability and security. Application Migration includes applications that are moved from legacy systems to new environments, often requiring reconfiguration. For example, moving an ERP system to a cloud-based SaaS platform involves rearchitecting workflows and adapting to cloud native capabilities. Cloud Migration refers specifically to transferring workloads and data to cloud platforms, whether public, private, or hybrid. It can also include moving between cloud providers. Business Process Migration focuses on transferring entire business processes to cloud-based systems, such as migrating supply chain management or CRM systems to platforms like Salesforce or SAP S/4HANA (Yu et al., 2010; Fernandez et al., 2012).

The planning process includes several key activities for identifying the most appropriate migration strategies. These are classified under the process element system evaluation and objective setting. One common approach is to analyze the legacy system's architecture and infrastructure to identify components that need modification or replacement for seamless integration into the cloud. The migration strategy may require one of several approaches: Rehosting, Refactoring, or Rebuilding. Each of these methods involves different levels of effort and resource allocation, depending on the complexity of the legacy system. In the case of Rehosting, organizations may opt for a "lift-and-shift" strategy where the legacy system is migrated to the cloud without any substantial changes. This approach is typically used for simple workloads where minimal adjustments are required. On the other hand, Refactoring involves modifying the legacy system's code to optimize it for cloud-native services, leveraging microservices or containerization to ensure that the system is more scalable and resilient. Finally, Rebuilding refers to completely redesigning the system to take full advantage of cloud infrastructure, which is often necessary for complex or outdated systems that do not meet modern performance or scalability standards. Another crucial aspect of the planning phase is addressing potential compatibility issues between legacy systems and cloud environments. For example, organizations may need to adapt or refactor application interfaces, data formats, and business logic to align with the cloud infrastructure. This process can involve modifying system codes or using cloud-native services to bridge gaps, ensuring that the system integrates seamlessly into the new cloud platform (Ahmad & Babar, 2014; Subashini & Kavitha, 2011; Yu et al., 2010; Fernandez et al., 2012; Ray et al., 2013).

Implementation involves dividing the migration into smaller, manageable phases to reduce risk. Initially, less critical workloads are migrated, followed by more integral systems once the process has been established. A primary approach during implementation is to Run Legacy and Cloud Systems in Parallel. This enables real-time validation of functionality and performance, ensuring that cloud systems operate as expected before fully decommissioning the legacy infrastructure. This parallel run allows for the identification and resolution of issues without interrupting critical business operations. To Minimize Downtime, Incremental Replication Techniques are employed. These techniques replicate data in stages, gradually shifting workloads to the cloud without causing significant disruption to operations. This approach ensures that most of the systems are operational during the migration process. Once the migration progresses, Rigorous Testing is conducted at every phase to confirm that each system functions correctly. This testing includes functional testing, performance testing and security testing. Post migration validation is performed to ensure that data integrity is intact and that the application functions seamlessly (Ahmad & Babar, 2014; Yu et al., 2010).

Migrating to the cloud is a transformative process, but it presents a series of challenges that require careful management. One of the key hurdles is ensuring the security and privacy of sensitive data, particularly during the transfer between legacy systems and cloud environments. Data encryption, both during transit and at rest, is critical to safeguarding information from potential breaches. Additionally, enforcing strong role-based access control (RBAC) and using effective monitoring tools can help ensure that only authorized users have access to sensitive data, addressing security risks and ensuring compliance with regulatory frameworks such as GDPR and HIPAA (Deloitte, n.d.; Fernandez et al., 2012; Ray et al., 2013).

Downtime and business disruptions during migration are also major concerns, as they can negatively affect business operations and customer experiences. To mitigate these risks, organizations often implement phased migration strategies, starting with non-critical systems and gradually progressing to more integral systems. By running legacy systems in parallel with cloud environments during the transition, businesses can validate the functionality of cloud systems while minimizing operational interruptions. Leveraging cloud-native features like autoscaling and failover mechanisms further ensures that services remain available even in the event of infrastructure issues, safeguarding business continuity (Yu et al., 2010; Fernandez et al., 2012).

Another significant challenge is ensuring compatibility between legacy systems and modern cloud platforms. Legacy systems, often designed with outdated technologies, can be difficult to integrate with cloud-based services. Addressing this requires refactoring legacy code, implementing middleware solutions, or developing integrators that act as an abstraction layer to bridge gaps between legacy systems and cloud environments. Additionally, migrating legacy data to cloud databases can lead to incompatibility issues, requiring data type conversions, schema transformations, and query adjustments to maintain functionality in the new cloud environment (Ahmad & Babar, 2014; Subashini & Kavitha, 2011).

The lack of in-house expertise in cloud technologies can further complicate migration efforts. Many organizations face skill gaps, particularly in areas like cloud architecture, security protocols, and containerization. To address this, companies often invest in cloud training programs and certifications for their IT teams. In some cases, organizations may bring in external consultants or cloud migration experts to guide the migration process and ensure that best practices are followed, reducing the risk of errors and delays (Yu et al., 2010; Kuo, 2011).

Finally, the migration process can lead to unforeseen financial implications, with costs escalating beyond initial estimates due to the complexity of migration, resource consumption, and the need for reconfiguration. To manage costs effectively, organizations should conduct thorough cost-benefit analyses before starting the migration. Using cloud cost management tools like AWS Cost Explorer and Azure Cost Management helps track spending and optimize resource usage. Post-migration optimization, such as right-sizing virtual machines and leveraging cloud-native auto-scaling, can further reduce ongoing costs, ensuring that migration delivers the expected return on investment (Amazon Web Services, 2023; Yu et al., 2010; Fernandez et al., 2012).

4.10 Integration with Legacy Systems

Integrating legacy systems with modern cloud platforms requires effective strategies to ensure seamless data flow and maintain compatibility without overhauling existing infrastructure. One primary solution is the use of middleware, which serves as a bridge between the legacy systems and cloud platforms, enabling data exchange without significant changes to the legacy setup. For example, integration engines like Mirth Connect can convert outdated HL7 messages from legacy EHRs into modern FHIR-compliant formats for cloud-based analytics, facilitating smoother communication between systems (Ahmad & Babar, 2014; Subashini & Kavitha, 2011; Yu et al., 2010; Fernandez et al., 2012).

Another key strategy is API-based integration, where modern cloud platforms such as AWS, Microsoft Azure, and Google Cloud provide APIs specifically designed for healthcare data integration. These APIs enable real-time communication between legacy systems and cloud platforms, ensuring that critical data, such as patient records, can be shared securely and efficiently. For instance, Azure's API for FHIR allows legacy EHRs to transmit patient data while maintaining interoperability with the cloud environment, supporting both security and regulatory compliance. To handle the intricacies of legacy data formats, data mapping and transformation are essential. Legacy systems often store data in proprietary formats, which need to be converted into standardized formats before cloud integration. Tools like ETL (Extract, Transform, Load) pipelines are commonly used to normalize this data, mapping it into FHIR or HL7 formats for compatibility with cloud systems. For example, Google Cloud's Healthcare Data Engine provides tools to transform raw EHR data into FHIR-ready formats, enabling easier integration into cloud platforms while ensuring data consistency (Ahmad & Babar, 2014; Yu et al., 2010; Fernandez et al., 2012).

Hybrid architecture offers another effective integration strategy, allowing organizations to retain critical legacy systems on-premises while leveraging cloud capabilities for enhanced analytics, scalability, and remote access. This approach enables healthcare providers to maintain control over core systems while benefiting from cloud-powered features. For instance, a hospital might keep its core EHR system on-premises for day-to-day operations but use AWS Health Lake for advanced predictive analytics, blending the best of both on-premises and cloud environments. Lastly, real-time data synchronization tools like Kafka or RabbitMQ are crucial for maintaining up-to-date information between legacy systems and cloud platforms. These tools enable the seamless transfer of data in real-time, reducing latency and ensuring that critical systems are always in sync. For example, synchronizing appointment schedules between an on-premises EHR and a cloud-based patient portal ensures that both systems have the latest information, improving operational efficiency and patient care (Subashini & Kavitha, 2011; Yu et al., 2010; Fernandez et al., 2012).

Integrating legacy systems into cloud environments presents several challenges, primarily due to compatibility issues, data silos, and workflow disruptions. Many legacies electronic health records (EHRs) use proprietary technologies that don't align with modern standards like HL7 or FHIR, making data exchange difficult. Additionally, legacy systems often store data in inconsistent formats, complicating data migration and mapping. Furthermore, these systems typically operate in isolated silos, hindering interoperability across different departments. Migrating such systems requires overcoming these silos to provide unified access to patient data. Cloud integration also demands workflow reengineering, which can disrupt operations, especially in critical areas like scheduling. Compliance with regulations like HIPAA and GDPR adds further complexity, as secure data sharing between legacy systems and cloud platforms must be ensured. Lastly, legacy systems are prone to scalability and performance bottlenecks, which can cause delays in high-demand scenarios, such as sharing large imaging files or processing high-volume data (Deloitte, n.d.; Ray et al., 2013).

4.11 Data Governance and Compliance

Data governance in the cloud involves developing frameworks and policies to ensure that data stored offsite is securely managed and remains compliant with various regulations. Unlike on-premises systems, cloud data governance becomes more complex due to the multi-region storage, diverse compliance laws, and increased data mobility. It focuses on key principles such as establishing data ownership and accountability, ensuring data quality throughout its lifecycle, enforcing access control and privacy through role-based or attribute-based access control (RBAC or ABAC), and complying with regulations like GDPR and HIPAA. The challenges arise from maintaining visibility and ownership of data, managing compliance across different jurisdictions, handling scalability issues, and mitigating the risk of data breaches. As data volumes grow, traditional governance models often struggle, requiring advanced tools like automated data discovery and dynamic data masking to address these challenges (Jamshidi et al., 2013; Fernandez et al., 2012).

To ensure effective governance, organizations adopt centralized governance frameworks that simplify policy enforcement across multi-cloud environments. Automated data discovery and classification tools, such as Immuta or Microsoft Purview, help in detecting and classifying sensitive data, reducing human error. Fine-grained access controls are essential for protecting sensitive information without disrupting operations. Real-time monitoring tools, like AWS CloudTrail or Azure Monitor, provide insights into data access patterns, helping identify anomalies and ensuring compliance. These governance frameworks are especially critical in industries like healthcare, where cloud platforms ensure compliance with HIPAA while maintaining secure access to sensitive health data, or in the financial sector, where centralized governance ensures adherence to GDPR and PCI DSS regulations. Overcoming barriers to effective cloud data governance involves ongoing training for staff and leveraging cloud-native tools to ensure scalability. Investing in comprehensive training for data stewards and engineers ensures smooth adoption of governance policies, while multi-layered security approaches—combining encryption, dynamic data masking, and real-time monitoring—help mitigate the risks associated with unauthorized access and data breaches (Jamshidi et al., 2013; Fernandez et al., 2012).

Continuous compliance ensures that organizations maintain adherence to evolving regulatory standards like GDPR, HIPAA, and ISO, integrating these requirements into their daily operations to mitigate the risk of penalties or breaches. Unlike one-time compliance efforts, continuous compliance involves dynamic strategies, ensuring that teams are accountable for specific aspects of compliance, automating monitoring, and using tools that offer real-time visibility and faster remediation. This approach helps organizations adapt to regulatory amendments, such as changes in GDPR, and streamlines the enforcement of policies across various compliance frameworks. GDPR mandates data localization and robust access controls, while HIPAA ensures the confidentiality of protected health information (PHI) with encrypted storage and audit logs. ISO 27001 sets the global standard for managing information security, emphasizing confidentiality, integrity, and availability of data (Fernandez et al., 2012).

5.0 SOLUTIONS AND RECOMMENDATIONS

5.1 Auditing Cloud based Healthcare Systems

Cloud auditing presents several unique challenges due to the shared responsibility model, limited physical access to infrastructure, encryption key management, multi-tenancy risks, dynamic cloud environments, and regulatory complexities. The shared responsibility model divides security duties between the cloud service provider (CSP) and the client, complicating accountability during audits, especially in environments like IaaS where CSP handles hardware, but clients are responsible for securing virtual machines and applications. Additionally, the reliance on CSP-provided reports, due to limited physical access to data centers, creates challenges in complying with standards that require physical audits. Managing encryption keys also introduces risks, as storing them with the CSP exposes them to potential insider threats, while managing them on the client side, especially in multi-cloud environments, can be operationally complex. Multi-tenancy in cloud environments further complicates auditing, as data leakage or privilege escalation risks arise when access controls are misconfigured (Fernandez et al., 2012; Ray et al., 2013).

To address these challenges, organizations can adopt several strategies. Leveraging cloud-specific standards like ISO/IEC 27017 and ISO/IEC 27018 provides auditors with tailored guidelines for evaluating cloud environments and ensuring compliance with cloud-specific security and privacy requirements. Tools like AWS

CloudTrail and Azure Security Center enable continuous monitoring and auditing, offering real-time visibility into activities, resource configurations, and security events, thus enhancing the efficiency and thoroughness of audits. Advanced access control models such as RBAC and ABAC help mitigate risks in multi-tenant environments by enforcing granular access based on user roles or attributes. Additionally, employing best practices for encryption, such as client-side encryption and using key management services (KMS) for secure storage and rotation of keys, helps ensure that sensitive data remains secure throughout its lifecycle (Takabi et al., 2010; Fernandez et al., 2012).

Automated compliance auditing tools play a crucial role in managing compliance across cloud environments. Azure Policy allows organizations to enforce standards like ISO 27001 and GDPR, providing real-time enforcement by blocking non-compliant resources at creation. AWS Config helps track resource configurations and provides real-time alerts and auto-remediation capabilities for compliance with frameworks like HIPAA and PCI DSS. Aqua CSPM offers continuous monitoring and automated remediation for multi-cloud environments, addressing misconfigurations and vulnerabilities. Additionally, Cloud Native Application Protection Platforms (CNAPPs) integrate compliance checks directly into DevOps pipelines, enabling real-time assessments for containerized and serverless applications, aligning with standards like NIST and PCI DSS (Takabi et al., 2010; Shahrabi & Ghaznavi-Ghoushchi, 2021).

The primary benefits of these tools include enhanced visibility across multiple cloud platforms, enabling centralized governance, and proactive remediation that reduces manual intervention. These tools help organizations maintain compliance with complex regulatory frameworks, ensuring alignment with standards like GDPR, CCPA, and ISO. However, implementing these tools can present challenges such as alert fatigue, where excessive alerts can lead to inefficiencies, and contextual gaps, where tools may fail to assess specific data types or use cases. Additionally, integrating these tools into existing workflows or multi-cloud environments can be technically challenging (Takabi et al., 2010; Shahrabi & Ghaznavi-Ghoushchi, 2021).

5.2 Opportunities During Healthcare Data Migration to the Cloud

The migration of healthcare data to the cloud presents an array of transformative opportunities. By leveraging cloud infrastructure, healthcare organizations can modernize their operations, improve data management, and unlock the potential of advanced technologies. The following sections elaborate on key aspects of healthcare data migration: data standardization and centralization, scalability and elasticity, disaster recovery and business continuity, integration with third-party applications, and advanced data analytics and AI integration (Amazon Web Services, 2023a; Amazon Web Services, 2023b; Argaw et al., 2020; Fernandez et al., 2012).

5.3 Data Standardization and Centralization

Medical information is dispersed across several systems, departments, and institutions and, therefore, it becomes difficult to achieve an integrated view. Data standardization standardizes formats, terminologies, and protocols to achieve consistency, while centralization integrates disparate datasets into a single repository.

Improved Data Quality: Structured data minimizes errors, redundancies, and inconsistencies and enables credible reporting and analysis.

Enhanced Interoperability: Standardized and centralized data can be shared more easily across providers, systems, and stakeholders.

Operational Efficiency: Consolidated data repositories reduce the inconvenience of dealing with multiple systems, saving time and resources.

Regulatory Compliance: Adherence to standardized forms ensures regulatory compliance with healthcare regulations such as HIPAA and GDPR.

Enhanced Patient Outcomes: Providers have a deeper understanding of patient history due to centralized information, which improves diagnosis and treatment planning (Argaw et al., 2020; Deloitte, n.d.; Fernandez et al., 2012).

5.4 Scalability and Elasticity

Cloud platforms offer unparalleled scalability and elasticity, enabling healthcare organizations to adjust resources according to demand. These capabilities are particularly vital for handling fluctuating workloads, such as during public health crises or seasonal peaks.

Cost Optimization: Pay-as-you-go models ensure that organizations only pay for the resources they use.

On-Demand Scaling: As healthcare needs grow, cloud infrastructure can easily scale to accommodate additional data and users without significant upfront investment.

Dynamic Resource Allocation: Elasticity allows systems to dynamically allocate resources during high-demand periods, ensuring uninterrupted service.

Future-Readiness: Scalable solutions prepare organizations for the integration of emerging technologies and expanding operations (Amazon Web Services, 2023a; Amazon Web Services, 2023b; Fernandez et al., 2012).

5.5 Increased Disaster Recovery and Business Continuity

Cloud migration enhances the ability to recover data and maintain operations during disruptions. With robust backup mechanisms and geographically dispersed data centers, cloud platforms offer superior disaster recovery solutions.

Continuous Availability: Automated backups and failover systems ensure critical data and services remain accessible.

Data Preservation: Regular snapshots and versioning preserve data accuracy and prevent loss during emergencies.

Regulatory Alignment: Disaster recovery plans aligned with HIPAA and other regulations safeguard sensitive healthcare data.

Service Resilience: Robust recovery solutions enable organizations to quickly resume services after incidents, protecting patient care and reputation (Amazon Web Services, 2023b; Fernandez et al., 2012).

5.6 Increased Integration with Third-party Applications

Modern healthcare relies on a variety of applications, including electronic health records (EHRs), telemedicine platforms, and wearable devices. Cloud platforms facilitate seamless integration with these third-party tools, enhancing functionality and interoperability.

Unified Experience: Integrated systems improve workflows and user interaction.

Service Expansion: Compatibility with various applications expands healthcare service offerings.

Reduced Error Rates: Automated data exchange lowers administrative overhead and human error.

Patient Empowerment: Integration with mobile apps helps patients manage their health more effectively (Amazon Web Services, 2023a; Amazon Web Services, 2023b; Argaw et al., 2020).

5.7 Advanced Data Analytics and AI Integration

Cloud platforms are well-suited for handling the computational demands of advanced data analytics and artificial intelligence (AI). These technologies enable predictive insights, personalized care, and operational optimization.

Forecasting: AI models can predict patient needs, disease outbreaks, and resource allocation.

Personalized Medicine: Data-driven insights facilitate tailored treatment plans.

Operational Efficiency: Analytics optimize workflows, resource usage, and cost control.

Medical Research: Cloud-based AI tools accelerate research by identifying patterns in large datasets.

Enhanced Accuracy: Integration improves diagnostic precision and treatment effectiveness (Amazon Web Services, 2023a; Amazon Web Services, 2023b; Argaw et al., 2020; Fernandez et al., 2012).

6.0 FUTURE RESEARCH DIRECTIONS

Integration of innovative technologies in healthcare cloud security creates new opportunities and challenges. Machine learning (ML) and artificial intelligence (AI) can enhance auditing and threat detection by monitoring large-scale system logs for anomalies and enabling predictive risk assessment.

Zero Trust Architecture (ZTA) is also gaining relevance, with emphasis shifting to constant verification of identity, devices, and data segments. Research indicated that AI-facilitated ZTA holds the potential to augment real-time threat evaluation, advanced behavior pattern detection, and overall security position. Such advancements have the potential to facilitate automating drudgework audit tasks and enable active compliance monitoring but introduce issues related to model explainability and governance as well.

Subsequent studies need to investigate how AI/ML-driven security analytics and zero-trust architecture can be validated and aligned with healthcare compliance requirements. Regulatory mandates continue to evolve, with fresh weights added to cloud governance. For example, in 2025 HHS proposed modifications to HIPAA's Security Rule (in a Notice of Proposed Rulemaking) to address modern-day cyber threats hitrustalliance.net. At the same time, the EU's General Data Protection Regulation (GDPR) remains stringent, with 4% global turnover fines emphasizing cloud-stored PHI responsibility. Industry standards like the HITRUST CSF attempt to align large-scale regulations: by incorporating HIPAA, GDPR, ISO, NIST and other controls, it provides a single, risk-based compliance framework. However, potential gaps persist in a few of the standards include cloud-native architectures, AI/ML auditability, or emerging technologies like the Internet of Medical Things in express terms. More work is needed to translate new regulatory guidance into cloud-specific controls for risk and identify where existing compliance models must pivot to cloud healthcare. Risks of operational migration must also be resolved. Vendor lock-in is a widely acknowledged hurdle: regulators like ENISA point out that proprietary cloud services can stifle interoperability and portability. Open standards or multi-cloud approaches are occasionally recommended to reduce this risk. Legacy system migration is another challenge. Care providers typically have mission-critical on-premises applications (e.g., EHRs) which must be re-architected for the cloud without affecting care. Although cloud platforms offer elastic recovery (e.g., automated backups, geo-redundancy), normal business continuity and disaster recovery planning is still required; for example, HITRUST incorporates a continuity domain to mandate operational resilience v-comply.com.

Such factors suggest research into applied migration planning, continuity assurance, and vendor/supply-chain risk management in healthcare clouds. With such trends, future research directions might include:

Risk-based audit automation platforms: Benchmark and compare health cloud-tuned automated compliance platforms. These solutions can utilize machine learning and real-time monitoring to highlight control discrepancies in real time, reducing the level of audit labor needed.

Privacy-preserving machine learning: Investigate federated learning, differential privacy or homomorphic encryption solutions for encrypted cloud-hosted health data. These methods can enable AI-enabled analytics without exposing patient information because it's always encrypted or anonymized, meeting HIPAA/GDPR compliances.

Adaptive multi-cloud compliance models: Develop governance schemas and standards that facilitate equal control of security across the providers. Explore sense-based standards-based audit proof and interfaces (e.g., identities, log and encryption key ones) in a bid to be lock-in-vendor-free and have cross-vendor commonality of compliance across AWS, Azure, GCP, etc.

Zero Trust deployment research: Analyze ZTA deployments for healthcare cloud infrastructure, e.g., metrics on continuous authentication and network segmentation. To illustrate, research can ascertain the effects of micro-segmentation and identity-based policies on auditability, breach detection, and regulatory compliance.

Future research will fill current audit, risk, and compliance gaps for healthcare cloud migration to make certain that new technology and evolving regulations are adequately addressed.

7.0 CONCLUSION

The transition to cloud-based systems within the healthcare industry signifies a transformative shift toward modernizing data management, improving patient care, and enhancing operational efficiencies. This evolution is not merely about adopting new technologies but fundamentally rethinking how data is stored, accessed, and utilized to achieve better outcomes for patients and healthcare organizations alike. Migration to the cloud presents numerous opportunities, such as scalability, integration with advanced analytics, and robust disaster recovery capabilities, while addressing challenges like data security, regulatory compliance, and compatibility with legacy systems (Argaw et al., 2020; Deloitte, n.d.; Fernandez et al., 2012).

One of the most significant advantages of cloud adoption in healthcare is the ability to scale resources dynamically to meet demand. Cloud platforms offer unparalleled elasticity, enabling healthcare organizations to handle fluctuations in workload, such as those experienced during public health crises or seasonal patient surges. This scalability is not only cost-effective but also ensures that critical services remain uninterrupted, supporting better patient outcomes and operational continuity. By employing pay-as-you-go models, healthcare providers can optimize their expenditure, investing in resources only as needed while preparing for future growth and technological advancements (Amazon Web Services, 2023a; Amazon Web Services, 2023b; Fernandez et al., 2012).

In addition to scalability, cloud migration facilitates integration with advanced analytics and artificial intelligence (AI) technologies, which have the potential to revolutionize healthcare delivery. Predictive analytics enabled by AI can provide actionable insights into patient care, such as identifying at-risk individuals, optimizing resource allocation, and forecasting disease outbreaks. Furthermore, personalized medicine, driven by AI-powered data analysis, allows healthcare providers to tailor treatments based on individual patient profiles, improving diagnostic accuracy and care delivery. These advancements underscore the transformative potential of cloud-enabled systems in enhancing patient care and operational efficiency (Amazon Web Services, 2023a; Amazon Web Services, 2023b; Argaw et al., 2020; Fernandez et al., 2012).

Another critical benefit of cloud migration is the enhancement of disaster recovery and business continuity planning. With data stored in geographically dispersed cloud data centers, healthcare organizations can ensure that critical information is backed up and accessible even in the event of natural disasters or cyberattacks. Automated backups, failover mechanisms, and real-time replication contribute to minimizing downtime and preserving data integrity, thereby safeguarding patient care and organizational reputation. Such robust disaster recovery solutions not only enhance resilience but also align with regulatory requirements, further solidifying trust in cloud-based systems (Amazon Web Services, 2023b; Fernandez et al., 2012).

Despite these opportunities, migration to cloud-based systems also presents several challenges, primarily centered around data security, privacy, and regulatory compliance. The sensitive nature of healthcare data necessitates stringent measures to ensure its confidentiality, integrity, and availability. Compliance with regulations like HIPAA, GDPR, and HITRUST CSF is non-negotiable, as these frameworks provide the foundation for protecting patient information and maintaining trust. Encryption of data both at rest and in transit, robust access controls, and continuous monitoring are essential to mitigating risks and addressing vulnerabilities during and after migration. Moreover, the shared responsibility model inherent in cloud services requires healthcare organizations to collaborate closely with cloud providers to ensure compliance and security across all layers of the infrastructure (Argaw et al., 2020; Deloitte, n.d.; Fernandez et al., 2012).

Compatibility with legacy systems is another significant hurdle in cloud migration. Many healthcare organizations rely on outdated systems that may not seamlessly integrate with modern cloud platforms. Addressing this challenge requires careful planning and execution, including strategies such as rehosting, refactoring, or rebuilding applications to ensure compatibility and functionality in the cloud environment. Middleware solutions, data mapping, and API-based integration can bridge gaps between legacy systems and cloud platforms, enabling seamless data exchange and reducing workflow disruptions. Hybrid architectures, which retain critical legacy systems on-premises while leveraging cloud capabilities, offer a pragmatic approach to balancing modernization with operational stability (Ahmad & Babar, 2014; Amazon Web Services, 2023a; Amazon Web Services, 2023b; Kuo, 2011).

To navigate these complexities successfully, risk management frameworks and IS auditing play a pivotal role. IS auditing ensuring that cloud migrations align with regulatory standards, secure sensitive data, and maintain system integrity. Continuous auditing and monitoring help healthcare organizations identify potential vulnerabilities, implement corrective measures, and ensure that cloud providers adhere to service-level agreements and best practices. The implementation of automated compliance tools further streamlines the auditing process, reducing manual intervention and enhancing efficiency (Fahmideh et al., 2016; Takabi et al., 2010; Fernandez et al., 2012; Shahrabi & Ghaznavi-Ghoushchi, 2021).

The journey to cloud adoption in healthcare is not solely a technological upgrade but a strategic pivot toward innovation and resilience. By leveraging cloud platforms, healthcare organizations can break down data silos, standardize and centralize information, and unlock the potential of emerging technologies. This migration enables healthcare providers to move beyond reactive care models, embracing proactive and predictive approaches that prioritize patient well-being and optimize resource utilization (Amazon Web Services, 2023a; Amazon Web Services, 2023b; Argaw et al., 2020; Fernandez et al., 2012).

However, the success of cloud migration hinges on the healthcare sector's ability to balance technological advancements with robust governance and compliance measures. Continuous monitoring, dynamic risk assessments, and alignment with evolving regulatory standards are essential to safeguarding sensitive data and maintaining trust among stakeholders. As cloud adoption deepens, the development of security frameworks and best practices tailored to the healthcare industry will be crucial in addressing emerging challenges and fostering a secure, efficient, and innovative ecosystem (Argaw et al., 2020; Jamshidi et al., 2013; Fernandez et al., 2012).

In conclusion, the migration of healthcare data to the cloud represents a paradigm shift in how healthcare organizations manage and utilize information. It offers a pathway to modernization, operational efficiency, and enhanced patient care, underpinned by the transformative potential of AI, analytics, and scalable infrastructure. By embracing strategic planning, robust risk management, and continuous compliance, the healthcare industry can harness the full potential of cloud computing to redefine patient care and operational excellence in a rapidly advancing digital landscape. This transition is not just about technology but about reimagining the future of healthcare delivery to create a resilient, innovative, and patient-centered ecosystem that meets the demands of the 21st century (Amazon Web Services, 2023a; Amazon Web Services, 2023b; Argaw et al., 2020; Deloitte, n.d.; Fernandez et al., 2012).

ACKNOWLEDGMENT

This research has not received funding from any specific grant through public, commercial, or not-for-profit research funding organizations. The authors would like to express their sincere appreciation to the faculty and mentors at the University at Buffalo for their intellectual guidance and encouragement throughout the development of this work.

Special thanks are extended to Professor Manish Gupta and Professor John Walp for their thoughtful feedback and valuable suggestions, which significantly enhanced the quality of this chapter.

The authors also wish to acknowledge Gopinath Sankara Narayanan, Saquan Grizzle, and Matt Kreuzer for their critical research input, collaborative effort, and dedication, all of which played a vital role in shaping the direction and scope of this paper.

REFERENCES

Ahmad, A., & Babar, M. A. (2014). *A framework for architecture-driven migration of legacy systems to cloud-enabled software*. In *Proceedings of the WICSA 2014 Companion Volume* (pp. 1–8). IEEE. DOI: 10.1145/2578128.2578232

Alder, S. (2023, September 22). Healthcare cloud usage grows but protecting PHI can be a challenge. *HIPAA Journal*. https://www.hipaajournal.com/healthcare-cloud-usage-grows-but-protecting-phi-can-be-a-challenge

Amazon Web Services. (2023). *MediSys replicates patient records and medical images to AWS*. https://aws.amazon.com/solutions/case-studies/medisys-case-study

Amazon Web Services. (2023). *Optimizing enterprise imaging in the cloud using Visage 7 PACS platform on AWS with Allina Health*. https://aws.amazon.com/solutions/case-studies/allinahealth-case-study

Argaw, S. T., Troncoso-Pastoriza, J. R., Lacey, D., Florin, M. V., & Flahault, A. (2020). Cybersecurity of hospitals: Discussing the challenges and working towards mitigating the risks. *BMC Medical Informatics and Decision Making*, *20*(146), 146. Advance online publication. DOI: 10.1186/s12911-020-01161-7 PMID: 32620167

Brodie, M., & Stonebraker, M. (1995). *Migrating legacy systems: Gateways, interfaces & the incremental approach*. Morgan Kaufmann Publishers Inc.

Deloitte. (n.d.). *Continuous monitoring and continuous auditing practices*. https://www2.deloitte.com/content/dam/Deloitte/uy/Documents/audit/Monitoreo%20continuo%20y%20auditoria%20continua.pdf

Fahmideh, M., Beydoun, G., & Atif, Y. (2016). Cloud migration process: A survey, evaluation framework, and open challenges. *Journal of Systems and Software*, *120*, 31–69. DOI: 10.1016/j.jss.2016.06.068

Fernandez, M., Cukier, J., Jones, T. S., & Khurana, R. (2012). Privacy and security in the cloud: A healthcare perspective. In *Proceedings of the IEEE HealthCom* (pp. 187–192). IEEE. https://doi.org/DOI: 10.1109/HealthCom.2012.6379435

Jamshidi, P., Ahmad, A., & Pahl, C. (2013). Cloud migration research: A systematic review. *IEEE Transactions on Cloud Computing, PP*, 1–1. https://doi.org/DOI: 10.1109/TCC.2013.10

Kuo, A. (2011). Opportunities and challenges of cloud computing to improve healthcare services. *Journal of Medical Internet Research*, *13*(3), e67. Advance online publication. DOI: 10.2196/jmir.1867 PMID: 21937354

Ray, I., Ray, I., & Kulkarni, N. (2013). Information assurance and security in healthcare cloud computing: Survey and challenges. *International Journal of Healthcare Information Systems and Informatics*, *8*(3), 57–74.

Shahrabi, A., & Ghaznavi-Ghoushchi, M. (2021). Application of machine learning in cloud computing security: A survey. *IEEE Access : Practical Innovations, Open Solutions*, *9*, 20732–20749. DOI: 10.1109/ACCESS.2021.3054783

Subashini, S., & Kavitha, V. (2011). A survey on security issues in service delivery models of cloud computing. *Journal of Network and Computer Applications*, *34*(1), 1–11. DOI: 10.1016/j.jnca.2010.07.006

Takabi, H., Joshi, J. B. D., & Ahn, G. J. (2010). Security and privacy challenges in cloud computing environments. *IEEE Security and Privacy*, *8*(6), 24–31. DOI: 10.1109/MSP.2010.186

Yu, S., Wang, C., Ren, K., & Lou, W. (2010). Achieving secure, scalable, and fine-grained data access control in cloud computing. In *Proceedings of the IEEE INFOCOM* (pp. 1–9). IEEE. https://doi.org/DOI: 10.1109/INFCOM.2010.5462174

ADDITIONAL READING

Agarwal, R., Gao, G., DesRoches, C., & Jha, A. K. (2010). The digital transformation of healthcare: Current status and the road ahead. *Information Systems Research, 21*(4), 796–809. DOI: 10.1287/isre.1100.0327

AWS. (2021). *Architecting for HIPAA Security and Compliance on AWS.* https://aws.amazon.com/compliance/hipaa-compliance/

Cloud Security Alliance. (2019). *Security guidance for critical areas of focus in cloud computing v4.0.* https://cloudsecurityalliance.org/artifacts/security-guidance-v4/

ENISA. (2022). *Guidelines on Securing the Supply Chain for Cloud Services.* https://www.enisa.europa.eu

Google Cloud. (2020). *Healthcare data protection and compliance on Google Cloud.* https://cloud.google.com/solutions/healthcare-compliance

ISACA. (2023). *COBIT 2019 Framework: Governance and Management Objectives.* ISACA.

National Institute of Standards and Technology. (2022). *SP 800-53 Revision 5: Security and Privacy Controls for Federal Information Systems and Organizations.* https://csrc.nist.gov/publications

Office for Civil Rights. (2013). *Guidance on Risk Analysis Requirements under the HIPAA Security Rule.* U.S. Department of Health & Human Services. https://www.hhs.gov

Shin, D., & Choi, M. (2015). Ecological views of big data: Perspectives and issues. *Telecommunications Policy, 39*(8), 780–789. DOI: 10.1016/j.telpol.2015.07.005

Takabi, H., Joshi, J. B. D., & Ahn, G. J. (2010). Security and privacy challenges in cloud computing environments. *IEEE Security and Privacy, 8*(6), 24–31. DOI: 10.1109/MSP.2010.186

KEY TERMS AND DEFINITIONS

Business Associate Agreement (BAA): A HIPAA-required legal contract between a cloud service provider and a healthcare organization for the protection and limited use of protected health information (PHI).

Cloud Migration: The process of moving data, applications, and services from traditional on-premises systems to cloud setups such as Infrastructure as a Service (IaaS), Platform as a Service (PaaS), or Software as a Service (SaaS).

Data Governance: A set of policies, procedures, and standards that data is managed properly in the areas of quality, integrity, security, and compliance during its whole lifecycle.

Disaster Recovery: A plan and set of procedures used by businesses to recover data and resume crucial activities after a system crash, data breach, or natural disaster.

Electronic Protected Health Information (ePHI): Any health information that is created, received, stored, or transmitted electronically and is protected under HIPAA regulations.

Health Insurance Portability and Accountability Act (HIPAA): A United States federal law that establishes standards for protecting sensitive patient data and mandates privacy, security, and breach notification safeguards.

Information Systems (IS) Auditing: An official evaluation of an organization's IT systems, controls, and processes to determine data integrity, security, and regulatory compliance.

Infrastructure as a Service (IaaS): A cloud computing paradigm where firms rent virtualized hardware and networking resources from a cloud provider but still run their own operating systems and applications.

Platform as a Service (PaaS): A model of cloud computing that provides a platform that allows customers to develop, run, and manage applications without the complexity of the underlying infrastructure management.

Shared Responsibility Model: A cloud computing security framework that outlines the sharing of responsibility between the cloud customer and provider in implementing cloud infrastructure and data security.

APPENDIX 1

Cloud Migration Checklist

The following checklist outlines key activities across each phase of a cloud migration project within healthcare or other compliance-driven environments.

Planning & Assessment

- Define business goals and expected outcomes
- Perform application inventory and dependency mapping
- Assess cloud readiness of applications and infrastructure
- Conduct cost-benefit and ROI analysis
- Choose the right cloud deployment model (public, private, hybrid, multi-cloud)
- Select the appropriate cloud service model (IaaS, PaaS, SaaS)
- Identify security, compliance, and regulatory requirements
- Develop a migration strategy (Rehost, Refactor, Rearchitect, Rebuild, Replace)

Design & Preparation

- Choose a cloud service provider (e.g., AWS, Azure, GCP)
- Design cloud architecture (VPC, IAM, storage, compute, etc.)
- Set up governance, access control, and monitoring framework
- Plan network connectivity (VPN, Direct Connect, etc.)
- Define backup, disaster recovery, and data retention policies
- Build a migration runbook and rollback plan

Migration Execution

- Set up landing zone (account structure, security baselines)
- Migrate in phases (start with pilot or low-risk applications)
- Use migration tools and services (AWS Migration Hub, Azure Migrate, etc.)
- Perform data migration and validation
- Conduct application performance testing
- Ensure security controls are active post-migration

Post-Migration Optimization

- Monitor application and infrastructure performance
- Optimize resource usage and cost (auto-scaling, reserved instances, etc.)
- Update documentation and knowledge base
- Train operations team and end-users
- Perform regular security audits and compliance checks
- Gather feedback and iterate for continuous improvement

Chapter 7
Multi-Cloud Environments:
Auditing for Security, Compliance, and Risk Mitigation

Varanasi Rahul
https://orcid.org/0000-0003-2407-7654
Jain University, India

N. Sathyanarayana
https://orcid.org/0000-0002-4185-7751
Jain University, India

L. B. Muralidhar
https://orcid.org/0000-0003-3453-613X
Jain University, India

Y. Fathima
https://orcid.org/0000-0002-0045-1421
Jain University, India

R. Shilpa
https://orcid.org/0009-0002-9805-1481
RJS Institute of Management Studies, India

ABSTRACT

The proliferation of multi-cloud environments, driven by the need for flexibility, redundancy, and cost efficiency, has introduced new challenges in managing security, compliance, and risk. This chapter explores integrative approaches to auditing within multi-cloud infrastructures, highlighting frameworks, tools, and methodol-

DOI: 10.4018/979-8-3373-3078-5.ch007

ogies necessary to ensure robust security and regulatory alignment. It examines key components such as identity and access management, data encryption, network security, and continuous monitoring. Additionally, the chapter outlines auditing practices for security and compliance, referencing international standards like NIST and GDPR. Risk mitigation strategies are discussed through real-world case studies, including risk assessment models and continuity planning. The discussion underscores the need for cohesive auditing mechanisms to address the complexity and fragmentation inherent in multi-cloud systems. By adopting a holistic audit perspective, organizations can safeguard critical assets, meet compliance demands, and build resilient digital ecosystems.

1. INTRODUCTION

1.1 The Rise of Multi-Cloud Environments

Over the past ten years, the technology landscape has evolved with cloud computing being the backbone of contemporary digital infrastructure. While organizations pursue the goal of being scalable, agile, and cost-effective, they embrace multi-cloud strategies—the use of two or more cloud computing offerings from various vendors, more and more. Unlike the use of both public and private clouds to create a so-called hybrid cloud environment, multi-cloud configurations use multiple public clouds (such as AWS, Microsoft Azure, Google Cloud) or a blend of public and private offerings to diversify workloads, avoid vendor lock-in, and improve the reliability of the services concerned. (Majumdar et al., 2022)

Multi-cloud setups have developed from being a tactical decision to a strategic necessity. Enterprises use such setups' flexibility to align various workloads to the most optimal cloud platforms, leverage region-based capabilities, and achieve competitive pricing models. The advantage of multi-cloud deployment is compounded by many complicating factors, especially in security, regulatory compliance, and risk management. Each cloud provider has unique architectures, tools, configurations, and security models with multiple complicating factors in providing visibility, control, and auditability across the IT ecosystem.

1.2 Security and Governance Issues

Security in multi-cloud is hardly a matter of defending a defined perimeter but rather of protecting several platforms with varied access control, audit trails, and threat models. Heterogeneity brings blind spots with it that can be exploited by an adversary. On top of this, cloud assets are inherently temporary in nature—ephemeral containers, automatically scaled-out VMs, and serverless functions—may necessitate a replacement for traditional security models and tools. (Kumar et al., 2023)

Governance is also affected when policy enforcement is disconnected. A compliance or security policy in one cloud might be incorrectly configured or put into effect in another cloud, generating gaps in the organization's defense. This is amplified by improper configuration, poor identity and access management (IAM), and a lack of uniform logging and monitoring controls by providers.

1.3 Regulatory Compliance in Multi-Cloud

Compliance is another top area of focus. Healthcare, finance, and government institutions must comply with increasingly lengthy lists of regulations and policies such as GDPR, HIPAA, PCI-DSS, and SOX, among numerous others. These regulations and policies are normally accompanied by stringent data residency, privacy, and security requirements that are a problem to meet in several clouds in a consistent manner. For instance, one cloud provider will store data in a region that is non-compliant to some of the requirements in law. While others will have particular levels of encryption and types of access controls. This implies that organisations must continually and stringently audit and check to ensure compliance is never compromised.

Auditing becomes a main mechanism for ensuring security controls are present, in effect, and functioning. (Akinade et al., 2024) Auditing is also an important means for detecting incidents, forensic analysis, compliance with laws, and contractual requirements. To be effective in multi-cloud scenarios, however, standardized processes able to correlate data across various platforms and utilize automation, AI, and centralized logging capabilities to provide a single pane of glass visibility to the clouds presence in an organization is essential.

1.4 The Role of Evolved Auditing Frameworks

Conventional IT auditing methodologies designed for on-premises and single-cloud deployments do not accommodate the' dynamic and distributed' nature of multi-cloud deployments. Auditing in such a context has to be more agile, automated, and ongoing in nature than discrete and manpower-consuming exercises from time to time. Risk-based auditing models should be embraced to prioritize assets and work based upon their business significance and sensitivity. Cloud-native controls and third-party platforms need to be engaged in order to ingest telemetry data, detect anomalies, and enforce compliance throughout the audit process. (Wang et al., 2024)

Cloud security posture management (CSPM) solutions, for instance, automatically detect misconfigurations and policy violations in multiple cloud accounts. Cloud access security brokers (CASBs) can also monitor data flow from cloud services to users, and security information and event management (SIEM) systems pool logs from multiple points to recognize threats in real time. These solutions must be supported with effective audit techniques, with focus being put on risk identification, assessment of controls, and continuous monitoring.

1.5 Multi-Dimensional Risk Landscape

Risk in multi-clouds covers a range of dimensions of operational risk, data security risk, compliance risks of vendors, and interoperability risk.Operational risks are a consequence of downtime, mismanagement, or misconfiguration as a result of the heavy reliance of services. Data security risks include unauthorized access breaches and loss resulting from a lack of sufficient encryption and access controls. Compliance risks occur in instances where an organization is unaware of gaps in regulations or compliance documents to standards.

Vendor risk is especially troublesome in multi-cloud scenarios in which support from several vendors may complicate accountability and undermine contractual guarantees. Additionally, non-standardization of cloud vendors introduces interoperability issues in the form of various APIs and support for various encryption protocols. It can also make enforcement of security and audit trails more problematic.

Accordingly, organizations must have a risk-based audit strategy that is in line with business priorities and risk profile. By setting and assessing each cloud platform's risk probability and corresponding impact, auditors are best able to customize their assessments and recommendations.

1.6 Auditing as an Enabler of Trust and Resilience

Fundamentally, auditing in the multi-cloud is more than a compliance activity; it is also a strategic facilitator of business resilience and digital trust. By having in place strict audit protocols, firms can be held to account, promote transparency to stakeholders and create trust in the trustworthiness of their clouds. Executive management and regulators receive empirical evidence of risk management and effectiveness of controls and ongoing improvement from the audit reports.

Furthermore, security audits also become a competitive advantage in an increasingly digitized economy and customer expectations of data privacy. Organizations that demonstrate evidence of compliance and implementing improved security measures reap higher customer trust and confidence, avoid reputational losses, and recover more rapidly in the event of a breach. By doing so, auditing plays a pivotal role in maintaining long-term business resilience and stakeholder trust.

2. UNDERSTANDING MULTI-CLOUD ENVIRONMENTS

2.1 Describing the Multi-Cloud Model

A multi-cloud model is an IT strategy that allows the organization to leverage the offerings of two or more cloud vendors concurrently. This can include public clouds (Amazon Web Services, Microsoft Azure, Google Cloud Platform), private clouds (hosted and/or internally hosted), or a hybrid model that combines on-prem equipment with cloud solutions. Unlike the interaction model between on-prem and cloud in a hybrid cloud model, the focus of a multi-cloud model is diversification and distribution—running distinct workloads in different clouds' environments based on performance needs, cost limitations, security requirements, and compliance mandates.

Multi-cloud strategies suddenly gained popularity due to their ability to curtail reliance on a single vendor. This not only keeps organizations from getting locked in with a specific vendor but also lets them take advantage of the unique strengths of different providers. For instance, a company can use AWS to scale computing power, Microsoft Azure to gain more in-depth integration with Office 365 and enterprise identity solutions, and Google Cloud to take advantage of advanced-level AI/ML solutions. (Hashim & Hussein, 2024)

2.2 Advantages of the Multi-Cloud Model

Organizations implement multiple-cloud deployments in response to various strategic and operational motivations:

- Flexibility and Optimization: Varying firms provide specialized services. Multi-cloud enables organizations to pick and choose those services that most appropriately fit their requirements, e.g., performance, geographic region coverage, and cost efficiency.
- Redundancy and Resilience: Having multiple applications and data spread over several different providers helps to increase system resiliency and disaster recovery. In case of an outage or security breach with one provider, business-critical workloads can operate uninterruptedly on other platforms.

- Regulatory and Sovereignty Needs: Nations may need certain data to reside locally. Organizations can fulfill those obligations by utilizing regional data centers from multiple cloud providers with a multi-cloud setup.
- Cost Management: Providers' pricing plans differ. Organizations can minimize their cloud costs by aligning their workloads to the least expensive platforms or negotiating the most competitive pricing in terms of use volumes.

These benefits render multi-cloud architecture attractive to various industries—from finance and health care to manufacturing and government.

2.3 The Inherent Challenges of Multi-Cloud Environments

Although the advantages are appealing, multi-cloud environments create a complex operational and security challenges matrix. The most prominent challenges come from the fact that the platforms lack uniformity in architecture, tools, APIs and governance models. (Folorunso et al., 2024)

2.3.1 Inconsistent Security Models

All cloud providers include various security controls, identity management tools, encryption methods, and logging facilities in the list of available security options and controls from which a customer can choose. For instance, AWS employs Identity and Access Management (IAM) technology, Azure employs Azure Active Directory (AAD), and Google Cloud employs its own version of IAM technology. These vary in their management of users, roles, and policies. Handling these differences can be time-consuming and error-prone and can result in misconfigurations, privilege creep, or missed vulnerabilities.

2.3.2 Fragmented Visibility and Control

One of the most fundamental challenges with operating in multiple clouds is being able to gain centralized visibility in all environments. Cloud vendors' monitoring tools and dashboards usually only cover their ecosystem. This leaves "islands of visibility" where organizations cannot achieve a unified view of security events, config drift, and utilization of resources in clouds.

Without integrated monitoring, the detection of anomalies, policy enforcement uniformity, and compliance becomes challenging. In addition to that, teams can employ various logging formats and standards, which make forensic investigation and incident response challenging. (Singh & Kumar, 2023)

2.3.3 Increased Attack Surface

With more platforms involved, there are more exposed services, endpoints, and configurations to manage. Each extra provider introduces complexity and points of weakness, particularly where services may be exposed to the Internet or misconfigured access controls exist. Cloud misconfigurations, insecure APIs, and exposed storage buckets are readily exploited by attackers—threats that multiply in multi-cloud environments.

2.3.4 Challenges in Meeting Compliance Requirements

Cloud offerings include broad industry approvals and regulations that are compliant with various frameworks. However, correlating the inherent capabilities with the organization's compliance responsibilities is hardly simple. Even with the shared responsibility model where the cloud provider secures the infrastructure, the customer should secure their data and applications; in return, there is greater complexity in the process.

For example, being compliant with storing personal health information (PHI) on AWS vs. Azure will necessitate different controls to achieve HIPAA compliance. Likewise, keeping personal data from exiting the European Economic Area in the case of GDPR may necessitate precise coordination of regions and services that vary by provider. (Reece et al., 2023a)

2.3.5 Auditing is the Cornerstone of Multi-cloud Governance

Auditing is critical to maintaining control in the disparate nature of multi-cloud environments. Audits allow organizations to confirm that:

- All platforms have adequate security policies enforced
- Regulatory standards are fulfilled irrespective of the provider
- Risks are addressed and mitigated before being exploited
- Access and modification of data are appropriately recorded and auditable

A successful audit approach in multi-cloud starts with asset discovery in detail. Organizations need to be aware of what assets they own, where they reside and how it is set up. Configuration assessment is next and here automated scanners verify if assets meet internal and external baselines of security. Last is continuous monitoring and real-time alerting which allows teams to react faster to policy breaches or malicious activity. (Reece et al., 2023b)

2.4 Standardizing Controls Across Platforms

Organizations can also leverage abstraction and normalization layers to tackle provider inconsistencies. Cloud security posture management (CSPM), cloud workload protection platforms (CWPP), and extended detection and response (XDR) platforms include functions that can consolidate control, visibility, and compliance in clouds.

Such tools function by

- Implementing uniform policies via APIs among providers
- Normalizing logs to a single format to be analyzed in unison
- Misconfigurations and non-compliance detection through rule engines
- Automation of remediation

As an example, a CSPM scanner may scan multiple cloud accounts to locate unencrypted storage buckets, publicly exposed databases and high-level IAM permissions and either automatically take action on them or raise audit alerts.

2.5 Human Factors and Skill Gaps

Managing a multi-cloud environment requires proficiency in multiple platforms and their associated terminology, management interfaces, and security models. This in turn creates skills gaps among IT teams and can come through in misconfigurations and response lags from incidents. These issues can be addressed with ongoing education, playbooks that are standardized, and cross-platform certifications (in the form of multi-cloud engineer tracks from cloud vendors).

Furthermore, cooperation between security, compliance, and operations teams is important to streamline auditing tasks. Having the teams utilize common frameworks—such as the NIST Cybersecurity Framework, ISO 27001, or COBIT—makes sure that audits are more than just checklist exercises and that they're indeed risk-mitigating measures.

2.6 Building a Multi-Cloud Governance Framework

Organizations should implement a governance model that encompasses the following factors in order to be able to manage and audit multi-cloud deployments effectively

- Policy Management: Maintaining standardized security and compliance policies that cover more than one cloud provider

- Role-Based Access Control (RBAC): Having least privilege access on various accounts and platforms
- Monitoring and Logging: Centralized logging and analysis implementation
- Automated Auditing: Use of scripts and tools to monitor configurations continuously and detect anomalies
- Documentation and Reporting: Maintaining complete audit trails, policies, and remediation plans for regulators and stakeholders

2.7 The role of Emerging Technologies

Increasingly emerging technologies like machine learning and AI are being employed to enhance auditing in multi-cloud setups. Machine learning is applied to detect patterns that imply insider threats, account compromise, and resource abuse. In contrast, robotic process automation (RPA) is applied to automate remediation, credential rotations, and compliance reports.

Blockchain is another technology with multi-cloud audit trail capability. Blockchain captures unalterable and timestamped proofs of things that happen on various cloud platforms that can build trust and reduce fraud in highly regulated environments.

3. KEY COMPONENTS OF MULTI-CLOUD SECURITY

Security in multi-cloud is far more complicated compared to traditional or single-cloud environments. Having constant and complete security on every platform is a formidable task with various cloud providers having different security models, APIs, and interfaces. However, security cannot be sacrificed in any way. Security breach in a single cloud environment can become a greater organization risk in seconds if the services and data become cross-linked.

Organizations should employ a layered and thorough security approach to protect all areas of the cloud infrastructure in order to successfully address these challenges. From identity management and encryption to safe networking and live monitoring, every component has a significant role in protecting multi-cloud environments. (Tian et al., 2025)

3.1 Identity and Access Management (IAM)

Identity and Access Management (IAM) forms the core of cloud security. In a multi-cloud setup, it is equally critical and complex. Each cloud provider has its own IAM (AWS IAM, Azure Active Directory, Google Cloud IAM) that can function differently in role granting, permission setting, or auditing access

Without proper IAM controls in place, users with unauthorized access can be allowed to gain access to privileged information or systems. Over-provisioned roles or inactive credentials can also be caused by inconsistent policies among different platforms.

The other emergent direction is to use identity federation and Just-in-Time (JIT) access delivery to restrict standing entitlements by offering transient access based on role and job function of the user. This reduces the attack surface dramatically and increases auditability. (Seetharamarao, 2023)

Moreover, IAM systems must be supplemented with audit logs and access analytics so that organizations can analyze historical patterns of access, detect anomalies and insider threats, and respond to account breaches.

3.2 Encryption and Protection of Privacy

Data is arguably the most precious resource in a multi-cloud setup, and safeguarding it is of the utmost importance. Encryption is critical to protecting data that is stored (at rest), in motion on networks (in transit), and being processed (in use).

All prominent cloud vendors deliver secure encryption facilities. But the actual challenge is that consistency in encryption policies, key management procedures, and privacy controls should be maintained across various platforms. Organizations should see to it that

- Encryption standards (such as AES-256) are applied to all cloud services
- All data in-transit on APIs and integrations is enforced with Transport Layer Security (TLS)
- Wherever feasible, policies that utilize Customer-Managed Keys (CMKs) or Bring Your Key (BYOK)
- Encryption key access is limited, audited and safeguarded by use of hardware security modules (HSMs)

Regulations such as GDPR, CCPA, and HIPAA require stringent rules around data residency, consent, and breach notification and necessitate that you institute data classification, tagging, and masking methods in order to monitor where sensitive data is located and guarantee that only those who should be permitted to will be allowed entry and decrypt it.

Moreover, tokenization and anonymization techniques can safeguard personal information during analytics and sharing so that organizations can use cloud-based insights without revealing raw identifiable data.

3.3 Network Security

Securing communication channels among services deployed on separate clouds—or in the case of cloud and on-premises deployments—is critical in a multi-cloud setup to avoid interception, tampering, or unauthorized access.

Network security in such a scenario demands a layered defense approach with a combination of perimeter defenses and internal controls. The primary elements include

- Virtual Private Networks (VPNs): Secure channels can be set up between clouds and corporate networks so that communication is encrypted. It is inconvenient to manage multiple VPN endpoints, and hence SD-WAN solutions are acquiring popularity with dynamic traffic routing and centralized management.
- Firewalls and Security Groups: All cloud providers offer native firewalls, but third-party cloud firewalls or Web Application Firewalls (WAFs) can offer uniform security across environments. Security groups should operate according to the principle of least privilege, only allowing required traffic and rejecting unused ports or services.
- Segmentation and Micro-Segmentation: Segmenting workloads with network segmentation reduces the lateral movement risk of attackers. With micro-segmentation, policies are applied at a granular level—even in the same cluster of applications—providing greater control over the interaction of workloads.
- Secure APIs: APIs usually serve as the conduit between clouds and services, yet can be a vulnerable point if not properly secured. Protection against typical threats such as data leakage, abuse of APIs, and man-in-the-middle attacks should be provided through enforcement of authentication tokens, limiting the rate of hits and data validation in input.

To handle the network complexity of cross-cloud environments, some use cloud-native network visibility tools, and others use multi-cloud networking platforms (MCNPs) that include unified policy enforcement, routing optimization, and telemetry in all connected networks. (Hazela et al., 2022)

3.4 Monitoring and Incident Detection

Unified visibility is the backbone of proactive cloud security. Nonetheless, unifying visibility in a multi-cloud setup is not easy with the presence of isolated logging mechanisms, multiple event formats, and multiple data retention policies.

A robust monitoring approach starts with log aggregation that is centralized. Cloud platforms' logs such as AWS CloudTrail, Azure Monitor, and Google Cloud Operations need to be gathered and normalized in a centralized platform such as Security Information and Event Management (SIEM) systems (for example, Splunk, IBM Q Radar, and Azure Sentinel).

Such systems monitor logs in real-time, correlate events between clouds and trigger alerts for

- Attempted unauthorized access
- Configuration modifications
  Data exfiltration
- Atypical user or load behavior

They can also be augmented with User and Entity Behavior Analytics (UEBA), which utilize machine learning to detect subtle patterns of departure from expected behavior. For instance, a user accessing from an unknown source IP or viewing privileged information outside of their traditional work schedule may raise an alarm to be looked into.

Security Orchestration, Automation and Response (SOAR) solutions can subsequently take action on SIEM alerts by automating responses like revoking access, isolating systems, or initiating alerts to the incident response group (Reddy, 2023)

Furthermore, threat intel feeds can be used with monitoring systems to indicate known malicious IPs, domains, or behaviors. Regulated industry organizations should also institute compliance dashboards to monitor critical risk indicators and give auditable proof of adherence to regulatory standards.

3.5 Integrating Security with DevOps: Introducing the Dev Sec Ops Approach

As multi-cloud deployments adopt agility through DevOps, security must be integrated into the development pipeline itself. This is what is also meant by the term DevSecOps where security controls, testing, and audits are part of every step of the software delivery pipeline.

For instance, Infrastructure-as-Code (IaC) templates used to provision cloud assets are scanned before deployment with security scanners such as Terraform Sentinel, Checkov, or Open Policy Agent (OPA). Containers' image vulnerabilities can be scanned before pushing them to production.

Integrating automated compliance validation, runtime security controls, and continuous monitoring into CI/CD pipelines enables organizations to minimize the attack surface of multi-cloud apps and deploy them securely much faster. (Singh, 2023)

Multi-cloud deployments bring unprecedented levels of flexibility and opportunity for innovation along with associated complex security issues to be addressed with a broad-ranging strategy. By focusing on key building blocks—identity and access management, encryption, network security, and continuous monitoring—companies can establish a solid security foundation in all clouds. These building blocks must operate in conjunction with each other through the assistance of automation, centralized visibility and policy enforcement to prevent attacks and also ensure compliance in an ever-changing threat environment.

4. AUDITING FOR SECURITY IN MULTI-CLOUD ENVIRONMENTS

As digital transformation gains speed in an ever-increasingly fast-paced world, multi-cloud setups are today at the center of IT strategy in enterprise companies. But with extensibility and adaptability come the additional demand for rigorous security audits. While in conventional configurations integrated control is a result of centralized infrastructures, multi-cloud installations are plagued with disparate visibility, decentralized controls and varied security paradigms

Auditing is the common thread between operational complexity and assurance of security. By conducting systematic checks for access controls, configuration, data-protection policies, and user habits, audits enable organizations to uncover weaknesses, avoid breaches, and apply standardized security controls to various platforms. For it to be effective, however, it should be both framework-based and technology-enabled and customized to handle the distinctive risks and architectures of multi-cloud services. (Liu, 2024)

4.1 Security Auditing Frameworks

Security audits gain organization and direction from industry-accepted frameworks. Frameworks provide a template of what to inspect with what regularity and to what level of detail. Frameworks in multi-cloud deployments normalize audit procedures between cloud providers and also act as a regulation and internal compliance benchmark.

4.1.1 Cloud Security Alliance

Cloud Security Alliance Cloud Controls Matrix (CCM) is one of the most comprehensive cloud-specific frameworks. It provides a complete control framework that maps security controls to industry standards like ISO/IEC 27001, COBIT, NIST, and GDPR. CCM defines over 130 control objectives in 16 domains that cover application security, encryption, governance, and identity and access management (Dobrinić, 2020)

The CSA STAR (Security, Trust, Assurance and Risk) program also facilitates transparency by allowing third-party audit reports and self-assessments to be shared by cloud providers and making provider-specific security procedures visible to customer organizations.

4.1.2 National Institute of Standards and Technology (NIST)

The NIST Cybersecurity Framework (CSF) is also a foundational global model of constructing secure systems. It has five major pillars of Identify, Protect, Detect, Respond, and Recover. For multi-cloud setups, NIST CSF has guidance to list down the risks involved in various cloud offerings and to implement layered protections and incident response planning.

A pertinent NIST document is SP 800-53, which includes detailed security and privacy controls that can be mapped by auditors to cloud provider configurations and practice.

Using these frameworks ensures that structured assessments are accomplished and enhances audit defensibility during regulatory inspections or legal audits.

4.2 Security Auditing Tools and Techniques

Manual audits only go so far in dynamic, ever-changing multi-cloud environments. Automation is key to scaling security assessments and providing real-time visibility. Cloud environments today are enhanced with native and third-party tools that allow continuous auditing among providers.

4.2.1 Native Cloud Auditing Tools

All major cloud vendors include built-in offerings to track user behavior, monitor configurations and enforce security policies

- CloudTrail from AWS: Tracks every call of the APIs in an AWS account so that auditors can track activity, monitor suspicious activity, and verify compliance against governance policies.
- Azure Security Center: Offers a single security management framework that provides threat coverage and compliance evaluations of hybrid and multi-cloud assets. It works with Azure Policy and Microsoft Defender to remediate automatically.
- Google Cloud Security Command Center (SCC): Consolidates findings of vulnerabilities, misconfigurations and threats in a single dashboard. SCC has support for real-time audit logging and can be paired with SIEM solutions.

4.2.2 Cross-Platform Auditing Tools

Organizations typically look to third-party products to gain uniform control over cloud providers by abstracting away from provider-specific variations:

- Cloud Security Posture Management (CSPM) tools such as Prisma Cloud, Wiz, or Orca Security automate security scanning by examining cloud environments for misconfigurations, insecure encryption, and overly privileged identities.
- Security Information and Event Management (SIEM) platforms such as Splunk, IBM QRadar, and Elastic Security collect logs from different sources and apply correlation rules to identify security incidents.
- Cloud Access Security Brokers (CASBs) like McAfee MVISION Cloud and Microsoft Defender for Cloud Apps monitor user activity in SaaS and IaaS to enforce data-protection policy

These tools also facilitate faster processing of auditing along with detection accuracy and policy enforcement consistency between different cloud platforms.

4.3 Security Breach Case Studies

Security breaches in the real-world situation demonstrate the need for stringent proactive audit measures. Insufficient audits without a follow-up may lead to undetected identifiable misconfigurations and weaknesses—resulting in colossal breaches adversely affecting numerous users. (Choudhary et al., 2023)

4.3.1 Capital One Breach

One of the most notable cloud-related hacks was in July 2019 and was carried out by an employee who exploited a misconfigured web application fire wall (WAF) in AWS and leaked customer-sensitive information. More than 100 million credit card applications and 140,000 Social Security numbers were exposed. The root causes were:

- Deficiency of WAF rule auditing
- Over-permissioned IAM roles
- Inadequate logging and anomaly detection

A solid audit approach—involving automated permissive role scans, network security setting monitoring, and real-time alerts on unusual access—would have prevented or substantially mitigated the effects of the breach.

4.3.2 Accenture Cloud Leak

In this case, Accenture left unsecured cloud storage buckets exposed on the internet, potentially leaking IP and confidential business information. Although no confirmed exploitation occurred, the incident highlighted a lack of automated auditing and misconfiguration detection, especially in large-scale multi-cloud deployments where storage services are often deployed in bulk and oversight is difficult.

4.3.3 Lessons Learned

They demonstrate the significance of:

- Least Privilege Auditing of IAM Policy
- Searching infrastructure-as-code templates for security vulnerabilities
- Monitor cloud storage for public exposure
- Forensic readiness through maintaining audit trails

They also demonstrate that gaps in audit practice—whether caused by poor tooling or lack of oversight—have the capacity to convert minor lapses into large data breaches.

4.4 Best Practices in Performing Security Audits

A good security audit in a multi-cloud setup is both strategic and procedural. It should be structured to achieve organization goals and be mindful of the technical differences in different clouds.

4.4.1 Set a Baseline with Frameworks

Audits should be based on widely accepted frameworks (e.g., CSA, NIST, ISO 27001). These determine audit scope, set priorities on controls, and allow security evaluations to be replicable and defensible.

4.4.2 Automate Where Possible

Automation tools can be employed to scan for

- Incorrectly configured security
- Unused credentials
- Over-provisioned IAM roles
- Non-compliant Encryption settings

Routine automation eliminates human mistakes and facilitates ongoing compliance checking.

4.4.3 Implement Continuous Monitoring

Audits need to transition from regular events to ongoing, real-time processes. SIEMs, CSPMs, and workload protection tools need to be set to report anomalies and trigger incident workflow instantly upon identification of abnormalities

4.4.4 Include Manual Reviews for Critical Systems

Some computers still need to be manually checked. These may be:

- Review of IAM policies relating to admin accounts
- Manual penetration testing of exposed APIs

- Encryption key management policy reviews

They provide depth and richness that may be missed by automated software.

4.4.5 Foster Cross-Team Collaboration

Security auditing should not be left to the IT security group alone. Include DevOps, compliance personnel, legal, and business owners so that audits align with operational priorities and regulatory mandates.

4.4.6 Document Everything

Keep thorough audit logs, evidence of remediations, and assessments of risk. These are used to confirm evidence of due diligence in case of audits conducted by regulators, partners, and clients.

Multi-cloud scenarios cannot have security auditing optional—security auditing is a strategic necessity. By integrating tried and tested methodologies, leveraging leading-edge tooling, and drawing inferences about real breaches, companies can define a process for audit that is as much about ensuring compliance as it is about ensuring cybersecurity breaches are minimized. A successful audit is more than a compliance tick box—it is a forward-looking way to build trust, resilience, and a market advantage in a complex cloud landscape.

5. COMPLIANCE IN MULTI-CLOUD ENVIRONMENTS

As cloud adoption is increasing, compliance is a top priority in organizations with multi-cloud infrastructures. From data privacy to industry regulations and compliance requirements, compliance controls storage, data access, data processing, and data transfer. Multi-cloud infrastructures complicate things even further—leaving us with operational diversity, geographical spread, and architectural fragmentation in the mix. (Frej, 2020)

Compared to traditional IT infrastructures where organisations previously owned and entirely controlled their own premises, multi-cloud infrastructures employ third-party platforms in different jurisdictions with differing compliance controls and geographical boundaries. This creates severe compliance challenges in meeting obligations in terms of law and regulation especially when data is dispersed across geography.

Organizational bodies must establish a strong and expandable compliance program applicable to all cloud providers with a view to audit and in accordance with applicable regulatory frameworks to be in compliance and to avoid fines.

5.1 Compliance with Laws and Regulations

Global and local laws govern the storage of information in the cloud, especially where personal information is stored or financial information is involved. Multi-cloud solutions pose yet another level of complexity because compliance will be needed in multiple jurisdictions and with multiple different service providers.

5.1.1 The Impact of GDPR

The General Data Protection Regulation (GDPR) of the European Union is one of the most powerful data privacy laws in the world. Organizations are mandated to process and store personal data of EU residents in fair, lawful, and transparent fashion. Main provisions include:

- Personal data should be stored in the EU or in countries that are deemed to offer sufficient safeguards.
- They should be provided with access to their information and the right to remove it (the "right to be forgotten").
- Breaches of data should be reported to officials within 72 hours.

Data residency is a primary concern in organizations where multi-cloud platforms are in use. It is critical to audit where data actually resides and verify that cloud services employed in multiple providers (for example, AWS, Azure, GCP) do not unintentionally shift or copy data out of compliant regions. (Apeh et al., 2023)

5.1.2 HIPAA, SOX, and Other Industry

Under HIPAA in the health industry, there is strict regulation of storage and transmission of Protected Health Information (PHI). Organizations should guarantee that their cloud vendors can protect clinical data with encryption, access controls, and logging of activity.

Financial institutions are also regulated by the Sarbanes-Oxley Act (SOX) that mandates data integrity and retention and the capacity to detect and report suspicious transactions. Auditable trails and tight controls over financial information are what the act mandates.

Multi-cloud environments need to be architected to allow segregation of duties, encrypt sensitive information, and auditable logs in order to comply with these industry-specific rules. Non-compliance may result in penalties, legal repercussions, and reputational harm.

5.2 Compliance Standards

Various established compliance standards offer frameworks of best practice to assist organizations in securing cloud operations. These standards also assist in helping auditors assess if cloud environments meet key security and privacy standards.

5.2.1 SOC 2 (System and Organisation Controls)

Created by the American Institute of CPAS (AICPA), SOC 2 addresses five trust principles of security, availability, processing integrity, confidentiality, and privacy. A SOC 2 audit validates that a service provider's system is properly designed and operated to satisfy the principles.

Organizations need to verify that their cloud vendors possess a current SOC 2 Type II certification. This accreditation measures controls over time (compared to Type I, which measures controls at a moment in time) and grants higher confidence that compliance is ongoing.

5.2.2 ISO/IEC 27001

This global standard offers a complete Information Security Management Systems (ISMS) model. It specifies requirements to set up, implement, monitor, and continually improve security management.

Most major cloud vendors happen to be certified to the ISO/IEC 27001 standard. Organizations should nonetheless verify that their own applications and settings in the cloud and user behaviour in the cloud environment meet this standard.

5.2.3 PCI-DSS

Compliance with the Payment Card Industry Data Security Standard (PCI-DSS) is mandatory for payment card data processing organizations. PCI-DSS includes controls like encryption, access controls, audit trails, and physical security.

Although some cloud providers do offer PCI-compliant hosting, shared responsibility is again the situation here. Cloud-hosted workloads and applications should be configured in compliant ways and cardholder data environments (CDEs) should be protected from untrusted networks.

5.3 Challenges Faced in Attaining Compliance

Multi-cloud compliance is a multi-layered and complex process. The individual providers all have different configurations, data management capabilities, and geographical reach. This diversity establishes a collection of shared obstacles:

5.3.1 Inconsistent Compliance Controls

Cloud providers will establish their own compliance policies and have varying levels of support for compliance with regulation. The provider may support data storage in a region but another may not have backup levels in a particular location. This is a difficulty when having a documented compliance policy.

5.3.2 Centralized Visibility is Missing

Monitoring compliance with multiple cloud providers is difficult without a shared dashboard technology or analytics technology in place. Many organizations also experience "shadow IT," where unauthorized use of services and compliance blind spots occur.

5.3.3 Data Movement that

Data may automatically transfer between regions in the event of redundancy and performance improvement—perhaps unbeknownst to the user. Transfers of these sorts with no controls and notification may infringe upon data residency laws and create regulatory violations.

5.3.4 Third-Party Risks

Compliance doesn't end with the cloud provider in itself. Third-party applications that most organizations use in cloud environments also represent a risk higher if those applications were not carefully reviewed beforehand. This necessitates due diligence in the vendor evaluations and contractual obligations with regard to data protection.

5.4 Auditing for Compliance

Organizations need to undertake regular and thorough compliance audits in order to tackle these challenges. These audits determine if the cloud setup is in accordance with laws and internal policy guidelines.

5.4.1 Content of Compliance Audits

Compliance audits in a multi-cloud setup usually assess

- Residency of data and sovereignty: Are data storage points in accordance with jurisdictional regulations?
- Access policies: Are IAM policies following the principle of least privilege? Are the access logs being monitored routinely?
- Encryption and key management: Are standards for encryption uniform? Are decryption keys securely stored?
- Logging and monitoring: Are logs centralized and secure? Are suspicious behaviors detected and responded to?
- Incident response: Does there exist a documented and tested breach notification and containment process?
- Vendor compliance: Are third-party vendors audited and contractually committed to being compliant?

5.4.2 Automated Compliance Tools

Automation is important to compliance in cloud environments due to their size and complexity. Current technology can automatically scan configurations and compare them against expected compliance standards in order to signal violations.

Popular tools include:

- AWSC and AWS Audit Manager: Ongoing tracking of resource configurations and evaluating compliance with best practice
- Azure Policy and Compliance Manager: Implement policy definitions and enforce compliance rules on resources.
- Google Cloud Assured Workloads: Provides compliant workloads with inbuilt constraints and monitoring tools.

Third-party scanning from vendors like Tenable, Qualys, and Rapid7 provides multiple cloud provider compliance scanning to simplify consistency in maintenance.

5.4.3 Reporting and Documentation

Following the identification of gaps or violations, organizations should create compliance reports that record:

- Non-conformities and root causes

- Corrective measures implemented
- Timeframes for remediation
- Ongoing monitoring plans

They are important to internal governance, external audit, and accountability to regulators and clients. Today, with the era of multi-cloud, regulatory compliance is not a project to be done once—it is ongoing and continuous in nature. Organizations need to create compliance programs that cut across multiple providers, geographies, and workloads so that all aspects of their cloud environment conform to legal and industry standards. By applying frameworks, taking advantage of automation capabilities and carrying out ongoing audits, firms can effectively handle compliance risk, gain the trust of the stakeholders and eschew expensive fines.

6. RISK MITIGATION STRATEGIES IN MULTI-CLOUD ENVIRONMENTS

Working in a multi-cloud environment offers very high flexibility, scalability and resilience benefits. With it comes a complex and a larger risk environment. Security breach, data loss and compliance failure are threat areas that are incurred through misconfigurations, inconsistent controls across different providers and visibility gaps. Risk mitigation in such a scenario is a recurring process rather than a one-time activity but constant in nature with continuous monitoring, review and optimizing. Organization must be proactive to discover future threat areas, map their impact and also adopt sufficient risk reduction steps compatible with multi-cloud infrastructures.

6.1 Models of Risk

Risk avoidance is initiated by a comprehensive and extensive process of risk assessment. The process of identifying potential risks, evaluating them in terms of their probability and prioritizing them in line of business impact is what successful mitigation strategies must be based on. Risk assessment models provide a place to begin in cases of multi-cloud environments where they are most valuable. (Meiran et al., 2021)

One of the best-known models is NIST Risk Management Framework (RMF). NIST RMF model has a step-by-step process with categorize information systems in it. This process involves identifying correct security controls to apply them, applying them in place, verifying they are operational in nature, authorizing systems for use, and continually monitor. The application of this model enables organization to align the controls with asset criticality and to apply controls over various cloud platforms consistently.

The ISO 31000 standard provides a more holistic enterprise approach towards risk management. It places a great emphasis on setting the risk context, setting and assessing threats, and deciding on alternatives to be considered and reviewing findings on a regular basis. ISO 31000 is widely used in integrating cloud-related risks with business plans. Organisations are made possible through these models to have a common risk register with storage of weaknesses, ownership assignment, and recording of action plans to mitigate them.

6.2 Implementing Mitigation Strategies

Once a risk has been identified and evaluated, organizations must put in place measures to mitigate it. For multi-cloud infrastructures, redundancy and failover planning is where it begins. By dispersing mission-critical functions and data across several cloud vendors, business uptime is assured for provider-related outages. For instance, object storage duplication between AWS and Google Cloud ensures access is never lost even in one of the platforms experiencing any form of outage

Both patch and vulnerability scanning are involved. The cloud environment is constantly changing and has new assets constantly coming out. Scanning tools such as Nessus, Qualys, or Tenable automatically detect exposed interfaces, improper permission setups, and old software. After detecting them, patch management products must be installed in order to have consistent security across different cloud systems. Constant updating will minimize exposure to known exploits and also ensure compliance with regulations.

One of the proactive steps is penetration testing. By mimicking cyber-attacks, organisations are able to discover underlying weaknesses in the form of overly liberal roles, insecure APIs, and vulnerable authenticating features. Such tests performed on a routine basis yield useful information regarding the efficacy of controls in place and help in reinforcing defences.

Disaster recovery and backup planning are essential risk management strategies. Third-party software or cloud-born options can be used to automate cross-cloud and cross-region backup to allow for rapid recovery in data loss scenarios. Organizational RTOs and RPOs must be clearly defined and recovery steps must be exercised on a regular basis to maintain resiliency in a critical situation. (Mohamed, 2024)

6.3 Risk Reporting And Risk Management Framework

Comprehensive risk management is not just about technical controls but also governance, communication, and record-keeping. Firms require tools to review and report risks and respond to them in a constructive and orderly manner.

The COSO Enterprise Risk Management (ERM) framework is among those frameworks used extensively to align risk practice with business goals. COSO ERM focuses on governance and culture, identifying and response planning for risks, and continuous monitoring. The inclusion of risk management in the strategic planning in COSO ERM ensures that risks in cloud computing are examined against general business impact.

The process is facilitated through the help of risk dashboards and reporting tools including ServiceNow, RSA Archer, and Power BI across most organizations. These combine real-time data received through cloud-based monitoring tools, vulnerability scanners, and audit logs to give visual presentations of prevailing risk levels, health of in-place mitigants, and escalations required. Constant and clear reporting helps to align executives and technical teams and guide deployment of resources towards most critical threats. (Bendicho, 2021)

Instituting a thoroughly documented risk governance framework ensures accountability and assists in fostering ongoing improvement and responsiveness to inside oversight and regulation compliance.

6.4 Risk Mitigation Case Study: Netflix

A prominent example of successful risk reduction in a multi-cloud environment is that of Netflix. Though Netflix operates predominantly on Amazon Web Services (AWS), it is also using Google Cloud in specific workloads. This multi-cloud strategy is less about achieving optimal performance—it's a security design to limit dependency upon one provider and ensure the reliability of the service.

Netflix architecture is fault resilient in design. Work is distributed over greater than one region and availability zone and can be migrated among cloud vendors if needed. Chaos engineering tools such as Chaos Monkey simulate failures and verify resilience in the systems. By causing sections of the system to fail in a way that is in their control, Netflix is ensuring that its applications recover very quickly from unplanned downtime.

Other than redundancy setups, Netflix also has scaling and failover automation and continuously checks its cloud environments for outliers. This approach was put to the test during regional AWS outages and was effective because Netflix users did not encounter major disruptions in their experience. Their approach is a demonstration of what multi-cloud risk management can achieve in ensuring continuity of service and protecting user experience even in the event of infrastructure-related downtime. (Banker et al., 2020)

Risk management in multi-cloud is a dynamic and continuous process. Adopting risk assessment standards such as NIST RMF and ISO 31000 helps organizations to methodologically identify and prioritize risks. Real-world solutions such as redundancy of data, vulnerability scanning, patch management, and penetration tests add to resilience even more. Governance frameworks such as COSO ERM help to align risk management with business decision-making, whereas concrete use case examples such as Netflix illustrate the way strategic use of multiple clouds can reduce operational risk by a massive margin.

At a time that sees digital offerings become increasingly critical to the operations of a business, organizations should look to risk prevention not just as a matter of defence but also as a proactive investment in long-term health and customer trust and compliance.

7. CONCLUSION

7.1 Auditing in Multi-Cloud Environments and its Strategic Importance

Multi-cloud is now a business-critical driver of flexibility, innovation and worldwide accessibility in the digital-first economy. Organizations currently utilize a blend of public and private cloud to disperse workloads, avoid relying on one specific vendor and to improve performance. For that reason, with added freedom of architecture in multi-cloud comes great complexity and particularly high complexity in the areas of security, compliance and risk management. (Annunziata et al., 2024)

Against such a scenario, auditing is a matter of strategic need and not of routine practice. Multi-cloud environments' decentralized and dynamic nature necessitates constant assurances that assets in the cloud remain secure, regulatory requirements are met, and organization risk is properly attended to. In traditional infrastructure where there is centralized management that allows easy visibility and management, multi-cloud operations traverse multiple platforms that each has its corresponding tools, policies, and rules of compliance in place. Auditing brings together the disparate landscapes of these in creating visibility, control, and accountability.

Organizations that adopt auditing in a proactive form—inextricably part of their cloud governance strategy—are far more likely to avoid not only breaches, but also to be seen to be taking due care to clients, partners, and regulatory authorities. (Jesudoss et al., 2021)

7.2 Integrating Security, Compliance and Risk into the Audit Lifecycle:

Security, risk mitigation and compliance consist of three pillars that require to be dealt with comprehensively through auditing. Security deals with controls of access restriction, encryption and detection of incidents to mention some. Compliance deals with regulations such as GDPR, HIPAA, SOX and so on that require stiff standards with regards to data residency, visibility of access and breach reporting just to mention some of them. Risk mitigation deals with detection and minimization of disruption of operations, security breach and non-compliance risk and chances.

Multi-cloud auditing is hence multi-faceted and continuous in nature. It is not only a matter of checking that technical controls are set correctly in each case, but of verifying that policies are implemented in identical fashion by all cloud providers. For example, what is the use of having a solid identity and access policy if it is implemented rigidly in one cloud environment and less rigorously in another. In a similar manner, standards compliance in encrypting storage space, databases and communication layers has to be implemented in a uniform fashion regardless of the provider. (Kim & Kim, 2022)

A life cycle of an integrated audit starts with planning and scoping—determining what assets, regulations, and threats come into play. It moves to evidence gathering and analysis where logs, configurations, and access histories are analyzed and finishes with reporting and remediation where gaps are addressed and results are provided to stakeholders.

7.3 Auditing Frameworks and Auditing Standards

A sound audit process is rooted firmly in well-recognized frameworks and standards that offer a structured means of assessing controls to facilitate remediation and to offer standardized reporting. Some of the most useful frameworks in this multi-cloud environment are NIST Risk Management Framework (RMF) and the Cloud Security Alliance's Cloud Controls Matrix (CSA CCM). These include comprehensive controls and mapping tools to align cloud practice both with external regulation and internal policy. (Yang et al., 2020)

Standards like ISO/IEC 27001, ISO 31000, and SOC 2 inform security control implementation, risk management processes, and monitoring in operations, and these are useful in cloud provider selection and diligence reviews. These also facilitate reporting requirements for compliance and certifying purposes and are therefore a critical component of an audit cycle.

By correlating multi-cloud deployments to these frameworks, companies are able to objectively measure the state of security and compliance maturity. Frameworks also serve to bring control expectations and risk terminology to a parity so departments are more in sync with technical teams, risk managers, and executive management.

7.4. Automation and Continual Monitoring: The Audit of Tomorrow

Manual audit processes reliant on cyclical review and older methodologies are less effective in fast-paced cloud landscapes. Where resources are continually being defined, changed and retired in always-changing landscapes, risk is changing in real time. Your company must employ automated audit tools offering real-time monitoring and instant notifications in order to be ahead of the game.

Cloud services like AWS CloudTrail, Azure Security Center and Google Cloud Security Command Center offer telemetry and logging to alert for misconfigurations, abnormalities and policy breaches. These can be integrated with SIEM products or with Cloud Security Posture Management (CSPM) products to collect data and correlate events across different vendors.

Besides detection, automation also provides self-healing. For instance, an automated process can rid the environment of unauthorized access through reconstituting insecure storage or automatically creating compliance reports without human assistance in so doing. This shortens remediation time and enables security controls and compliance to be sustained even in changing infrastructures. (Ali et al., 2024)

As multi-cloud systems continue to scale and become more complex, machine learning and artificial intelligence will increasingly have a part to play. These can identify patterns, anticipate vulnerability and suggest action based on behaviour baselines—delivering a degree of insight and agility unavailable to traditional approaches.

7.5 Risk Mitigation through Strategic Design and Resilience

One of the critical purposes of auditing is to enable risk mitigation—both technical and organization-wise. For multi-cloud setups, besides securing the workloads, it also means that the system should be resilient against failures, outages, and malicious attacks without disrupting business operations.

Organizations should institute multiple risk reduction measures, e.g., data redundancy, geo-graphic failover, and infrastructure diversification. These should be guided by risk assessment models such as NIST RMF or ISO 31000 to prioritize controls by impact and likelihood.

Audits play a key part in confirming the effectiveness of these risk mitigation measures. For instance, disaster recovery plans need to be tested and checked, backup routines audited and penetration tests analyzed for systemic vulnerabilities. In the lack of these verification measures, even the most complete risk mitigation plan can come up short during a real-world scenario.

Examples in the real world that include Netflix's utilization of AWS and Google Cloud to achieve high availability illustrate the way auditing and automation can complement each other to limit the dependency on a particular provider and continue service delivery in case of outages. Such case studies form a usable benchmark for organizations to implement resilience in multi-cloud operations. (Naveena et al., 2020)

7.6 Compliance as a Moving Target: Why Agility is Needed

Regulatory compliance is not static any more. Laws and standards remain to change according to technological developments, geopolitical events, and heightened privacy demands. Emergence of laws such as the General Data Protection Regulation (GDPR), the California Consumer Privacy Act (CCPA), and the Personal Information Protection Law in China (PIPL) has made the landscape of compliance global, disjointed, and rapidly changing.

Compliance rules in a multi-cloud environment must be monitored, translated and enforced in real-time. Cloud data may be required to be relocated or locked down in response to changing data sovereignty legislation, to cite just one example. Service providers will also need to renew their certifications or reporting technology in order to meet heightened audit expectations in similar fashion. (Dhotay et al., 2024)

Organizations must adopt agile compliance programs with the help of automation tools, policy modularity, and ongoing training in order to pace themselves with the speed of the situation. Audits of compliance should not just verify current practice but also project forward to anticipated change. Alignment with legal, compliance, and risk teams ensures that responses from technology and regulators become harmonized.

7.7 Business Advantages of Sound Auditing Practices

Beyond the legal and technical dimensions of auditing, auditing also delivers concrete business value. Good auditing procedures give rise to customer trust, improve partnership and partnership opportunities, and reinforce market credibility. Organizations with a good audit trail in place stand a greater chance of weathering external audit scrutiny, avoiding penalties, and fulfilling government or enterprise-level contracts. (Oqaily et al., 2021)

Internally, cost is optimized by auditing with the identification of idle assets, redundant services and inefficient access controls.These include being cognizant of emerging threats, auditing DevOps and CI/CD pipelines, and implementing tools that offer predictive and prescriptive analytics. Organizations should also establish a security and compliance culture—audit outcomes should not be considered to be in error but seen as opportunities to learn and be resilient.

REFERENCES

Akinade, A. O., Adepoju, P. A., Ige, A. B., & Afolabi, A. I. (2024). Cloud security challenges and solutions: A review of current best practices. *International Journal of Multidisciplinary Research and Growth Evaluation*, *6*(1), 26–35. DOI: 10.54660/. IJMRGE.2025.6.1.26-35

Ali, H., Abidin, S., & Alam, M. A. (2024). Auditing of outsourced data in cloud computing: An overview. *2024 11th International Conference on Computing for Sustainable Global Development (INDIACom)*, 111–117. https://doi.org/DOI: 10.23919/INDIACom61295.2024.10498177

Annunziata, G., Sheykina, A., Palomba, F., De Lucia, A., Catolino, G., & Ferrucci, F. (2024). Security risk assessment on cloud: A systematic mapping study. *Proceedings of the 28th International Conference on Evaluation and Assessment in Software Engineering*. https://doi.org/DOI: 10.1145/3661167.3661287

Banker, R., Li, X., Maex, S., & Shi, W. (2020). The audit implications of cloud computing. *Accounting Horizons*, *34*(4), 1–31. Advance online publication. DOI: 10.2308/HORIZONS-19-166

Bendicho, C. (2021). Cyber security in cloud: Risk assessment models. In *Cybersecurity and Privacy in Cyber Physical Systems* (pp. 471–482). Springer., DOI: 10.1007/978-3-030-80119-9_28

Choudhary, C., Vyas, N., & Lilhore, U. K. (2023). Cloud security: Challenges and strategies for ensuring data protection. *2023 3rd International Conference on Technological Advancements in Computational Sciences (ICTACS)*, 669–673. https://doi.org/DOI: 10.1109/ICTACS59847.2023.10390302

Dhotay, M., Mitra, A., Suryawanshi, A. S., Bangare, S. L., & Tiwari, A. (2024). Securing cloud infrastructures: A multi-layered approach to data protection. *Computer Fraud & Security*, 126–133. Advance online publication. DOI: 10.52710/cfs.69

Dobrinić, D. (2020). *Conceptual model for cloud computing acceptance in the audit profession*. Informatologia., DOI: 10.32914/i.53.3-4.6

Folorunso, A., Babalola, O., Nwatu, C. E., & Adedoyin, A. (2024). A comprehensive model for ensuring data compliance in cloud computing environment. *World Journal of Advanced Research and Reviews*, *24*(2), 3514. Advance online publication. DOI: 10.30574/wjarr.2024.24.2.3514

Frej, M. B. H. (2020). Light-weight accountable privacy-preserving protocol in cloud computing based on a third-party auditor. *[Conference name or journal missing]*.

Hashim, W., & Hussein, N. A. K. (2024). *Securing cloud computing environments: An analysis of multi-tenancy vulnerabilities and countermeasures*. SHIFRA., DOI: 10.70470/SHIFRA/2024/002

Hazela, B., Gupta, S. K., Soni, N., & Saranya, C. (2022). Securing the confidentiality and integrity of cloud computing data. *ECS Transactions*. https://doi.org/DOI: 10.1149/10701.2651ecst

Jesudoss, A., Lakshmanan, L., & Christy, A., MercyTheresa, M., & Jayaprakash, S. (2021). Public auditing in cloud environment for secure data sharing. *Proceedings of the First International Conference on Advanced Scientific Innovation in Science, Engineering and Technology (ICASISET)*. https://doi.org/DOI: 10.4108/eai.16-5-2020.2303943

Kim, D., & Kim, K. S. (2022). Privacy-preserving public auditing for shared cloud data with secure group management. *IEEE Access, PP*, 1–1. https://doi.org/DOI: 10.1109/ACCESS.2022.3169793

Kumar, M., Maple, C., & Chand, S. (2023). An efficient and secure identity-based integrity auditing scheme for sensitive data with anti-replacement attack on multi-cloud storage. *Journal of King Saud University. Computer and Information Sciences*, *35*(9), 101745. DOI: 10.1016/j.jksuci.2023.101745

Liu, Y. (2024). Build an audit framework for data privacy protection in cloud environment. *Procedia Computer Science*, *247*, 166–175. Advance online publication. DOI: 10.1016/j.procs.2024.10.020

Majumdar, S., Chawla, G., Alimohammadifar, A., Madi, T., Jarraya, Y., Pourzandi, M., Wang, L., & Debbabi, M. (2022). ProSAS: Proactive security auditing system for clouds. *IEEE Transactions on Dependable and Secure Computing*, *19*(4), 2517–2534. DOI: 10.1109/TDSC.2021.3062204

Meiran, G., Unkašević, T., Banjac, Z., & Milosavljevic, M. (2021). Automated compliance system for service organizations. *Sinteza*, 21–27. https://doi.org/DOI: 10.15308/Sinteza-2021-21-27

Mohamed, M. M. (2024). The impact of cloud computing on activating the role of risk-based internal audit and its reflection on the organization's financial performance - An empirical study. https://doi.org/DOI: 10.21608/atasu.2024.348955

Naveena, P., Soundarya, R. S., & Mohanapriya, K. A. (2020). Light weight secure auditing scheme for shared data in cloud storage. *International Journal of Engineering Research & Technology (Ahmedabad)*, •••, 8.

Oqaily, M., Jarraya, Y., Mohammady, M., Majumdar, S., Pourzandi, M., Wang, L., & Debbabi, M. (2021). SegGuard: Segmentation-based anonymization of network data in clouds for privacy-preserving security auditing. *IEEE Transactions on Dependable and Secure Computing*, *18*, 2486–2505. DOI: 10.1109/TDSC.2019.2957488

Reddy, H. M. (2023). *Cloud security compliance: Challenges, solutions, and impact on enterprises*. International Journal for Multidisciplinary Research., DOI: 10.36948/ijfmr.2023.v05i04.19118

Reece, M., Lander, T., Mittal, S., Rastogi, N., Dykstra, J., & Sampson, A. (2023). Emergent (in)security of multi-cloud environments. *arXiv, abs/2311.01247*. https://doi.org//arXiv.2311.01247DOI: 10.48550

Reece, M., Lander, T., Stoffolano, M., Sampson, A., Dykstra, J., Mittal, S., & Rastogi, N. (2023). Systemic risk and vulnerability analysis of multi-cloud environments. *arXiv, abs/2306.01862*. https://doi.org//arXiv.2306.01862DOI: 10.48550

Seetharamarao, R. Y. (2023). A unified approach towards security audit and compliance in cloud computing environment. *2023 16th International Conference on Developments in eSystems Engineering (DeSE)*, 623–629. https://doi.org/DOI: 10.1109/DeSE60595.2023.10469536

Singh, A. (2023). Secure auditing and deduplicating data in cloud. *International Journal for Research in Applied Science and Engineering Technology*, *11*(5), 6530–6534. Advance online publication. DOI: 10.22214/ijraset.2023.53343

Singh, T., & Kumar, A. M. (2023). Analyzing security and privacy issues for multi-cloud service providers using Nessus. *2023 Fifth International Conference on Electrical, Computer and Communication Technologies (ICECCT)*, 1–8. https://doi.org/DOI: 10.1109/ICECCT56650.2023.10179727

Tian, H., Wang, M., Quan, H., Chang, C.-C., & Vasilakos, A. V. (2025). TEEMRDA: Leveraging trusted execution environments for multi-replica data auditing in cloud storage. *Computers & Security*, *150*, 104250. DOI: 10.1016/j.cose.2024.104250

Wang, S., Yu, M., Zhao, M., & Wang, H. (2024). Blockchain-based cloud data auditing scheme in multi-cloud storage service environment. *2024 27th International Conference on Computer Supported Cooperative Work in Design (CSCWD)*, 669–674. https://doi.org/DOI: 10.1109/CSCWD61410.2024.10580186

Yang, X., Wang, M., Li, T., Liu, R., & Wang, C. (2020). Privacy-preserving cloud auditing for multiple users scheme with authorization and traceability. *IEEE Access : Practical Innovations, Open Solutions*, *8*, 130866–130877. DOI: 10.1109/ACCESS.2020.3009539

Chapter 8
Auditing IT Applications for Risk Management and Strategic Optimization

Varun Razdan
https://orcid.org/0009-0002-7069-2009
University at Buffalo, SUNY, USA

Aman Modi
University at Buffalo, SUNY, USA

Dinesh Kanna Aranganathan
https://orcid.org/0009-0007-3117-0538
University at Buffalo, SUNY, USA

Manish Gupta
University at Buffalo, SUNY, USA

Raj Sharman
https://orcid.org/0000-0001-5838-7330
University at Buffalo, SUNY, USA

ABSTRACT

This chapter presents a comprehensive strategy for auditing IT application portfolios to mitigate risks, enhance governance, and drive strategic optimization. Targeted at IT auditors, risk professionals, and enterprise architects, it integrates frameworks such as CISA, COBIT, ITIL, SOC 2, NIST, and ISO 27001 to guide practices in inventory validation, business alignment, cost-effectiveness, technical risk, and cloud readiness. Structured tools like checklists, the TIME model, and dashboards support a systematic audit process. A hypothetical case study illustrates practical

DOI: 10.4018/979-8-3373-3078-5.ch008

application across multi-industry and multi-region settings, demonstrating how audit-driven insights can uncover redundancies, improve lifecycle health, and strengthen operational resilience. This chapter per the authors emphasizes that a well-governed application portfolio audit not only ensures compliance and risk mitigation but also enables substantial cost savings and better alignment with modernization goals.

INTRODUCTION

Modern enterprises rely on a vast array of software applications to support business processes, but unmanaged growth of the application portfolio can lead to *application sprawl* – duplicated functions, rising costs, and increased operational risk (Theseira, 2024; Faddom, 2023). *Application Portfolio Management (APM)* is the discipline that governs applications throughout their lifecycle to maximize business value delivery (Global Affairs Canada, 2022). Effective APM involves maintaining a comprehensive inventory of applications and continuously assessing each for its business value, technical health, cost, and risk, so that informed decisions can be made on which applications to **keep, modernize, or eliminate** (Global Affairs Canada, 2022; CIO Council & C&I CoP, 2020). In practice, however, many organizations struggle with incomplete application inventories, siloed ownership, outdated systems, and misaligned resources, prompting the need for rigorous auditing of the application portfolio.

Auditing an IT application portfolio is a systematic approach to evaluating how well an organization catalogs, governs, and optimizes its software applications. Unlike a one-time project, portfolio auditing is often a continuous or periodic activity woven into IT governance and risk management programs (Theseira, 2024). The goal is twofold: **assurance** – verifying that controls and best practices are in place for managing the portfolio, and **advisory** – identifying opportunities to streamline and enhance the portfolio for better business alignment and cost-effectiveness.

This paper examines strategies for auditing application portfolios effectively. It bridges *practical techniques* (like inventory validation, scoring models, and tool-supported analysis) with *theoretical frameworks* that auditors and IT managers commonly use. Frameworks such as ISACA's CISA and COBIT 2019, ITIL 4's Portfolio Management practice, AICPA's SOC 2 trust principles, NIST's Cybersecurity Framework and Risk Management Framework, and ISO/IEC 27001's controls on asset management all inform the standards for a well-governed application portfolio. By aligning the audit approach with these recognized frameworks, auditors can ensure comprehensive coverage of governance, risk, and compliance aspects (Wiseman, 2025).

Key focus areas addressed include: verifying the *accuracy and completeness of application inventories* (as a foundation for any optimization), evaluating *business alignment and value* of applications (ensuring each system supports organizational objectives), assessing *cost-effectiveness* and *total cost of ownership (TCO)*, scrutinizing *technical risks* such as outdated technologies reaching end-of-service-life, identifying *functional redundancies* in the portfolio (duplicate or overlapping applications), and reviewing *operational resilience* (the ability of critical applications to withstand and recover from disruptions). Given the accelerating shift to cloud computing, the audit strategies also cover *cloud migration readiness* assessments and the complexities of *multi-cloud environments*. We discuss how auditors can approach these areas, supported by illustrative tools like checklists, scoring matrices (including the Gartner **TIME** quadrant – Tolerate, Invest, Migrate, Eliminate – for categorizing applications (Bittler & Kreizman, 2010)), and automated dashboards for portfolio analytics.

Throughout the paper, we incorporate examples and a hypothetical case study to ground the concepts in real-world context. We reference an integrated toolkit (similar in capabilities to a Technology Portfolio Strategy toolkit used in industry) to demonstrate a cohesive approach to data gathering, analysis, and reporting, without naming any proprietary product. This hypothetical scenario, along with multi-industry and multi-region considerations, illustrates how the audit strategies can be adapted to different organizational contexts – from highly regulated sectors (e.g. finance or healthcare) to global enterprises operating across diverse jurisdictions.

In summary, an *effective audit of the IT application portfolio* serves as both a **governance mechanism** – ensuring that management has accurate insights and controls over their applications – and a **value optimization lever** – spotlighting opportunities to reduce costs (often by up to 30% of portfolio TCO through rationalization (Grant Thornton Bharat, 2021)), mitigate risks, and improve the alignment of IT capabilities with business strategy. The following sections provide a structured exploration of these strategies, guidelines for implementation, and references to established best practices and standards.

Frameworks and Governance Standards for Portfolio Auditing

Before diving into specific audit techniques, it is important to understand the governance frameworks and standards that set expectations for managing and auditing IT application portfolios. These frameworks provide principles and controls that auditors can use as benchmarks for evaluating an organization's portfolio management practices:

- **COBIT 2019 (Control Objectives for Information and Related Technology):** COBIT is a widely used IT governance framework that includes guidance on managing IT investments and portfolios. COBIT emphasizes aligning IT resources and projects with enterprise goals and optimizing value delivery. For instance, COBIT's process *APO05 Manage Portfolio* highlights the importance of maintaining an up-to-date portfolio of IT investments (including applications) to ensure they align with the overall business strategy (Kempwad, 2024). Effective portfolio management under COBIT enables informed decision-making, resource optimization, and value maximization (Kempwad, 2024). An audit of application portfolio optimization will often check for COBIT-aligned practices, such as governance structures assigning clear accountability for the portfolio, evaluation of application value against business objectives, and regular reporting on portfolio performance.
- **ITIL 4 Service Portfolio Management:** In ITIL (Information Technology Infrastructure Library), managing the service portfolio is a key practice to ensure that the IT service provider has the *right mix of services (and underlying applications)* to meet business needs at an appropriate level of investment (IT Process Wiki, n.d.). ITIL's guidance is that organizations should continuously assess their service and application portfolio to eliminate obsolete services and invest in those that deliver value. Auditors might leverage ITIL principles by checking if the organization periodically reviews its application portfolio for viability and alignment, and whether *service portfolio reviews* occur to keep the portfolio aligned with business outcomes (IT Process Wiki, n.d.). For example, ITIL recommends regular portfolio review meetings to ensure the application landscape remains economically viable and strategically aligned (IT Process Wiki, n.d.).
- **CISA and IT Audit Framework:** The Certified Information Systems Auditor (CISA) framework and ISACA's IT Assurance Framework (ITAF) provide standards for how IT audits should be planned and executed. A core principle is a **risk-based audit approach** (Cooke, 2019). Auditors should assess the risk profile of the application portfolio (considering factors like criticality of applications, known security vulnerabilities, compliance requirements, etc.) and allocate audit resources accordingly (Cooke, 2019). CISA guidance also underscores evaluating IT governance, ensuring that processes like application portfolio management have proper oversight by senior management and alignment with enterprise risk management. In practice, when auditing application portfolios, a CISA-certified auditor will verify that the organization has policies and procedures for application lifecycle management, that roles and responsibilities for portfolio decisions are defined, and that there's a process to regularly assess application performance and risks. If the organization

employs frameworks like COBIT or ITIL, the auditor will map controls and activities to those best practices.

- **NIST Cybersecurity Framework & NIST SP 800-53:** The NIST CSF's first function, **Identify**, includes *Asset Management* – maintaining an inventory of hardware and software assets (including applications) to manage cybersecurity risk (Wiseman, 2025). An accurate application inventory is foundational for security and risk management, as one cannot protect or optimize what is not known. NIST SP 800-53 (Rev. 5) provides specific controls such as CM-8 "System Component Inventory," which requires organizations to develop and maintain an inventory of information system components (like applications), with attributes such as owner, version, and status. For an application portfolio audit, NIST provides criteria to check against: Does the organization have a documented inventory of all applications including those in cloud environments? Is it updated regularly? Are there procedures to identify and track *End-of-Life software* and ensure timely upgrades or mitigation? NIST guidance also ties inventory to risk assessments – e.g., identifying which applications are critical or contain sensitive data. Thus, auditors often check compliance with NIST-based policies: for example, verifying that *all applications and their supporting infrastructure are inventoried and classified* (perhaps in a configuration management database) as required by internal policy or standards like NIST CSF (Wiseman, 2025).
- **ISO/IEC 27001 (Information Security Management) and ISO 27002:** ISO 27001 includes controls for asset management (Annex A.8 in ISO 27001:2013, updated in ISO 27002:2022) which require organizations to have an inventory of information assets (including application software) and assign ownership (Wiseman, 2025). The purpose is to ensure each application is accounted for and has an owner responsible for its security and value. In the context of portfolio optimization, ISO 27001's focus is on protecting information assets, so an auditor will ensure that applications especially those supporting critical or sensitive processes are identified in the asset register, have owners, and have classification (e.g., confidentiality, integrity, availability requirements) documented. Furthermore, ISO 27001's controls around change management and system acquisition (Annex A.14) imply that new applications should go through a formal process – an area which an audit might examine to see if *portfolio governance* is integrated with project governance (i.e., avoiding random acquisition of redundant applications without proper review). An auditor might cite ISO standards to support recommendations like: *Establish and maintain a formal application inventory, as required by international security standards, to underpin both security and optimization efforts* (Wiseman, 2025).

- **SOC 2 (Service Organization Control 2) Reports:** SOC 2 is a framework for auditing service organizations against Trust Services Criteria (security, availability, processing integrity, confidentiality, privacy). For companies providing cloud services or operating critical systems, a SOC 2 audit will examine how well they manage their software environment. One criterion under **security** and **availability** is having an inventory of system components and managing changes. SOC 2 emphasizes that organizations identify and manage applications that process customer data (Wiseman, 2025). In an enterprise's internal context, SOC 2 principles can be applied to assess if applications (especially those impacting financial reporting or customer data) are documented and controlled. If an organization or its auditors are looking to align with SOC 2, they will want to see evidence that the application portfolio is not an unknown black box – it should show that management knows what applications exist, what data they handle, and what their reliability and security postures are. For example, SOC 2 compliance would support having **up-to-date inventories and documentation for all in-scope applications** as part of demonstrating proper control over technology that stores or processes sensitive data (Wiseman, 2025).
- **Other Regulatory Frameworks:** Depending on industry, there are additional standards: e.g., **PCI-DSS** (for payment systems) explicitly requires maintaining an inventory of system components including software that is in the cardholder data environment (Wiseman, 2025). **HIPAA** in healthcare expects covered entities to track systems that handle electronic protected health information (Wiseman, 2025). Auditors in regulated industries must incorporate these specific requirements into the portfolio audit. For instance, an audit of a hospital's application portfolio must ensure that any application touching patient data is identified and has proper controls per HIPAA, and any unsupported legacy software is flagged as a compliance risk.

In summary, frameworks like COBIT and ITIL provide *best-practice benchmarks* for value alignment and process governance, while standards like NIST, ISO, and SOC 2 provide *control requirements* especially around inventory and risk management. An effective portfolio audit uses these frameworks as a lens: **Does the organization have the structures, processes, and data required by these standards to optimize and control its application portfolio?** The next sections translate these high-level principles into concrete audit focus areas and methodologies.

AUDIT METHODOLOGY AND KEY FOCUS AREAS

Auditing an IT application portfolio is not a one-size-fits-all task; it requires a structured, risk-based methodology that systematically addresses inventory completeness, business alignment, cost, technical health, and future readiness. This section outlines a streamlined, yet effective approach grounded in widely accepted frameworks like COBIT, ITIL, and ISO 27001. Each audit step is designed to yield insights that support rationalization, risk mitigation, and optimization of the application landscape.

1. Planning and Scoping

The audit begins with planning and risk scoping. This phase sets the foundation for the entire engagement by defining what will be audited, the rationale for the selection, and the approach that will be taken. Auditors prioritize high-risk areas such as applications supporting financial reporting, customer data, regulatory functions, or those undergoing major changes (e.g., migration to cloud, integration due to M&A). Inputs like existing inventories, business roadmaps, previous audit reports, and stakeholder interviews help shape the scope.

Key stakeholders include business application owners, IT operations, enterprise architects, finance controllers, and information security teams. The audit team defines evaluation criteria for business fit, technical health, cost, and risk exposure. This ensures consistency across the portfolio and allows scoring or heat maps to be produced later. The planning process should also establish thresholds (e.g., "retire if score < X") to guide actionable recommendations (Cooke, 2019).

Best practice recommends conducting portfolio audits at least annually, with shared ownership between the IT PMO, enterprise architecture, and internal audit functions to maintain accountability and momentum. The audit methodology should also integrate with broader IT governance and risk management programs to ensure findings translate into enterprise-level risk mitigation and investment decisions.

2. Inventory Validation

An accurate and up-to-date application inventory is the foundation of portfolio audit. However, many organizations struggle to maintain a single source of truth. Common issues include:

- Duplicate records across departments
- Applications with no assigned technical or business owner
- Inconsistent data on cost, platform, version, or support status

- "Ghost apps" (retired systems still listed)
- Shadow IT (tools in use but not listed)

The audit validates the inventory through cross-referencing CMDBs, financial systems, cloud billing tools, and security systems. Automated discovery tools (e.g., ServiceNow Discovery, Device42) can help identify running systems. Interviews with IT owners also reveal discrepancies or legacy systems missed by scanning. According to Global Affairs Canada (2022), 7% of applications lacked a defined business owner, and many still had references to outdated technology stacks. Maintaining a validated inventory is also a compliance requirement under ISO 27001 Annex A.8 and SOC 2 CC1.2 (Wiseman, 2025).

Auditors should also examine integration points and dependencies between applications. Mapping upstream/downstream data flows, shared infrastructure, and API usage is critical for impact analysis, especially when recommending retirement, consolidation, or cloud migration.

3. Business Value and Strategic Alignment

Each application must be tied to a business capability or process to justify its place in the portfolio. This step evaluates business fit using criteria such as:

- Alignment with strategic objectives
- Support for revenue-generating or mission-critical processes
- User satisfaction and adoption metrics
- Contribution to regulatory or risk functions

Auditors conduct interviews with business owners and process leads to assign qualitative or quantitative scores to each application. The Gartner TIME model (Tolerate, Invest, Migrate, Eliminate) is often used to categorize applications (LeanIX, n.d.). For instance, an outdated mobile app with low user ratings and high maintenance costs may fall into the Eliminate quadrant, while a scalable, well-rated app might qualify for further investment.

As Theseira (2024) notes, aligning APM with evolving business strategy is essential. Regular scoring ensures agility in reprioritizing investments and helps avoid sunk cost bias.

Auditors should also consider each application's position in its lifecycle, whether it's in early adoption, active growth, maturity, or decline. Applications in decline with rising maintenance costs and low business value are usually prime candidates for retirement.

4. Cost Assessment and Redundancy

Cost visibility is frequently poor in large enterprises, particularly for SaaS and internal tools funded through indirect budgets. The audit assesses:

- Licensing costs (actual vs. entitled usage)
- Infrastructure and hosting costs (on-prem vs. cloud)
- Application-specific project spending
- Staff effort for maintenance and support

Underused applications, where license utilization is <50% may be classified as shelfware. Redundancy checks often reveal multiple tools performing similar functions (e.g., five analytics tools, three CRM platforms). Auditors may create a heatmap or rationalization table to group overlapping tools.

Torii (2023) notes that rationalization of underused or redundant software can reduce TCO by up to 30%. However, initial savings often range from 10–15% depending on organizational readiness (Grant Thornton Bharat, 2021). Cost reduction should be balanced against user disruption, vendor lock-in, and data migration risks.

Some organizations are also beginning to assess application sustainability by measuring energy usage and infrastructure footprint. Retiring high-energy legacy systems or migrating to greener cloud platforms can support broader ESG goals.

5. Technical Risk and Lifecycle Status

Technical debt is one of the most overlooked risk areas in application portfolios. This audit dimension evaluates:

- End-of-life (EOL) or unsupported components
- Number of incidents or downtime events
- Code quality and maintainability
- Architecture compliance (e.g., microservices, containers, cloud-native)

Tools like the Application Portfolio Health Index (APHI) aggregate business, technical, and financial indicators to provide an overall health score (Global Affairs Canada, 2022). LeanIX (2022) highlights that outdated frameworks and unpatched systems pose significant security and operational risks.

Auditors also check whether applications have current patching practices, automated CI/CD pipelines, and technical roadmaps. Findings here often influence prioritization in modernization plans.

In addition, audits should verify access control hygiene, ensuring that role-based access control (RBAC), single sign-on (SSO), and identity federation are in place and aligned with corporate IAM standards.

6. Operational Resilience

Resilience assessment focuses on whether business-critical applications can survive outages, disasters, or cyber events. The audit examines:

- Existence of disaster recovery (DR) plans
- Frequency and outcomes of DR tests
- Recovery time objectives (RTOs) and recovery point objectives (RPOs)
- Hosting arrangements (on-prem, multi-region cloud, hybrid)

Global Affairs Canada (2022) found that only 6 out of 10 critical apps had documented DR plans. Audits may also uncover single points of failure, such as all backups stored onsite or multiple critical systems hosted in a single data center. These risks can be mitigated by secondary hosting, cloud backups, or active-active configurations.

Auditors should also verify the presence of logging, monitoring, and audit trails for applications handling sensitive data or subject to regulatory oversight. These capabilities are essential for post-incident forensics and compliance reporting.

7. Cloud Readiness and Multi-Cloud Governance

With most organizations pursuing cloud-first strategies, audits must examine how cloud decisions are being made. Key questions include:

- Has a cloud readiness assessment been completed?
- Are migration plans backed by data (e.g., cost, latency, complexity)?
- Are tagging, access, and policy controls consistent across cloud providers?

AWS Prescriptive Guidance recommends a six-step cloud migration model, starting with discovery and readiness scoring (Goncalves & Berner, 2024). Auditors also check if governance frameworks exist for SaaS onboarding, IaaS security, and cost reporting.

Multi-cloud environments introduce additional risks, New Horizons (2024) note that organizations often lack unified monitoring or tagging, making visibility and cost tracking difficult. Auditors flag non-compliant configurations (e.g., EU data stored in U.S. regions) as data sovereignty risks, referencing GDPR and ISO 27001.

TOOLS AND TECHNIQUES FOR AUDITING APPLICATION PORTFOLIOS

Auditing an IT application portfolio benefits greatly from structured tools and repeatable methodologies. These tools bring consistency, objectivity, and the ability to handle complex and large-scale environments. This section outlines and elaborates on essential categories of tools used in portfolio audits: checklists, scoring models, visualization techniques, automation, and reporting mechanisms. When combined, they enable auditors to uncover critical gaps, rationalize redundant systems, and guide strategic IT decisions. Tool selection and audit depth may vary depending on the organization's portfolio size, regulatory environment, and digital maturity.

When selecting tools and techniques for an application portfolio audit, several factors should be considered: portfolio size, regulatory exposure, cloud maturity, available in-house expertise, integration capabilities, and budget. For example, a large enterprise operating across multiple geographies may benefit from an enterprise-grade APM suite with GRC integration, while a mid-sized organization may rely on Excel templates paired with discovery tools and lightweight visualization platforms.

1. Checklists and Assessment Frameworks

Checklists grounded in COBIT, ITIL, ISO 27001, NIST CSF, and SOC 2 provide a reliable structure to audit a wide range of dimensions:

- Inventory Validation: Auditors use structured prompts to validate whether an application inventory exists, is up to date, and includes attributes such as owner, platform, version, and cost. Common questions include: “Is the inventory centralized and current?”, “Are both business and technical owners assigned?”, and “Have CMDB or discovery tools been reconciled with manual inventories?” (Wiseman, 2025; Global Affairs Canada, 2022).
- Business Alignment: Questions focus on whether each application supports a defined business capability, contributes to KPIs, or aligns with strategic priorities. Auditors verify if business owners have validated application value recently and whether value scores are linked to enterprise goals (Theseira, 2024).
- Cost and License Use: Checklists confirm whether usage is tracked, licenses are right-sized, and whether multiple tools overlap in functionality. This helps flag shelfware and rationalization targets (Torii, 2023).
- Technical Health and Security: These evaluate support status (e.g., end-of-life components), patch currency, code review status, and adherence to architecture standards. Frameworks like ISO 27001 A.9 and SOC 2 CC6 are refer-

enced to assess identity and access management, patching, and vulnerability monitoring (LeanIX, 2022; VMware Tanzu Labs, 2023).

- Cloud Readiness and Resilience: Auditors check for cloud strategy documentation, completed readiness assessments, multi-cloud policy enforcement, DR testing history, and region-specific compliance like GDPR data residency (Goncalves & Berner, 2024).

Checklists also serve a critical documentation function, enabling auditors to show adherence to standards and traceability of recommendations. Results from checklist audits can be aggregated into a compliance heatmap or checklist scorecard, allowing executives to see control maturity briefly. Additionally, many frameworks offer pre-built toolkits or templates to accelerate checklist development.

2. Scoring Models and Matrices

Scoring introduces a structured way to compare and prioritize applications. Models allow subjective stakeholder input and objective data to be synthesized:

- Gartner TIME Model: A widely used framework plotting applications based on Technical Condition and Functional Value. Apps in the Eliminate quadrant often exhibit low value and high maintenance cost; Invest apps offer strategic or innovation potential (Bittler & Kreizman, 2010).
- Business Value vs. Cost Matrix: This model helps isolate applications that are high-cost but low-value, often prime candidates for retirement or consolidation. Conversely, low-cost, high-value applications may qualify for further investment.
- Risk Heat Maps: Applications are scored across likelihood and impact dimensions (e.g., security risk, operational failure), and then plotted visually to highlight priority areas for mitigation.
- Application Portfolio Health Index (APHI): Combines metrics such as business fit, technical health, lifecycle stage, funding status, and compliance posture into a single, trackable score (Global Affairs Canada, 2022).

Auditors should validate that the scoring logic is consistent, that source data is current, and that outliers are investigated. Scoring frameworks may be customized organizations often weigh cost, security risk, or business value differently depending on audit goals. Visualization of scoring (e.g., bubble charts, quadrant plots) helps drive stakeholder conversations and decision-making.

3. Automation and Discovery Tools

Automation is vital in portfolios with hundreds or thousands of applications. Tools assist in data collection, validation, visualization, and issue tracking:

- Discovery and Inventory: Tools like ServiceNow Discovery, Lansweeper, and Device42 scan networks and environments to identify running applications, platforms, dependencies, and hosts. This is essential for reconciling against manual lists.
- Application Portfolio Management Suites: LeanIX, ServiceNow APM, and BizzDesign allow centralized tracking of lifecycle status, business alignment, TCO, and risk scores. These platforms support integration with EA, finance, and GRC systems.
- Dependency Mapping Tools: Products like Faddom or Auvik help visualize app-to-app and app-to-database dependencies, useful for impact analysis, cloud migration, and redundancy detection.
- Data Collection Templates: Auditors often design structured Excel or online forms to capture consistent inputs from application owners, covering ownership, cost, users, licensing, integrations, and known issues.
- Issue and Follow-Up Management: Audit observations and remediation plans are tracked via platforms like Jira, ServiceNow GRC, or specialized audit software to ensure accountability.

Automation reduces audit fatigue, speeds up validation, and allows auditors to spend more time on insight and recommendations. Emerging APM platforms are incorporating AI to suggest rationalization candidates, flag outliers, and auto-classify applications based on usage and metadata. AI-enabled platforms can also perform predictive analysis, for instance, flagging applications likely to exceed budget based on past cost trends or identifying candidates for retirement based on usage patterns, lifecycle stage, and redundancy mapping.

Despite their value, tool integration can pose challenges. Data inconsistencies across CMDBs, licensing systems, and cloud platforms often require manual reconciliation. Moreover, security and access controls may restrict discovery tooling from reaching certain segments of the environment, requiring creative workarounds or business engagement.

4. Visualization Techniques

Effective visualization helps communicate audit findings to stakeholders who may not be technical or familiar with risk frameworks. Popular visualization formats include:

- Heat Maps: Used to depict compliance status, technical debt levels, lifecycle stages, or audit scoring across business units or domains.
- TIME Quadrant or Value-Risk Plots: A bubble chart showing where each app stands based on risk, value, and size of cost (bubble size). It clearly communicates which apps are critical, overspending, or obsolete.
- Application Roadmaps: Visual timelines (e.g., Gantt charts) that show when applications will be retired, modernized, migrated, or replaced.
- Stack Diagrams: Show how applications are layered by business function, infrastructure, and integration. Useful for identifying duplication or concentration.

These tools support not only executive reporting but also workshop discussions during strategy or budgeting cycles. Interactive dashboards (e.g., via PowerBI or Tableau) enable real-time portfolio workshops, helping teams simulate "what-if" scenarios and prioritize actions collaboratively.

5. Reporting and Communication

Well-structured reporting is essential to translate audit findings into organizational action. Formats typically include:

- Executive Summary Dashboards: Condense audit status into a single page showing number of apps, % with DR coverage, % redundant, estimated savings, and compliance gaps.
- Detailed Findings Tables: For each issue, include affected applications, risk rating, recommended action, estimated cost/impact, and responsible team.
- Scoring Appendices: Show full matrices of business fit, technical risk, and lifecycle scores, supporting transparency and follow-up.
- Checklist Compliance Reports: Show pass/fail results by ISO or SOC 2 control, useful for integrated audits.
- Use Case Snapshots: Include anonymized or illustrative mini-cases like "Two CRMs serving the same region," "Legacy app with unsupported database," or "Customer portal with no assigned owner."

These reports become critical inputs for annual IT planning, funding requests, and CIO briefings. Tailoring reports to different audiences - executives, enterprise architects, and risk managers, ensures each group receives the level of detail and context they need to act.

HYPOTHETICAL CASE STUDY: PORTFOLIO AUDIT IN PRACTICE

Background: *FinServe Corp* is a hypothetical financial services company operating in multiple regions (North America, Europe, and Asia). Over decades, it accumulated ~250 applications, ranging from core banking systems to customer-facing mobile apps and numerous internal support systems. FinServe has grown through acquisitions, resulting in overlapping systems (for instance, two online banking platforms from different acquired banks) and a mix of technologies (mainframe COBOL systems, .NET applications, Java microservices, and a growing number of SaaS subscriptions). The CIO of FinServe has flagged application rationalization as a priority to reduce costs (IT budget is heavily consumed by maintaining legacy apps) and to improve agility (developers complain that integrating new digital services is slow due to the complex legacy environment). An internal audit is initiated to assess the IT application portfolio and recommend optimization strategies, aligning with corporate goals of cloud-first modernization and improved operational resilience, while of course maintaining compliance with stringent financial regulations.

Audit Process: The internal audit team follows the methodology outlined in previous sections:

1. **Planning:** Audit scope is enterprise-wide but will focus on business-critical applications and areas of known pain (like the post-merger overlaps). The audit team references COBIT and CISA guidelines to ensure a risk-based approach (Cooke, 2019)– for example, prioritizing auditing the core banking and payment systems (very high impact), while sampling some less critical internal tools. They assemble initial data: existing CMDB entries, a list of applications by the IT department, and previous risk assessments. Right away, they notice discrepancies – the IT list shows 240 applications, but an inventory from a recent consultancy report mentioned "approximately 300 applications" in use. This raises a red flag about inventory completeness. The audit team plans to use a survey and automated scan to reconcile this.
2. **Data Collection:** The auditors deploy an **automated discovery tool** on FinServe's network and cloud accounts. This tool finds 260 distinct application deployments. Some turned out to be different instances of the same application, but it

also uncovers a few shadow IT systems – e.g., a marketing-run SaaS platform for customer analytics that was not in the official IT inventory. Meanwhile, the auditors circulate a questionnaire (based on an APM template) to each business unit and application owner. Questions cover the basics (name, purpose, owner), as well as ratings for business satisfaction and known issues. The team also asks: "If you could get rid of two applications without any loss of functionality, which would they be?" to gauge which apps are seen as redundant or burdensome by staff. The response rate is high (since leadership mandated cooperation). Through this, auditors compile a unified inventory of 275 applications, reconciling names (some duplicates were just naming differences). They conclude the true portfolio size is 275, of which 20 were previously undocumented – a significant find confirming the need for better inventory management.

3. **Inventory Validation Finding:** FinServe had no single owner for the application inventory. Various spreadsheets existed in different departments. The audit finds that *no formal process ensures new applications (especially SaaS) are recorded* – they note this as a governance gap. Citing ISO 27001's requirement for maintaining an asset register (Wiseman, 2025), the auditors recommend establishing a configuration management database or APM system as the authoritative source, with quarterly updates. Management, surprised by the discovery of 20 "unknown" apps (including a legacy MS Access based system still used in HR for niche reporting), agrees to assign the IT PMO responsibility for maintaining the inventory going forward.
4. **Business Alignment and Redundancy:** Using the collected data, the auditors map applications to 15 top-level business capabilities (like Retail Banking, Commercial Banking, Investment Services, Corporate Functions, etc.). They create a diagram showing each capability with the apps supporting it. Immediately, clear redundancies appear in Retail Banking: FinServe has two mobile banking apps (one from the original company and one from an acquired bank, both still running) and three different analytics tools used by various teams to analyze customer behavior. Interviews confirm overlap: the digital banking team admits they support two mobile apps but would prefer to retire one and focus on a single platform, only that some regional customers haven't migrated. Similarly, analytics teams in different regions independently subscribed to different SaaS analytics services. The audit quantifies the cost of these: maintaining two mobile apps costs double development effort (approx. $2M vs. could be $1M annually if unified), and the analytics tools collectively cost $400k/year, likely ~$200k could be saved by consolidating to one.

Business value assessment shows the mobile apps are both critical (high value, high customer impact) but one is clearly more modern and better rated by users (as per app store reviews and internal user feedback). The auditors rate the legacy mobile app as low technical fit (it has frequent bugs, older tech) and medium business fit, whereas the new app is high on both. This positions the legacy app in the **Eliminate** quadrant of TIME (Bittler & Kreizman, 2010). Audit recommendation: **Move all customers to the new mobile app within 12 months and decommission the legacy one**. They support this with a success story from another bank (citing industry best practice: one bank saved significant maintenance costs by consolidating online banking platforms, which aligns with Gartner's note on 30% TCO reduction by rationalization) (Grant Thornton Bharat, 2021).

For analytics tools, the audit recommendation is to form a cross-functional task force to choose a single analytics platform (perhaps negotiate enterprise licensing for one) and phase out the others, to reduce redundant spend and consolidate data for better insights. This aligns with ITIL's idea of providing the right mix of services at optimal investment (IT Process Wiki, n.d.).

5. **Cost Analysis:** The auditors compile cost data. FinServe's IT accounting wasn't fully broken down by app, but major applications had known costs. They find the top 20% of applications account for 80% of the spend (Pareto principle holds). These are mostly core systems (core banking, trading platform, ERP, CRM). Most of these are necessary, but some cost anomalies emerge. For example, an old trade finance system supporting a diminishing business line still incurs high maintenance fees (~$500k/year) despite low transaction volume. The business confirms that product line is being phased out in two years. Audit suggests accelerating that decommission or shifting remaining clients to a manual process to retire the system earlier, saving $1M (next two years) that would be wasted on keeping it alive. Finance stakeholders agree in principle – this becomes a quick win recommendation: **Retire TradeFin system by end of year**, migrate any active contracts to the main core banking system which has a module to handle trade finance (maybe with slight process change). This is a direct optimization: eliminating a low-value, high-cost application (Torii, 2023).

The audit also identifies that software maintenance contracts have not been renegotiated in a while. They note that by reducing redundancy (like cutting out one CRM system and one document management system that were duplicates), the company can also consolidate vendors and possibly negotiate better terms (industry practice shows volume consolidation can cut license costs 10-15%). They quantify potential savings of around $300k/year through vendor consolidation.

6. **Technical Risk Assessment:** The audit finds that 30 applications (about 11% of the portfolio) use technologies that are either already out of support or will be within 18 months. Notably, the core banking system runs on a mainframe platform scheduled for vendor end-of-support next year. This is a known big-ticket issue – there's a project underway to modernize it, but it's behind schedule. Auditors highlight the urgency: running a bank on unsupported software is not only risky but could draw regulator ire. They cite security risks of EOL software (LeanIX, 2022) and recommend management develop contingency plans (like extended support contracts or accelerating the replacement project by allocating more resources). They assign this a high risk rating in the audit.

Another example: one of the CRM systems (the one planned for phase-out) runs on Windows Server 2012, which is past end-of-support. The audit notes this and actually treats it as a compelling reason to speed up migrating those users to the other CRM which is on a modern platform. Essentially, technical risk findings reinforce the rationalization moves by adding a risk mitigation rationale, not just cost.

Security-wise, the audit, working with the infosec team, performed vulnerability scans on a sample of web applications. They found a couple of medium severity issues and one high-severity issue in an internal HR app (an outdated open-source library). These were reported and already in process to be patched, but it showed a pattern: legacy apps not regularly patched. They recommend instituting a quarterly security review of all applications, perhaps integrating with the portfolio management process so that each app's technical owner certifies key controls (like patching) are up to date – aligning with SOC 2 criteria for security control and inventory (Wiseman, 2025). This also ties into CISA audit practices of ensuring continuous control monitoring.

7. **Operational Resilience:** FinServe, being in finance, is subject to regulations for continuity. The audit reviews BCP documents and finds that for most critical systems, recovery time objectives (RTOs) of 4 hours are defined, and DR infrastructure is in place (a secondary data center). Test records show annual DR tests have been mostly successful; however, two newer cloud-based applications (a customer chatbot service and a data lake) have no documented DR test or clear recovery plan. The teams assumed the cloud is inherently resilient, but the audit reminds them that they still need plans for cloud outages. This is a learning moment for FinServe – they need to extend their continuity planning to cloud (perhaps by using multi-region deployments or backup instances). Auditors reference an industry incident where a cloud region failure caused hours of downtime, stressing multi-cloud or multi-region setups for critical customer-facing services (New Horizons, 2024).

Another resilience gap discovered: the incident management logs showed that when the legacy mobile app went down one weekend, it wasn't immediately clear who was responsible to bring it back (since digital team was focused on the new app). This caused a 4-hour delay in response. The audit identified this as a roles and responsibilities issue rooted in portfolio complexity – too many overlapping apps causing confusion in support. They recommend clearly assigning operational ownership even for systems slated to retire, until they are decommissioned, to avoid such support lapses.

FinServe's multi-region presence means they also worry about data sovereignty (client data in EU must stay in EU, etc.). The audit checks cloud deployments and finds all European customer data is indeed stored in EU data centers except one backup for an ancillary system which was going to a US region. They flag that as non-compliant with EU regulations (ISACA News, 2024) and it's corrected by switching to an EU backup. This was a detail that could have been missed without a portfolio-wide audit.

8. **Cloud Readiness and Multi-Cloud:** FinServe had a cloud strategy to move 50% of apps to cloud in 3 years. Two years in, only about 20% have moved. The audit investigates why. They find that certain apps had much higher migration complexity than anticipated – notably the core banking (not moved for good reason – it's huge and a replacement is being built instead) and some older systems with data entanglements. However, some medium complexity apps (like internal portals, mid-tier services) that could have been lifted to cloud were not tackled yet, possibly due to resource constraints and lack of a detailed plan. The audit suggests using a structured approach (like AWS's six-step assessment model) to systematically evaluate the remaining portfolio (Goncalves & Berner, 2024). They demonstrate this by picking one application – a customer notifications system – and doing a quick cloud readiness survey: results show it's a good candidate (built on modern tech, few external dependencies). They present this as a pilot example and recommend prioritizing it in the next migration wave.

On multi-cloud, FinServe uses AWS for most, Azure for some MS-specific workloads, and a number of SaaS like Salesforce and Workday. The audit finds no overarching governance document that covers all; each is managed in silo. For instance, AWS and Azure each have separate teams and security configurations. The audit points out risks: inconsistent security policies and monitoring gaps. They reference the need for centralized governance across multi-cloud environments (New Horizons, 2024). As a result, FinServe's CIO decides to establish a *Cloud Center of Excellence (CCoE)* that will set unified policies (e.g., both AWS and Azure must have encryption, similar tagging, and feed into a single SIEM for logs). The audit also suggests adopting a Cloud Management Platform to get a single pane of glass for cost and asset tracking.

On costs, auditors observe the cloud spend has grown 30% year-over-year but without equivalent decommissioning of on-prem costs, indicating some inefficiency – cloud was added on top of existing costs. They underscore the importance of decommissioning old infrastructure in tandem (for example, after moving a development environment to cloud, they found the on-prem dev servers were still running, essentially double spending). This example emphasizes portfolio discipline: when an app moves, update inventory, and retire legacy resources.

Audit Outcomes: The audit report for FinServe Corp is delivered with around 40 recommendations. Key ones include:

- **Establish a centralized application portfolio management function** – assign ownership, implement a single inventory repository, and carry out annual portfolio reviews with business leadership (addresses governance and data quality issues) (Global Affairs Canada, 2022).
- **Retire or consolidate 15 specific applications** over the next 12-18 months, which is projected to cut portfolio costs by ~$3 million (about 10% of the IT application spend) and reduce complexity (the exact list includes the duplicate mobile app, one CRM, the trade finance system, two analytics tools, and several minor apps with niche usage). This aligns with the industry estimate of up to 30% TCO reduction for aggressive rationalization, but the auditors took a conservative, feasible set yielding ~10% savings initially (Grant Thornton Bharat, 2021).
- **Invest in modernizing or replacing 5 high-risk/high-value applications**, notably the core banking and a few others, and in the interim ensure robust compensating controls (extended support, additional failovers). Essentially, move these to the "Invest" or "Migrate" category – invest in cloud-native replacements or major upgrades. The case for each is backed by risk and value analysis.
- **Improve operational resilience** by addressing gaps in DR planning for cloud systems, conducting more frequent continuity tests that include third-party SaaS scenarios, and clarifying support ownership during the transition period where old and new systems coexist. Also by closing the data residency compliance gap found in backup configuration (ISACA News, 2024).
- **Enhance multi-cloud management** – unify security monitoring, cost tracking, and compliance checks across all environments. This included implementing a tagging policy where every cloud resource is tagged with the application name and environment, enabling easier portfolio-wide reporting (e.g., one could query "show me all resources related to Application X across

AWS/Azure"). Regular cloud configuration audits were recommended, echoing that auditors should perform or IT should self-audit cloud setups due to the complexity and dynamic nature (New Horizons, 2024).

Management at FinServe responds positively. They create a task force to execute on application consolidation (co-chaired by the enterprise architect and head of applications). Within 6 months, they report to the board that 5 applications have been retired with minimal business impact, saving $800k already, and plans are underway for the others. The CIO also reports that for the first time they have a truly complete view of their application landscape, thanks to the audit-driven inventory effort, which is now maintained in a live dashboard. They also note improved alignment: some business units volunteered additional candidates for retirement once they saw the audit findings, as they realized they had more systems than needed.

From an audit perspective, this case demonstrates how applying a comprehensive audit strategy yields tangible optimization results. It validates that an audit can go beyond compliance checking – it can directly facilitate IT strategy by identifying inefficiencies and guiding action. FinServe's example, though hypothetical, is reflective of real-world outcomes where such audits have eliminated millions in waste and significantly strengthened IT environments (CIO Council & C&I CoP, 2020).

MULTI-INDUSTRY AND MULTI-REGION CONSIDERATIONS

While the core principles of application portfolio auditing remain consistent, different industries and regions impose unique requirements and challenges that auditors must consider:

Industry Variations

- **Highly Regulated Industries (Finance, Healthcare, Government):** These sectors often have additional oversight and specific criteria. For example, banks and insurers face regulations for technology risk (such as the Basel Committee's operational risk guidelines, EU's Digital Operational Resilience Act, etc.) that require demonstrable control over IT assets and resilience. An audit in these industries must ensure that portfolio management aligns with regulatory expectations like maintaining an updated inventory of systems that impact critical services, rigorous change management for any system that could affect financial reporting (tie to Sarbanes-Oxley in the US), and strong disaster recovery capabilities. In healthcare, HIPAA and related laws necessitate tracking any application handling ePHI (patient data) and ensuring they meet security standards (Wiseman, 2025). Thus, auditors in these industries might add checks for compliance mapping – e.g., verifying each application is categorized for the type of data it holds (PII, financial data, health data) and that required controls (encryption, access logs, etc.) are in place. Also, industry regulators may require audits themselves; for instance, US federal agencies follow playbooks like the Application Rationalization Playbook and report progress on optimization (as part of initiatives like Cloud Smart) (CIO Council & C&I CoP, 2020). Auditors need to align findings with such mandated frameworks, and sometimes the audit report becomes part of regulatory submissions.

- **Manufacturing and Energy:** These industries often have a mix of IT and OT (Operational Technology) systems. The application portfolio might include industrial control systems, SCADA, etc., which have different lifecycles and risk profiles (they may be kept running for decades, often past typical EOL, due to operational necessity). Auditing such portfolios means dealing with more *end-of-service-life* occurrences and judging risk differently – sometimes you cannot simply retire a system without plant downtime planning. Auditors will focus on mitigation plans (like network isolations, compensating controls for legacy OT). Additionally, these industries might not have as stringent data regulations as finance/health, but downtime can be even more directly costly (e.g., factory stoppage). So the emphasis on resilience and maintenance planning is high.
- **Technology and Software Companies:** Ironically, tech companies might have sprawling portfolios due to innovative cultures – lots of internal apps and tools spun up by developers. The challenge here is usually *shadow IT and uncontrolled growth.* Auditors may find a lack of formal process, but also these organizations might be more open to modern solutions (like using automated tools, cloud, etc.). Auditing a tech company's portfolio might focus on streamlining and eliminating pet projects that are not providing value, and instituting just enough governance to keep sprawl in check without stifling innovation (maybe implementing an internal "app store" concept or approval process for new tools). The risk tolerance might be higher for running open-source or latest tech (with less worry about legacy), so EOL might be less an issue, but security might be (ensuring all these new apps follow secure coding and data practices).
- **Retail and Consumer Services:** These industries focus heavily on customer-facing applications (e.g., e-commerce platforms, mobile apps, loyalty systems). Performance and user experience are critical business value factors. An audit in retail might incorporate more metrics on response times, scalability, and the ability of apps to handle peak loads (like Black Friday traffic).

Redundancy could be an issue if, for example, different regions or brands within a company developed separate e-commerce systems – consolidation could yield a unified customer experience. Also, these industries often leverage many SaaS (for marketing, CRM, etc.), so portfolio audits will handle a lot of vendor management aspects. Data privacy laws (GDPR, CCPA) strongly affect them, so ensuring each app that collects customer data has proper compliance (consent management, deletion processes) is key – tying into the audit.

Regional Considerations

- **Data Sovereignty and Privacy Laws:** Different countries have different laws on data storage and processing (e.g., GDPR in Europe, data localization laws in Russia, China, India, etc.). A multi-region organization's portfolio audit must track where each application's data resides and flows. For instance, if a European subsidiary uses a SaaS app that stores data in the US, the audit needs to flag that for GDPR compliance review (ISACA News, 2024). We saw in the case study an example of adjusting backup location. Auditors might need to consult legal requirements per region or ensure that local IT teams have done so. Sometimes a solution is required: e.g., using EU-only instances of certain applications for EU data. If a global portfolio is centrally managed, the audit may recommend segmentation or deployment of separate instances to satisfy local laws (which could increase complexity, showing the trade-off between optimization and compliance that management must navigate).
- **Localization and Regional Duplication:** Companies operating in different regions might have separate portfolios per region (due to historical reasons or local vendors). An audit can encourage global standardization where feasible (for example, a multinational could save money by using one global HR system rather than different ones in each region). However, auditors must also consider legitimate reasons for differences: local language support, local vendor dominance, or regulatory certification (some countries require using domestic software for certain public sector processes, etc.). The audit should engage local IT management to understand these factors. Perhaps North America and Europe can unify a system, but Asia might need a different one due to local conditions. The audit report can still highlight this and possibly suggest a long-term strategy (e.g., "Three ERP systems exist across regions; while NorthAm and EMEA could consolidate, APAC's system must remain separate due to local compliance. Ensure all three are integrated at the data level for corporate reporting to mitigate fragmentation impact.").

- **Follow-the-sun operations and cultural aspects:** Multi-region operations often have support handed off between regions (for 24/7 support). The audit might consider if the portfolio data (like inventory and documentation) is equally accessible and understandable by teams globally. If not, recommend making it so, to improve support. Additionally, different corporate cultures might treat audits differently – e.g., some regions might be less forthcoming about problems. Ensuring a consistent audit approach sometimes requires tailored communication (for instance, APAC subsidiaries might need communications in local languages or assurance that the audit is not a punitive exercise by HQ). The audit team composition with multi-lingual auditors or regional audit reps can help.
- **Compliance Standards by Region:** Aside from data laws, there are regional standards like Europe's **ENISA guidance** for cybersecurity, or country-specific mandates (e.g., MAS in Singapore has tech risk guidelines for banks). The audit should align with any such region-specific requirements if the company operates there. For instance, if Singapore operations are under MAS TRM guidelines, the audit should incorporate checks from those guidelines (they require an updated inventory of systems, risk assessments, etc., which dovetails with our process).
- **Outsourcing and Offshoring:** Many global companies outsource application development or maintenance to different countries. The audit might need to check how that affects portfolio control – e.g., if an app is maintained by an offshore vendor, is knowledge retained in-house? Is documentation up to date? If the contract ends, can we transition easily? This is part of risk – an app could be technically fine but if it's solely understood by an external team with a contract ending, that's a risk to continuity. Regions with heavy outsourcing (India, Eastern Europe, etc., for IT services) might have these patterns.

Multi-industry/region example to illustrate: Consider a global manufacturing firm with HQ in Germany, plants in US, China, Brazil. An audit finds that in Germany/US they use SAP as the main ERP, but in China they use a local ERP product to comply with some local accounting rules and government integration, and in Brazil they use an older Oracle JD Edwards system from a past era. The audit would not naively say "one ERP to rule them all" without considering that China might need to keep its system. Instead, the recommendation might be: consolidate Germany and US on one SAP instance (if not already), plan a migration for Brazil to SAP (since nothing stops that except effort), and interface the China system with SAP for group reporting while monitoring if future Chinese regulations allow a move. Also, ensure all these systems adhere to the company's global security policy and that inventories of each are centrally visible (Global Affairs Canada, 2022; ISACA News, 2024). The audit might also involve local audit teams to check that, for instance, the China ERP is properly licensed and up to date (perhaps the local team finds it's 2 versions behind – an issue to fix).

Another scenario: a North American retailer expanding to EU must adapt its systems to GDPR. The audit in year 1 of expansion might heavily focus on checking every customer-facing application for GDPR compliance (consent, data deletion, local hosting). Multi-region audits thus often have an element of compliance audit integrated.

In general, **the audit strategies described in this paper are applicable across industries**, but the emphasis and key risk areas will shift based on the context. Recognizing these nuances ensures the audit provides relevant and value-added recommendations. Auditors should customize their checklists and evaluation criteria to include industry-specific controls (e.g., PCI-DSS checks for retailers with point-of-sale systems, or FDA validation status for software used in pharma manufacturing, etc.).

CONCLUSION

Optimizing an IT application portfolio is a complex undertaking that requires balancing business needs, technological possibilities, cost constraints, and risk management. Through a comprehensive auditing approach, organizations can shine a light on this complexity and derive a clear roadmap for improvement. This paper detailed how an audit – grounded in industry frameworks and augmented with robust tools – can evaluate and enhance the effectiveness of application portfolio management.

In summary, effective portfolio auditing encompasses: ensuring a complete and accurate inventory of applications (the foundation for all optimization) (Wiseman, 2025); analyzing each application's alignment with business objectives and value contribution (so that IT investments support what the organization truly needs) (Info-Tech Research Group, n.d.); assessing cost-effectiveness and eliminating waste (driving down maintenance of redundant or low-value apps to reallocate resources to innovation) (CIO Council & C&I CoP, 2020); scrutinizing technical risks such as outdated technologies and security vulnerabilities (to prevent incidents and enforce a modern, supportable tech stack) (LeanIX, 2022); identifying functional redundancies and opportunities for consolidation (simplifying the landscape to reduce complexity and cost) (Faddom, 2023); and evaluating operational resilience and cloud readiness (ensuring continuity of critical services and smooth adoption of future-state architectures like cloud and multi-cloud) (New Horizons, 2024; Goncalves & Berner, 2024).

By leveraging frameworks like COBIT and ITIL, the audit ensures that recommendations align with recognized best practices in IT governance and service management. COBIT's emphasis on value and resource optimization and ITIL's focus on having the right mix of services at the right investment level underpin many audit criteria (Kempwad, 2024; IT Process Wiki, n.d.). Simultaneously, standards such as NIST, ISO 27001, and SOC 2 provide concrete benchmarks for controls (for example, inventory management, access control, and continuity planning) (Wiseman, 2025). The audit in effect becomes a tool to verify compliance with these standards while also driving improvements.

One of the key insights from this exploration is that auditing for portfolio optimization is not a one-off project but part of a **continuous improvement cycle**. Technology and business needs evolve rapidly – what was an optimal portfolio two years ago may be suboptimal now due to new solutions in the market or shifts in strategy. Therefore, organizations should treat the application portfolio as a living ecosystem that requires ongoing monitoring. Establishing metrics like an Application Portfolio Health Index (Global Affairs Canada, 2022) or regular portfolio review boards (with representation from both IT and business) helps maintain momentum. Audit functions can integrate portfolio risk into their annual plans, revisiting the highest risk areas more frequently. Over time, as redundant and risky applications are retired, the audit focus can shift more towards optimizing the remaining portfolio and ensuring new additions adhere to architecture principles (preventing the cycle of sprawl from repeating).

The use of automated tools and data analytics in audits – as detailed with checklists, scoring models, and dashboards – greatly enhances both the efficiency of the audit and the clarity of its findings. Visualization of complex data (like via the TIME quadrant or cost-value graphs) allows decision-makers to grasp issues quickly and take action. The hypothetical case study of FinServe Corp illustrated that when armed with solid audit findings, management was able to act decisively, yielding cost savings and risk reduction within months. This underscores that **audits should not only find problems but also illuminate solutions**. The inclusion of a toolkit-like approach (surveys, analysis templates, dashboards) in the audit ensures that recommendations are accompanied by the data and tools needed to execute them.

Multi-industry and multi-region considerations remind us that context matters – an optimal solution in one environment might not fit another due to regulatory or cultural differences. Nonetheless, the overarching audit approach remains valid everywhere: know what you have, know how it's performing, know what it costs, and know the risks – then use that knowledge to guide optimization decisions. By tailoring the approach to local needs, auditors can provide relevant guidance while maintaining global standards.

In conclusion, *auditing strategies for IT application portfolio optimization* are an essential part of modern IT governance. They bridge the gap between high-level digital transformation goals and the on-the-ground reality of legacy systems and fragmented applications. When done thoroughly and with the right tools, such audits produce actionable intelligence that drives both immediate improvements (like cost cuts and quick wins on redundancies) and long-term strategic alignment (like shaping the roadmap for modernization and cloud migration). The result is an application portfolio that is leaner, more aligned with the business, more secure, and more resilient – enabling IT to be not just a cost center, but a true enabler of business innovation and agility (Info-Tech Research Group, n.d.; Theseira, 2024).

FinServe's journey (and similar real-world cases) demonstrate that this is achievable: they turned audit insights into tangible business value. For any organization embarking on optimizing its IT application landscape, the methodologies and considerations outlined in this paper can serve as a blueprint for conducting a professional, comprehensive audit that sets the foundation for effective portfolio management and continuous improvement.

REFERENCES

Bittler, R., & Kreizman, G. (2010). Gartner's TIME model for application portfolio analysis. Gartner (Archived). https://www.leanix.net/en/wiki/apm/gartner-time-model#:~:text=The%20Gartner%C2%AE%20TIME%20framework%20,planning%20and%20executing%20application%20rationalization

CIO Council & C&I CoP. (2020). Application rationalization playbook (Version 1.1). U.S. Federal CIO Council. https://www.cio.gov/assets/files/Application-Rationalization-Playbook.pdf#:~:text=business%20applications%20across%20an%20organization,whole%20to%20eliminate%20redundancies%2C%20lower

Cooke, I. (2019). Developing the IT audit plan using COBIT 2019. ISACA Journal, 3. https://www.isaca.org/resources/isaca-journal/issues/2019/volume-3/developing-the-it-audit-plan-using-cobit-2019#:~:text=The%20IT%20Assurance%20Framework%20,can%20this%20be%20improved%20upon

Faddom. (2023). Application portfolio management: Essential elements and 7 critical best practices. Faddom Blog. https://faddom.com/application-portfolio-management-essential-elements-and-7-critical-best-practices/#:~:text=Mitigate%20Security%20and%20Compliance%20Vulnerabilities

Global Affairs Canada. (2022). Application portfolio health index (APHI) description. https://www.international.gc.ca/transparency-transparence/audit-evaluation-verification/2022/2022-11-it-ti.aspx?lang=eng

Global Affairs Canada. (2022). Audit of IT application portfolio management. https://www.international.gc.ca/transparency-transparence/audit-evaluation-verification/2022/2022-11-it-ti.aspx?lang=eng

Goncalves, G., & Berner, M. (2024). Application portfolio assessment strategy for AWS cloud migration. AWS Prescriptive Guidance. Amazon Web Services. https://docs.aws.amazon.com/prescriptive-guidance/latest/strategy-application-portfolio-assessment-migration/introduction.html#:~:text=At%20a%20high,priorities%2C%20and%20accelerates%20business%20outcomes

Grant Thornton Bharat. (2021). Simplifying the enterprise application portfolio. Insights Blog. https://www.grantthornton.in/insights/blogs/simplifying-the-enterprise-application-portfolio-to-make-the-most-of-your-organisational-investments/#:~:text=Gartner%20estimates%20that%20organisations%20following,significant%20saving%20in%20IT%20budget

Info-Tech Research Group. (n.d.). Rationalize your application portfolio (Blueprint). https://www.infotech.com/research/ss/rationalize-your-application-portfolio

ISACA News. (2024). Cloud data sovereignty: Governance and risk implications. ISACA Industry News. https://www.isaca.org/resources/news-and-trends/industry-news/2024/cloud-data-sovereignty-governance-and-risk-implications-of-cross-border-cloud-storage#:~:text=the%20global%20public%20cloud%20services,compliance%20measures%20to%20ensure%20successful

Kempwad, A. (2024). COBIT APO05.04 – Maintain portfolios. ITSM Docs. https://www.itsm-docs.com/blogs/cobit-framework/cobit-apo05-04-maintain-portfolios#:~:text=COBIT%20APO05,optimize%20resources%2C%20and%20maximize%20value

Lean, I. X. (2022). EOL vs. EOS in software: Meaning & business impact. LeanIX Blog. https://www.leanix.net/en/wiki/trm/what-is-end-of-life-vs-end-of-support#:~:text=Using%20software%20after%20it%20reaches,EoL%20poses%20several%20risks

Lean, I. X. (n.d.). Gartner TIME framework for application rationalization. LeanIX Wiki. https://www.leanix.net/en/wiki/apm/gartner-time-model#:~:text=The%20Gartner%C2%AE%20TIME%20framework%20,planning%20and%20executing%20application%20rationalization

New Horizons. (2024). Multi-cloud challenges: Best practices and strategies (T. Karl, Ed.). https://www.newhorizons.com/resources/blog/multi-cloud-challenges#:~:text=,cloud%20management

Process Wiki, I. T. (n.d.). ITIL service portfolio management. https://wiki.en.it-processmaps.com/index.php/Service_Portfolio_Management#:~:text=Service%20Portfolio%20Review

ServiceNow. (2025). Application portfolio management – Cloud assessment (Vancouver release). https://www.servicenow.com/docs/bundle/vancouver-application-portfolio-management/page/product/application-portfolio-management/concept/apm-cloud-readiness-score-prof.html#:~:text=Log%20in%20to%20get%20a,better%20experience

Theseira, D. (2024). What is application portfolio management (APM)? The guide to success & best practices. Ardoq Knowledge Hub. https://www.ardoq.com/knowledge-hub/application-portfolio-management#:~:text=Application%20Portfolio%20Management%20,overall%20value%20to%20the%20business

Torii. (2023). Application rationalization: How to optimize your software stack. Torii Blog. https://www.toriihq.com/blog/application-rationalization-made-easy#:~:text=Elimination%20of%20Redundant%20Applications

VMware Tanzu Labs. (2023). Introducing the open source application portfolio auditor. VMware Tanzu Blog. https://blogs.vmware.com/tanzu/introducing-application-portfolio-auditor/#:~:text=consistently%20assess%20cloud%20readiness%2C%20quality%2C,up%20to%2015%20software%20analyzers

Wiseman, R. (2025). List of standards and regulations requiring an application inventory. Orchid Security Blog. https://www.orchid.security/blog/list-of-standards-and-regulations#:~:text=Requirement%3A

Chapter 9
Data-Driven IT Audits in Higher Education:
Leveraging Big Data and AI for Enhanced Governance and Compliance

Tshepo Maota
https://orcid.org/0009-0001-0475-5801
University of South Africa, South Africa

Audrey Legodi
https://orcid.org/0000-0001-5311-7307
University of South Africa, South Africa

ABSTRACT

This study examines the data-driven IT audit landscape within six South African higher education institutions (HEIs), focusing on IT governance, AI integration, big data analytics, digital transformation, data governance, and cybersecurity. It analyses publicly available reports to understand how these HEIs are leveraging data and AI in their IT audits, using specific frameworks to identify trends in technology adoption. Findings show that while some institutions demonstrate strong IT governance and strategic AI adoption, others are still building basic digital skills. Challenges remain in operating AI, fostering data-driven cultures, and mitigating cybersecurity risks, although external reports add objectivity. Practical implications include formalising governance structures, enhancing data literacy, and leveraging real-time audit insights to strengthen resilience. The study points out that it requires ongoing improvements, stakeholder engagement, and regionally relevant research to support sustainable digital transformation in South African HEIs.

DOI: 10.4018/979-8-3373-3078-5.ch009

1. INTRODUCTION

"Digital transformation is not about technology – it's about change."
— Peter Weill and Stephanie Woerner.

The global landscape of higher education institutions (HEIs) is undergoing significant changes due to swift digital transformation, emerging cybersecurity concerns, and increasing demands for accountability and compliance (Mah & Gross, 2024). Over the past twenty years, HEIs have evolved from traditional campus-based operations to sophisticated digital ecosystems that facilitate online learning, hybrid classrooms, virtual collaboration, and data-intensive research environments (Benavides et al., 2022; Divjak et al., 2022; Rojas et al., 2025). This evolution has broadened educational options while simultaneously increasing the complexity and risk landscape encountered by higher education institutions.

Historically, IT audits in higher education used manual, checklist-orientated, and compliance-centric approaches (Aliyu et al., 2020; Benavides et al., 2022). Nonetheless, these conventional audit methodologies have found it challenging to adapt to the rapidity of digital transformation and the extensive quantity of data produced in contemporary academic settings. In 2020, the COVID-19 epidemic precipitated a significant acceleration of digital adoption in the sector, as numerous universities transitioned rapidly to online learning and virtual administration (Maota, 2024). This transition revealed substantial deficiencies in digital governance, cybersecurity resilience, and IT risk management.

The digital expansion is exacerbated by the increasing hazards of data breaches and cyberattacks (Akacha & Awad, 2023; Lallie et al., 2023; Rojas et al., 2025). Recent worldwide education reports reveal a 30% increase in cybersecurity incidents within higher education from 2021 to 2023 (Gadhi et al., 2024; Lallie et al., 2023), indicating the susceptibility of university IT infrastructures to external threats and internal data governance deficiencies. The implementation of the Protection of Personal Information Act (POPIA) in South Africa in 2021 has heightened regulatory oversight on HEIs, necessitating a reassessment of their data governance and IT audit protocols. In 2025, cybercrime has become the predominant threat in South Africa, surpassing persistent problems like load shedding and political instability (Daily Investor, 2025). This transition highlights the increasing peril of cyber incidents, such as ransomware attacks, data breaches, and IT outages, which have emerged as the foremost worldwide business risk for the fourth consecutive year. Recent high-profile intrusions have heightened worries regarding cybersecurity preparedness and the potential for substantial disruptions across multiple sectors. A significant Malaysian institution experienced a substantial data breach, leading to the internet exposure of personal information belonging to over one million persons (Ganesen et al., 2022). The hack revealed confidential information, including student names, identification numbers, addresses, contact information, and academic records, raising significant concerns over data protection protocols (Masmali & Miah, 2022).

The changing laws and technology highlight the need to change how IT audits are done, moving from traditional methods to using data-driven and AI-powered techniques. Big data analytics, machine learning, and prediction algorithms offer innovative avenues for the proactive identification of hazards, the optimisation of audit processes, and the assurance of real-time compliance monitoring (Sun et al., 2024). AI can identify irregularities in financial systems, machine learning models can predict IT problems, and big data can convert static audit reports into actionable intelligence dashboards.

Furthermore, the implementation of governance frameworks such as COBIT, ISO 27001, and NIST standards provides a solid basis for integrating data-driven audit processes into the governance structures of higher education. These frameworks, established over the last twenty years and enhanced through iterative revisions (COBIT 2019 and ISO 27001:2022), offer a systematic methodology for managing IT risks, assessing control efficacy, and aligning audit processes with business objectives.

This chapter explores the integration of data-driven audits and higher education governance, contending that the use of AI and big data constitutes not merely a technological enhancement but a strategic need. HEIs must adopt predictive, data-driven audits to enhance accountability to stakeholders and regulators, protect sensitive academic data, comply with changing requirements, and strengthen governance procedures. This research fills a significant gap in current auditing literature and practice, providing insights that are recent, pertinent, and the digital resilience of HEIs in the future.

2. BACKGROUND

As HEIs expedite the integration of digital technologies, such as artificial intelligence (AI), big data analytics, and cloud computing, these innovations present both strategic advantages and emerging concerns (George & Wooden, 2023; Moşteanu, 2023). AI and machine learning are increasingly integrated into several academic and operational processes, facilitating adaptive learning, data-informed decision-making, and predictive analytics. Nonetheless, these advancements also present risks related to the magnitude, diversity, and speed of data handled by HEIs (Klímová & Pikhart, 2025), encompassing algorithmic bias, data privacy issues, and emerging cybersecurity threats (Karpouzis, 2024; Onesi-Ozigagun et al., 2024; Roshanaei et al., 2023).

The COVID-19 pandemic in 2020 expedited digital adoption, revealing deficiencies in data governance, cybersecurity, and regulatory compliance (Maota, 2024). Internationally, legislation such as South Africa's Protection of Personal Information Act (POPIA), the EU's General Data Protection Regulation (GDPR), and the U.S. Family Educational Rights and Privacy Act (FERPA) highlight the necessity for comprehensive data governance frameworks to mitigate these risks (Borgman, 2018; Marcucci et al., 2023; Reis et al., 2024).

Despite this advancement, conventional IT audits, typically reliant on checklists and conducted periodically, are inadequate for managing the dynamic, real-time hazards present in the contemporary digital environment (Ghorashi et al., 2023). Modern auditing techniques using big data analytics and AI-driven tools are progressively acknowledged as essential for anticipating and mitigating these hazards (Klímová & Pikhart, 2025; Roshanaei et al., 2023). Frameworks such as COBIT and ISO 27001, perpetually enhanced through revisions (e.g., COBIT 2019 and ISO 27001:2022), provide systematic direction for aligning digital governance with strategic objectives and fostering resilience (Atrinawati et al., 2021; ISO, 2022).

The rise of cybercrime as South Africa's foremost concern in 2025 (Daily Investor, 2025) has heightened the necessity for real-time IT governance capable of proactively identifying vulnerabilities and ensuring compliance. This chapter examines how HEIs can use data-driven audits not only for compliance but also as a strategic instrument to protect sensitive data, fulfil regulatory requirements, and enhance governance in a continuously evolving digital landscape.

3. PROBLEM STATEMENT

As higher education institutions (HEIs) rapidly embrace digitisation, traditional IT audit methodologies encounter difficulties in adeptly addressing the emerging risks linked to sophisticated technologies such as big data, artificial intelligence, and machine learning. These developing technologies have transformed academic delivery, research management, and administrative processes in HEIs; yet they also introduce unprecedented risks and complexities that frequently exceed the parameters of traditional audit frameworks.

Current IT audit methods mainly rely on checklists and look back at past events, which do not provide the timely risk assessments and forward-looking insights needed to effectively manage IT weaknesses and ensure compliance with regulations.

Many HEIs continue to use outdated manual audit methods focused on compliance, which cannot keep up with the rapid pace and large amounts of digital data, resulting in problems with governance, cybersecurity, and regulatory oversight. This imbalance renders institutions susceptible to considerable dangers, including data breaches, algorithmic bias, AI-induced vulnerabilities, and non-compliance with data protection regulations such as POPIA, GDPR, and FERPA (Jakkula, 2024; Marri et al., 2024).

The absence of AI and big data analytics integration in IT audits restricts HEIs' capacity to proactively identify vulnerabilities and maintain real-time governance (Alaran et al., 2025; Mbonye et al., 2024). In the absence of data-driven audit methods, HEIs are inadequately prepared to oversee evolving IT systems, resulting in reactive instead of proactive risk management.

The absence of a definitive strategy for using data science and AI in IT audits in higher education establishes a significant deficiency in both scholarly research and institutional implementation. This chapter examines the gap by exploring how data-driven, AI-enhanced auditing approaches, supported by COBIT, ISO 27001, and NIST standards, might convert IT audits from static compliance activities into dynamic governance instruments. The study aims to deliver actionable insights and pragmatic recommendations for improving IT governance, cybersecurity resilience, and compliance in HEIs, assuring their adaptability and sustainability in a rapidly evolving digital landscape.

4. STUDY AIM

This chapter explores the integration of data-driven IT audit practices, enhanced by big data, artificial intelligence, and predictive analytics, within governance frameworks in higher education. The objective is to identify effective practices, challenges, and opportunities for using emerging technologies to improve risk management, cybersecurity resilience, and regulatory compliance in HEIs. The study looks at how well current practices match with established frameworks like COBIT, ISO 27001, and NIST to create a plan for changing traditional IT audits into active, real-time monitoring systems. The chapter aims to expand one's knowledge about data-centric auditing by connecting theoretical frameworks with practical applications, offering helpful tips to policymakers, IT auditors, and leaders in higher education.

5. STUDY METHODOLOGY

5.1 Research approach

This chapter looks at how big data analytics, AI, and IT governance frameworks are combined into data-driven IT audit processes in HEIs using a method that carefully analyses written documents. The study examines six South African universities: HEI 1[1], HEI 2, HEI 3, HEI 4, HEI 5, and HEI 6, by using the COBIT framework, disruption management theory, and the diffusion of innovations model. Qualitative document analysis, a careful research method that involves looking closely at publicly available written documents to find patterns, themes, and insights related to the research goals (Morgan, 2022) was used. This methodology is especially appropriate for analysing the intricate and diverse characteristics of IT audit processes in HEIs, as it enables the researcher to contextualise results within organisational practices, regulatory frameworks, and sector-specific difficulties (Mohamed et al., 2019).

5.2 Research design

The study relies solely on document analysis and uses an exploratory and interpretative research approach (Bowen, 2009). The purpose of this study is to gain a better understanding of the ways in which IT audits within HEIs governance frameworks make use of big data, AI, and predictive modelling. This chapter takes a methodical look at reports that are out in the public domain to find governance gaps, best practices, and new trends in data-driven IT auditing. These reports include institutional audits, ICT strategies, policy frameworks, and sectoral assessments.

5.3 Data sources and collection

The data for this study will be obtained from publicly accessible documents on institutional websites and through the Council on Higher Education (CHE) portals. This information encompasses annual audit reports, ICT governance frameworks, digital transformation strategies, and sectoral benchmark reports from professional organisations such as the IIA, ISACA, and CHE. The data gathering process entails a methodical search, classification, and arrangement of these documents to create a thorough dataset for analysis.

5.4 Data analysis

The chapter uses thematic content analysis to systematically identify recurring themes and patterns throughout the documents (Colorafi & Evans, 2016; Popenoe et al., 2021). Qualitative analysis software, NVivo, was used to code and categorise documents, identifying key themes, including the utilisation of big data analytics and AI in IT audits, the adoption of governance frameworks like COBIT, ISO 27001, and NIST, as well as the obstacles and challenges encountered by HEIs in implementing these advanced auditing methodologies. The theme study will concentrate on the emerging risks linked to AI and big data, examining how IT audits might alleviate these risks and enhance digital resilience in HEIs.

5.5 Institutional focus

The study will evaluate various HEIs to offer comparative insights into differing levels of digital audit maturity. The subject matter encompasses one institution with extensive implementation of AI and data-driven auditing processes, one in the process of integrating these tools, and one with limited adoption. This comparison method enhances comprehension of how institutions at varying levels of digital maturity manage the intricacies of IT audit transformation.

5.6 Ethical considerations

This study complies with data protection principles and ethical research standards because it does not obtain personal data from individuals but instead uses publicly available data. This method offers an open, evidence-based examination of data-driven audit methods in HEIs while protecting the privacy of stakeholders. Furthermore, we protected the identities of the institutions by using pseudonyms, even though the reports are open to the public.

5.7 Contribution of the methodology

This chapter uses qualitative document analysis to fill in a significant gap in our knowledge about how big data, AI, and predictive modelling can change how HEIs do their IT checks. It provides a structured, evidence-based look at how these technologies can change IT audits from one-time compliance checks to ongoing, real-time monitoring systems that deal with cybersecurity, governance, and compliance issues in the sector before they happen.

6. THEORETICAL FRAMEWORK

This study is based on a multi-theoretical framework that combines IT governance, disruption management theory, and technological innovation frameworks to investigate how data-driven and AI-enhanced IT audits might improve oversight and resilience in HEIs.

The framework's foundation is the COBIT (Control Objectives for Information and Related Technologies) governance model, which offers a systematic method for aligning IT plans with organisational objectives (Isaca, 2012). The principles of risk optimisation, resource management, and performance assessment in COBIT provide a framework for assessing the integration of AI and big data in audit processes, ensuring accountability and strategic alignment in HEIs (Fitrani & Ginardi, 2019; Samsinar & Sinaga, 2022).

The disruption management theory highlights the ability of institutions to foresee, endure, and adjust to disruptions in their operational contexts (Serpil & KESİM, 2024). As AI and data analytics rapidly grow across IT ecosystems, HEIs encounter novel disruptions, including data breaches, AI-driven threats, and legal changes. This paradigm emphasises the necessity for proactive auditing processes capable of identifying and addressing emerging risks in real time.

The technological innovation frameworks, particularly the diffusion of innovations (Rogers, 2003), explain the adoption curve of AI and big data in IT audits within the higher education sector. The framework facilitates an examination of the barriers, facilitators, and strategic enablers for digital transformation in HEI governance by explaining the adoption and integration of new technology in audit processes. These interconnected theories offer an effective analytical framework for analysing how data-driven IT audits can transcend conventional compliance roles and evolve into dynamic, real-time supervisory systems. The study also evaluates the institutional preparedness and adaptability of HEIs in implementing AI-enhanced audit procedures. This theoretical framework supports the review of documents and comparisons, guiding how results are understood and helping to create practical suggestions for strong, forward-looking governance in higher education.

7. LITERATURE REVIEW

7.1 Introduction

The digital transformation of HEIs has presented complex difficulties in IT governance, cybersecurity, and compliance (Masmali & Miah, 2022; Sengik et al., 2022). Traditional IT audit methodologies, which are typically manual and focused on compliance, are becoming inadequate for addressing the evolving risks associated with emerging technologies such as big data analytics and AI. This study examines how to use data-driven approaches in IT audits at HEIs, drawing on concepts from COBIT, disruption management theory, and the spread of new ideas.

7.2 Theoretical frameworks

7.2.1 COBIT framework

COBIT (Control Objectives for Information and Related Technologies) is a comprehensive framework for IT governance and management that offers a systematic method for aligning IT plans with organisational objectives (Khther & Othman, 2013). It highlights risk optimisation, resource management, and performance assessment, making it an appropriate framework for assessing the incorporation of AI and big data in auditing operations. Within the realm of HEIs, COBIT functions as a fundamental framework for evaluating and improving IT audit processes (Marcela & Fianty, 2023; Nurdin & Lubis, 2023).

By using COBIT's principles, HEIs can carefully check how well they manage their IT, find areas that need improvement, and set up controls that match their goals. The framework's domains, Evaluate, Direct and Monitor (EDM); Align, Plan and Organise (APO); Build, Acquire and Implement (BAI); Deliver, Service and Support (DSS); and Monitor, Evaluate and Assess (MEA), provide a systematic methodology for managing IT operations. This systematic methodology is crucial for incorporating emerging technologies such as AI and big data analytics into audit activities, guaranteeing that these innovations align with the institution's goal and adhere to regulatory standards.

7.2.2 Disruption management theory

Disruption management theory emphasises an organization's capacity to anticipate, endure, and adapt to disruptions in its operational environment (Gerber & Matthee, 2019; Zubizarreta et al., 2020). Within HEIs, the swift integration of AI and data analytics signifies a technological disruption that requires proactive auditing techniques to successfully manage emerging risks (Prosci, 2023). This theoretical framework is essential for comprehending the transformation of data-driven IT audits from reactive compliance activities to proactive risk management approaches.

Moreover, HEIs are increasingly facing disruptions caused by swift technological breakthroughs, including the integration of artificial intelligence and big data analytics in both administrative and academic procedures (Onesi-Ozigagun et al., 2024).

This paper uses the theory to analyse how HEIs might proactively mitigate the risks linked to the integration of these technologies in IT audit operations. It highlights the necessity of cultivating resilience and adaptability within institutional frameworks to address technological changes. By identifying possible disruptions early, HEIs can execute strategic plans that reduce risks and capitalise on opportunities offered by emerging technology, thus ensuring strong governance and compliance standards.

7.2.3 Diffusion of innovations

Rogers' diffusion of innovations theory explains the mechanisms by which new ideas and technologies disseminate within a social system (Foster et al., 2020). This study identifies factors influencing adoption, such as perceived advantages, compatibility, complexity, trialability, and observability (Anton et al., 2023; Choi et al., 2020; Prescott, 1995; Rogers, 1962). This framework facilitates comprehension of the adoption curve of AI and big data in IT audits within HEIs.

The diffusion of innovation theory facilitates the analysis of AI and big data analytics adoption patterns in IT audits within HEIs. Understanding these patterns allows the study to identify barriers to adoption and formulate strategies for the integration of innovative audit practices (Kokina et al., 2025; O'Donnell, 2024). Institutions that recognise the significant comparative advantage and compatibility of data-driven audits with their current systems are more inclined to adopt these technologies. Furthermore, offering trial opportunities and showcasing measurable benefits can enhance adoption rates among faculty and administrative personnel.

7.3. Emergence of data-driven IT audits

The traditional approach to IT audits at HEIs has primarily been manual, emphasising compliance and the study of historical data. The growing complexity of IT environments and the volume of data produced require a transition to data-driven audits (Aditya et al., 2018; Sun & Qu, 2020). These audits use big data analytics and artificial intelligence to deliver real-time insights, predictive risk evaluations, and improved decision-making abilities.

Research shows that using big data analytics in internal auditing helps with ongoing checks, finding fraud, and spotting potential risks before they happen (Adelakun et al., 2024; Patil, 2025; Udeh et al., 2024). This transition corresponds with the COBIT framework's focus on real-time governance and performance evaluation.

7.4. Integration of AI in IT audits

AI technologies, including machine learning and natural language processing, can change IT audits by automating routine tasks, finding problems, and providing helpful predictions. The use of AI in auditing procedures improves efficiency, effectiveness, and precision, allowing auditors to concentrate on strategic analysis and decision-making.

The integration of AI in auditing signifies that auditors in the digital age acquire specialised skills and uphold the essential ethical standards of the profession (Leocádio et al., 2024).

The integration of AI in auditing presents new issues, including the necessity for ethical AI use, the preservation of transparency, and the management of risks linked to algorithmic decision-making. These issues highlight the necessity of strong governance frameworks, like COBIT, to direct the ethical and efficient incorporation of AI into auditing practices (Dhopte & Bagde, 2023; Kandasamy, 2024).

7.5. Challenges in adopting data-driven audits

Notwithstanding potential benefits, the implementation of data-driven audits in HEIs encounters numerous obstacles. These encompass opposition to change, insufficient technical skills, data privacy issues, and the necessity for substantial investment in technology and training (Kokina et al., 2025; Lois et al., 2020). The diffusion of innovation theory identifies these barriers as obstacles to the adoption of innovative technologies in organisations (Durodolu & Olumide, 2016; Pandjaitan, 2024; Rogers, 1962).

Moreover, the swift advancement of technology may exceed the ability of HEIs to adjust their auditing processes properly. Disruption management theory stresses the necessity for institutions to cultivate resilience and adaptability to effectively navigate disruptions (Prosci, 2023).

7.6. Regulatory and compliance considerations

HEIs function within a multifaceted regulatory framework, with data protection legislation, including the GDPR (James, 2022) and the POPIA, imposing rigorous mandates on data governance and security (Palada et al., 2024). Data-driven audits can improve compliance through real-time monitoring and reporting functionalities. Nonetheless, they also express concerns over data privacy and the ethical use of AI, hence necessitating the formulation of extensive governance structures to tackle these concerns.

7.7. Best case scenarios

Various industries, such as the financial sector, started the integration of data-driven methodologies into their auditing methods. Some institutions have adopted continuous auditing systems that use big data analytics to monitor transactions in real time, enabling the early identification of abnormalities and possible fraud (Bình, 2025; Kaban, 2020; Sun & Qu, 2020; Udeh et al., 2024). Others used AI-driven solutions to automate standard audit activities, thereby reallocating resources for strategic analysis.

These examples illustrate the capacity of data-driven audits to improve governance, risk management, and compliance in HEIs. They emphasise the necessity of integrating audit methods with established frameworks, like COBIT, to ensure their effective implementation and oversight.

The integration of big data analytics and AI into IT audits can significantly enhance the governance capacities of higher education institutions. Using frameworks like COBIT, disruption management theory, and the diffusion of innovations, institutions can effectively address the obstacles of technology adoption. By adopting data-driven audit methodologies, HEIs can improve their capacity to manage risks, maintain compliance, and adjust to the swiftly changing digital environment.

8. FINDINGS AND DISCUSSION

8.1. Introduction

The digital revolution of South African HEIs is altering governance, risk management, and compliance processes (Ajigini, 2022; Sityata et al., 2021; Smidt et al., 2022). Employing Braun and Clarke's (2006) methodology alongside open code, we examined the six HEIs (HEI 1 to HEI 6) publicly accessible reports to explain their treatment of IT governance, AI integration, big data utilisation, digital transformation, data governance, and cybersecurity.

8.2. Thematic synthesis

8.2.1 IT governance

IT governance has become a key concern in universities, indicating a shared understanding of the importance of technology in achieving strategic goals. HEI 1 aligns with COBIT principles by establishing a dedicated Technology and Information Governance Committee for oversight. HEI 2 implements established standards and controls to ensure the security and management of IT operations. HEI 3 employs a top-down approach, as demonstrated by the Council's endorsement of an ICT digitalisation strategy in 2022 aimed at addressing previous governance criticisms. HEI 4's integrated systems facilitate governance; however, external auditors recommend the establishment of a cohesive digital governance strategy. HEI 5's ICT services exhibit integration yet faces challenges due to rapid growth, whereas HEI 6's governance structures are suitable for its size and context. The findings highlight the necessity for universities to periodically assess IT governance practices to accommodate emerging technologies and environmental changes (Bianchi et al., 2021).

8.2.2 Integration of AI

Various educational institutions use AI in different ways. HEI 2's chatbots and mailbots handled over 73,500 application queries, demonstrating the use of AI in their environment. HEI 1 hasn't fully implemented AI yet, but it sees it as an important part of its long-term goal to be an innovator. Through its 4IR and Data Science Research Unit, HEI 3's AI work is mostly focused on building up the skills of academics and researchers. HEI 4, HEI 5, and HEI 6 don't mention AI in their reports, which may mean they are new to it or lack resources. These different levels of AI use show that different institutions have different goals and abilities, which shows how important it is to match AI strategies with available resources. Patel and Ragolane (2024) say that strategically introducing AI into higher education is important for making administration more efficient and improving service delivery.

8.2.3 Use of big data and analytics

Big data analytics practices vary from advanced to emerging stages. The Data and Analytics Strategy and Operating Model (DASOM) at HEI 1 demonstrates a commitment to data-driven decision-making at the institutional level. The HEI 2 uses analytics in education via its Centre for Teaching and Learning, directly connecting data to curriculum renewal. HEI 4 possesses systems and a Data Analytics Working Group; however, it has not fully utilised these capabilities. HEI 3 is enhancing its BI systems to align with the breadth of its distance education objectives, whereas HEI 6 is in the preliminary phases, focusing on establishing reliable data to facilitate student success. HEI 2 does not delineate specific applications of big data, indicating that it may not be a primary area of emphasis. The observed variations highlight the necessity for universities to enhance their data strategies and effectively utilise analytics for strategic insights.

In higher education, particularly within non-public universities, the integration of intelligent technologies frequently aligns with a comprehensive strategy that establishes priorities (Owoc et al., 2021). Artificial intelligence and machine learning improve institutional security and operational efficiency, providing a versatile computing environment and fostering collaborative learning (Kuleto et al., 2021). Higher education is increasingly utilising AI for automated learning and information support, automated essay scoring, and personalised learning (O'Dea & O'Dea, 2023). Adaptive AI systems in university courses enhance student motivation and course completion rates, highlighting the transformative potential of these technologies in higher education (Merino-Campos, 2025). South African universities are investigating AI-powered tools to enhance teaching and learning, considering the challenges and opportunities associated with technological adoption and AI integration in the global South (Bosch et al., 2023).

8.2.4 Digital transformation

Digital transformation is a key concern for all institutions, influenced by the COVID-19 epidemic and the necessity for distant and hybrid education. HEI 1 demonstrates a comprehensive approach, integrating digital transformation with employee development and competitive edge. HEI 3's digitalisation initiatives address delayed ICT projects and the necessity to maintain online education. HEI 4 emphasises adaptive teaching and learning and advocates the formulation of a more extensive digital infrastructure strategy. HEI 5 has invested in digital infrastructure but must address resource constraints. HEI 6's emphasis on infrastructure preparedness brings attention to essential digital competencies. The report does not reference the digital revolution at HEI 2. Universities must consistently evaluate and analyse digital transformation activities to guarantee enhancements in pedagogical and academic achievements (Alenezi & Akour, 2023).

8.2.5 Data governance and quality

Institutions recognise the importance of data governance for effectively leveraging big data and maintaining compliance. HEI 2 complies with data protection standards in accordance with POPIA and COBIT, whereas HEI 1 establishes data governance through DASOM and council oversight. HEI 4 maintains data integrity by implementing stringent quality checks and advocating improved data utilisation. The stable ICT infrastructure at HEI 5 ensures data reliability, while HEI 3's policies, such as the Digital Preservation Policy, enhance investments in cybersecurity. While still in development, HEI 6 maintains reliable data systems and advises enhancing data engagement among faculty and students. Data privacy and ethical usage are critical factors, especially as institutions enhance their AI and data analytics capabilities (George & Wooden, 2023).

8.2.6 Cybersecurity

Cybersecurity methods emphasise both proactive and reactive measures in response to escalating risks. HEI 1 recognises cybersecurity as a primary risk and has established a thorough cybersecurity strategy that includes incident response capabilities. The HEI 2 has contracted a 24/7 cybersecurity service provider and provides training for staff and students to enhance resilience. HEI 3's Managed Cyber Security Infrastructure project rectifies previous vulnerabilities, whereas HEI 4, HEI 5, and HEI 6 reference security only tangentially through robust ICT infrastructure. This highlights disparities in perceived risk levels and the availability of resources for specialised security activities. Universities encounter several cybersecurity threats, such as malware, phishing, and denial-of-service attacks.

Identifying vulnerabilities and establishing procedures to prevent the misuse of critical records is essential (Masmali & Miah, 2022). PRISM, a cybersecurity risk management system designed to address the specific challenges and requirements of the institution, can enhance organisational cyber policies and risk mitigation strategies and practices (Lamarca, 2020). The implementation of cybersecurity is crucial for safeguarding university networks and data in cyberspace (Badamasi & Utulu, 2021). Higher education institutions have important research data and personal information of more than three million staff and students, as well as millions of alumni, rendering them appealing targets for cyberattacks (Lallie et al., 2023). These networks are intricate, with multiple users retrieving data from diverse locations and devices, thereby heightening susceptibility (Lallie et al., 2023). IT governance can improve security processes to avert breaches that may jeopardise valuable academic and personal information (Masmali & Miah, 2022).

8.3. Comparative visualization

Table 1 below presents a comparative summary of institutional approaches across key themes. This visual mapping outlines prominent practices (e.g., HEI 1's strategic oversight, HEI 2's operational AI adoption), emerging areas (e.g., HEI 4's call for a unified digital strategy), and fundamental efforts (e.g., HEI 6's emphasis on infrastructure). Comparative insights encourage the development of focused strategies aimed at enhancing IT governance, conducting data-driven audits, and improving digital resilience within HEIs.

Table 1. Comparative visualization of HEI's IT governance

Themes	HEI 1	HEI 2	HEI 3	HEI 4	HEI 5	HEI 6
IT Governance	Explicit alignment with COBIT, strong oversight	Documented standards and controls	Top-level digital strategy governance	Integrated systems, audit urges comprehensive strategy	Integrated ICT services, risk of growth strain	Basic governance with well-managed ICT
Integration of AI	Strategic focus, innovation and future-oriented	Operational AI (chatbots, mailbots)	Research-focused AI (4IR Unit)	No explicit AI use noted	No explicit AI mention	No AI adoption noted
Use of Big Data	Mature data analytics strategy (DASOM)	Integrated data systems, noted use of analytics	Developing data analytics and BI systems	Systems in place, data analytics working group	Data analytics for teaching improvement	Foundational data systems, credible data
Digital Transformation	Holistic digital transformation with staff training	Digital transformation for inclusion, strategic adoption	Responsive digital transformation (CODeL focus)	Teaching-focused digital transformation	Modern facilities, digitalisation plan	Emphasis on infrastructure readiness
Data Governance & Quality	Formal DASOM and council oversight	Data protection standards for privacy and control	Data preservation and research data policies	Data quality checks, recommended utilization improvement	Stable infrastructure, quality-focused	Recommendations for student/staff data engagement
Cybersecurity	Top risk priority, dedicated response team	Managed 24/7 cybersecurity service	Addressing weaknesses with new infrastructure	Cybersecurity not highlighted	Secure infrastructure mentioned	No explicit mention, likely built-in security

Source: Researchers' own compilation

The thematic analysis indicates that although all six universities acknowledge the significance of digital transformation and data-driven governance, they are at varying degrees of adoption and maturity. Early adopters such as HEI 1 and HEI 2 amalgamate strategic and operational technology efforts, whereas HEI 3 concentrates on remediation and capacity enhancement. HEI 5, HEI 4, and HEI 6 demonstrate foundational to intermediate involvement, reconciling resource limitations with digital ambitions. This comparative theme synthesis, grounded in solid theoretical frameworks, enhances the knowledge of how South African HEIs are managing the intricacies of digital governance in a swiftly changing educational environment.

8.4 Comparative insights and international best practices for South African HEIs

The integration of advanced technologies and effective IT governance in HEIs is crucial for achieving operational efficiency, regulatory compliance, and competitive advantage (Patel & Ragolane, 2024; Sengik et al., 2022). This analysis integrates findings from the thematic examination of six South African universities: HEI

2, HEI 3, HEI 1, HEI 4, HEI 5, and HEI 6, and juxtaposes these with global best practices. This section examines literature and global case studies to illustrate how South African HEIs can improve their strategies regarding IT governance, AI adoption, big data analytics, digital transformation, data governance, and cybersecurity.

8.5 IT Governance: Establishing comprehensive frameworks

Effective IT governance ensures that technological investments are in alignment with institutional missions and comply with regulatory requirements (Sengik et al., 2022). The thematic analysis indicated that HEI 1 exhibits strong IT governance in accordance with COBIT principles, whereas HEI 2 depends on established standards to uphold data privacy and operational integrity. HEI 3, addressing previous governance deficiencies, has instituted a comprehensive IT digitalisation strategy at the highest level. On the other hand, HEI 4 and HEI 5 exhibit developing governance structures, accompanied by suggestions for stronger frameworks.

Across the globe, European universities regularly implement frameworks like COBIT and ISO/IEC 38500 to standardise IT processes and improve decision-making (Armas & Taherdoost, 2025; Sulasula, 2023). The University of Edinburgh, for instance, uses these frameworks to ensure strategic use of technology in teaching, learning, and administration (University of Edinburgh, 2024). The evidence indicates that HEIs in South Africa, especially those that continue to depend on conventional governance frameworks, have the opportunity to enhance their IT governance by integrating globally acknowledged models. This integration would help ensure better management and alignment with the school's goals, which would lower the risks associated with fast changes in technology.

8.6 AI Integration: From research to administration

The integration of AI in South African HEIs shows significant variability. The HEI 2 has implemented AI-driven chatbots and mailbots to enhance administrative efficiency, showcasing initial operational application. HEI 3 positions artificial intelligence as a strategic avenue for future innovation, whereas the HEI 1 focuses its AI initiatives on academic research via its Fourth Industrial Revolution and Data Science Research Unit. HEI 4, HEI 5, and HEI 6 have not yet developed strategies for AI adoption.

The Massachusetts Institute of Technology (MIT) serves as a model for effectively utilising AI to tailor learning experiences and implement predictive analytics to enhance student success (MIT Media Lab, 2024). These applications illustrate the potential of AI to improve student engagement and institutional effectiveness. South African HEIs can learn from MIT by incorporating AI into research and strategic planning, as well as into current operational processes to enhance administrative efficiency and educational outcomes.

8.7 Big Data Analytics: Transforming decision-making

Big data analytics emerged as a prominent theme across all six universities. HEI 1's Data and Analytics Strategy and Operating Model (DASOM) represent a thorough framework for employing analytics in strategic decision-making. HEI 5 employs analytics to guide curriculum development and teaching methodologies, whereas HEI 4 and HEI 3 are at preliminary phases of analytics integration, demonstrating existing data infrastructure yet failing to leverage its capabilities fully. HEI 6's initiatives are fundamental, creating reliable data systems as a prerequisite for the application of advanced analytics.

The University of Edinburgh's application of data analytics to assess student engagement and forecast academic performance serves as a model for the integration of big data in academic decision-making (University of Edinburgh, 2024). The university can utilise real-time data analytics to customise interventions aimed at supporting at-risk students and improving academic outcomes. South African universities can implement analogous data-driven strategies to enhance student success, optimise resource distribution, and inform policy formulation.

8.8 Digital transformation: Building future-ready institutions

The COVID-19 pandemic expedited the necessity for digital transformation, which is acknowledged by all six South African HEIs. HEI 1's comprehensive digital transformation strategy, which encompasses staff training and infrastructure modernisation, is a significant model. HEI 3 is enhancing its online learning environment, whereas HEI 4 and HEI 5 are addressing curriculum modernisation and infrastructure requirements. HEI 6, being a relatively new institution, emphasises the establishment of foundational digital infrastructure to facilitate future transformations.

The Open University in the UK exemplifies digital transformation by transitioning to a fully online model, thereby providing flexible and accessible learning opportunities (The Open University, 2024). South African HEIs can adopt this model by incorporating blended and online learning platforms to improve flexibility and accessibility for varied student demographics, especially in rural or underserved regions. Aligning digital transformation strategies with institutional missions and student needs is essential for sustainable innovation.

8.9 Data governance and quality: Enabling compliance and trust

Data governance is necessary for maintaining data quality, security, and adherence to requirements such as South Africa's Protection of Personal Information Act (POPIA). HEI 2 and HEI 1 demonstrate systematic data governance, with HEI 1's DASOM exemplifying oversight at the council level. HEI 4 and HEI 5 possess robust data management policies yet have difficulties in maximising their data for institutional planning and decision-making. HEI 3's data rules and HEI 6's foundational practices highlight the recognition of data stewardship as a fundamental governance value.

Stanford University's extensive data governance frameworks, including data stewardship responsibilities and data quality standards, exemplify how organised governance may protect data integrity and facilitate data-driven decision-making (Stanford University, 2024). South African universities can set up similar systems to clarify who is responsible for data, making sure that insights from data lead to effective plans and comply with new regulations.

8.10 Cybersecurity: Strengthening resilience in a digital age

Cybersecurity stands as a paramount concern for digitally advanced institutions, such as HEI 1 and HEI 2, both of which have committed resources to specialised incident response systems and managed cybersecurity services. HEI 3 is addressing previous audit findings by implementing a managed cybersecurity infrastructure, while HEI 4, HEI 5, and HEI 6 maintain secure ICT infrastructure but do not specifically emphasise cybersecurity initiatives.

Universities across the United States widely adopt the National Institute of Standards and Technology (NIST) Cybersecurity Framework to effectively manage and mitigate cybersecurity risks (NIST, 2024). Through the adoption of established cybersecurity standards and the execution of regular risk assessments, South African HEIs can enhance their digital resilience and safeguard sensitive academic and administrative information from increasing cyber threats.

This discussion emphasises that while South African HEIs are exploring various paths in digital governance, international best practices offer distinct avenues for enhancement. Utilising frameworks such as COBIT and ISO/IEC 38500 can enhance IT governance and ensure alignment among institutions. Implementing AI and big data analytics can improve decision-making in both academic and administrative contexts, while having structured data governance and cybersecurity measures is vital for preserving trust and ensuring compliance. By studying global exemplars, South African universities can cope with this disruption with strategic oversight, making sure that digital transformation serves as a catalyst for enhanced academic outcomes and institutional sustainability.

9. OVERCOMING CHALLENGES IN SOUTH AFRICAN HEIS: STRATEGIES FOR IMPLEMENTATION

Although the findings and conversations indicate promising opportunities, South African HEIs encounter numerous enduring hurdles in their digital governance endeavours. The difficulties encompass constrained resources, disjointed governance frameworks, data silos, digital disparities among personnel and students, and emerging cybersecurity risks. Addressing these difficulties necessitates a blend of strategic, operational, and cultural transformations.

9.1 Strengthening strategic alignment and capacity building

A persistent challenge is the absence of cohesive strategies in certain institutions, such as HEI 4 and HEI 5, where digital initiatives tend to be fragmented. By using the holistic approaches observed at HEI 1 and globally at institutions such as the Open University, HEIs in South Africa can establish formal digital strategies that correspond with institutional objectives and stakeholder requirements. This process involves the formation of digital transformation task forces comprising IT leaders, academic personnel, and student representatives to ensure that plans are thorough and feasible.

Capacity-building initiatives are essential. Institutions should allocate resources for staff training and upskilling to facilitate effective engagement with new systems and data-driven decision-making processes. HEI 2's staff training for digital transformation represents a local best practice with potential for sector-wide scalability.

9.2 Enhancing data-driven cultures

Although most institutions have data analytics capabilities (for example, HEI 1's DASOM), there is still a barrier to integrating data-driven decision-making into institutional cultures. Internationally, the University of Edinburgh's use of learning analytics for continual student engagement enhancement provides a model (University of Edinburgh, 2024). South African HEIs might follow suit by increasing data literacy among their staff and incorporating data insights into academic and administrative procedures.

9.3 Breaking down data silos

Establishing centralised data repositories and cross-functional data governance teams can mitigate the existence of data silos, such as HEI 4. These teams can facilitate the seamless transfer of data between systems, hence enhancing comprehensive decision-making. Insights from Stanford University's data stewardship methodology (Stanford University, 2024) point out the value of explicit data responsibilities and standards, which South African universities can emulate by establishing data ownership and accountability frameworks.

9.4 Balancing innovation and ethical considerations

The adoption of AI and big data analytics presents ethical and regulatory difficulties, such as data privacy, algorithmic bias, and transparency. Using MIT's responsible AI projects (MIT Media Lab, 2024), South African HEIs can formulate ethical AI rules and guarantee that emerging technologies adhere to the principles of justice and inclusivity. Forming ethics review groups for technology implementation might mitigate unforeseen outcomes.

9.5 Closing the digital divide

The digital divide, worsened by economic inequality, continues to be a substantial hurdle. Universities may alleviate this issue by investing in inexpensive internet connections for students, distributing low-cost digital gadgets, and implementing blended learning methods that account for connectivity limits. For example, HEI 6's emphasis on ICT infrastructure and dependable internet access serves as a basic step that other institutions might follow and build upon.

9.6 Strengthening cybersecurity resilience

Given the increased cyber dangers faced by digitally mature institutions such as HEI 1, all universities must take proactive cybersecurity measures. Implementing recognised frameworks, such as the NIST Cybersecurity Framework (NIST, 2024) and conducting frequent vulnerability assessments can aid in the identification and mitigation of possible threats. Furthermore, building a culture of cyberawareness among staff and students through regular training is critical, as human error is frequently the weakest link in security defenses.

9.7 Leveraging external partnerships

Strategic partnerships with the private sector, government agencies, and international collaborators can effectively address financial and technical constraints. Partnerships can offer collaborative expertise, financial resources, and technology solutions specifically designed for the South African context. Collaborating with regional ICT companies to develop secure, locally relevant platforms can assist HEIs with modernisation while maintaining budgetary constraints.

9.8 Promoting continuous improvement and feedback loops

Ultimately, as demonstrated by global leaders such as the Open University, effective digital transformation is an iterative process necessitating ongoing monitoring and adjustment (The Open University, 2024). South African HEIs can implement feedback loops by regularly evaluating the effectiveness of digital initiatives and making evidence-based adjustments. Institutional research units can assess the effects of new technologies on teaching, learning, and operational performance.

9.9 Charting a sustainable path forward

Thus, although South African HEIs differ in digital maturity and capability, there is a collective acknowledgement of the necessity for strong governance, data-informed decision-making, and safe digital environments. Studying global best practices—such as the extensive digital strategies of the Open University, Stanford's data stewardship, and MIT's creative application of AI—can offer essential assistance. Nonetheless, local settings are significant: effective implementation will rely on institutional endorsement, adaptive leadership, and a dedication to inclusivity and ongoing enhancement.

By actively addressing problems like poor governance, unequal access to technology, isolated data systems, and security risks, South African HEIs can use digital transformation to improve academic quality, help students succeed, and ensure long-term stability.

10. THEORETICAL AND PRACTICAL IMPLICATIONS

10.1 Theoretical implications

This study integrates global frameworks (COBIT, ISO/IEC 38500, disruptive innovation theories, and the diffusion of innovations model) to analyse the adoption of digital governance in South African HEIs. The analysis indicates that certain institutions are early adopters of advanced IT governance and data-driven practices, while others fall behind due to contextual factors. This finding supports the idea that the adoption of innovation is nonlinear and influenced by institutional capacity, strategic priorities, and external pressures (Kohl, 2023). The findings contribute to the discussion of digital maturity in HEIs by contextualising South African experiences with global trends.

10.2 Practical implications

This study offers South African HEIs a framework for improving IT governance, integrating AI, utilising big data analytics, advancing digital transformation, managing data governance, and strengthening cybersecurity. By emphasising comparative practices and insights from worldwide exemplars like MIT, Stanford, and the Open University, it provides pragmatic ways to enhance digital resilience and operational efficiency. The practical consequences encompass:

- The strategic alignment of IT governance frameworks with institutional missions is achieved through the use of established frameworks like COBIT.
- AI is being implemented to improve administrative efficiency and student assistance.
- Fostering data-driven cultures by enhancing data literacy and dismantling data silos.
- Enhancing cybersecurity measures through NIST-compliant frameworks and awareness programs.
- Utilising collaborations for collective knowledge and resource efficiency.

11. THE LIMITATIONS OF THE STUDY

The use of externally created reports alleviates the specific limitations of this study. The research is based on publicly accessible executive summaries and audit reports produced by external auditors and oversight entities, including the CHE. Although these other sources offer a degree of independence and impartiality that enhances the credibility of their findings, they remain subject to the frameworks and criteria established by these organisations. Therefore, an aspect of institutional framing may persist, not solely attributable to overt institutional bias, but rather because external auditors frequently prioritise compliance and strategic alignment, potentially neglecting the quotidian intricacies or cultural obstacles associated with the implementation of digital governance.

Secondly, notwithstanding the external autonomy of these reports, the study did not integrate direct contributions from internal stakeholders, like academic personnel, IT auditors within the institutions, or students. Even though external audits and CHE evaluations provide organised, evidence-based information about digital governance and transformation efforts, they often do not capture the real experiences and working conditions of the people who actually use the digital systems. Conducting direct interviews, surveys, or focus groups with staff and students would enhance the analysis, offering personal opinions about the implementation of digital governance frameworks and identifying potential shortcomings not fully apparent from external evaluations.

However, using independent and verified audit and CHE reports is a significant advantage of this study, providing a trustworthy way to understand digital governance processes in South African HEIs.

Future research can expand upon this basis by incorporating internal stakeholder viewpoints and triangulating institutional narratives and external oversight with the actual realities of individuals impacted by digital governance strategies.

12. FUTURE RESEARCH DIRECTIONS

This study's conclusions suggest numerous future research opportunities to further our understanding of digital governance inside South African HEIs. Longitudinal studies could monitor the evolution of digital governance and IT audit procedures over time, especially as institutions enhance their digital transformation goals and adapt to persistent technological challenges. These studies could highlight both the progress made and the challenges faced in keeping up with changes, offering a more active view than what is usually found in yearly reports and audits.

Secondly, case study research exploring the lived experiences of staff, students, and IT governance executives would yield essential qualitative insights to enhance the externally validated quantitative data. Such studies could investigate the effects of digital transformation programs on daily teaching, learning, and administrative activities, revealing cultural or organisational obstacles to adoption that may not be adequately represented in institutional narratives.

Thirdly, comparative study across other African or Global South contexts would contextualise South African HEIs within a wider continental or international framework. The results will clarify whether the digital governance difficulties and accomplishments reported in South Africa correspond with broader regional trends or are distinctly influenced by local circumstances. Such comparisons may elucidate regionally pertinent tactics and enhance theoretical frameworks for comprehending digital governance in resource-limited or swiftly changing environments.

Ultimately, research concentrated on cybersecurity represents a viable domain for further exploration. This study recognised cybersecurity as a key concern for prominent South African HEIs, although additional research could comprehensively delineate the unique threats and vulnerabilities confronting the sector. This type of work may encompass technical vulnerability assessments, surveys on staff and student awareness, or evaluations on the localisation of global cybersecurity frameworks such as NIST within the South African higher education context.

Future research might expand upon this work by exploring how South African universities manage the interplay between digital innovation, governance, and the fulfilment of their academic missions.

CONCLUSION

In conclusion, this study provides a nuanced, comparative perspective on how South African HEIs are navigating the complexities of IT governance and digital transformation. By applying global best practices and theoretical frameworks, it highlights both the progress made and the challenges that remain—particularly around AI integration, data-driven decision-making, and cybersecurity. As digital disruption continues to reshape higher education globally, South African universities have a unique opportunity to leverage lessons from international exemplars while crafting contextually relevant strategies that promote inclusivity, resilience, and academic excellence.

REFERENCES

Adelakun, B. O., Majekodunmi, T. G., & Akintoye, O. S. (2024). AI and ethical accounting: Navigating challenges and opportunities. *International Journal of Advanced Economics*, *6*(6), 224–241. DOI: 10.51594/ijae.v6i6.1230

Aditya, B. R., Hartanto, R., & Nugroho, L. E. (2018). The Role of IT Audit in the Era of Digital Transformation. *IOP Conference Series. Materials Science and Engineering*, *407*, 12164. DOI: 10.1088/1757-899X/407/1/012164

Ajigini, O. A. (2022). Towards a Model on Digital Transformation within the Higher Education Sector. https://digitalcommons.kennesaw.edu/cgi/viewcontent.cgi?article=1067&context=acist

Akacha, S. A.-L., & Awad, A. I. (2023). Enhancing Security and Sustainability of e-Learning Software Systems: A Comprehensive Vulnerability Analysis and Recommendations for Stakeholders. *Sustainability (Basel)*, *15*(19), 14132. DOI: 10.3390/su151914132

Alaran, M., Lawal, S. K., Jiya, M. H., Egya, S. A., Ahmed, M. M., Abdulsalam, A., Haruna, U. A., Musa, M. K., & Lucero-Prisno, D. E.III. (2025). Challenges and opportunities of artificial intelligence in African health space. *Digital Health*, *11*, 20552076241305915. Advance online publication. DOI: 10.1177/20552076241305915 PMID: 39839959

Alenezi, M., & Akour, M. (2023). Digital Transformation Blueprint in Higher Education: A Case Study of PSU. *Sustainability (Basel)*, *15*(10), 8204. DOI: 10.3390/su15108204

Aliyu, A., Μαγλαράς, Λ., He, Y., Yevseyeva, I., Boiten, E., Cook, A., & Janicke, H. (2020). A Holistic Cybersecurity Maturity Assessment Framework for Higher Education Institutions in the United Kingdom. *Applied Sciences (Basel, Switzerland)*, *10*(10), 3660. DOI: 10.3390/app10103660

Anton, T. S., Trupp, A., Stephenson, M. L., & Chong, K. L. (2023). The Technology Adoption Model Canvas (TAMC): A Smart Framework to Guide the Advancement of Microbusinesses in Emerging Economies. *Smart Cities*, *6*(6), 3297–3318. DOI: 10.3390/smartcities6060146

Armas, R., & Taherdoost, H. (2025). Building a Cybersecurity Culture in Higher Education: Proposing a Cybersecurity Awareness Paradigm. *Information (Basel)*, *16*(5), 336. DOI: 10.3390/info16050336

Atrinawati, F., Gerl, H., Von Der Heyde, M., Groß, M., Seck, D., & Watkowski, R. (2021). Applying COBIT 2019 to IT Governance in Higher Education. Retrieved from https://www.researchgate.net/publication/349440036ResearchGate+1DLGI+1

Badamasi, B., & Utulu, S. C. A. (2021). Framework for Managing Cybercrime Risks in Nigerian Universities. arXiv (Cornell University). https://doi.org//arxiv .2108.09754DOI: 10.48550

Benavides, L. M. C., Arias, J. A. T., Burgos, D., & Martens, A. (2022). *Measuring digital transformation in higher education institutions – content validity instrument*. Applied Computing and Informatics., DOI: 10.1108/ACI-03-2022-0069

Bianchi, I. S., Sousa, R. D., & Pereira, R. (2021). Information Technology Governance for Higher Education Institutions: A Multi-Country Study. *Informatics (MDPI)*, *8*(2), 26. DOI: 10.3390/informatics8020026

. Bình, N. T. T. (2025). Transforming Auditing in the AI Era: A Comprehensive Review [Review of Transforming Auditing in the AI Era: A Comprehensive Review]. Information, 16(5), 400. Multidisciplinary Digital Publishing Institute. DOI: 10.3390/info16050400

Borgman, C. L. (2018). Open Data, Grey Data, and Stewardship: Universities at the Privacy Frontier. arXiv (Cornell University). https://doi.org//arXiv.1802.02953DOI: 10.48550

Bosch, T., Jordaan, M., Mwaura, J., Nkoala, S., Schoon, A., Smit, A., Uzuegbunam, C. E., & Mare, A. (2023). South African University Students' Use of AI-Powered Tools for Engaged Learning. SSRN Electronic Journal. DOI: 10.2139/ssrn.4595655

Bowen, G. A. (2009). Document analysis as a qualitative research method. *Qualitative Research Journal*, *9*(2), 27–40. DOI: 10.3316/QRJ0902027

Braun, V., & Clarke, V. (2006). Using thematic analysis in psychology. *Qualitative Research in Psychology*, *3*(2), 77–101. DOI: 10.1191/1478088706qp063oa

Choi, D., Chung, C. Y., Seyha, T., & Young, J. (2020). Factors Affecting Organizations' Resistance to the Adoption of Blockchain Technology in Supply Networks. *Sustainability (Basel)*, *12*(21), 8882. DOI: 10.3390/su12218882

Colorafi, K., & Evans, B. C. (2016). Qualitative Descriptive Methods in Health Science Research. *HERD*, *9*(4), 16–25. DOI: 10.1177/1937586715614171 PMID: 26791375

Daily Investor. (2025, April 15). *One threat bigger than load-shedding in South Africa*. Retrieved from https://dailyinvestor.com/business/85980/one-threat-bigger-than-load-shedding-in-south-africa/

Dhopte, A., & Bagde, H. (2023). *Smart Smile: Revolutionizing Dentistry With Artificial Intelligence* [Review of Smart Smile: Revolutionizing Dentistry With Artificial Intelligence]. Cureus. Cureus, Inc., DOI: 10.7759/cureus.41227

. Divjak, B., Rienties, B., Iniesto, F., Vondra, P., & Žižak, M. (2022). Flipped classrooms in higher education during the COVID-19 pandemic: findings and future research recommendations [Review of Flipped classrooms in higher education during the COVID-19 pandemic: findings and future research recommendations]. International Journal of Educational Technology in Higher Education, 19(1). Springer Nature. DOI: 10.1186/s41239-021-00316-4

Durodolu, O. O., & Olumide, O. (2016). Technology Acceptance Model as a predictor of using information system' to acquire information literacy skills. Library Philosophy and Practice. https://digitalcommons.unl.edu/cgi/viewcontent.cgi?article=4029&context=libphilprac

Fitrani, L. D., & Ginardi, R. V. H. (2019). Analysis Improvement of Helpdesk System Services Based on Framework COBIT 5 and ITIL 3rd Version (Case Study: DSIK Airlangga University). *IPTEK Journal of Proceedings Series*, *1*(1), 28. DOI: 10.12962/j23546026.y2019i1.5102

Foster, E., Mphil, M., Nkyi-Asamoah, J., Klutse, E. K., & Kwadwo, M. (2020). Technology in Music Education: A Survey of Computer Usage in Teaching Music in Selected Colleges of Education in Ghana. *Journal of Education and Practice*. Advance online publication. DOI: 10.7176/JEP/11-3-15

Gadhi, A., Gondu, R. M., Chaudhary, H., & Abiona, O. (2024). Cyber Resilience through Real-Time Threat Analysis in Information Security. *International Journal of Communications, Network and Systems Sciences*, *17*(4), 51–67. DOI: 10.4236/ijcns.2024.174004

Ganesen, R., Bakar, A. A., Ramli, R., Rahim, F. A., & Zawawi, M. N. A. (2022). Cybersecurity Risk Assessment: Modeling Factors Associated with Higher Education Institutions. *International Journal of Advanced Computer Science and Applications*, *13*(8). Advance online publication. DOI: 10.14569/IJACSA.2022.0130843

George, B., & Wooden, O. S. (2023). Managing the Strategic Transformation of Higher Education through Artificial Intelligence. *Administrative Sciences*, *13*(9), 196. DOI: 10.3390/admsci13090196

Gerber, A., & Matthee, M. (2019). Design Thinking for Pre-empting Digital Disruption. In Lecture notes in computer science (p. 759). Springer Science+Business Media. DOI: 10.1007/978-3-030-29374-1_62

Ghorashi, S. R., Zia, T., Bewong, M., & Jiang, Y. (2023). An Analytical Review of Industrial Privacy Frameworks and Regulations for Organisational Data Sharing. *Applied Sciences (Basel, Switzerland)*, *13*(23), 12727. DOI: 10.3390/app132312727

Isaca. (2012). Cobit 5. https://dl.acm.org/citation.cfm?id=2361913

Jakkula, A. R. (2024). Ensuring Data Privacy and Security in AI-Enabled E-commerce Platforms. *Journal of Artificial Intelligence & Cloud Computing*, *3*(1), 1–3. DOI: 10.47363/JAICC/2024(3)288

James, M. (2022). International Student Recruitment During the Pandemic: The Unique Perspective of Recruiters from Small to Medium-Sized Higher Education Institutions. *Higher Education Policy*, *36*(3), 510–528. DOI: 10.1057/s41307-022-00271-3 PMID: 35465058

. Kaban, İ. (2020). Central audit activities as a continuous audit approach in the Turkish banking sector: A case study about frauds in savings accounts. Öneri Dergisi, 15(53), 254. DOI: 10.14783/maruoneri.676406

Kandasamy, U. C. (2024). Ethical Leadership in the Age of AI Challenges, Opportunities and Framework for Ethical Leadership. arXiv (Cornell University). https://doi.org//arxiv.2410.18095DOI: 10.48550

Karpouzis, K. (2024). Artificial Intelligence in Education. *Ethical Considerations and Insights from Ancient Greek Philosophy.*, *1*, 1–7. Advance online publication. DOI: 10.1145/3688671.3688772

Khther, R. A., & Othman, M. (2013). Cobit Framework as a Guideline of Effective it Governance in Higher Education: A Review [Review of Cobit Framework as a Guideline of Effective it Governance in Higher Education: A Review]. *International Journal of Advanced Information Technology*, *3*(1), 21–29. DOI: 10.5121/ijitcs.2013.3102

. Klímová, B., & Pikhart, M. (2025). Exploring the effects of artificial intelligence on student and academic well-being in higher education: a mini-review [Review of Exploring the effects of artificial intelligence on student and academic well-being in higher education: a mini-review]. Frontiers in Psychology, 16. Frontiers Media. DOI: 10.3389/fpsyg.2025.1498132

Kohl, R. D. (2023). Key factors for advancing innovations to scale: Evidence from multiple country case studies of agricultural innovations. *Frontiers in Sustainable Food Systems*, *7*, 1053152. Advance online publication. DOI: 10.3389/fsufs.2023.1053152

Kokina, J., Blanchette, S., Davenport, T. H., & Pachamanova, D. A. (2025). Challenges and opportunities for artificial intelligence in auditing: Evidence from the field. *International Journal of Accounting Information Systems*, *56*, 100734. DOI: 10.1016/j.accinf.2025.100734

Kuleto, V., Ilić, M., Dumangiu, M. A., Ranković, M., Martins, O., Păun, D., & Mihoreanu, L. (2021). Exploring Opportunities and Challenges of Artificial Intelligence and Machine Learning in Higher Education Institutions. *Sustainability (Basel)*, *13*(18), 10424. DOI: 10.3390/su131810424

Lallie, H. S., Thompson, A., Titis, E., & Stephens, P. (2023). Understanding Cyber Threats Against the Universities, Colleges, and Schools. arXiv (Cornell University). https://doi.org//arXiv.2307.07755DOI: 10.48550

Lamarca, B. I. J. (2020). Cybersecurity Risk Assessment of the University of Northern Philippines using PRISM Approach. *IOP Conference Series. Materials Science and Engineering*, *769*(1), 12066. DOI: 10.1088/1757-899X/769/1/012066

Leocádio, D., Malheiro, L., & Reis, J. (2024). Artificial Intelligence in Auditing: A Conceptual Framework for Auditing Practices. *Administrative Sciences*, *14*(10), 238. DOI: 10.3390/admsci14100238

Lois, P., Drogalas, G., Karagiorgos, A., & Tsikalakis, K. (2020). Internal audits in the digital era: Opportunities risks and challenges. *EuroMed Journal of Business*, *15*(2), 205–217. DOI: 10.1108/EMJB-07-2019-0097

Mah, D.-K., & Gross, N. (2024). Artificial intelligence in higher education: Exploring faculty use, self-efficacy, distinct profiles, and professional development needs. *International Journal of Educational Technology in Higher Education*, *21*(1), 58. Advance online publication. DOI: 10.1186/s41239-024-00490-1

Maota, T. (2024). A conceptual framework for private higher educational institutions to respond to disruptions in South Africa. Available online: https://researchspace.ukzn.ac.za/items/404b7a1f-e593-490a-a749-09c00f6d9e07

Marcela, E. D., & Fianty, M. I. (2023). Performance Evaluation IT Governance on Universities: COBIT 2019 Approach with Measurement Capability Levels. *Indonesian Journal of Computer Science*, *12*(4). Advance online publication. DOI: 10.33022/ijcs.v12i4.3353

Marcucci, S., Alarcon, N. G., Verhulst, S., & Wüllhorst, E. (2023). Mapping and Comparing Data Governance Frameworks: A benchmarking exercise to inform global data governance deliberations. arXiv (Cornell University). https://doi.org//arXiv.2302.13731DOI: 10.48550

Marri, R., Dabbara, L. N., & Karampuri, S. (2024). AI security in different industries: A comprehensive review of vulnerabilities and mitigation strategies [Review of AI security in different industries: A comprehensive review of vulnerabilities and mitigation strategies]. *International Journal of Science and Research Archive, 13*(1), 2375–2393. DOI: 10.30574/ijsra.2024.13.1.1923

Masmali, H. H., & Miah, S. J. (2022, July). Emergent insight of the cyber security management for Saudi Arabian universities: a content analysis. In Proceedings of Seventh International Congress on Information and Communication Technology: ICICT 2022, London, Volume 2 (pp. 153-171). Singapore: Springer Nature Singapore.

Mbonye, V., Moodley, M., & Nyika, F. (2024). Examining the applicability of the Protection of Personal Information Act in AI-driven environments. *South African Journal of Information Management, 26*(1). Advance online publication. DOI: 10.4102/sajim.v26i1.1808

. Merino-Campos, C. (2025). The Impact of Artificial Intelligence on Personalized Learning in Higher Education: A Systematic Review [Review of The Impact of Artificial Intelligence on Personalized Learning in Higher Education: A Systematic Review]. Trends in Higher Education, 4(2), 17. Multidisciplinary Digital Publishing Institute. DOI: 10.3390/higheredu4020017

MIT Media Lab. (2024). *Generative AI for Personalized Learning & Self-Development*. Retrieved from https://www.media.mit.edu/projects/generative-ai-for-personalized-learning/overview/

Mohamed, E. A., Elshareif, E., & El, . (2019). Designing a Generic Information Systems Audit Framework to Improve the Quality of Audit in Higher Education. *Journal of Computational Science, 15*(5), 664–672. DOI: 10.3844/jcssp.2019.664.672

Morgan, H. (2022). Conducting a Qualitative Document Analysis. *The Qualitative Report*. Advance online publication. DOI: 10.46743/2160-3715/2022.5044

. Moşteanu, N. R. (2023). Building a sustainable future: how intelligent automation Is transforming higher education's sustainability efforts. E3S Web of Conferences, 420, 10009. DOI: 10.1051/e3sconf/202342010009

National Institute of Standards and Technology (NIST). (2024). *Cybersecurity Framework*. Retrieved from https://www.nist.gov/cyberframework

Nurdin, A., & Lubis, M. (2023). The IT Governance Measurement using Cobit 5 Framework in Quality Assurance Department. *Jurnal Informatika Dan Rekayasa Perangkat Lunak*, *5*(1), 80. DOI: 10.36499/jinrpl.v5i1.7963

O'Dea, X., & O'Dea, M. (2023). Is Artificial Intelligence Really the Next Big Thing in Learning and Teaching in Higher Education? A Conceptual Paper. *Journal of University Teaching & Learning Practice*, *20*(5). Advance online publication. DOI: 10.53761/1.20.5.06

O'Donnell, J. B. (2024). Auditing Transformation: A Model of Artificial Intelligence Adoption. *Journal of Applied Business and Economics*, *26*(6). Advance online publication. DOI: 10.33423/jabe.v26i6.7390

. Onesi-Ozigagun, O., Ololade, Y. J., Eyo-Udo, N. L., & Ogundipe, D. O. (2024). Revolutionizing education through AI: A comprehensive review of enhancing learning experiences. International Journal of Applied Research in Social Sciences, 6(4), 589. Fair East Publishers. DOI: 10.51594/ijarss.v6i4.1011

Owoc, M. L., Sawicka, A., & Weichbroth, P. (2021). Artificial Intelligence Technologies in Education: Benefits, Challenges and Strategies of Implementation. In IFIP advances in information and communication technology (p. 37). Springer Science+Business Media. DOI: 10.1007/978-3-030-85001-2_4

Palada, B., Chandan, V. S., & Gowda, C. P. (2024). The Role of Augmented Reality (AR) in Education. *International Journal for Research in Applied Science and Engineering Technology*, *12*(3), 1400–1408. DOI: 10.22214/ijraset.2024.59079

Pandjaitan, R. H. (2024). The Social Media Marketing Mix Trends in Indonesia for 2024: Communication Perspective. *Jurnal Komunikasi Ikatan Sarjana Komunikasi Indonesia*, *9*(1), 251–269. DOI: 10.25008/jkiski.v9i1.1005

Patel, S., & Ragolane, M. (2024). The Implementation of Artificial Intelligence in South African Higher Education Institutions: Opportunities and Challenges. *Technium Education and Humanities*, *9*, 51–65. DOI: 10.47577/teh.v9i.11452

Patil, D. (2025). Artificial Intelligence In Financial Risk Assessment And Fraud Detection: Opportunities And Ethical Concerns. DOI: 10.2139/ssrn.5057434

Popenoe, R., Langius-Eklöf, A., Stenwall, E., & Jervaeus, A. (2021). A practical guide to data analysis in general literature reviews. *Nordic Journal of Nursing Research*, *41*(4), 175–186. DOI: 10.1177/2057158521991949

Prescott, M. B. (1995). Diffusion of innovation theory. *The Data Base for Advances in Information Systems*, *26*(2-3), 16–19. DOI: 10.1145/217278.217283

Prosci. (2023). Managing Disruptive Changes in Higher Education. Retrieved from https://www.prosci.com/blog/managing-disruptive-changes-in-higher-ed

. Reis, O., Eneh, N. E., Ehimuan, B., Anyanwu, A., Olorunsogo, T., & Abrahams, T. O. (2024). Privacy law challenges in the digital age: A global review of legislation and enforcement. International Journal of Applied Research in Social Sciences, 6(1), 73. Fair East Publishers. DOI: 10.51594/ijarss.v6i1.733

Rogers, E. M. (1962). Diffusion of Innovations. https://blogs.unpad.ac.id/teddykw/files/2012/07/Everett-M.-Rogers-Diffusion-of-Innovations.pdf

Rojas, Ó. A. C., Contero, M., & Hincapié, M. (2025). Personalized and Timely Feedback in Online Education: Enhancing Learning with Deep Learning and Large Language Models. *Multimodal Technologies and Interaction*, *9*(5), 45. DOI: 10.3390/mti9050045

Roshanaei, M., Olivares, H., & Lopez, R. R. (2023). Harnessing AI to Foster Equity in Education: Opportunities, Challenges, and Emerging Strategies. *Journal of Intelligent Learning Systems and Applications*, *15*(4), 123–143. DOI: 10.4236/jilsa.2023.154009

Samsinar, S., & Sinaga, R. (2022). Information Technology Governance Audit at XYZ College Using COBIT Framework 2019. *BERKALA SAINSTEK*, *10*(2), 58. DOI: 10.19184/bst.v10i2.30325

Sengik, A. R., Lunardi, G. L., Bianchi, I. S., & Wiedenhöft, G. C. (2022). Using design science research to propose an IT governance model for higher education institutions. *Education and Information Technologies*, *27*(8), 11285–11305. DOI: 10.1007/s10639-022-11088-3 PMID: 35528756

Serpil, H., & Kesim, E. (2024). Understanding the Application of AI in Higher Education Systems: Global Perspectives From a Local AI Ecosystem. *Open Praxis*, *16*(4), 645–662. DOI: 10.55982/openpraxis.16.4.725

Sityata, I., Botha, L., & Dubihlela, J. (2021). Risk Management Practices by South African Universities: An Annual Report Disclosure Analysis. *Journal of Risk and Financial Management*, *14*(5), 195. DOI: 10.3390/jrfm14050195

. Smidt, L., Pretorius, C., & Nest, D. P. van der. (2022). Current Use of the Risk Register to Integrate Strategy and Risk- and Performance Management: A Case of a University of Technology in South Africa. Journal of Accounting Finance and Auditing Studies. DOI: 10.32602/jafas.2022.031

Stanford University. (2024). *Data Governance Center*. Retrieved from https://datagovernance.stanford.edu/

Stanford University. (2024). *Data Governance Center*. Retrieved from https://datagovernance.stanford.edu/

Sulasula, J. (2023). Exploring the viability of Smart Public Universities in the Philippines' Zamboanga Peninsula Region. DOI: 10.31219/osf.io/tu5qs

. Sun, M., & Qu, Y. (2020). IT Audit Education Implemented Under the Cloud Accounting. DOI: 10.2991/assehr.k.200801.009

Sun, Y., Li, J., Lu, M., & Guo, Z. (2024). Study of the Impact of the Big Data Era on Accounting and Auditing. *Frontiers in Business, Economics and Management, 13*(3), 44–47. DOI: 10.54097/0fa7xk79

The Open University. (2024). *Distance Learning and Online Courses*. Retrieved from https://www.open.ac.uk/courses/what-is-distance-learning

Udeh, E. O., Amajuoyi, P., Adeusi, K. B., & Scott, A. O. (2024). The role of big data in detecting and preventing financial fraud in digital transactions. *World Journal of Advanced Research and Reviews, 22*(2), 1746–1760. DOI: 10.30574/wjarr.2024.22.2.1575

University of Edinburgh. (2024). *Learning Analytics - Information Services*. Retrieved from https://information-services.ed.ac.uk/learning-technology/more-about-learning-technology/learning-analytics

Zubizarreta, M., Ganzarain, J., Cuadrado, J., & Lizarralde, R. (2020). Evaluating Disruptive Innovation Project Management Capabilities. *Sustainability (Basel), 13*(1), 1. DOI: 10.3390/su13010001

ENDNOTES

1 HEI 1-6 – a pseudonym was used to protect the identity of the universities.

Chapter 10
Ensuring Compliance in Cloud Native Assurance and IT Audits

Harini Shankar
https://orcid.org/0009-0007-6891-8669
Independent Researcher, USA

ABSTRACT

This chapter fundamentally redefines compliance strategies for cloud-native environments, moving away from traditional audit practices that no longer align with the ephemeral and automated nature of modern infrastructure. Rather than relying on manual, after-the-fact evidence collection, the chapter advocates integrating compliance directly into development and deployment workflows. Approaches such as Infrastructure as Code and Policy-as-Code are emphasized, alongside automated enforcement mechanisms, immutable audit trails, and robust observability to support ongoing regulatory adherence. However, technology alone is not sufficient—success also hinges on fostering cross-functional collaboration, upskilling teams, and driving cultural change so that compliance becomes an intrinsic part of day-to-day operations. By aligning governance with the agility demanded by contemporary software delivery, this framework supports audit readiness, mitigates risk, and helps organizations maintain trust with stakeholders.

INTRODUCTION

Modern enterprises choose cloud-native architecture because it provides them with agility together with scalability and operational efficiency in the current digital transformation period. The combination of microservices with containers

DOI: 10.4018/979-8-3373-3078-5.ch010

and serverless functions and declarative infrastructure makes innovation faster and reduces market response times. The introduction of new technological advancements presents organizations with substantial obstacles in their efforts to keep systems compliant and audit-ready.

Traditional IT audits operated on monolithic systems that experienced rare infrastructure changes while maintaining direct traceability. Cloud-native systems operate with Continuous Integration and Continuous Deployment (CI CD) pipelines that execute thousands of code changes, deployments and configuration updates every week because they represent dynamic systems (IBM, n.d.). Complex systems create problems for conventional audit methods when trying to establish reliable controls.

Modern regulatory frameworks such as SOX (Sarbanes-Oxley Act), HIPAA (Health Insurance Portability and Accountability Act) enforce stricter requirements for documentation and traceability and system integrity. The adaptation of cloud-native environments requires both technical adjustments and fundamental changes in organizational culture to fulfill these requirements. Public cloud platforms present challenges to compliance because organizations need to establish clear definitions of internal control ownership within their shared responsibility model (Amazon Web Services, n.d.).

The rapid growth of cloud adoption among finance and healthcare industries together with retail and public sector organizations has led auditors to expect instant monitoring of systems and automated evidence collection alongside continuous control tracking. Static screenshots, spreadsheets, and point-in-time reviews are no longer sufficient. The development lifecycle needs to incorporate compliance through practices including DevSecOps and Infrastructure-as-Code (IaC) and Policy-as-Code and observability (Open Policy Agent, n.d.; Drata, n.d.).

The implemented tools and methodologies allow organizations to adopt a "compliance-as-a-product" model which automatically produces audit artifacts while continuously monitoring compliance status. Quality assurance teams used to function independently from governance have started working together with security and compliance functions to authenticate both functional and performance capabilities and regulatory adherence.

Organizations should handle compliance as an ongoing capability that involves collaboration between teams instead of treating it as an outside requirement. The transformation requires organizations to redefine how roles operate and their responsibilities together with their selection of tools. Compliance officers need to master both CI/CD pipeline operations and cloud control mechanisms while engineers require mastery of regulatory standards and control management systems. Operational resilience emerges from the unification of independent organizational functions that previously operated separately.

This chapter explains how Business Intelligence and DevOps and Cloud Assurance work together to transform compliance into a proactive force which enables digital trust. The framework establishes a method for using automation and policy-driven governance and resilient control design to link modern engineering practices with audit requirements.

Key topics include:

- Traditional audit practices need transformation to support cloud-native systems
- The implementation of Policy-as-Code and automated validation systems enables compliance checks in CI/CD pipelines.
- The integration of observability tools enables organizations to develop real-time compliance dashboards alongside tamper-proof audit trails.
- Organizations must achieve both cultural evolution and multidisciplinary teamwork to maintain continuous compliance.

This content addresses the complex cloud governance challenges that technology leaders, compliance officers, cloud architects and DevOps engineers and auditors must handle. Organizations at every stage of their cloud deployment journey can implement these principles to develop compliance systems that operate as secure automated intelligent components throughout software delivery processes.

Organizations achieve better audit risk management while developing competitive advantages through compliance strategy alignment with engineering velocity. The demonstration of real-time control enforcement together with traceability and data integrity establishes trust relationships between organizations and their regulators as well as their customers and internal stakeholders. Highly regulated industries benefit from market access expansion and faster certification processes and simplified vendor evaluation.

The essential nature of cloud-native environment compliance emerges from a combination of regulatory evolution alongside rising cyber threats and heightened customer expectations. Organizations that prosper recognize compliance as an integrated system that generates continuous resilience alongside trust and innovation capabilities.

Organizations need to move away from isolated tooling and manual checkpoints by building unified automation-driven compliance ecosystems. Organizations should use Infrastructure-as-Code for both infrastructure provisioning prediction and pre-deployment security and compliance setting validation. Developers should incorporate Policy-as-Code into their workflows to identify violations early during the development phase while maintaining delivery speed. These practices reduce friction between engineering and audit teams by aligning control enforcement with everyday development processes.

The implementation of observability and telemetry systems which track compliance metrics in real time stands as a vital necessity. The traditional logging methods no longer fulfill enterprise requirements because organizations need tamper-proof contextual audit trails that establish links between policy violations and code commits and user actions and deployment events. The combination of enhanced audit readiness with early risk detection capabilities and accelerated responses and improved team accountability emerges from these collected insights.

The approach toward compliance needs to undergo a complete transformation. Organizations should recognize compliance as a shared ongoing responsibility which product teams and engineering and security functions must jointly manage. When integrated into the genetic makeup of cloud-native operations compliance becomes both sustainable and expandable.

This chapter establishes fundamental principles to shape organizational mindsets while providing leadership tools for implementing enduring change.

THE SHIFTING LANDSCAPE OF IT AUDITS IN CLOUD-NATIVE ENVIRONMENTS

The widespread adoption of cloud-native architectures led to major changes in the way IT audits operate. Traditional monolithic systems combined with on-premise infrastructure provided audits which followed predictable patterns. The infrastructure stayed fixed while organizations had restricted timeframes for modification and they could check access controls through standard templates and manual log analysis. All audit trails existed as physical records while approvals moved through established hierarchical structures and documentation remained paper-based yet simple to verify through centralization. The legacy models functioned well within governance frameworks because these standards emerged in an era where IT administrators maintained full control over systems which changed at a manageable rate.

Cloud-native environments operate through fundamental design principles that include decentralization and automation and velocity. Application development and deployment and management now happen through microservices combined with containers and ephemeral environments and Infrastructure-as-Code (IaC) and Continuous Integration/Continuous Deployment (CI/CD) pipelines. The dynamic nature of these environments supports daily implementation of hundreds or even thousands of modifications. Observability and logging systems need to be designed specifically to detect the fast creation and destruction of virtual machines and containers because these systems leave minimal trace. The current IT audit methods which focus on manual reviews along with static screenshots and compliance spreadsheets fail to manage complex environments at high speeds (Open Policy Agent [OPA], n.d.; OpenControl, n.d.).

Figure 1. Compliance Risks in Cloud-Native Development Lifecycle

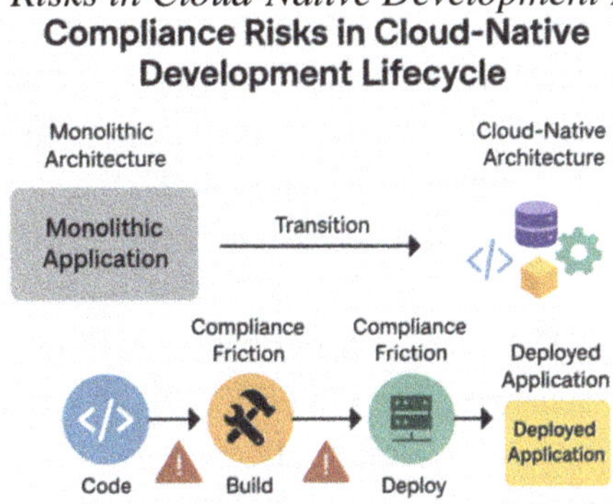

This diagram demonstrates the significant friction traditional compliance methods encounter within contemporary CI/CD cloud-native pipelines. It juxtaposes monolithic and cloud-native architectures, highlighting specific audit and compliance challenges that arise throughout the stages of code development, building, testing, and deployment. The visualization underscores how legacy approaches often struggle to adapt to the dynamic, distributed nature of modern cloud environments.

Auditors must now address questions which were unimportant in previous systems which maintained static states. Auditors need to determine if access controls operated properly in systems that only lasted five minutes. Auditors need to verify that security scans occurred prior to deployment although no manual tickets were issued. The declared policy can be proved only through automated pipelines because each configuration line resides in Git. These questions reveal the primary challenge because engineering speed requires compliance to adapt at the same rate (Secureframe, n.d.).

The transition has transformed IT audit professionals into professionals with expanded duties and heightened expectations. Auditors no longer have the option to inspect only selected controls together with static log reviews. Their work requires them to learn operational expertise about DevOps pipelines as well as IaC tools Terraform, CloudFormation and source control platforms such as GitHub. The understanding of CI/CD workflows has become essential for all organizations. Organizations now practice "shift-left" compliance through automated policy validations integrated into development workflows to detect and fix issues pre-deployment (HashiCorp, n.d.).

The shared responsibility model of cloud computing introduces new levels of complexity into IT systems. Businesses need to manage configurations and implement identity and access management (IAM) controls and encryption policies as well as network segmentation but public cloud providers AWS, Azure and GCP handle the base infrastructure security. The auditor needs to identify what responsibilities belong to the cloud provider and which responsibilities belong to the organization. The process of auditing these aspects requires strong evidence of boundary controls together with tenant isolation and third-party service governance yet these elements prove challenging to verify without automated tools.

Organizations which achieve successful audit modernization implement three essential changes:

From Point-in-Time to Continuous Monitoring

Traditional IT audits perform assessments only at scheduled intervals which occur either quarterly or annually. Cloud-native audits need continuous monitoring because they operate in a different environment. Enterprises can utilize AWS Config alongside Azure Policy and OPA (Open Policy Agent) to identify policy breaches in real-time which sends notifications to stakeholders before security issues become serious risks. The transition enables better monitoring and ensures rapid development maintains proper compliance posture.

From Manual Evidence to Automated Audit Trails

The generation of automatic audit evidence has replaced the manual collection process of emails and screenshots and approvals. All changes to infrastructure receive automated tracking through Git which includes security risk scanning and timestamped logs that record approver information and pipeline results. The records exist in tamper-proof logs or immutable storage systems which make internal and external audits easy to access (IBM, n.d.).

From Compliance as an External Function to an Embedded Practice

The practice of compliance transformed from its status as a separate external duty into an integral operational practice.The responsibility for compliance no longer belongs exclusively to internal audit teams and GRC departments. The responsibility for compliance now rests jointly with engineering staff and security personnel and operations teams. DevSecOps practices make it possible to embed security and compliance controls into version-controlled application code through its codification process (Center for Internet Security [CIS], 2021).

The market has given rise to modern tools which provide auditing functions that engineers can use alongside auditors. Compliance automation platforms such as Evident and Drata and JupiterOne and Tugboat Logic enable real-time dashboards to track control effectiveness at scale through their integration with cloud services. The platforms function as bridges that translate system telemetry data into audit-ready insights between engineering systems and audit frameworks.

IT audit expectations underwent a permanent transformation because of the cloud-native paradigm. Organizations face reduced opportunities for manual intervention because their dependence on ephemeral and highly automated infrastructure systems continues to grow. The speed of code requires compliance to become an embedded practice which operates continuously through automated systems. The new audit model requires both technical adaptation alongside cultural change and skill transformation and deep cross-functional collaboration. Organizations can build trust while demonstrating resilience and meeting future regulatory demands by redefining audit as an enabling function rather than a blocking one.

KEY COMPONENTS OF CLOUD-NATIVE COMPLIANCE ARCHITECTURE

Cloud-native environments need more than tool implementation for compliance success because they require an architectural strategy that integrates automation with traceability and policy enforcement across all layers. This section explains the essential components of a contemporary compliance-oriented architecture which provides real-time assurance and secure software delivery and audit readiness capabilities.

Infrastructure as Code (IaC) as the Compliance Backbone

Cloud-native governance depends on Infrastructure as Code (IaC) as its core foundation. Organizations implement Terraform and Pulumi and AWS CloudFormation and Azure Bicep to develop version-controlled declarative templates which define infrastructure resources such as VPCs and IAM roles and storage policies and Kubernetes clusters. The method allows organizations to create standardized and auditable infrastructure provisioning that repeats consistently.

Key benefits of IaC for compliance include:

- **Automated Control Enforcement**: Security groups, access restrictions, and encryption policies can be codified and reused consistently across environments.
- **Version Control and Traceability**: Every infrastructure change becomes traceable, with full metadata (who, what, when) logged through Git commits.
- **Policy-as-Code Integration:** Compliance checks can be embedded as CI/CD gatekeepers using tools like Open Policy Agent (OPA) or HashiCorp Sentinel.

IaC functions as a DevOps best practice and serves as a strategic tool for implementing auditability and control governance in regulated industries.

CI/CD Pipelines with Embedded Compliance Gates

CI/CD pipelines operate as the core management system of cloud-native delivery through automated build, test and deployment process execution. The contemporary compliance architecture implements continuous validation within these pipelines which transforms compliance from a post-deployment checklist into an active enforcement mechanism.

Common pipeline controls for compliance include:

- **Static Code Analysis for Security Violations**: Security tools Checkmarx Snyk and SonarQube use automatic code scanning to detect vulnerabilities and misconfigurations before deployment (Secureframe, n.d.).
- **Infrastructure Policy Scanning**: The IaC template enforcement tool Terrascan uses guardrails to stop non-compliant configuration settings from being deployed (Terraform Compliance, n.d.).
- **Evidence Capture for Audits**: The system collects build logs and approvals and test results and configuration hashes as immutable audit records (Drata, n.d.; IBM, n.d.).

The embedded validations function as "compliance gates" which block non-conforming code or infrastructure from reaching production to decrease risk and accelerate audit readiness.

Figure 2. CI/CD Pipelines with Built-In Compliance Gates

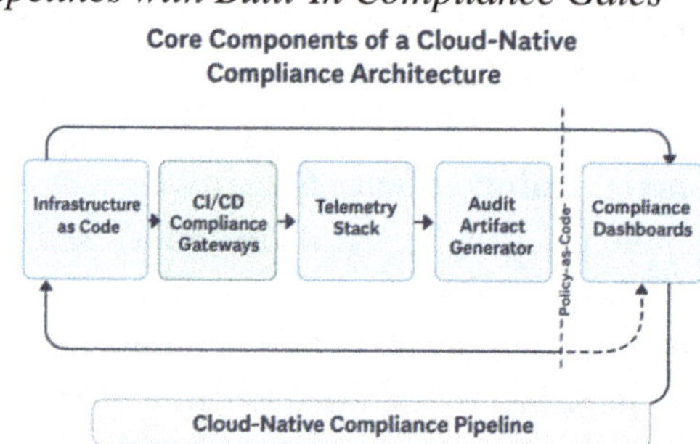

This diagram demonstrates how compliance is integrated directly within CI/CD pipelines, moving beyond the traditional post-deployment audit approach. At each stage—beginning with code commit and continuing through to deployment—automated compliance gates are present. These include static code analysis, infrastructure policy scanning, and continuous audit artifact collection. Each phase interacts with policy-as-code validations and audit checkpoints, ensuring that compliance is maintained as an intrinsic, real-time component of the development process rather than an afterthought. This approach enables organizations to uphold rigorous standards throughout the pipeline, streamlining both compliance and delivery.

Declarative Infrastructure and Immutable Audit Trails

Cloud-native compliance depends on declarative infrastructure as its core foundation which uses human-readable configuration files (YAML, JSON, HCL) to define infrastructure. The combination of Git version control with this approach enables built-in traceability and immutability. Standard software development workflows allow tracking and peer-review and approval of every change to infrastructure components including networking and security groups and storage policies and compute resources.

This practice supports audit needs in multiple ways:

- **Versioned History**: Auditors are able to review the exact infrastructure definitions that were deployed at any point of time (AWS, n.d.).
- **Change Attribution**: Git metadata such as commit history and authorshi are able to offer more accountability.
- **Reproducibility**: Environment can be recreated or tested in isolated sandboxes to verify compliance behavior since it is defined in code.

The declarative method allows automated policy scanning through tools like Sentinel which check code compliance with defined guardrails before production deployment. The GitOps deployment model integrates policy checks into the deployment process because it uses pull requests to drive infrastructure changes.

Figure 3. Policy-as-Code Enforcement in CI/CD Pipelines

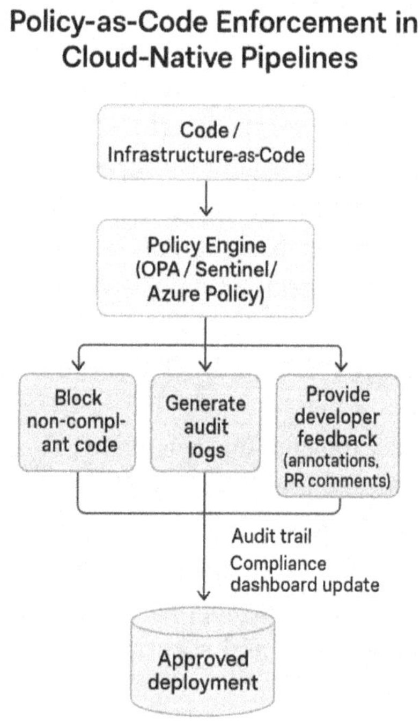

This diagram illustrates how compliance rules codified in Policy-as-Code (PaC) frameworks are automatically evaluated during CI/CD workflows. It visualizes how policy checks are triggered during code commits and deployments, with pass/fail gates feeding back to developers in real time. This enforces consistent governance while reducing manual review effort and aligning development with regulatory standards.

Integrating QA with Compliance Validation

Quality Assurance (QA) and compliance operate as independent workflows within numerous organizations. The isolated management of these processes creates gaps because functionality validation does not ensure regulatory or security posture compliance. Forward-thinking engineering teams now extend QA testing to include compliance-specific test cases for regulated industries.

Examples include:

- Verifying that logs are generated for sensitive operations
- Asserting that encryption configurations are enforced across services (PCI Security Standards Council, 2022)
- Ensuring APIs respond with proper data masking or redaction

The integration of these checks into automated test suites and CI/CD pipelines enables QA to function as the first line of defense for detecting compliance drift and preventing audit failures before they become major issues.

Organizations need to establish evidence generation and transmission as their primary architectural priority to achieve continuous compliance in cloud-native environments. Organizations should create secure automated pipelines which treat compliance artifacts at the same level of importance as code and infrastructure. The pipelines record logs and configuration snapshots and security scan results and policy violations and test execution records in a tamper-proof manner (OpenControl, n.d.). Every artifact requires timestamping and cryptographic hashing and WORM (Write Once Read Many) repository storage to maintain integrity. The evidence requires contextualization by establishing direct links to build deployments and environments to maintain complete and traceable audit trails across the DevOps lifecycle. Role-based access controls provide necessary security measures to allow authorized users to access or export evidence while maintaining enterprise security standards.

Figure 4. Core Components of a Continuous Compliance Framework

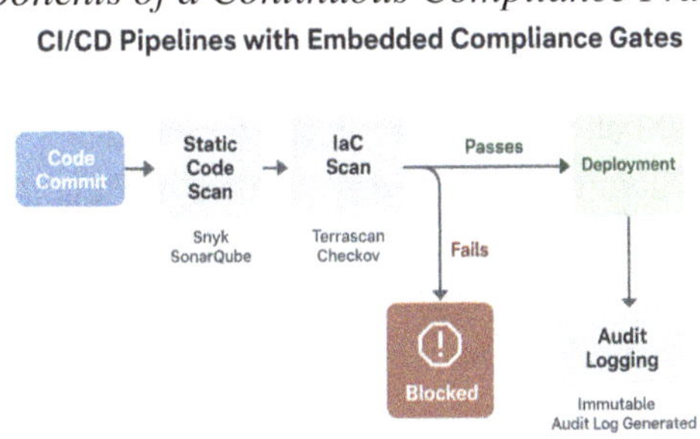

This diagram demonstrates the integration of essential components—such as policy-as-code, compliance checkpoints within CI/CD pipelines, observability frameworks, audit artifact generators, and comprehensive compliance dashboards—to construct a robust cloud-native compliance architecture. The visualization emphasizes that compliance is not relegated to a final step, but is systematically embedded throughout the development lifecycle. This approach facilitates automation, enhances traceability, and supports ongoing assurance within regulated environments.

Organizations need to establish multiple layers of controls throughout their cloud-native stack to achieve audit readiness. Policy-as-code gates serve as preventive controls which stop non-compliant configurations from moving through CI/CD pipelines(OPA, n.d.). Cloud configuration scanners together with observability tools enable detective controls to detect both approved baseline deviations and drifts. The system uses corrective controls to automatically fix violations through automated scripts or to trigger alerts which require manual intervention for resolution. The multi-tiered approach builds resilience because it maintains detection and mitigation capabilities through multiple layers even when one control fails or gets bypassed. The software release process integration of these control types enables compliance to become a scalable proactive capability which matches the velocity and complexity of cloud-native ecosystems.

Policy-as-Code and the Shift to Declarative Compliance

The traditional compliance approach depended on manual procedures which included checklists and human approvals together with point-in-time assessments. The basic assurance provided by these methods in static on-premises environments does not match the requirements of modern cloud-native systems which operate in a fluid manner. Organizations that adopt DevOps and infrastructure-as-code have developed Policy-as-Code (PaC) as a new approach which enables organizations to establish compliance rules through machine-readable policies integrated into their pipelines and infrastructure definitions. This model transforms compliance from a manual burden into a scalable version-controlled discipline Open Policy Agent [OPA], n.d.; HashiCorp, n.d.; AWS, n.d.).

Policy-as-Code establishes a software-defined approach to transform compliance into a process. The evaluation of policies written in Rego (Open Policy Agent), HashiCorp Sentinel and YAML (Azure Policy and AWS Config) happens automatically instead of requiring manual auditor review for storage bucket encryption and resource deployment authorization. The policies can be incorporated into CI/CD workflows to enforce security baselines and validate naming conventions and restrict deprecated service usage and enforce tagging for cost allocation and traceability. The process of codification and versioning and peer-review of these policies at the same level as application code makes compliance testable and auditable and fully integrated with the development lifecycle (Drata, n.d.; IBM, n.d.).

Use Cases of Policy-as-Code in Cloud-Native Compliance

- **Preventing Non-Compliant Deployments:** Policies in CI/CD pipelines can block infrastructure changes that violate regulatory or security guidelines (e.g., deploying databases without encryption).
- **Tag Enforcement:** Ensures resources carry mandatory metadata such as owner, cost center, or data classification for traceability and audit tracking.

The successful implementation of PaC depends on developing a governance framework together with a cultural transformation. Policy creation together with testing needs active collaboration between development personnel and compliance staff. Each policy must link directly to particular regulatory standards and stakeholders need access to complete enforcement transparency. Developers receive immediate feedback through Policy-as-Code integration into their developer workflow because this system tells them about configuration and code policy violations at the beginning of the lifecycle for easy self-remediation. Organizations develop continuous compliance through automated checks of every pull request and deployment and infrastructure update for conformance.

Enterprises that implement policy engines with regulatory intent and operational safeguards can achieve powerful compliance management across thousands of microservices and cloud accounts and environments. The combination of automated governance with human error prevention creates essential tools for the current fast-moving digital environment which demands both repeatable and provable compliance solutions.

Policy-as-Code (PaC) provides explainability capabilities that meet audit requirements in addition to its enforcement functions. PaC frameworks produce detailed reports and logs that explain which policies succeeded and failed and provide failure explanations. Organizations need this audit trail to prove the design and effectiveness and enforcement of internal controls during both regular audits and post-incident investigations. The version control system for these policies enables teams to display their evolving compliance safeguards throughout time which proves beneficial for both new regulation compliance and audit response.

Policy-as-Code delivers the capability to evaluate policy effects before their actual implementation. Teams utilize advisory policy mode to discover which present infrastructure elements would not comply with regulations. The feature enables smooth deployment transitions by supporting sequential policy deployments which engages developers rather than disrupting their work. Teams receive policy violation feedback through pull request comments and pipeline annotations which eliminates deployment-time surprises while decreasing traditional governance-related delays.

The Policy-as-Code approach enables teams to share policy modules across different environments making it suitable for organizations operating in multi-cloud and federated structures. Policy modules which enforce encryption on S3 buckets or deny public IP assignment can be applied uniformly across all accounts and business units and regions. Compliance and security teams should review centrally managed libraries that contain approved policies which teams maintain. Standardized policy baselines exist through shared collections but organizations can implement local policy modifications when their business requirements demand such changes.

Organizations can transition from monitoring compliance reactions to actively preventing risks through Policy-as-Code implementation. The inclusion of policies throughout development workflows and infrastructure operations makes compliance a built-in automated feature that developers can easily work with. The essential principle of scalable governance in cloud-native environments requires maintaining trust instead of imposing it (NIST, 2018; Center for Internet Security [CIS], 2021).

IMPLEMENTATION FRAMEWORKS FOR CONTINUOUS COMPLIANCE IN CLOUD-NATIVE SYSTEMS

Organizations must adopt new methods to achieve compliance because traditional manual and siloed approaches no longer work for cloud-native architectures (NIST, 2018; Secureframe, n.d.). The evolution of compliance requires it to become an automated process which runs continuously throughout the software development lifecycle. A unified framework must unite process transformation with toolchain integration and cross-functional ownership to achieve this goal. This section presents a functional framework for continuous compliance in cloud-native environments which provides scalable traceability and auditability and governance capabilities.

Defining Compliance as Code

A scalable compliance strategy requires the fundamental principle of "Compliance as Code." The Compliance as Code concept expands the Infrastructure as Code (IaC) philosophy by transforming compliance policies and rules and controls into versioned testable auditable code artifacts. Organizations can validate configurations and enforce security policies through codified compliance requirements which provide a living testable source of truth for regulatory adherence.

The enforcement of Compliance as Code depends on policy definition languages and engines which include Open Policy Agent (OPA) and HashiCorp Sentinel and Rego. The tools enable teams to create policies which check infrastructure and deployment plans and runtime behaviors against enterprise controls. The integration of these checks within CI/CD pipelines performs automatic compliance risk evaluations on every commit and deployment and configuration change before production deployment (Secureframe, n.d.).

The method allows compliance checks to happen at the beginning of the development cycle through code commit and pre-deployment gate evaluation. The system stops non-compliant code from reaching production while developing a governance culture among developers and DevOps engineers.

Embedding Controls in CI/CD Pipelines

The effective operationalization of compliance requires its integration into the continuous integration and deployment (CI/CD) toolchain. The CI/CD pipeline functions as an enforcement tool for controls which enables organizations to check code and infrastructure and configuration changes throughout the delivery lifecycle (Drata, n.d.).

Two types of controls are typically implemented in CI/CD:

- **Preventative Controls:** These checks prevent non-compliant changes from progressing to the next stage. The IaC validation for tagging standards along with secret scanning and unauthorized resource types serve as examples of preventative controls.
- **Detective Controls:** These capture metrics and generate logs or alerts when compliance anomalies are detected, such as drift from baseline configurations or policy violations in test environments.

The implementation of these controls through CI/CD pipeline tools including GitHub Actions, GitLab CI, Azure DevOps and Jenkins enables teams to enforce compliance automatically without human involvement. The approach reduces audit workloads significantly in regulated industries while preserving organizational agility.

The pipeline telemetry system enables the development of a compliance dashboard which provides real-time visibility into enforcement rates and historical trends and current violations. The system supports both operational monitoring and audit reporting.

The traditional quality assurance approach to functional validation becomes essential for compliance assurance when it includes non-functional requirements such as policy adherence and access control and infrastructure validation. Test automation suites use InSpec and Chef Compliance frameworks together with custom scripts to run compliance test cases. Organizations can use automated checks to confirm data stores have encryption enabled and verify that all compute resources belong to approved security groups and access logs are active for cloud storage buckets and IAM roles and privileges match pre-approved organizational baselines. The automated pipelines run compliance validations together with unit and integration tests to produce artifacts which fulfill both quality and compliance requirements. The dual-purpose method ensures technical release compliance while generating auditable time-stamped evidence of control enforcement. Test automation functions as a fundamental tool for continuous compliance by connecting engineering execution to audit assurance.

Key Components of a Continuous Compliance Framework

A complete compliance framework for cloud-native environments requires the following components to integrate all available capabilities.

- **Policy Management System:** Functions as a central repository which stores version-controlled compliance policies through code-based implementation (OPA, n.d.).
- **CI/CD Compliance Gateways:** Middleware or plugins that enforce policy checks during build and deploy stages.
- **Telemetry and Observability Stack:** Consists of Prometheus alongside Datadog and ELK Stack which monitor compliance-related metrics and anomalies.
- **Audit Artifact Generator:** functions as an automated system which collects and timestamps and archives compliance evidence.
- **Compliance Dashboards:** Real-time visualizations for tracking control effectiveness, violations, and audit readiness metrics.

Organizations can transition from reactive compliance to continuous governance through the integration of these elements into a unified framework which enforces controls while measuring their effectiveness for continuous improvement.

Cross-Functional Collaboration and Ownership Models

The transition to continuous compliance requires both cultural and organizational changes beyond technical modifications. The distribution of compliance responsibility needs to span across different teams while engineering and security and legal and audit functions must work together (Center for Internet Security [CIS], 2021).

Engineering teams maintain compliance code through their ownership while compliance officers and auditors use automated system evidence to validate policy effectiveness. DevSecOps teams function as integration points which connect control logic to delivery pipelines.

The implementation of shared dashboards and regular syncs enables teams to maintain alignment through tracking of policy pass/fail rates per sprint and audit evidence coverage and control gaps discovered during post-mortems. The model establishes visibility and accountability across stakeholders which converts compliance from an innovation barrier into a strategic tool for secure trusted software delivery.

The model transforms compliance from an innovation obstacle into a delivery enabler which supports secure trusted delivery.

Benefits of an Embedded Compliance Framework

Organizations operating in complex regulated environments achieve strategic benefits through successful implementation of continuous compliance frameworks. The implementation of automated evidence trails cuts down audit preparation time which leads to efficient data access-based audit processes. The development pipeline includes preventative controls that enhance risk posture through early detection of policy violations before they become production problems. Organizations that integrate compliance validation into developer workflows reduce developer friction while improving productivity which enables engineers to deliver features without compromising governance standards (AWS, n.d.; IBM, n.d.). Real-time dashboards increase regulatory confidence through transparent and updated compliance status views which stakeholders and auditors can easily access. Organizations that establish continuous compliance beyond regulatory requirements develop trust and operational excellence while gaining the ability to move swiftly and securely in fast-changing markets.

Challenges and Pitfalls in Cloud-Native Compliance

The implementation of continuous compliance in cloud-native environments presents significant advantages yet the process contains multiple obstacles. Organizations tend to underestimate the amount of work needed to transform their technical operations and organizational design and compliance principles for this new paradigm (NIST, 2018; Secureframe, n.d.). The following section identifies typical obstacles that occur when implementing compliance within modern dynamic systems and provides guidance on their resolution.

Fragmented Tooling and Integration Complexity

The most widespread challenge in building continuous compliance frameworks stems from the fragmented nature of tooling across development and operations environments. Different teams operate with separate technology stacks that include CI/CD platforms and cloud providers and infrastructure management tools and testing frameworks and monitoring dashboards which frequently lack standard integration points. Security teams employ different tools for access policy management while DevOps teams use different tools for infrastructure provisioning and compliance teams maintain evidence records through spreadsheets and custom portals. The absence of integration between systems results in redundant work and inconsistent measurements which creates substantial challenges for engineers who need to connect these systems.

Enterprises need to develop a unified architecture strategy which standardizes compliance data pipelines while enabling systems to exchange artifacts without restrictions. The integration of middleware platforms with centralized logging solutions and cloud-native compliance hubs (AWS Config, Azure Policy, Open Policy Agent) functions as connective tissue. The integration process requires intentional design with defined cross-functional ownership from the beginning to guarantee stakeholders use the same sources of truth.

Skill Gaps and Mindset Barriers

The implementation of cloud-native compliance demands engineers who possess both technical expertise and regulatory understanding and automation capabilities. The current workforce of QA, DevOps and compliance professionals lacks the necessary skills to connect these domains. QA teams lack understanding about audit trails and control mappings while compliance officers demonstrate insufficient technical knowledge to read evidence logs and IaC validation reports. The cultural practice of treating compliance as an afterthought persists as a deeply ingrained habit throughout many organizations among skilled engineers (HIPAA Journal, 2023; Drata, n.d.).

The solution to this gap needs both training programs and a complete change in perspective. Compliance needs to transform into a shared engineering responsibility which continues throughout development instead of functioning as a simple verification process. The internal champions serve as essential advocates to promote this mindset. The group consists of DevSecOps engineers and cloud architects and senior QA leads who grasp both regulatory requirements and software delivery procedures. These professionals act as connectors between departmental languages and expectations to demonstrate how embedded compliance should be implemented.

Inadequate Policy Design and Overly Rigid Controls

Organizations with established DevOps practices encounter difficulties when they attempt to convert regulatory frameworks into technical controls that can be enforced. The natural language structure of compliance policies makes them suitable for legal interpretation but challenging to transform into testable logic. The process of policy translation results in overly strict implementation which slows down development speed and triggers preventable build failures. Developers frequently view compliance tools as obstacles instead of tools that enable their work.

The resolution requires policy designers to receive engineering feedback during their initial development stage. The policy should be divided into small, automated testable controls which can be evaluated by continuous automation engines. Policy-as-code frameworks including Open Policy Agent and HashiCorp Sentinel enable organizations to write governance logic in flexible version-controlled code. Organizations should implement these steps to create policies that maintain effectiveness while remaining developer-friendly:

- Break policies into modular, testable rules that can be mapped directly to CI/CD steps.
- Use risk scoring or tiered enforcement instead of binary pass/fail thresholds whenever possible.
- The documentation of policies should include both human-readable and machine-readable formats to help users understand and debug the system.

This method decreases team resistance and enables better policy iteration when regulations change or business priorities adjust.

Incomplete Visibility and Poor Audit Trail Integrity

The main objective of compliance requires organizations to establish the capability to track user activities through time and their associated reasons. Many organizations struggle to produce tamper-proof end-to-end audit trails within their cloud-native systems. Auditors face blind spots because cloud-native systems use ephemeral infrastructure together with event-based scaling and decentralized access patterns. The evidence collection process results in missing data that exists across multiple tools and requires manual entry into non-integrity-based formats (AWS, n.d.; OpenControl, n.d.).

Observability needs to be transformed into a capability which supports compliance requirements. All logs need to be protected from tampering while being stored in a central location with cryptographic signatures when available. The basic audit capabilities of AWS CloudTrail and Azure Monitor and GCP Audit Logs need additional context from CI/CD platforms and test suites and access control systems. The combination of automated resource tagging with deployment and ownership metadata and pipeline-triggered evidence snapshots creates substantial improvements in audit readiness.

Compliance Fatigue and Alert Overload

Highly dynamic environments produce numerous compliance alerts which include many false positives and low-priority warnings. The continuous stream of alerts leads teams to disregard signals which results in alert fatigue and allows policy violations to go undetected.

The solution requires organizations to establish smart alerting systems which prioritize alerts effectively. The level of urgency for non-compliant states varies because some need immediate response but others can be tolerated temporarily or automatically fixed. Engineering teams should direct their attention to the most critical areas through violation tiering which considers severity levels and business impact and potential consequences. The design of dashboards needs to be strategic to prevent information overload for stakeholders by presenting relevant summaries that match their responsibilities.

Organizational Resistance to Change

The implementation of technology infrastructure does not guarantee progress because organizational inertia can still prevent advancement. The implementation of compliance programs demands teamwork between engineering and security departments and risk management and audit and legal departments. The different groups within the organization maintain separate timelines and risk tolerance levels and success criteria. The absence of executive backing together with an unclear unified strategy leads to the abandonment of continuous compliance initiatives during their implementation phase (Drata, n.d.; Secureframe, n.d.).

Executive sponsorship combined with business goal alignment serves as the essential method to defeat resistance. The organization achieves better buy-in when compliance is presented as a trust-building and security-enhancing practice which also supports customer retention instead of being viewed as a cost center. The demonstration of compliance dashboards together with success metrics and early achievements at regular intervals helps maintain stakeholder interest and momentum.

Organizational Readiness and Skill Development

Organizations need more than technical tools and frameworks to achieve successful continuous compliance in cloud-native environments because they must develop prepared adaptive teams with proper people and processes and cultural mindset. The responsibility for compliance extends beyond audit and risk teams because modern software delivery demands shared competency among engineering, operations, security and legal functions (Drata, n.d.; CIS, 2021). This section defines what it means for an organization to be "compliance-ready" in the cloud era by specifying necessary capabilities and providing methods to evaluate current maturity and develop team skills for continuous assurance.

Evolving the Definition of Readiness

In the past, audit readiness for IT was mostly about following a checklist—documenting controls, grabbing screenshots, and generating reports after everything was done. It was reactive and manual, pretty much. With cloud-native systems, though, the focus has shifted to continuous, real-time compliance. Organizations need to prove they're compliant at any moment, not just when an audit is coming up. So, readiness isn't just a prep step anymore; it's an ongoing operational state that's built into daily workflows.

This shift impacts every layer of delivery. Infrastructure now needs to be provisioned with Infrastructure as Code (IaC), which means changes are versioned and fully traceable. Delivery pipelines are required to generate test artifacts and logs that stick around and can't be tampered with. Quality assurance? It has to check for more than just basic functionality—access controls, encryption, and policy enforcement need to be validated automatically. Leadership's role changes, too: compliance has to be integrated as a core system feature, not treated like some external checkpoint (AWS, n.d.; OPA, n.d.).

So, organizational readiness turns into a multi-layered evaluation. It covers technical maturity (what tools and infrastructure you've got), process alignment (your governance and change management), and whether the culture's actually bought in (role clarity, willingness to adapt). All these dimensions need to be reviewed thoroughly and routinely to make sure compliance efforts aren't just a one-off but can actually last long-term.

Conducting a Compliance Capability Assessment

Prior to initiating any major transformation, it's crucial for organizations to get a clear-eyed view of their current compliance landscape. An honest baseline assessment helps pinpoint strengths, weaknesses, and those awkward gray areas that need attention. Without this, you're basically flying blind. So, organizations should systematically examine the following key aspects:

- **Tooling Assessment:** Which compliance-related tools are presently in use within the organization, and to what extent are these tools integrated with the CI/CD pipeline? Additionally, do these systems generate evidence in a format that is readily machine-readable, or does evidence collection require manual intervention?

- **Process Alignment**: To what degree are security, legal, and compliance teams embedded within the development lifecycle? Is their involvement proactive and continuous, or do they primarily engage in post-release reviews and assessments?
- **Skill Inventory**: Do QA and DevOps personnel possess a comprehensive understanding of key regulatory frameworks such as SOX, GDPR, and HIPAA? Furthermore, are they equipped to translate policies into actionable and testable cases within the development process?
- **Audit Practices**: What mechanisms are currently in place for the collection of audit evidence? Is this process automated, version-controlled, and traceable to specific deployments, or does it rely on manual compilation and retrospective documentation?
- **Governance Frameworks**: Are organizational policies codified and enforced programmatically across all environments, ensuring consistency and minimizing variance in compliance adherence?

Addressing these questions can illuminate areas of vulnerability, including excessive reliance on manual controls, insufficient training for developers regarding compliance obligations, or a disjointed set of tools and processes. Identifying such gaps is essential for constructing a strategic roadmap toward greater compliance maturity.

Building Cross-Disciplinary Skills

In today's cloud-native environment, compliance is no longer just the responsibility of auditors or risk managers. Instead, it has evolved into an ongoing concern for engineering teams across the organization. To meet this challenge, teams must develop a combination of skills—merging software engineering, security best practices, and a functional understanding of regulatory frameworks.

Critical areas for team development include:

- **Policy Interpretation:** Developers and QA professionals need to move beyond simple familiarity with compliance policies. They must interpret and translate requirements such as "least privilege" and "encryption at rest" into actionable technical controls (CIS, 2021; HIPAA Journal, 2023).
- **Tooling Proficiency:** Engineering teams should become adept with policy-as-code solutions (e.g., OPA, Sentinel), infrastructure-as-code platforms

(such as Terraform and Pulumi), and compliance automation tools (like AWS Config and Azure Policy).

- **Evidence Generation and Management:** It is essential for teams to recognize and produce valid audit evidence, automate its collection, and ensure the integrity and immutability of compliance records.
- **Continuous Monitoring and Metrics:** Stakeholders must develop the ability to analyze compliance dashboards, evaluate the effectiveness of technical controls, and proactively address potential violations.

Integrating this upskilling into onboarding procedures, structured training programs, and routine team activities—such as retrospectives and incident reviews—is vital. Where internal expertise is limited, organizations should invest in cross-training initiatives, targeted workshops, or external certification programs focused on DevSecOps and compliance automation. This holistic approach is fundamental for maintaining compliance in complex, cloud-native environments.

Redefining Roles and Responsibilities

As the integration of continuous compliance deepens within DevOps practices, established roles are undergoing notable transformation. Quality assurance professionals are no longer confined to the narrow function of drafting test cases; instead, they are evolving into quality engineers tasked with hands-on control validation. Developers, in turn, assume heightened responsibility for the security aspects of their own services, rather than deferring such concerns. Compliance officers transition from peripheral oversight to strategic advisory positions embedded within product and platform teams, actively shaping outcomes from within. Meanwhile, DevOps and platform engineers are now expected to architect infrastructure with compliance as a foundational default, moving beyond the traditional focus on system availability.

To support this transformation, clear role definitions and accountability models must be established. For example:

- QA engineers own policy-based test automation.
- DevSecOps engineers build reusable compliance templates and dashboards.
- Cloud architects define guardrails via IaC.
- Security teams review code for control misconfigurations.
- Product managers include compliance status in release readiness criteria (CIS, 2021; NIST, 2018).

To ensure genuine shared ownership, it's essential to clearly document the model, integrate it into team objectives, and connect it directly to performance evaluations. Without these concrete steps, commitment to distributed ownership risks remaining superficial.

Change Management and Cultural Buy-In

If compliance initiatives fail to align with organizational culture, their chances of success are slim. Individuals within the organization need to perceive compliance as meaningful, not merely a bureaucratic hurdle. This calls for more than basic communication or routine training sessions; rather, it requires strategies that ground compliance in tangible business value—be it increased customer trust, streamlined audits, risk mitigation, or competitive differentiation.

Having dedicated compliance advocates embedded in each team can be instrumental. These individuals offer peer-level support and help reinforce best practices. Leadership plays a crucial role as well, not only by highlighting achievements such as audit successes or improved risk metrics, but also by maintaining transparency around compliance data. Open forums and accessible feedback channels empower team members to share concerns and contribute to the ongoing process.

Ultimately, the objective is to integrate compliance into the organization's collective identity so that it is embraced rather than merely tolerated. When developers routinely verify access controls, QA teams incorporate policy reviews into their workflows, and security officers collaborate proactively on release decisions, compliance evolves from an obligation to an organic, continuous practice.

REGULATORY MAPPING AND MULTI-FRAMEWORK ALIGNMENT

As cloud-native technologies continue to expand across geographic regions and industry sectors, organizations increasingly encounter the multifaceted challenge of complying with a broad array of regulatory standards. The landscape is far from straightforward: enterprises may simultaneously manage financial data subject to Sarbanes-Oxley (SOX), safeguard health information under HIPAA, uphold the privacy of individuals in accordance with policies, and fulfill the rigorous demands of payment data (HIPAA Journal, 2023; PCI Security Standards Council, 2022; European Parliament and Council, 2016). Navigating this regulatory labyrinth, companies must architect cloud-native environments capable of demonstrating adherence to these varied frameworks. This section examines strategies for constructing such systems, focusing on regulatory mapping, abstraction of controls, automation of compliance tasks, and methods to enhance the efficiency of cross-framework audits.

The Challenge of Overlapping Regulations

Every regulatory framework comes with its own specialized language and set of requirements. SOX is primarily centered on ensuring the integrity of financial data, establishing strict access controls, and managing changes with precision. HIPAA, on the other hand, is designed to safeguard the confidentiality and security of protected health information, demanding detailed audit trails. GDPR's focus is on minimizing unnecessary data collection, requiring explicit user consent, and granting individuals the right to have their information erased (European Parliament and Council, 2016).

Despite these differences, these standards are ultimately aligned in their broader objectives: safeguarding sensitive data, preserving data integrity, and maintaining traceability. The real challenge, though, lies in the discrepancies in terminology, scope, and the level of detail demanded by each framework. This lack of uniformity can lead to what is commonly termed "compliance fatigue," where organizations find themselves repeatedly mapping the same technical controls to multiple regulations, often manually. Such redundancies increase inefficiency and can result in overlooked gaps, especially during audits, undermining both compliance efforts and overall security posture.

Managing compliance across numerous regulatory frameworks can be quite the labyrinth, but organizations have found a clever workaround by abstracting technical controls into what are called "canonical controls." These function as reusable blocks—think of "encryption at rest" as a classic example. Rather than creating a bespoke solution for every regulation, one control can be mapped across different frameworks. For instance, the same encryption control might satisfy HIPAA, GDPR, and PCI-DSS requirements simultaneously, reducing the need for redundant implementations.

Organizations typically maintain a comprehensive matrix that links each canonical control to the relevant regulatory clauses. This approach not only streamlines compliance reporting—since the same evidence can be repurposed for different frameworks—but also clarifies responsibility for shared controls and enables more efficient tracking of changes. Ultimately, connecting technical controls directly to compliance narratives fosters greater organizational alignment and operational efficiency. It's a practical strategy that bridges the gap between technical teams, compliance officers, and auditors, making the entire process far less fragmented and more academically robust.

Automation of Control Mapping

Modern compliance automation platforms have significantly streamlined the process of managing multiple regulatory frameworks. These solutions offer robust functionalities, such as automated control mapping, centralized evidence tracking, and dynamic report generation. Collectively, they reduce the administrative burden traditionally associated with compliance management, enhancing both efficiency and accuracy in organizational processes. Some of the features are:

- Automated control-to-framework mapping using built-in catalogs
- Unified evidence collection linked to multiple regulations
- Dynamic questionnaires that adjust based on framework selection

Open-source and vendor-neutral tools have become increasingly important for managing multi-framework compliance. For instance, IBM's Compliance-Trestle offers organizations the ability to structure compliance data, which streamlines automation and supports integration across disparate systems. Likewise, OpenControl enables teams to maintain version-controlled control catalogs through the use of YAML, fostering consistency, traceability, and reusability throughout various audits and regulatory requirements.

Furthermore, integrating these tools with CI/CD pipelines and cloud configuration scanners—such as AWS Config, OPA, or Terraform Compliance—enables organizations to automatically evaluate the impact of infrastructure or application changes on multiple compliance domains in real time (AWS, n.d.; OPA, n.d.; Terraform Compliance, n.d.). This approach not only improves operational efficiency but also strengthens ongoing compliance efforts across evolving technological landscapes.

Evidence Tagging and Metadata Enrichment

For effective cross-framework traceability, it is essential to ensure that all compliance artifacts are accompanied by comprehensive metadata. Each item—whether it be a screenshot, configuration file, pipeline log, or test result—should be systematically enriched with relevant descriptive information to facilitate robust tracking and alignment across frameworks.

- **Control ID(s)**
- **Framework(s) covered**
- **Timestamp and environment**
- **Change source (e.g., commit hash, PR number)**
- **Owner and reviewer information**

When a Terraform plan is validated against Sentinel policies, the resulting compliance report includes key metadata such as:

- "Encrypted S3 buckets – HIPAA, GDPR, PCI-DSS,"
- The relevant commit ID (for example, d2f5b6a)
- The associated date and pipeline run identifier
- Hash of the evidence file to ensure integrity

This metadata enables efficient categorization of evidence based on relevant regulations, deployment contexts, or specific audit requirements. By doing so, it significantly simplifies and expedites the preparation of organized compliance documentation.

Managing Regulatory Drift

Regulatory requirements evolve on a frequent basis due to amendments and new data protection laws. These regulatory updates must be treated by organizations as a type of system change that requires version control and validation.

Best practices for managing drift would include:

- **Subscribing to regulatory change feeds** (e.g., IAPP, government websites)
- **Using versioned policy libraries** with clear linkage to framework versions
- **Periodic crosswalk reviews** to assess impact on shared controls
- **Change management processes** to ensure updated controls are tested and communicated

When organizations treat regulatory updates with priority to the compliance lifecycle, organizations can stay ahead of audit expectations. This helps reduce last-minute remediation during audits.

Real-World Scenario: Control Harmonization in Practice

Consider a large-scale cloud provider facing the demands of compliance. Instead of approaching each framework with isolated, fragmented programs, the organization adopts a unified control model. By consolidating requirements, they create a streamlined compliance structure, reducing redundancy and operational friction. This integrated approach not only optimizes resource allocation but also supports consistent governance across multiple regulatory regimes (OPA, n.d.; OpenControl, n.d.; IBM, n.d.).

- Encryption controls are standardized across services
- IAM policies enforce role-based access with audit trails
- CI/CD pipelines embed compliance gates using OPA
- All evidence is centralized in an immutable compliance vault with multi-framework tags

This approach enables internal audit teams to efficiently produce reports tailored to each framework by leveraging a shared set of evidence. As a result, both administrative burden and audit preparation time are notably minimized.

Benefits of Multi-Framework Mapping

Organizations that effectively implement regulatory mapping realize several significant advantages.

- **Operational efficiency**: a single control measure may address multiple regulatory requirements, eliminating unnecessary duplication of effort. This streamlines operations and enhances overall efficiency.
- **Audit acceleration**: Evidence collection is expedited and manual work is reduced, which enables organizations to complete audits with greater speed and accuracy.
- **Lower compliance risk**: Mitigating compliance risk is another key benefit. By standardizing control implementations, organizations decrease the likelihood of inconsistencies or oversights that could result in non-compliance.
- **Strategic alignment**: From a strategic perspective, such a framework equips organizations to adapt swiftly to new regulatory demands, fostering agility in an evolving environment.

By aligning their compliance architecture with a versatile, automation-ready model, enterprises transform regulatory complexity into a manageable and scalable system of trust

Multi-framework alignment stands as a fundamental aspect of contemporary compliance engineering. In an era where cloud-native systems are rapidly expanding and intersecting with a labyrinth of evolving global regulations, the capacity to establish standardized controls, automate the mapping between frameworks, and generate evidence dynamically becomes a distinct competitive advantage. This approach not only alleviates the complexities and redundancies associated with fragmented compliance practices but also enables organizations to enhance transparency, respond with agility, and maintain robust audit readiness amid persistent regulatory uncertainty.

BUILDING A CONTINUOUS ASSURANCE OPERATING MODEL

In the contemporary landscape where cloud-native environments underpin digital enterprises, traditional, periodic approaches to compliance are increasingly inadequate. Continuous Assurance emerges as a paradigm shift, embedding compliance mechanisms directly into the fabric of software development and operational processes. Rather than relegating compliance to periodic audits, CA ensures that controls are persistently monitored, enforced, and validated throughout the lifecycle (Secureframe, n.d.; NIST, 2018). This section delineates the foundational principles, structural components, and practical strategies of a Continuous Assurance Operating Model, outlining a comprehensive framework for evolving compliance into an adaptive, scalable organizational capability.

Core Principles of a Continuous Assurance Operating Model

A robust Continuous Automated Operations Monitoring (CAOM) framework is built upon five key, interrelated principles

1. **Always-On Monitoring:** Ensures that compliance controls are evaluated on a continual basis, not merely during designated audit periods. This persistent vigilance enables organizations to identify and address issues proactively rather than reactively.
2. **Evidence as a Byproduct:** Streamlines compliance by generating audit artifacts automatically as an inherent part of everyday engineering workflows. This approach minimizes manual intervention and reduces the operational overhead often associated with compliance documentation.
3. **Federated Ownership:** Distributes accountability for controls among product, platform, and compliance teams. Such shared responsibility fosters cross-functional collaboration and avoids the pitfalls of siloed oversight.
4. **Integrated Toolchains:** Represent the incorporation of compliance validation directly within existing Continuous Integration/Continuous Deployment (CI/CD), Infrastructure as Code (IaC), and observability pipelines. Embedding these processes ensures that compliance is maintained seamlessly throughout the software delivery lifecycle.
5. **Feedback-Driven Improvement:** Leverages incidents and exceptions as opportunities for learning, using these occurrences to iteratively refine and enhance control mechanisms.

These principles form a compliance framework that aligns with the rapid cadence of contemporary software development, supporting both agility and regulatory rigor.

Figure 5. Continuous Assurance Operating Model Framework

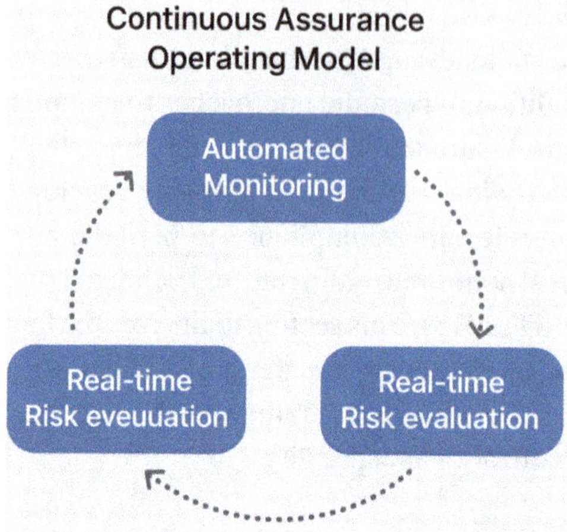

The visual demonstrates the integration of fundamental concepts such as persistent monitoring, embedded toolchains, distributed ownership, and feedback-oriented refinement in sustaining ongoing compliance within cloud-native frameworks. Rather than presenting these elements in isolation, the diagram depicts them as a cohesive system interwoven throughout each phase of the DevOps lifecycle. This approach underscores the importance of automation, comprehensive traceability, and collective accountability among team members to ensure robust and reliable compliance practices.

Operationalizing Control Ownership

In the Continuous Assurance Operating Model (CAOM), responsibility for compliance controls is intentionally distributed rather than centralized within the Governance, Risk, and Compliance team. Each functional area is tasked with oversight appropriate to its domain expertise. Platform engineering teams administer critical infrastructure elements, including identity and access management, encryption protocols, and network segmentation. DevSecOps teams are charged with maintaining compliance tooling, developing automation rules, and conducting security scans to ensure ongoing adherence to standards. Quality Assurance (QA) teams integrate compliance test cases alongside functional testing to confirm regulatory requirements are met throughout the software development lifecycle. Product teams manage tagging, cost attribution, and user-level data classification, ensuring organizational data is appropriately categorized and traceable. Meanwhile, internal audit functions continuously assess control effectiveness, identify compliance gaps, and prepare the organization for external audits. This distributed ownership model is supported by comprehensive documentation, structured onboarding checklists, and dashboards, all of which enhance visibility and accountability for control health throughout the organization (CIS, 2021; IBM, n.d.).

Embedding Compliance into Agile Delivery

In organizations exhibiting a high level of operational maturity, compliance is no longer treated as a peripheral concern but is instead systematically embedded within agile delivery methodologies. This integration manifests in several notable ways: compliance-related user stories are incorporated directly into sprint backlogs, and control reviews are regularly addressed during sprint retrospectives. Furthermore, the "definition of done" is intentionally broadened to encompass both security and compliance validations.

Teams also adopt quantitative approaches to compliance oversight, analogous to code coverage metrics such as tracking the proportion of services adhering to tagging protocols, implementing encryption, or generating requisite audit logs. The responsibility for compliance is distributed across roles; product managers evaluate compliance status as a core criterion for release readiness, while engineering leads continuously monitor for policy deviations or exceptions throughout the development lifecycle. Ultimately, compliance emerges not as a discrete function but as an integral, collective obligation embedded within the team's daily operations.

Use of Runbooks and Playbooks

When compliance breaches come to light, organizations must employ systematic protocols. Having a set of well-defined procedures is essential. Typically, two primary mechanisms form the backbone of an effective response.

- **Runbooks**: Runbooks function as automated scripts designed to swiftly address misconfigurations or halt problematic deployments. For instance, if an unencrypted storage volume is detected, the runbook initiates an automatic reversion to enforce security standards without requiring manual intervention.
- **Playbooks**: Playbooks are structured, human-oriented guides that detail the appropriate investigative steps, escalation protocols, and documentation processes. For example, in the event of unauthorized role assumption, a playbook provides a clear procedural framework for response, ensuring that incidents are managed systematically and in accordance with organizational policy.

These runbooks and playbooks provide a structured approach to incident response, facilitating consistency and auditability. Additionally, they contribute to more efficient resolution by minimizing the time required to address issues.

Leveraging CI/CD as a Compliance Gateway

CI/CD pipelines function as pivotal mechanisms for ensuring continuous compliance throughout the software delivery lifecycle. Pre-commit hooks act as the initial checkpoint, scrutinizing code and infrastructure definitions for potential policy violations prior to code integration. During the build phase, systematic tests are employed to validate Infrastructure-as-Code (IaC) templates and configuration files, thereby enforcing established compliance standards.

At the deployment stage, gating mechanisms serve to verify the presence of critical safeguards—such as accurate resource tagging, encryption protocols, access control provisions, and audit logging. Widely adopted tools, including Sentinel and Checkov, facilitate comprehensive policy-as-code enforcement by rigorously analyzing each code submission.

The pipeline automatically archives pertinent artifacts (e.g., build logs, test results, records of policy violations), producing a tamper-evident audit trail. This degree of automation minimizes the need for manual evidence collection, enhances traceability, and strengthens organizational audit readiness.

Continuous Assurance Metrics and Dashboards

Measuring the effectiveness of a CAOM requires new types of metrics:

- **Policy Pass Rate:** Indicates the proportion of deployments that successfully meet all compliance requirements.
- **Control Coverage:** Represents the percentage of cloud resources managed under at least one automated policy, ensuring comprehensive oversight.
- **Time to Remediation:** Measures the average duration required to address and resolve compliance violations.
- **Open Violations by Severity:** Categorizes unresolved compliance issues by their level of severity, supporting effective prioritization.
- **Audit Readiness Score:** Serves as an indicator of the organization's ability to provide accurate, up-to-date compliance evidence and maintain traceability (Secureframe, n.d.; Drata, n.d.).

Dashboards developed through Grafana, Power BI, or custom web portals provide critical insights into compliance health across teams, individual systems, and the organization as a whole. By offering a comprehensive overview, these visual tools enable stakeholders to identify and address potential issues proactively, supporting effective compliance management at every level.

Governance, Training, and Change Management

To effectively operationalize CAOM, organizations must implement comprehensive governance mechanisms.

- Establish a **compliance steering committee** with cross-functional representation.
- Maintain a **compliance calendar** aligned with sprint and release cadences.
- Define **training paths** for engineers to learn policy-as-code, compliance automation, and evidence generation.
- Use quarterly **compliance maturity reviews** for identifying gaps and prioritizing investments.

Senior leadership must actively promote compliance as a core organizational value, embedding it within the cultural fabric rather than relegating it to a mere legal obligation (NIST, 2018; CIS, 2021).

Benefits and Long-Term Outcomes

When effectively implemented, a Continuous Assurance Operating Model provides organizations with:

- **Sustainable compliance**: A framework for compliance, which scales alongside increasing complexity.
- **Reduced audit fatigue:** Automated, ready-to-use evidence reduces the strain of audit preparation, streamlining processes and minimizing the risk of so-called "audit fatigue."
- **Improved time-to-market:** Rather than serving as a bottleneck late in the development cycle, compliance becomes integrated into operational workflows, expediting time-to-market and reducing last-minute obstacles.
- **Stronger cross-team collaboration:** Stronger collaboration between teams by fostering a shared understanding of risk and clearly delineating responsibilities.

- **Higher auditor and regulator confidence:** This transparency and traceability not only improve internal coordination but also enhance the confidence of auditors and regulators.

Ultimately, the adoption of a CAOM transforms compliance from a reactive, periodic exercise into a continuous, collaborative process. It aligns governance practices with innovation, particularly in cloud-native environments where speed and complexity are standard. By embedding controls into developer workflows, ensuring clear ownership of responsibilities, and continuously measuring outcomes, organizations are better equipped to meet regulatory requirements while maintaining agility, security, and audit readiness.

CONCLUSION: REDEFINING COMPLIANCE FOR THE CLOUD-NATIVE ERA

In the evolving landscape of enterprise digital transformation, the paradigm of compliance must shift fundamentally. No longer can organizations rely on static checklists or retrospective audits, these approaches simply cannot keep pace with the rapid, ephemeral nature of cloud-native environments. The complexity and velocity inherent in such systems render traditional audit models obsolete.

A sustainable approach necessitates embedding compliance within the core processes of software development, deployment, and operation. Foundational technical shifts like Infrastructure as Code, Policy-as-Code, and Continuous Assurance now enable organizations to integrate governance directly into CI/CD pipelines. Through automation, evidence generation becomes continuous, and systems can achieve audit readiness at scale. In this context, compliance transitions from a perceived bottleneck to a catalyst for trust, quality, and competitive differentiation.

Yet, technological innovation alone is insufficient. Maturing an organization's compliance posture requires cross-functional collaboration, strong executive sponsorship, and a culture that empowers every team to view governance as an intrinsic responsibility. Developers, quality assurance professionals, platform engineers, and compliance officers must work in concert, unified by shared objectives of security, traceability, transparency, and ongoing improvement.

Regulatory landscapes are only growing more intricate, and public trust increasingly depends on demonstrable accountability. The ability to navigate governance seamlessly without impeding delivery will define which organizations can innovate effectively.

Ultimately, those organizations that treat compliance as a central competency, engineered with the same rigor as their core software, will be best positioned for the future. In doing so, they will not only satisfy audit requirements, but also establish resilient, scalable, and trustworthy systems capable of enduring in a rapidly changing world.

REFERENCES

Amazon Web Services (AWS). (n.d.). *AWS Config – Track AWS resource configurations and changes.* https://aws.amazon.com/config/

Center for Internet Security (CIS). (2021). *CIS Controls v8.* https://www.cisecurity.org/controls/cis-controls-list

Drata. (n.d.). *Automate your compliance journey.* https://drata.com/

European Parliament and Council. (2016). *Regulation (EU) 2016/679 of the European Parliament and of the Council – General Data Protection Regulation (GDPR).* https://eur-lex.europa.eu/eli/reg/2016/679/oj

HashiCorp. (n.d.). *Sentinel – Policy as code framework.* https://www.hashicorp.com/sentinel

IBM. (n.d.). *Compliance-Trestle.* https://github.com/IBM/compliance-trestle

Journal, H. I. P. A. A. (2023). *What is HIPAA compliance?* https://www.hipaajournal.com/hipaa-compliance/

National Institute of Standards and Technology (NIST). (2018). *Framework for improving critical infrastructure cybersecurity, version 1.1.* U.S. Department of Commerce. https://www.nist.gov/cyberframework

Open Policy Agent (OPA). (n.d.). *Policy-based control for cloud-native environments.* https://www.openpolicyagent.org/

OpenControl. (n.d.). *OpenControl – Compliance made simple.* https://github.com/opencontrol

PCI Security Standards Council. (2022). *Payment Card Industry Data Security Standard: Requirements and Security Assessment Procedures, version 4.0.* https://www.pcisecuritystandards.org/

Secureframe. (n.d.). *Compliance automation for modern enterprises.* https://secureframe.com/

Terraform Compliance. (n.d.). *Terraform compliance framework.* https://terraform-compliance.com/

Chapter 11
Fortifying Municipal Governance:
Leveraging IT Audits and Disruption Management for Sustainable Public Services

Tshepo Maota
https://orcid.org/0009-0001-0475-5801
University of South Africa, South Africa

ABSTRACT

This study examines how IT audits and disruption management might improve municipal administration and public service delivery in South Africa. Based on the 2024 Governance Performance Index, digital innovations and ethical leadership affect institution performance, specifically money mismanagement and poor service delivery. The study analyses municipal audit reports, oversight results, and worldwide best practices from Finland, Switzerland, and Singapore using qualitative document analysis. Research shows that most municipalities lack digital infrastructure, early-warning systems, and qualified personnel to manage disturbances. IT audits ensure compliance and transparency, while AI-driven disruption solutions reduce risk and plan continuity. Practical recommendations include institutionalising digital audits; decentralising e-governance; investing in cybersecurity and staff development; and encouraging citizen-centric involvement. This research recommends flexible, technology-driven governance structures to address complex and evolving service demands.

DOI: 10.4018/979-8-3373-3078-5.ch011

INTRODUCTION

"The test of good governance is not how institutions function in times of stability, but how resilient and responsive they remain amidst disruption."

Effective municipal governance involves not only the administration of public services but also the strategic management of the complex interactions among economic, sociological, and urban processes, necessitating a comprehensive and adaptable strategy (Das, 2024). Delivering sustainable public services in this complex environment requires a comprehensive framework that incorporates information technology (IT) audits and disruption management strategies, thereby protecting operational integrity and enhancing resilience to unexpected challenges (Das, 2024; Motubatse, Ngwakwe, & Sebola, 2020). The modern framework of municipal administration requires a shift towards citizen-focused, data-informed, and performance-oriented approaches, facilitated by improvements in information and communication technologies. Well-executed data management policies can equip cities for a transformational technological era (Blauer, 2017). Information technology audits are essential for assessing the efficiency, security, and compliance of IT systems and infrastructure, and they offer critical insights for process optimisation and risk mitigation. Disruption management involves the proactive identification, evaluation, and alleviation of potential disruptions, including natural disasters and cyber-attacks, to ensure the continuity of essential services and reduce negative effects on citizens and the community (Amaglobeli, 2023). Digital transformation in local government facilitates a transition from reactive to proactive, citizen-centric service delivery (Mhlongo & Thomas, 2024).

The integration of IT audits and disruption management is essential for cultivating sustainable public services, as it allows towns to optimise resource allocations, improve service delivery, promote transparency and accountability, and boost resilience against unforeseen events. The goal is to explore how IT audits and disruption management work together in local government, showing how they both help make public services more sustainable and effective in the long run. The Fourth Industrial Revolution requires local government officials to have a comprehensive awareness of their responsibilities in service delivery and the transformations associated with technological breakthroughs (Mhlongo & Thomas, 2024). Robust governance frameworks must be established on the basis of technology comprehension and readiness. Local governments can utilise strategic analysis approaches derived from the private sector to determine the necessary resources, capabilities, and management strategies for effectively addressing the changing environment (Sánchez & Zuntini, 2019). This discourse seeks to furnish concrete insights for municipal leaders and practitioners by examining real-world examples, best practices, and emerging trends to improve governance frameworks and foster more resilient and sustainable communities.

BACKGROUND

Growing urban complexity and residents' expectations for efficient, open, and responsible public services drive the need for strengthening municipal governance. Important for ensuring the well-being and quality of life of their residents, municipalities are charged with delivering a wide range of necessary services, including water and sanitation, transportation, public safety, and healthcare. These services, however, are frequently provided in a difficult and resource-limited setting marked by ageing infrastructure, financial constraints, and changing society demands. By means of resource management, local governments can promote law compliance and more open public policies, therefore enhancing the quality of life of citizens by ensuring essential services like education, safety, and health, especially for those who depend only on the local government (Thesari, Trojan, & Batistus, 2019). Moreover, it affects the environment via garbage disposal and sanitation services as well as taxation and infrastructure, which influence urban development. The growth of digital technologies and their increasing dependence on IT systems have significantly transformed the landscape of municipal government, offering new opportunities for creativity and efficiency, but also introducing new risks and vulnerabilities.

A thorough risk management system includes IT audits and disturbance management, which help municipalities to proactively spot, evaluate, and reduce possible dangers to their service delivery and operations. IT audits help identify weaknesses, inefficiencies, and compliance gaps that could endanger the confidentiality, integrity, and availability of vital data and systems by providing an independent and impartial evaluation of an organization's IT infrastructure, policies, and procedures. Conversely, disruption management includes a variety of strategies and techniques meant to prevent, minimise, and recover from disturbances like natural disasters, cyberattacks, and pandemics; therefore, it guarantees the continuity of vital services and reduces negative effects on people and the community. To manage facilities properly, local governments have to regularly repair and enhance infrastructure, oversee hazardous facilities, and control disaster-prone areas.

Smart cities, where technology is used to improve the quality of life, increase resource efficiency, and support sustainable development, make the convergence of IT audits and disruption management very pertinent. As municipalities become increasingly dependent on digital technology, the potential effects of IT failures and disruptions increase, highlighting the need for robust risk management systems that integrate IT audits and disruption control. In terms of infrastructure, transport, energy supply, and administration, technology will accelerate city expansion, enabling them more efficient and effective (Fajriyah & Djunaedi, 2021). The integration of digital technology into city operations offers possibilities for efficiency and creativity as well as new hazards and vulnerabilities, hence stressing the need for a comprehensive approach.

These emergency management systems will actually handle a range of urban-scale data, a vital element of the smart cities idea (Costa et al., 2022). Consequently, to create safer and more resilient cities, emergency management systems have included several technologies to automate different phases of the emergency management cycle and provide detection, alerting, and mitigation services (Costa et al., 2022). Urban safety and improved regulatory efficiency call for an active emergency command system driven by smart technology (Lyu et al., 2023). Addressing these gaps will help cities to better resist and recover from disturbances, hence guaranteeing the continuity of vital services and supporting the long-term viability of their communities (El-Maissi, Kassem, & Nazri, 2024). Smart cities generate a great deal of real-time data that guides policy and decision-making for efficient and effective public service delivery by means of technology, especially digital ones. To become a smart municipality, digital transformation is first required (Hoogen et al., 2024).

Furthermore, the integration of data analytics into municipal operations and automation of emergency responses are changing public administration and influencing urban resilience in the face of increasing unpredictability (Fajriyah & Djunaedi, 2021; El-Maissi et al., 2024). These changes highlight the importance of a comprehensive approach, in which IT governance and risk readiness are not isolated activities but rather complementary components of a forward-looking municipal organisation.

South African municipalities are at a crossroads: they may either welcome digital innovation together with strict risk management or run the danger of entrenching inefficiencies and weaknesses. Rethinking municipal governance approaches is justified by this twofold need to use IT audits for internal enhancement and to institutionalise disturbance management for external shocks.

PROBLEM STATEMENT

Ageing infrastructure, limited funds, and a growing reliance on IT systems converge to make efficient public service delivery more difficult for municipalities all over the world, especially in South Africa. Changing society demands for openness, responsibility, and continuous access to vital services only serve to aggravate these difficulties. Although ICT offers changing possibilities for enhanced production and service efficiency, South African municipalities have found it difficult to turn these potentials into real changes in governance results (Motubatse et al., 2020; Sibanda & Solms, 2018; Oyelana & Thakhathi, 2015). The regularity of service delivery protests, which indicate community discontent with municipal performance and institutional responsiveness, reflects this ongoing disparity.

Many local governments in South Africa still struggle to encourage awareness of risks, proactive management, and teamwork on digital transformation goals, even though they have made changes at the structural, strategic, and systems levels. Critical obstacles include insufficient ICT knowledge among municipal staff members, poor documentation and information management practices, and the absence of formalised IT project methodologies and testing environments, all of which undermine institutional readiness to adopt and control digital systems (Oyelana & Thakhathi, 2015; Nel-Sanders, 2018).

Furthermore, a weak IT environment is caused by financial limitations, low technical capacity, and scattered implementation strategies, which therefore heighten susceptibility to cyber-attacks, data breaches, and operational interruptions. The lack of strong IT audit policies and disturbance management systems aggravates this fragility; hence, cities are underprepared to protect data integrity, guarantee service continuity, or react quickly to crises.

These difficulties emphasise how important it is to include IT governance and risk management more strategically in the municipal ecosystem. Developing robust, responsible, and future-ready municipalities in South Africa depends on an understanding of how IT audits and disruption management interact with more general governance practices, particularly in light of worldwide trends towards digital government and smart city development.

STUDY AIM

This study aims to investigate ways for cities to enhance governance and ensure the long-term profitability of public services by means of IT audits and disturbance management. The aim is to assess present techniques, identify challenges and possibilities, and propose feasible remedies that would help cities to safeguard data, enhance service delivery, and lower risks.

The study will also provide feasible ideas to help cities address the issues impeding staff performance in using information and communication technologies, including poor document management, a lack of an adopted IT project management methodology, and the unavailability of a testing facility (Mahmud, 2020; Oyelana & Thakhathi, 2015). By means of literature analysis and an empirical survey of service providers in Limpopo province municipalities, the study aims to close this gap and give readers the views of important actors and recommendations for improving service delivery in South African municipalities (Mudzusi et al., 2024; Emily & Muyengwa,

2021). The major objectives of this study are to assess the effectiveness of present techniques, identify challenges and possibilities, and propose feasible remedies.

STUDY METHODOLOGY

To investigate how IT audits and disruption management support municipal governance and allow long-term public service sustainability, this paper uses a qualitative document analysis approach, methodically reviewing various case studies, academic literature, and industry reports. The study, which will focus on identifying best practices, identifying common implementation issues, and highlighting emerging global trends, situates itself at the intersection of technology, risk governance, and municipal management (Tonmoy et al., 2020).

Governance trends, performance indicators, and disruption management techniques were methodically extracted from publicly available secondary data sources, such as municipal annual reports, AGSA audit results, and audit committee reports. Thematic coding identified recurring governance shortcomings and innovative ideas. There was no primary data gathering with human subjects.

The study connects local governance issues to a global discussion by analysing both South African examples and practices from around the world, allowing for comparisons that help create specific recommendations for different contexts. This method provides a detailed analysis of how municipalities may use risk-based disruption strategies and IT audits to strengthen governance systems, improve service delivery continuity, and create community resilience. The study addresses the growing need for municipal innovation by specifically focusing on areas with infrastructure deterioration, climate risk, and digital capability deficits as is typically the case in South Africa's local government scene.

Moreover, the results of this study will have practical use for city officials and legislators. The report provides concrete ideas on how cities may match digital control with proactive risk management by drawing on data from a variety of sources, achieving efficient resource use, legal compliance, and open policy execution. Particularly for underprivileged and vulnerable populations, these foundations of government are vital as they directly affect people's access to basic services, including healthcare, education, water, and public safety. Through infrastructure investment, environmental stewardship, tax policies, and sustainable service delivery systems, local governments also significantly influence urban growth (Sánchez & Zuntini, 2019).

THEORETICAL FRAMEWORK

This study is based on two complementary theoretical frameworks: Public Value Governance (PVG) and Digital Era Governance (DEG).

Public Value Governance (PVG)

PVG, as articulated by Stoker (2006) and subsequently expanded upon by Bryson, Crosby, and Bloomberg (2014), underscores a transition from conventional top-down governmental frameworks to interconnected, collaborative governance systems. According to the PVG, municipalities are responsible for generating "public value" by providing services that fulfil the requirements and expectations of their inhabitants (Aswin, Ariesmansyah, & Indrianie, 2022; Liva et al., 2020). This strategy necessitates openness, civic engagement, ethical governance, and interorganisational cooperation. Within the framework of municipal administration in South Africa, PVG emphasises the necessity of reinstating legitimacy via performances that correspond with community priorities (Kanyane et al., 2020; Nzewi & Sibanda, 2023).

Digital Era Governance (DEG)

DEG, as delineated by Dunleavy et al. (2006) and further elaborated by Margetts and Dunleavy (2013), promotes the digital transformation of governmental functions to attain enhanced efficiency, responsiveness, and integration. DEG underscores the reintegration of previously disjointed services, the automation of processes, real-time data analysis, and a citizen-focused approach in service provision. Recent studies show that DEG principles are crucial for building strong towns that can prepare for challenges, handle risks effectively, and build public trust through clear and digital governance methods.

PVG and DEG collectively offer a comprehensive framework for examining the convergence of IT audits, disruption management, and municipal service delivery, facilitating institutional renewal and improved public value generation in the South African local government sector.

LITERATURE REVIEW

Overview of Municipal Governance

Municipal governance includes the rules, institutions, and procedures that determine how local decisions are taken, carried out, and watched over to make sure that public services are delivered effectively and the community is healthy (Curtis, 1999). Local governments in South Africa are required by the constitution to provide basic services, support socio-economic development, and make sure that democracy is open to everyone (Ndevu & Müller, 2018). But structural problems, including corruption, mismanagement of resources, weak leadership, and broken institutions, often get in the way of these aspirations (Govender & Reddy, 2019). Often interrupted services lead to community protests and a loss of trust in the government.

Disproportionate power arrangements, internal political tensions, and a lack of responsiveness to community demands all make governance less successful (Ngumbela, 2022). To get past these systemic problems, municipalities need to adopt governance models based on democracy, openness, participation, decentralisation, and legal certainty (Kasmawati, Aprilianti, & Dauri, 2022). To make this change happen, we need to do more than just plan ahead and build up our skills. We also need to use technology as a tool for governance.

The Strategic Role of IT Audits in Local Governments

IT audits are essential for checking how well municipal IT systems work, how safe they are, and whether they follow the rules. These audits look at infrastructure, controls, data governance, and digital assets in a methodical way to find weaknesses and inefficiencies that could affect service delivery or put municipalities at risk of cyber threats (Mofolo, 2012; Nadiyah et al., 2024; Sun & Qu, 2020; Khale & Worku, 2013).

In South Africa, where digital maturity in local government is still uneven, IT audits can help make the best use of resources, make sure that laws are followed (such as the MFMA and POPIA), and help people make decisions based on facts (Khasodi, Mahlala, & Hofisi, 2023; Pieterse, 2021). IT audits provide towns unbiased information on operational gaps, which helps them run more smoothly, keep private data safe, and provide better services to citizens (Curtis, 1999; Khale & Worku, 2013).

Management of Disruptions for Service Continuity

Disruption management is a proactive and holistic strategy for anticipating, managing, and recovering from service interruptions resulting from events like cyber-attacks, natural disasters, or system failures. Local governments are responsible for overseeing hazardous facilities, managing areas susceptible to disasters, and developing contingency plans to mitigate the economic and social impacts of disruptions (Terblanche et al., 2022).

Effective disruption management strategies are essential for preserving infrastructure integrity and public confidence. When properly executed, these methods guarantee that vital services remain accessible and equitable, even during crises. As municipalities confront climate change, digital reliance, and operational vulnerability, the integration of IT governance and disruption management is essential.

The Potential of E-Government in Revolutionising Public Service Delivery

E-government denotes the application of information and communication technologies to enhance public sector operations, service provision, and citizen participation (Mirandilla-Santos, 2008). Worldwide, e-government platforms have facilitated greater transparency in bureaucracies, improved administrative efficiency, and diminished potential for corruption via system automation and audit trails (Iverson & Barbier, 2021).

In South Africa, the advantages of digital governance are limited by deficiencies in ICT skills, insufficient infrastructure, and inadequate implementation strategies (Oyelana & Thakhathi, 2015). Moreover, despite the existence of strategic and institutional support measures, there is a deficient risk culture and insufficient buy-in among municipal employees (Nel-Sanders, 2018). These inherent deficiencies impede the adoption of e-government solutions and diminish the prospects for enduring digital transformation.

Digital technology can revolutionise governance by transitioning it from a reactive to proactive approach. Governments globally are enhancing productivity, reducing administrative burdens, and aligning with Sustainable Development Goals through cloud computing, open data portals, and AI-based systems (Alenezi, 2022). Nonetheless, ethical challenges, data privacy issues, and socioeconomic inequalities in access persist as significant obstacles to comprehensive digital transformation (Liva et al., 2020; Al-Ansi et al., 2024).

Digital Governance: Integrating Technology, Trust, and Accountability

The transition to digital governance signifies a wider trend necessitating public authorities to reevaluate their roles, responsibilities, and operational frameworks (Liva et al., 2020; Katsonis & Botros, 2015). This change is not merely technological; it is also cultural and institutional. Through the integration of e-government tools, municipalities can promote citizen-focused service design, improve transparency in reporting, and stimulate public engagement in policymaking (Manoharan, Melitski, & Holzer, 2022; Deni, Husain, & Deni, 2020; Akman et al., 2005).

Furthermore, digital governance frameworks increase internal operations via e-administration, which streamlines "back-office" processes, and e-services, which improve "front-office" contacts with the public (Riany, 2021). When connected with integrated risk management, these methods facilitate evidence-based policymaking, resilience planning, and responsiveness to community requirements.

The Significance of Public Trust, Stakeholder Involvement, and Innovation

Governments must increasingly partner with the corporate sector and civil society to jointly find solutions for intricate social issues, especially in urban development, infrastructure, and service delivery (Kamara & Rabie, 2021). In this context, cultivating multi-stakeholder relationships is crucial for innovation and accountability.

The cultivation of public trust is equally significant, closely associated with the quality and reliability of municipal services. Municipalities may enhance citizen trust and institutional legitimacy through transparent governance, participatory platforms, and dependable digital services.

FINDINGS AND DISCUSSIONS

Financial mismanagement, political unrest, and inadequate service delivery define a multi-dimensional dilemma confronting South African municipal government. The Auditor-General South Africa (AGSA, 2023) has observed a persistent decrease in audit results, which expose systematic weaknesses in internal controls and governance structures. In this context, IT audits and disruption management stand out as important tools for change (Erasmus & Matsimela, 2021; Khasodi et al., 2023). This paper investigates how these tools may be used to strengthen governance in municipal organisations and support sustainable public service delivery.

The theoretical perspectives of Public Value Governance (PVG) and Digital Era Governance (DEG) influence the analysis. While DEG promotes using digital tools and teamwork to make government more responsive and stronger, PVG focusses on working together with citizens to create results that the public values.

Governance Deficiencies and Internal Control Weaknesses

The AGSA's 2022/23 Municipal Finance Management Act (MFMA) report offers a stark analysis of the state of governance throughout municipalities. Despite numerous requests for accountability, only 34 municipalities have reported clean audits, resulting in a disappointing 13% success rate (AGSA, 2023). Performance reporting, infrastructure upkeep, and financial control all showed notable shortcomings. Most cities still struggle with internal audit functions, risk management, and audit committee efficiency.

The Audit Committee report of the Ba-Phalaborwa Municipality (2024) clearly demonstrates these issues. It points out inadequate duty segregation, capacity limits, and partial execution of audit results. Though the internal audit unit was deemed "generally conformant," 44% of the risk mitigation plans remained unimplemented. These results highlight the gap between policy frameworks and operational execution, a major issue in public value governance theory where performance legitimacy is important (Dzomira, 2020).

Information Technology Audits and Strategic Governance Facilitators

Information Technology (IT) audits, when conducted, have revealed significant inefficiencies. Johannesburg's audit findings indicated inadequate execution of the Municipal Standard Chart of Accounts (mSCOA), restricted use of automated tools such as Power BI, and delays in risk reporting—elements that obstruct data-driven decision-making and responsiveness (City of Johannesburg, 2024).

Conversely, organisations like SALGA (the South African Local Government Association) exhibited strong internal audit integration and utilised project management dashboards, resulting in consistently favourable audit outcomes (SALGA, 2024). SALGA's methodology is consistent with DEG principles, it utilises technology to enhance governance procedures and enable real-time monitoring and accountability (Margetts & Dunleavy, 2013).

Disruption Management: Transitioning From Reactive to Resilient Governance

Disruptions in municipal services, whether due to infrastructure breakdown, political instability, or environmental pressures, necessitate proactive risk management. The Polokwane Municipality's 2022/23 Annual Report recognises issues in water distribution due to deteriorating infrastructure and insufficient coordination with provincial water agencies. Notwithstanding several initiatives via intergovernmental forums, structural deficiencies persist (Polokwane Municipality, 2024).

The Audit Committee report of Senqu Municipality (2024) reiterated the necessity for frequent updates and oversight of the risk register. Nevertheless, the execution of risk strategies remains inconsistent, indicating a persistent disparity between risk identification and action. DEG theory suggests that governments should use a systems-thinking approach, which includes IT audits and predictive analytics, to foresee problems and reduce their impact (Cordella & Paletti, 2019).

Material Anomalies and Governance Vulnerabilities

The widespread problem of material anomalies, particularly in procurement, signifies weakened internal controls and ethical failures. The City of Johannesburg reported R4.9 billion in SCM deviations under Regulation 36, citing insufficient consequence management and control deficiencies for conflict of interest declarations (City of Johannesburg, 2024). This violates MFMA stipulations and diminishes institutional legitimacy.

The LGELI (Local Government Ethical Leadership Initiative) Code, 2024 promotes integrity in leadership, delineates political and administrative boundaries, and emphasises competence in oversight frameworks (The Ethics Institute, 2024). Nonetheless, ethical governance continues to be aspirational in several towns owing to inadequate enforcement tools.

The findings validate theoretical assertions that public value cannot be produced without institutional integrity and systemic accountability. Municipalities lack the requisite circumstances to provide essential services valued by the public, such as clean water, waste management, and economic infrastructure. Information technology audits and ethical leadership are crucial for transitioning from "control-based" to "performance-based" governance.

Digital era governance provides a framework for this shift by promoting the reintegration of disparate services, the digitalisation of internal processes, and data-driven supervision. Municipalities using these concepts, such as SALGA, exhibit enhanced resilience, transparency, and operational continuity.

Comparative Findings: International Best Practices

When looking at worldwide best practices, the example of Tallinn, Estonia, stands out as a model for municipal government excellence. Tallinn has effectively put in place a thorough e-government infrastructure, including digital identity systems, real-time data platforms, and automated service delivery (European Commission, 2022). Key factors supporting Tallinn's success are:

- End-to-end digitisation of municipal services lets people access services online 24/7 and helps to cut bureaucratic bottlenecks.
- Active citizen involvement is encouraged by citizen-centric platforms like e-Residency, e-Taxation, and e-Voting, which also help to build openness and streamline state-resident interactions.
- Predictive analytics in urban management—such as monitoring infrastructure health and traffic flows—allows for proactive decision-making and resource allocation (Kattel & Takala, 2021).
- The Estonian model shows that sustainable digital governance is enabled by high degrees of digital literacy, robust legal systems, and ongoing cybersecurity investment.

Likewise, Hangzhou, China, offers a wonderful example with its "City Brain" initiative.

Hangzhou uses cloud computing, large data analytics, and artificial intelligence (AI) to enhance metropolitan administration. Key points are:

- Emergency vehicles, real-time traffic management greatly lowers congestion and emergency response times.
- IoT sensors environmental monitoring by use of Internet of Things (IoT) sensors provides real-time updates on air quality and waste management efficacy.
- Integrated urban command centres let city officials oversee and coordinate several services at once, ranging from public safety to public utilities (Shen & Zhang, 2024).

Hangzhou's strategy emphasises the need for cross-sector data integration and predictive governance to improve municipal resilience and public happiness.

Furthermore, as seen in the Chandler Good Government Index (Chandler Institute of Governance, 2021) and other global ratings, Finland, Switzerland, and Singapore often placed among the top countries for outstanding governance. Their governance systems provide useful ideas for improving municipal governance in South Africa.

The table 1 below summarises the strategic pillars from these countries.

Table 1. Countries for good governance key pillars

Country	Key pillars of governance	Technology/IT practices	Lessons for SA municipalities
Finland	Trust, Decentralization, Fiscal Stewardship	Digital public services, citizen e-participation, foresight tools	Empower local digital platforms, use foresight-driven disruption planning
Switzerland	Direct Democracy, Subsidiarity, Consensus	Decentralized e-governance tools, local autonomy in decision-making	Enable citizen digital voting/ input mechanisms and devolve services
Singapore	Meritocracy, Anticipatory Governance, Anti-Corruption	AI-driven City Brain, real-time dashboards, predictive analytics	Adopt smart systems for audits, service monitoring, and risk forecasting.

Source: Author's own compilation

The above thoughts on the pillars are further discussed in the following sections.

Finland: Institutional Strength and Trust-Based Governance

High degrees of public confidence, openness, and strong institutional structures define Finland's system of government. The Chandler Good Government Index identifies seven foundations that support Finland's outstanding government:

- Proactive and visionary leadership anticipating future obstacles.
- Strong laws & policies: Finland's comprehensive legal systems ensure justice and responsibility.
- Independent and effective institutions that support democratic ideals are strong ones.
- Prudent fiscal management guaranteeing economic stability defines financial stewardship.
- An appealing market creates an environment that fosters creativity and entrepreneurship.
- Active participation in international events contributes to a positive global reputation.
- Policies meant to promote social mobility and lower inequality help people rise (OECD, 2023a).
- A decentralised government system supports these pillars by giving local governments great independence; hence, it improves responsiveness and service delivery at the city level.

Switzerland: Direct Democracy and Decentralisation

Switzerland's government stands out for its federal system and dedication to direct democracy. Mainstays are:

- Decentralised administration: Autonomy given to cantons and municipalities lets them create adapted policies that fit local needs.
- Direct democracy: By use of referendums and initiatives, citizens may shape laws.
- Making decisions based on consensus. Political culture emphasises collaboration and consensus among various organisations.
- The Swiss Federal Department of Foreign Affairs (OECD, 2023b) makes decisions at the most immediate level, consistent with their resolution.

In promoting strong citizen involvement and confidence in public institutions, this approach supports good government and social cohesion.

Singapore: Strategic Foresight and Meritocracy

Principles of meritocracy, strategic planning, and zero tolerance for corruption form the basis of Singapore's governing system. Singapore's good governance has six principles:

- Meritocracy: Ability and performance determine appointments and promotions.
- The policies promote social harmony within a multicultural society.
- Honest government – Open public administration and rigorous anti-corruption policies.
- A strong judicial system ensures the maintenance of justice and order.
- Political leadership's ongoing development and succession planning is leadership renewal.
- Proactive identification and handling of future issues defines anticipatory governance. This includes references to Ling (2024) and the Lee Kuan Yew School of Public Policy.

Singapore's focus on strategic foresight and creativity has driven it to the forefront of digital governance and public service quality.

ADDRESSING GOVERNANCE FAILURES IN SOUTH AFRICAN MUNICIPALITIES: LESSONS FROM GLOBAL BEST PRACTICES

The 2024 Governance Performance Index (GPI) from Corruption Watch shows that South Africa's municipalities are not doing well. The research says that pervasive corruption, bad financial management, poor service delivery, and incompetent administration are still hurting governance and public trust in the local government sector (Corruption Watch, 2024). These problems make it very difficult to change the economy and society, especially in communities that rely on municipal services.

Identified Key Challenges

One of the biggest problems is still poor financial management. For example, Eskom, an electricity provider took the assets of Emfuleni Local Municipality because it owed more than R3 billion, which shows that the municipality didn't keep track of its finance well (Eskom, 2024). In the same way, the Auditor General's recurrent audit disclaimers show that there are problems with the way finances are controlled and reported (Parliamentary Monitory Group, 2025).

Failures in service delivery are just as common. Municipalities like Lekwa have had a difficult time getting people clean water, working toilets, and consistent electricity. Backlogs in infrastructure, lack of maintenance, and misallocation of resources have hurt the environment and made people less healthy (National Treasury, 2021; Corruption Watch, 2024).

Corruption and a lack of accountability have made a culture of impunity strong. The GPI shows that many local governments have problems with nepotism, political influence, and improper procurement practices. Corruption Watch (2024) says that weak internal audit units and municipal public accounts committees (MPACs) can't do enough to stop wrongdoing. Furthermore, poor human resource capacity makes it harder to govern well. Many high-level officials don't have the skills, expertise, and certifications needed to handle complicated service delivery and compliance tasks. This keeps policies from moving forward and makes the government less efficient.

Lessons for South African Municipalities: Aligning IT Audits and Disruption Management for Sustainable Public Services

The 2024 Governance Performance Index (GPI) (Corruption Watch, 2024) shows that South African municipalities have long-term problems with governance, such as bad financial controls, pervasive corruption, unqualified workers, and service infrastructure that is getting worse. To fix these problems, municipalities need to not only improve their institutions' capability but also use IT audits and disruption management technologies as strategic levers for long-term success.

The following response techniques can help strengthen municipal governance in South Africa by using the best practices from Finland, Switzerland, and Singapore:

- Make IT audits a regular part of municipal governance, like they are in Singapore. These audits should be real-time performance evaluation. This digital monitoring can be very helpful in finding problems, making internal controls better, and cutting down on spending that isn't authorised or isn't needed.

- Decentralised digital governance: Give local governments more power through digital autonomy, just like Finland and Switzerland did. Decentralised ICT platforms can help service providers deal with problems in a way that makes sense for each situation. They can also make things more open by using open data portals and mechanisms for citizen feedback.
- Use predictive disruption management: Take inspiration from Finland's forward-thinking government and Singapore's proactive approach by implementing systems that monitor potential disruptions. Municipalities should use AI-powered solutions to deal with issues like water shortages, infrastructure failures, or power outages before they happen. These tools can also help with early-warning systems and becoming ready for disasters (Bari et al., 2023; Munawar et al., 2022).
- Encourage digital participation and direct democracy: Municipalities should set up digital ways for citizens to give their opinions on budgets, service ratings, and local policy decisions, just like Switzerland does with direct democracy. This not only builds trust in the government, but it also makes sure that digital policies are in line with local needs (Park, 2023).
- Make municipal platforms cyber-resilient: Municipalities need to protect their digital infrastructure, as witnessed in Singapore and Estonia. This includes teaching employees about cyber hygiene, employing encrypted systems to protect public data, and using blockchain to check purchases (Fiore & Mongiello, 2023; Ter, 2018).
- Invest in People for Digital Transformation: Using Singapore's merit-based civil service model as a guide, cities should focus on training and planning for the future of officials who run audit and risk systems. Capacity-building programmes should focus on teaching people how to do things like analyse data, buy things online, and predict risks (Pennington, 2023; Zhen-qi, 2021). Digital transformation is not merely about technology adoption but about fundamentally reshaping governance processes to enhance efficiency, transparency, and citizen engagement (Alenezi, 2022). Digital technologies can improve infrastructure, service delivery, and governance, fostering smart sustainable cities (Das, 2024).

Looking at the above practices, integrating them with IT audits and disruption management, South African municipalities may move from a reactive, fragmented system of governance to one that is proactive, integrated, and based on technology.

This change is necessary to make sure that public services are sustainable, resilient, and fair, even if infrastructure and budget problems worsens.

Ethical leadership, risk-based planning, and smart technology can all work together to help municipalities grow and build trust in the government again. There are many things that South African municipalities can learn from these best practices from around the world:

- Empowering local governments with more authority will improve responsiveness and responsibility.
- Direct citizen involvement can help build democracy and confidence.
- Appointments Based on Merit— Filling public service posts depending on ability will help enhance service delivery.
- Strategic Planning: Long-term planning and anticipatory governance can help cities get ready for problems that may come up in the future.
- Accountability and openness: To build public trust, it is important to set up strong anti-corruption structures.
- South African towns can strengthen their governance systems by using these concepts together. This will lead to better service delivery and more trust from the public.

THEORETICAL AND PRACTICAL IMPLICATIONS

Theoretical Implications

By applying the Public Value Governance (PVG) and Digital Era Governance (DEG) frameworks to the South African municipal setting, this study provides an important theoretical contribution. PVG emphasises the need to work together to create value through ethical leadership, collaborative governance, and a citizen-centered approach to service delivery (Stoker, 2006; Bryson et al., 2014). On the other side, DEG focuses on how digital technology may change things by bringing services back together, making them more open, and allowing government to work more quickly (Dunleavy et al., 2006; Cordella & Paletti, 2019).

The study indicates that digital transformation and disruption preparedness are not just technical improvements but also important ways to renew governance. This is shown by applying these frameworks to the situation in South African local government, which is marked by systemic financial mismanagement, service delivery backlogs, and institutional fragility. In particular, it shows how IT audits may be used strategically to find problems with controls, make things clearer, and make sure that institutions are meeting public expectations.

Adding predictive disruption management to the PVG and DEG frameworks helps us understand better how municipalities may move from reactive governance to planning and creating resilience based on foresight. This suggests that future research should focus on creating hybrid models that combine digital governance theory with adaptive risk governance in new and unstable municipal settings.

Practical Implications

The report gives municipal leaders, lawmakers, internal auditors, and oversight groups like MPACs and audit committees useful strategies that they can use right away. It that municipalities need to make digital governance tools a part of their daily operations and administration if they want to move towards providing services in a way that is both sustainable and trustworthy. This includes:

- Making IT audits a part of the business: Using technology-based audit systems lets you keep track of your finances in real time, keep an eye on compliance, and find abnormal spending early. These tools also help audits cover more ground at a lower cost, which is especially important for municipalities that don't have a lot of money to spend.
- Strengthening internal controls and ethical leadership: The 2024 Governance Performance Index (Corruption Watch, 2024) reported widespread failures in governance. This study calls for codes of conduct, making sure there is independent oversight, and enforcing accountability mechanisms that follow the LGELI Code of Ethics.
- Using predictive analytics to control disruptions: Singapore and Finland show how useful anticipatory governance can be. South African cities can use machine learning, GIS, and data dashboards to keep an eye on service pressures, stop problems before they happen (such as infrastructure failure or water shortages), and help them decide how to use their resources before a crisis happens.
- Encouraging digital services that put citizens first: The adoption of e-governance platforms can boost public involvement, make policies more responsive, and restore public faith in local government, important for local realities and participation.
- Investing in digital skills and cybersecurity: As municipalities become more dependent on ICTs, they need to train their staff in cybersecurity, data management, and system administration to protect against cyber attacks and make sure that data is safe when providing services and doing audits.

This study indicates that a digital infrastructure that is both technically sound and ethically led is becoming more and more important for long-term municipal governance. It connects theory and practice by putting IT audits and disruption management at the centre of strategic efforts to not only comply with the law but also build municipalities that are adaptable, open, and aligned with citizens in the digital age.

THE LIMITATIONS OF THE STUDY

The study's dependence on secondary data limits its ability to capture the intricacies of internal municipal operations. The approach is also context-specific to South Africa, limiting its direct applicability to other governance settings. To gain a more profound understanding, future studies could include original data from interviews or case studies.

FUTURE RESEARCH DIRECTIONS

Future research needs to explore the integration of Public Value Governance (PVG), Digital Era Governance (DEG), and adaptive risk frameworks in the context of South African municipalities. It's becoming more important to create governance models that bring together digital tools, ways for citizens to get involved, and plans for handling disruptions in a clear system for municipalities that face high risks and have limited resources. Research should look into how effective IT audits are at improving financial rules, openness, and service quality, as well as how well local governments manage disruptions. Additionally, research may evaluate the impact of digital platforms on public trust, accountability, and civic participation, thus helping to clarify e-governance adoption. The integration of artificial intelligence (AI) and automation in enhancing audit oversight and facilitating predictive risk management represents a significant area for further research. Longitudinal studies assessing capacity-building and professionalisation initiatives in IT governance, data ethics, and digital resilience would provide valuable insights for institutional reform. These research directions are essential for creating a resilient, transparent, and digitally proficient local government sector that effectively addresses present challenges and anticipates future uncertainties.

ETHICAL CONSIDERATIONS

This study exclusively uses publicly available documents and secondary data sources, such as government reports, municipal annual reports, and audit committee conclusions. Moreover, this study didn't include any people; thus, it didn't need ethical approval. All of the data used came from publicly available repositories and official websites, which are in line with academic standards for analysing secondary data.

CONCLUSION

This study has highlighted the pressing necessity to enhance municipal governance in South Africa by strategically incorporating IT audits and disruption management. The research indicates that sustainable governance is unattainable without digital transformation and ethical leadership, informed by local issues like pervasive financial mismanagement and inadequate service delivery, as well as global best practices from nations such as Finland, Switzerland, and Singapore.

This study theoretically broadens the applicability of public value governance and digital era governance within municipalities, positioning IT-enabled monitoring and predictive risk instruments as fundamental facilitators of institutional efficacy and public trust. The report offers pragmatic ideas, including institutionalising IT audit processes, implementing predictive disruption models, and investing in human resources and cybersecurity infrastructure.

The 2024 Governance Performance Index findings indicate that conventional compliance-based strategies are insufficient to tackle the entrenched issues within South African local government. A transition to anticipatory, technology-driven, and citizen-responsive governance is necessary. By adopting insights from international models and adapting them through local innovation, municipalities may regain credibility, enhance resilience, and fulfil their constitutional obligation to provide sustainable public services to all.

REFERENCES

Akman, İ., Yazıcı, A., Mishra, A., & Arifoğlu, A. (2005). E-Government: A global view and an empirical evaluation of some attributes of citizens. *Government Information Quarterly*, *22*(2), 239–257. DOI: 10.1016/j.giq.2004.12.001

Al-Ansi, A. M., Garad, A., Jaboob, M., & Ansi, A. A. -. (2024). Elevating E-Government: Unleashing the Power of AI and IoT for Enhanced Public Services. https://doi.org/DOI: 10.1016/j.heliyon.2024.e40591

Alenezi, M. (2022). Understanding Digital Government Transformation. arXiv (Cornell University). https://doi.org//arxiv.2202.01797DOI: 10.48550

Amaglobeli, D. (2023). Transforming Public Finance Through GovTech. In IMF staff discussion note (Vol. 2023, Issue 4, p. 1). International Monetary Fund. DOI: 10.5089/9798400245480.006

Aswin, A., Ariesmansyah, A., & Indrianie, M. (2022). Collaborative Governance Model in the Development Center of Economic Empowerment and Community Creativity in Bandung City. *Formosa Journal of Multidisciplinary Research*, *1*(5), 1189–1208. DOI: 10.55927/fjmr.v1i5.1071

Auditor-General South Africa (AGSA). (2023) *Integrated Annual Report 2022–2023*. Pretoria: AGSA. Available at: https://www.agsa.co.za/Reporting/AnnualReport.aspx (Accessed: 22 April 2025).

Ba-Phalaborwa Municipality. (2024) Final Audit Committee Report as of 30 June 2024. Ba-Phalaborwa Local Municipality. Available at: https://www.phalaborwa.gov.za/docs/reports/ANNEXURE%20-%206%20-%20Final%20AC%20Report%20(JNM)-%2030%20June%202024.pdf (Accessed: 22 May 2025)

Bari, L. F., Ahmed, I., Ahamed, R., Zihan, T. A., Sharmin, S., Pranto, A. H., & Islam, M. (2023). Potential Use of Artificial Intelligence (AI) in Disaster Risk and Emergency Health Management: A Critical Appraisal on Environmental Health. *Environmental Health Insights*, *17*, 11786302231217808. Advance online publication. DOI: 10.1177/11786302231217808 PMID: 38089525

Blauer, B. (2017). Building the Data City of the Future. In The Annals of the American Academy of Political and Social Science (Vol. 675, Issue 1, p. 151). SAGE Publishing. DOI: 10.1177/0002716217746359

Bryson, J. M., Crosby, B. C., & Bloomberg, L. (2014). Public Value Governance: Moving beyond Traditional Public Administration and the New Public Management. *Public Administration Review*, *74*(4), 445–456. DOI: 10.1111/puar.12238

Chandler Institute of Governance. (2021). *Finland Takes Top Spot in 2021 Chandler Good Government Index*. Retrieved from https://www.chandlerinstitute.org/news/finland-takes-top-spot-in-2021-chandler-good-government-index

City of Johannesburg. (2024) Oversight Report on the 2022/23 Annual Report and Its Annexures. Johannesburg: City of Johannesburg Metropolitan Municipality. Available at: https://joburg.org.za/documents_/Documents/Oversight-report-on-the-2022-23-Annual-Report-and-its-annexures.pdf (Accessed: 22 May 2025).

Cordella, A., & Paletti, A. (2019). Government as a platform, orchestration, and public value creation: The Italian case. *Government Information Quarterly*, *36*(4), 101409. DOI: 10.1016/j.giq.2019.101409

Corruption Watch. (2024) *The state of South Africa's municipalities revealed in 2024 GPI*. Available at: https://www.corruptionwatch.org.za/the-state-of-south-africas-municipalities-revealed-in-2024-gpi/ (Accessed: 19 May 2025).

Costa, D. G., Peixoto, J. P. J., Jesus, T. C., Portugal, P., Vasques, F., Rangel, E. O., & Peixoto, M. (2022). A Survey of Emergencies Management Systems in Smart Cities. *IEEE Access : Practical Innovations, Open Solutions*, *10*, 61843–61872. DOI: 10.1109/ACCESS.2022.3180033

Curtis, D. (1999). Performance management for participatory democracy: Thoughts on the transformation process in South African local government. *International Journal of Public Sector Management*, *12*(3), 260–273. DOI: 10.1108/09513559910267413

Das, D. K. (2024). Exploring the Symbiotic Relationship between Digital Transformation, Infrastructure, Service Delivery, and Governance for Smart Sustainable Cities. In Smart Cities (Vol. 7, Issue 2, p. 806). Multidisciplinary Digital Publishing Institute. https://doi.org/DOI: 10.3390/smartcities7020034

Deni, S., Husain, T., & Deni, A. (2020). Bureaucracy and Challenges in Digital Era: A New Concept of Information Technology Integration in the Archipelagic Country. *Journal of Public Policy and Administration*, *4*(4), 71. DOI: 10.11648/j.jppa.20200404.12

. Dunleavy, P. & Margetts, H. (2013) 'The Second Wave of Digital Era Governance: a quasi-paradigm for government on the web', Philosophical Transactions of the Royal Society A, 371(1987).

Dunleavy, P., Margetts, H., Bastow, S., & Tinkler, J. (2006). New public management is dead—Long live digital-era governance. *Journal of Public Administration: Research and Theory*, *16*(3), 467–494. DOI: 10.1093/jopart/mui057

Dzomira, S. (2020). Corporate Governance and Performance of Audit Committee and Internal Audit Functions in an Emerging Economy's Public Sector. *Indian Journal of Corporate Governance*, *13*(1), 85–98. DOI: 10.1177/0974686220923789

El-Maissi, A. M., Kassem, M. M., & Nazri, F. M. (2024). Resilient critical infrastructures: An innovative methodological perspective for critical infrastructure (CI) integrated assessment models by inducing digital technologies during multi-hazard incidents. *MethodsX*, *12*, 102561. DOI: 10.1016/j.mex.2024.102561 PMID: 38292313

Emily, M. M., & Muyengwa, G. (2021). Maintenance of Municipality Infrastructure: A Case Study on Service Delivery in Limpopo Province at South Africa. *American Journal of Operations Research*, *11*(6), 309–323. DOI: 10.4236/ajor.2021.116019

Erasmus, L. J., & Matsimela, T. (2021). The Municipal Audit Committee Self-review Threat: The South African Dilemma. *Southern African Business Review*, *24*. Advance online publication. DOI: 10.25159/1998-8125/6332

Eskom (2024) Eskom has attached Emfuleni Municipality's bank accounts to recover R8 billion in arrear debt after the municipality failed to comply with the Debt Relief Program. Available at: https://www.eskom.co.za/eskom-has-attached-emfuleni-municipalitys-bank-accounts-to-recover-r8-billion-in-arrear-debt-after-the-municipality-failed-to-comply-with-the-debt-relief-program/ (Accessed: 2 May 2025).

European Commission. (2022). *2022 European Semester: Country Report – Estonia*. Brussels: European Commission. Available at: https://commission.europa.eu/system/files/2022-05/2022-european-semester-country-report-estonia_en.pdf (Accessed: 3 April 2025).

Fajriyah, N. O., & Djunaedi, A. F. (2021). The Transformation of Smart City Concept in Urban Development (Case Study: Semarang City). *IOP Conference Series. Earth and Environmental Science*, *764*(1), 12028. DOI: 10.1088/1755-1315/764/1/012028

Fiore, M., & Mongiello, M. (2023).. . *Blockchain for Smart Cities Improvement: an Architecture Proposal.*, *1*, 1–5. Advance online publication. DOI: 10.1109/ICCSM60247.2023.00009

Govender, N., & Reddy, P. S. (2019). Effectiveness of governance towards digitalisation at eThekwini Metropolitan Municipality in KwaZulu-Natal province, South Africa. *Africa's Public Service Delivery and Performance Review*, *7*(1). Advance online publication. DOI: 10.4102/apsdpr.v7i1.336

Iverson, T., & Barbier, E. B. (2021). National and Sub-National Social Distancing Responses to COVID-19. *Economies*, *9*(2), 69. DOI: 10.3390/economies9020069

Kamara, R. D., & Rabie, B. (2021). The Efficacy of Policy and Legal Framework for Cooperative Governance and Local Economic Development (LED) in Small Towns in a Selected Region in South Africa. *Zarządzanie Publiczne*, *7*(1 (53)), 7–26. Advance online publication. DOI: 10.4467/20843968ZP.21.001.14134

Kasmawati, , Aprilianti, , & Dauri, . (2022). Kasmawati, Aprilianti, & Dauri, D. (2022). Urgency of Electronic Licensing Management Licensing Services in Improving the Community Economy. Advances in Social Science, Education and Humanities Research. *Advances in Social Science, Education and Humanities Research*. Advance online publication. DOI: 10.2991/assehr.k.220102.013

Katsonis, M., & Botros, A. (2015). Digital Government: A Primer and Professional Perspectives. *Australian Journal of Public Administration*, *74*(1), 42–52. DOI: 10.1111/1467-8500.12144

. Kattel, R., & Takala, V. (2021). Dynamic capabilities in the public sector: The case of the UK's Government Digital Service.

Khale, S., & Worku, Z. (2013). Factors that Affect Municipal Service Delivery in Gauteng and Northwest Provinces of South Africa. *African Journal of Science, Technology, Innovation and Development*, *5*(1), 61–70. DOI: 10.1080/20421338.2013.782143

. Khasodi, M. S., Mahlala, S., & Hofisi, C. (2023). Assessment of clean audit outcomes as an effective determinant of good service delivery: a case study of Midvaal Local Municipality. International Journal of Research in Business and Social Science (2147-4478), 12(9), 338. https://doi.org/DOI: 10.20525/ijrbs.v12i9.3012

Lee Kuan Yew School of Public Policy. (n.d.). *The Six Principles of Good Governance in Singapore*. Retrieved from https://lkyspp.nus.edu.sg/gia/article/the-six-principles-of-good-governance

Ling, F. (2024) 'Efficiency and integrity: The pillars of Singapore's public service'. Medium. Available at: https://medium.com/@feiwuling/efficiency-and-integrity-the-pillars-of-singapores-public-service-55e0b186a727 (Accessed: 19 May 2025).

Ling, F. (2024). *Efficiency and Integrity: The Pillars of Singapore's Public Service*. Retrieved from https://medium.com/@feiwuling/efficiency-and-integrity-the-pillars-of-singapores-public-service-55e0b186a727

. Liva, G., Codagnone, C., Misuraca, G., Gineikyte, V., & Barcevičius, E. (2020). Exploring digital government transformation. 502. https://doi.org/DOI: 10.1145/3428502.3428578

Lyu, J., Zhou, S., Liu, J., & Jiang, B. (2023). Intelligent-Technology-Empowered Active Emergency Command Strategy for Urban Hazardous Chemical Disaster Management. *Sustainability (Basel)*, *15*(19), 14369. DOI: 10.3390/su151914369

. Mahmud, T. A. (2020). Implementation of E-Government Policy in Banten Province. https://doi.org/DOI: 10.2991/assehr.k.200303.016

Manoharan, A., Melitski, J., & Holzer, M. (2022). Digital Governance: An Assessment of Performance and Best Practices. *Public Organization Review*, *23*(1), 265–283. DOI: 10.1007/s11115-021-00584-8

Mhlongo, T. P., & Thomas, P. (2024). An examination of the Fourth Industrial Revolution in the context of the South African local government. *Africa's Public Service Delivery and Performance Review*, *12*(1). Advance online publication. DOI: 10.4102/apsdpr.v12i1.807

Mirandilla-Santos, M. G. (2008). Promoting E-Government in the Context of New Public Management: The Case of the Local Government of Cebu, Philippines. SSRN Electronic Journal. DOI: 10.2139/ssrn.1558948

Mofolo, M. A. (2012). Strengthening Performance Management System Implementation in South African Municipalities. *Africa's Public Service Delivery and Performance Review*, *1*(1), 73. DOI: 10.4102/apsdpr.v1i1.25

Motubatse, K., Ngwakwe, C., & Sebola, M. P. (2020). Internal Control as a Catalyst for Clean Audit Outcomes in the Local Government. The Moderating Role of Information Technology. In International Journal of Recent Technology and Engineering (IJRTE) (Vol. 9, Issue 4, p. 204). DOI: 10.35940/ijrte.B4036.119420

Mudzusi, T. N., Munzhedzi, P. H., & Mahole, E. (2024). Governance challenges in the provision of municipal services: In the Vhembe District Municipality. *Africa's Public Service Delivery and Performance Review*, *12*(1). Advance online publication. DOI: 10.4102/apsdpr.v12i1.749

. Munawar, H. S., Hammad, A. W. A., & Waller, S. T. (2022). Remote Sensing Methods for Flood Prediction: A Review [Review of Remote Sensing Methods for Flood Prediction: A Review]. Sensors, 22(3), 960. Multidisciplinary Digital Publishing Institute. https://doi.org/DOI: 10.3390/s22030960

Nadiyah, F. A., Maharani, B., & Rahmatika, D. N. (2024). Pengaruh Audit Teknologi Infomasi Terhadap Kualitas Audit. *Ekonomi Keuangan Syariah Dan Akuntansi Pajak.*, *1*(3), 236–253. DOI: 10.61132/eksap.v1i3.278

National Treasury. (2021) *Final Financial Recovery Plan for Lekwa Local Municipality*. Pretoria: National Treasury. Available at: https://www.treasury.gov.za/comm_media/press/2021/LekwaFRP/02%20Final%20Lekwa%20LM%20FRP%20 Report.pdf (Accessed: 12 May 2025)

Ndevu, Z., & Müller, K. (2018). Operationalising performance management in local government: The use of the balanced scorecard. *SA Journal of Human Resource Management, 16*. Advance online publication. DOI: 10.4102/sajhrm.v16i0.977

Nel-Sanders, D. (2018). Risk management in the South African local government and its impact on service delivery. In International Journal of Management Practice (Vol. 12, Issue 1, p. 60). Inderscience Publishers. DOI: 10.1504/IJMP.2019.096683

Ngumbela, X. G. (2022). *The relationship between policy, governance and service delivery in local government in South Africa*. International Journal of Innovative Technologies in Social Science., DOI: 10.31435/rsglobal_ijitss/30062022/7810

Nzewi, O., & Sibanda, M. M. (2023). Local Government's Existential Challenge: 25 Years of the White Paper on Local Government (1998–2023). Journal of Local Government Research and Innovation, 4. https://doi.org/DOI: 10.4102/jolgri.v4i0.168

OECD. (2023a) 'Government at a Glance 2023: Finland'. Available at: https://www.oecd.org/en/publications/government-at-a-glance-2023_c4200b14-en/finland_d1080a88-en.html

OECD. (2023b) 'Government at a Glance 2023: Switzerland'. Available at: https://www.oecd.org/en/publications/government-at-a-glance-2023_c4200b14-en/switzerland_8f88ce47-en.html

Park, S.-C. (2023). Smart Cities: Striking a Balance Between Urban Resilience and Civil Liberties. arXiv (Cornell University). https://doi.org//arXiv.2303.14597DOI: 10.48550

Pennington, J. (2023). Singapore's Administrative Service – a model from which ASEAN should adopt? https://www.aseantoday.com/2017/09/singapores-administrative-service-a-model-from-which-asean-should-adopt/

Pieterse, H. (2021). The Cyber Threat Landscape in South Africa: A 10-Year Review [Review of The Cyber Threat Landscape in South Africa: A 10-Year Review] [AJIC]. *The African Journal of Information and Communication, 28*. Advance online publication. DOI: 10.23962/10539/32213

Polokwane Municipality. (2024) *Final Draft Annual Report for 2022–2023*. Polokwane: Polokwane Local Municipality. Available at: https://www.polokwane.gov.za/wp-content/uploads/2024/02/FINAL-DRAFT-ANNUAL-REPORT-FOR-2022-2023.pdf (Accessed: 12 April 2025).

Riany, K. G. (2021). Influence of Electronic Administration on Public Service Delivery among State Agencies in Kenya. *European Journal of Business Management and Research*, *6*(2), 39–43. DOI: 10.24018/ejbmr.2021.6.2.712

Sánchez, M. A., & Zuntini, J. I. (2019). Digital readiness in government: the case of Bahía Blanca municipal government. In International Journal of Electronic Governance (Vol. 11, Issue 2, p. 155). Inderscience Publishers. DOI: 10.1504/IJEG.2019.101500

Shen, Y., & Zhang, B. (2024). Advancing the Emergency Industry: Policy, Innovation, and Implications for National Security. *Journal of the Knowledge Economy*, *16*(2), 1–23. DOI: 10.1007/s13132-024-02018-4

Sibanda, M. M., & von Solms, R. (2018). Devising a strategy for IT governance implementation in municipalities. A case study of South Africa. *The Electronic Journal on Information Systems in Developing Countries*, *85*(2), e12067. Advance online publication. DOI: 10.1002/isd2.12067

South African Local Government Association (SALGA). (2024) *Annual Performance Plan 2024–2025*. Pretoria: SALGA. Available at: https://www.salga.org.za/Documents%20and%20Publications%20APP.html (Accessed: 18 April 2025).

Stoker, G. (2006). Public value management: A new narrative for networked governance? *American Review of Public Administration*, *36*(1), 41–57. DOI: 10.1177/0275074005282583

. Sun, M., & Qu, Y. (2020). IT Audit Education Implemented Under the Cloud Accounting. https://doi.org/DOI: 10.2991/assehr.k.200801.009

Swiss Federal Department of Foreign Affairs. (n.d.). *Switzerland promotes governance*. Retrieved from https://www.fdfa.admin.ch/content/dam/deza/en/documents/themen/anwaltschaft-regierungsfuehrung/FS-Gouvernanz_EN.pdf

Ter, K. L. (2018). Singapore's cybersecurity strategy. *Computer Law & Security Review*, *34*(4), 924–927. DOI: 10.1016/j.clsr.2018.05.001

. Terblanche, T., Sousa, L. O. de, & Niekerk, D. van. (2022). Disaster resilience framework indicators for a city's disaster resilience planning strategy [Review of Disaster resilience framework indicators for a city's disaster resilience planning strategy]. Jàmbá Journal of Disaster Risk Studies, 14(1). AOSIS. https://doi.org/ DOI: 10.4102/jamba.v14i1.1264

The Ethics Institute. (2024) *Code for Ethical Leadership in Local Government*. Pretoria: The Ethics Institute. Available at: https://www.tei.org.za/wp-content/uploads/2024/02/LGELI-Code-for-Ethical-Leadership-in-LG.pdf (Accessed: 1 April 2025).

Thesari, S. S., Trojan, F., & Batistus, D. R. (2019). A decision model for municipal resources management. *Management Decision*, *57*(11), 3015–3034. DOI: 10.1108/MD-05-2017-0500

Tonmoy, F., Hasan, S., & Tomlinson, R. (2020). Increasing Coastal Disaster Resilience Using Smart City Frameworks: Current State, Challenges, and Opportunities. *Frontiers in Water*, *2*, 3. Advance online publication. DOI: 10.3389/frwa.2020.00003

van der Hoogen, A., Fashoro, I., Calitz, A. P., & Luke, L. (2024). A Digital Transformation Framework for Smart Municipalities. *Sustainability (Basel)*, *16*(3), 1320. DOI: 10.3390/su16031320

Zhen-qi, W. (2021). Review of Government Performance Management in the Big Data Era: Practice, Issues and Prospects. Advances in Social Science, Education and Humanities Research. *Advances in Social Science, Education and Humanities Research*. Advance online publication. DOI: 10.2991/assehr.k.210519.076

Compilation of References

Abualhaija, S.. (2022, November). COREQQA: A compliance requirements understanding using question answering tool. In *Proceedings of the 30th ACM Joint European Software Engineering Conference and Symposium on the Foundations of Software Engineering* (pp. 1682–1686). ACM. DOI: 10.1145/3540250.3558926

Adadi, A., & Berrada, M. (2018). Peeking inside the black-box: A survey on explainable artificial intelligence (XAI). *IEEE Access : Practical Innovations, Open Solutions*, *6*, 52138–52160. DOI: 10.1109/ACCESS.2018.2870052

Adelakun, B. O. (2022). Ethical Considerations in the Use of AI for Auditing: Balancing Innovation and Integrity. European Journal of Accounting, Auditing and Finance Research, 10(12), 91-108. Retrieved from https://tudr.org/id/eprint/3072/

Adelakun, B. O., Majekodunmi, T. G., & Akintoye, O. S. (2024). AI and ethical accounting: Navigating challenges and opportunities. *International Journal of Advanced Economics*, *6*(6), 224–241. DOI: 10.51594/ijae.v6i6.1230

Aditya, B. R., Hartanto, R., & Nugroho, L. E. (2018). The Role of IT Audit in the Era of Digital Transformation. *IOP Conference Series. Materials Science and Engineering*, *407*, 12164. DOI: 10.1088/1757-899X/407/1/012164

Ahmad, A., & Babar, M. A. (2014). *A framework for architecture-driven migration of legacy systems to cloud-enabled software*. In *Proceedings of the WICSA 2014 Companion Volume* (pp. 1–8). IEEE. DOI: 10.1145/2578128.2578232

Ahmed, T., ... (2023, May). Recommending root-cause and mitigation steps for cloud incidents using large language models. In 2023 IEEE/ACM 45th International Conference on Software Engineering (ICSE) (pp. 1737–1749). IEEE. DOI: 10.1109/ICSE48619.2023.00149

AI Risk Management Framework | NIST. (2025, March 27). NIST. https://www.nist.gov/itl/ai-risk-management-framework

Aitchison, J., & Dunsmore, I. R. (1975). *Statistical Prediction Analysis.* DOI: 10.1017/CBO9780511569647

Aitkazinov, A. (2023). The role of artificial intelligence in auditing: Opportunities and challenges. International Journal of Research in Engineering, Science and Management, 6(6), 117-119. Retrieved from https://journal.ijresm.com/index.php/ijresm/article/view/2740

Ajigini, O. A. (2022). Towards a Model on Digital Transformation within the Higher Education Sector. https://digitalcommons.kennesaw.edu/cgi/viewcontent.cgi?article=1067&context=acist

Akacha, S. A.-L., & Awad, A. I. (2023). Enhancing Security and Sustainability of e-Learning Software Systems: A Comprehensive Vulnerability Analysis and Recommendations for Stakeholders. *Sustainability (Basel), 15*(19), 14132. DOI: 10.3390/su151914132

Akinade, A. O., Adepoju, P. A., Ige, A. B., & Afolabi, A. I. (2024). Cloud security challenges and solutions: A review of current best practices. *International Journal of Multidisciplinary Research and Growth Evaluation, 6*(1), 26–35. DOI: 10.54660/.IJMRGE.2025.6.1.26-35

Akman, İ., Yazıcı, A., Mishra, A., & Arifoğlu, A. (2005). E-Government: A global view and an empirical evaluation of some attributes of citizens. *Government Information Quarterly, 22*(2), 239–257. DOI: 10.1016/j.giq.2004.12.001

Aktas, E. U.. (2023, November). Issue report validation in an industrial context. In *Proceedings of the 31st ACM Joint European Software Engineering Conference and Symposium on the Foundations of Software Engineering* (pp. 2026–2031). DOI: 10.1145/3611643.3613887

Al-Ansi, A. M., Garad, A., Jaboob, M., & Ansi, A. A. -. (2024). Elevating E-Government: Unleashing the Power of AI and IoT for Enhanced Public Services. https://doi.org/DOI: 10.1016/j.heliyon.2024.e40591

Alaran, M., Lawal, S. K., Jiya, M. H., Egya, S. A., Ahmed, M. M., Abdulsalam, A., Haruna, U. A., Musa, M. K., & Lucero-Prisno, D. E.III. (2025). Challenges and opportunities of artificial intelligence in African health space. *Digital Health, 11*, 20552076241305915. Advance online publication. DOI: 10.1177/20552076241305915 PMID: 39839959

Al-Baity, H. H. (2023). The artificial intelligence revolution in digital finance in Saudi Arabia: A comprehensive review and proposed framework. *Sustainability (Basel), 15*(18), 13725. https://www.mdpi.com/2071-1050/15/18/13725. DOI: 10.3390/su151813725

Albawwat, I., & Frijat, Y. A. (2021). An analysis of auditors' perceptions towards artificial intelligence and its contribution to audit quality. *Accounting*, 755–762. DOI: 10.5267/j.ac.2021.2.009

Alder, S. (2023, September 22). Healthcare cloud usage grows but protecting PHI can be a challenge. *HIPAA Journal*. https://www.hipaajournal.com/healthcare-cloud-usage-grows-but-protecting-phi-can-be-a-challenge

Alenezi, M., & Akour, M. (2023). Digital Transformation Blueprint in Higher Education: A Case Study of PSU. *Sustainability (Basel), 15*(10), 8204. DOI: 10.3390/su15108204

Ali, H., Abidin, S., & Alam, M. A. (2024). Auditing of outsourced data in cloud computing: An overview. *2024 11th International Conference on Computing for Sustainable Global Development (INDIACom)*, 111–117. https://doi.org/DOI: 10.23919/INDIACom61295.2024.10498177

Aliane, N., & Zakariya, A. (2023). Enhancing cyber security resilience in the industrial sector: A comprehensive framework for third-party risk management. *International Journal of Cyber Criminology*, *17*(2), 262–283.

Aliyu, A., Μαγλαράς, Λ., He, Y., Yevseyeva, I., Boiten, E., Cook, A., & Janicke, H. (2020). A Holistic Cybersecurity Maturity Assessment Framework for Higher Education Institutions in the United Kingdom. *Applied Sciences (Basel, Switzerland), 10*(10), 3660. DOI: 10.3390/app10103660

Alles, M. G., Kogan, A., & Vasarhelyi, M. A. (2008). Audit automation for implementing continuous auditing: Principles and problems. Rutgers Business School, 1, 1-24. Retrieved from https://raw.rutgers.edu/MiklosVasarhelyi/Resume%20Articles/RESEARCH%20&%20W ORKING%20PAPERS/audit%20automation.pdf

Allgeier, H. (2020, August 27). Jennifer Bisceglie honored as EY Entrepreneur of the Year® 2020 Mid-Atlantic Award finalist. Interos Inc. Retrieved December 12, 2020, from https://www.interos.ai/bisceglie-ey-entrepreneur-of-the-year/

Alotaibi, E. M. (2023). Cloud computing to audit quality–evidence from Saudi Arabia. *International Journal of Applied Economics. Finance and Accounting*, *17*(1), 18–29.

Amaglobeli, D. (2023). Transforming Public Finance Through GovTech. In IMF staff discussion note (Vol. 2023, Issue 4, p. 1). International Monetary Fund. DOI: 10.5089/9798400245480.006

Amazon Web Services (AWS). (n.d.). *AWS Config – Track AWS resource configurations and changes.* https://aws.amazon.com/config/

Amazon Web Services. (2023). *MediSys replicates patient records and medical images to AWS.* https://aws.amazon.com/solutions/case-studies/medisys-case-study

Amazon Web Services. (2023). *Optimizing enterprise imaging in the cloud using Visage 7 PACS platform on AWS with Allina Health.* https://aws.amazon.com/solutions/case-studies/allinahealth-case-study

Annunziata, G., Sheykina, A., Palomba, F., De Lucia, A., Catolino, G., & Ferrucci, F. (2024). Security risk assessment on cloud: A systematic mapping study. *Proceedings of the 28th International Conference on Evaluation and Assessment in Software Engineering.* https://doi.org/DOI: 10.1145/3661167.3661287

Anton, T. S., Trupp, A., Stephenson, M. L., & Chong, K. L. (2023). The Technology Adoption Model Canvas (TAMC): A Smart Framework to Guide the Advancement of Microbusinesses in Emerging Economies. *Smart Cities*, *6*(6), 3297–3318. DOI: 10.3390/smartcities6060146

Appelbaum, D. (2017). Audit analytics and continuous audit: Looking toward the future. *The CPA Journal*, *87*(6), 19–25. https://scholar.google.com/scholar_lookup?title=The+impact+of+cloud+computing+on+auditing+practices&author=Appelbaum,+D.&publication_year=2017

Arazzi, M., ... (2023). NLP-based techniques for cyber threat intelligence. arXiv preprint arXiv:2311.08807.

Argaw, S. T., Troncoso-Pastoriza, J. R., Lacey, D., Florin, M. V., & Flahault, A. (2020). Cybersecurity of hospitals: Discussing the challenges and working towards mitigating the risks. *BMC Medical Informatics and Decision Making*, *20*(146), 146. Advance online publication. DOI: 10.1186/s12911-020-01161-7 PMID: 32620167

Arisa, R., Tomoharu, M., & Shinji, H. (2023). "Advancing AI Audits for Enhanced AI Governance." *arXiv*. https://arxiv.org/pdf/2312.00044

Armas, R., & Taherdoost, H. (2025). Building a Cybersecurity Culture in Higher Education: Proposing a Cybersecurity Awareness Paradigm. *Information (Basel)*, *16*(5), 336. DOI: 10.3390/info16050336

Arnold, V., Collier, P. A., Leech, S. A., & Sutton, S. G. (2004). Impact of intelligent decision aids on expert and novice decision-makers judgments. *Accounting and Finance*, *44*(1), 1–26. DOI: 10.1111/j.1467-629x.2004.00099.x

Arora, S., & Ramteke, V. (2024, November). Revolutionizing Third Party Risk Management Using Generative AI and RAG. In *2024 First International Conference on Data, Computation and Communication (ICDCC)* (pp. 16-22). IEEE. DOI: 10.1109/ICDCC62744.2024.10961910

Arun, K. (2024). ARTIFICIAL INTELLIGENCE INVESTMENT, REALISTIC REPORTS, AND FINANCIAL LOSS. *Denetişim*, (31), 117–128. DOI: 10.58348/denetisim.1519501

Ashton, R. H. (1990). Pressure and performance in accounting decision settings: Paradoxical effects of incentives, feedback, and justification. *Journal of Accounting Research*, *28*, 148. DOI: 10.2307/2491253

Aswin, A., Ariesmansyah, A., & Indrianie, M. (2022). Collaborative Governance Model in the Development Center of Economic Empowerment and Community Creativity in Bandung City. *Formosa Journal of Multidisciplinary Research*, *1*(5), 1189–1208. DOI: 10.55927/fjmr.v1i5.1071

Atrinawati, F., Gerl, H., Von Der Heyde, M., Groß, M., Seck, D., & Watkowski, R. (2021). Applying COBIT 2019 to IT Governance in Higher Education. Retrieved from https://www.researchgate.net/publication/349440036ResearchGate+1DLGI+1

AuditBoard. (2024, June 14). *5 steps to assess the cyber and privacy risk of generative AI*. AuditBoard. Retrieved from https://www.auditboard.com/blog/5-steps-to-assess-the-cyber-and-privacy-risk-of-generative-ai

Auditor-General South Africa (AGSA). (2023) *Integrated Annual Report 2022–2023*. Pretoria: AGSA. Available at: https://www.agsa.co.za/Reporting/AnnualReport.aspx (Accessed: 22 April 2025).

Baldwin, A. A., Brown, C. E., & Trinkle, B. S. (2006). Opportunities for artificial intelligence development in the accounting domain: The case for auditing. *Intelligent Systems in Accounting, Finance & Management*, *14*(3), 77–86. DOI: 10.1002/isaf.277

Banker, R. D., Chang, M. H., & Lee, C. (2020). The audit implications of cloud computing. *Accounting Horizons*, *34*(4), 1–31. DOI: 10.2308/HORIZONS-19-166

Ba-Phalaborwa Municipality. (2024) Final Audit Committee Report as of 30 June 2024. Ba-Phalaborwa Local Municipality. Available at: https://www.phalaborwa.gov.za/docs/reports/ANNEXURE%20-%206%20-%20Final%20AC%20Report%20(JNM)-%2030%20June%202024.pdf (Accessed: 22 May 2025)

Bari, L. F., Ahmed, I., Ahamed, R., Zihan, T. A., Sharmin, S., Pranto, A. H., & Islam, M. (2023). Potential Use of Artificial Intelligence (AI) in Disaster Risk and Emergency Health Management: A Critical Appraisal on Environmental Health. *Environmental Health Insights, 17*, 11786302231217808. Advance online publication. DOI: 10.1177/11786302231217808 PMID: 38089525

Baxter, C. (2024, January 1). *IS audit in practice: A collaborative approach to assessing AI risk*. ISACA Journal, 2024(1). https://www.isaca.org/resources/isaca-journal/issues/2024/volume-1/a-collaborative-approach-to-assessing-ai-risk

Bell, T. B., & Carcello, J. V. (2000). A decision aid for assessing the likelihood of fraudulent financial reporting. *Auditing, 19*(1), 169–184. DOI: 10.2308/aud.2000.19.1.169

Benavides, L. M. C., Arias, J. A. T., Burgos, D., & Martens, A. (2022). *Measuring digital transformation in higher education institutions – content validity instrument*. Applied Computing and Informatics., DOI: 10.1108/ACI-03-2022-0069

Bendicho, C. (2021). Cyber security in cloud: Risk assessment models. In *Cybersecurity and Privacy in Cyber Physical Systems* (pp. 471–482). Springer., DOI: 10.1007/978-3-030-80119-9_28

Bertolli, L. (2019). Blockchain records: Is the evidence admissible? A challenge for EU member states. *Civil Procedure Review*, (3–4), 53–64.

Bharadhwaj, H., Huang, D.-A., Xiao, C., Anandkumar, A., & Garg, A. (2021, September 25). Auditing AI models for verified deployment under semantic specifications. *arXiv*. https://arxiv.org/abs/2109.12456

Bianchi, I. S., Sousa, R. D., & Pereira, R. (2021). Information Technology Governance for Higher Education Institutions: A Multi-Country Study. *Informatics (MDPI), 8*(2), 26. DOI: 10.3390/informatics8020026

Bilski, A. (2011). *A review of Artificial intelligence Algorithms in Document Classification*. International Journal of Electronics and Telecommunications - PAS Journals. https://journals.pan.pl/dlibra/doccontent?id=86895

Biondi, J., & Marchi, A. (2021). Blockchain and the future of financial reporting and assurance. *Accounting, Auditing & Accountability Journal, 34*(10), 2567–2594.

BitSight Technologies Inc. et al. (2020). Understand your security rating | BitSight Security Ratings. Retrieved December 12, 2020, from https://www.bitsight.com/understand-your-rating

BitSight Technologies. (2022). BitSight Security Ratings Platform [White paper].

Bittler, R., & Kreizman, G. (2010). Gartner's TIME model for application portfolio analysis. Gartner (Archived). https://www.leanix.net/en/wiki/apm/gartner-time-model#:~:text=The%20Gartner%C2%AE%20TIME%20framework%20,planning%20and%20executing%20application%20rationalization

Blauer, B. (2017). Building the Data City of the Future. In The Annals of the American Academy of Political and Social Science (Vol. 675, Issue 1, p. 151). SAGE Publishing. DOI: 10.1177/0002716217746359

Bommasani, R., ... (2022, July 12). On the opportunities and risks of foundation models. *arXiv*. https://doi.org//arXiv.2108.07258DOI: 10.48550

Borenstein, M., Hedges, L. V., Higgins, J. P. T., & Rothstein, H. R. (2009). *Introduction to meta-analysis*. Wiley. DOI: 10.1002/9780470743386

Bosch, T., Jordaan, M., Mwaura, J., Nkoala, S., Schoon, A., Smit, A., Uzuegbunam, C. E., & Mare, A. (2023). South African University Students' Use of AI-Powered Tools for Engaged Learning. SSRN Electronic Journal. DOI: 10.2139/ssrn.4595655

Bowen, G. A. (2009). Document analysis as a qualitative research method. *Qualitative Research Journal*, *9*(2), 27–40. DOI: 10.3316/QRJ0902027

Braun, V., & Clarke, V. (2006). Using thematic analysis in psychology. *Qualitative Research in Psychology*, *3*(2), 77–101. DOI: 10.1191/1478088706qp063oa

Brodie, M., & Stonebraker, M. (1995). *Migrating legacy systems: Gateways, interfaces & the incremental approach*. Morgan Kaufmann Publishers Inc.

Bryson, J. M., Crosby, B. C., & Bloomberg, L. (2014). Public Value Governance: Moving beyond Traditional Public Administration and the New Public Management. *Public Administration Review*, *74*(4), 445–456. DOI: 10.1111/puar.12238

Carrns, A. (2012, May 10). Is that credit score a FICO, or a FICO 8? Bucks Blog. Retrieved December 12, 2020, from https://bucks.blogs.nytimes.com/2012/05/10/is-that-credit-score-a-fico-or-a-fico-8/

Center for Internet Security (CIS). (2021). *CIS Controls v8*. https://www.cisecurity.org/controls/cis-controls-list

Chandler Institute of Governance. (2021). *Finland Takes Top Spot in 2021 Chandler Good Government Index*. Retrieved from https://www.chandlerinstitute.org/news/finland-takes-top-spot-in-2021-chandler-good-government-index

Changchit, C., & Holsapple, C. W. (2004). The development of an expert system for managerial evaluation of internal controls. *Intelligent Systems in Accounting, Finance & Management*, *12*(2), 103–120. DOI: 10.1002/isaf.246

Chiappini, D. (2024). The Legal Definition of Artificial Intelligence: A Comparative Perspective. *European Journal of Comparative Law and Governance, 11*(3), 360–387. DOI: 10.1163/22134514-bja10071

Chimwanda, E., Miller, K., & DeRoche, T. (2024). *CISA Official Review Manual* (28th ed.). ISACA.

Choi, D., Chung, C. Y., Seyha, T., & Young, J. (2020). Factors Affecting Organizations' Resistance to the Adoption of Blockchain Technology in Supply Networks. *Sustainability (Basel), 12*(21), 8882. DOI: 10.3390/su12218882

Choi, G.-Y., & Kim, A. G. (2024, April 18). *Firm-level tax audits: A generative AI-based measurement* (Chicago Booth Research Paper No. 23-23). *SSRN*. Retrieved from https://ssrn.com/abstract=4645865 or DOI: 10.2139/ssrn.4645865

Chou, D. C. (2015). Cloud computing risk and audit issues. *Computer Standards & Interfaces, 42*, 137–142. DOI: 10.1016/j.csi.2015.06.005

Choudhary, C., Vyas, N., & Lilhore, U. K. (2023). Cloud security: Challenges and strategies for ensuring data protection. *2023 3rd International Conference on Technological Advancements in Computational Sciences (ICTACS)*, 669–673. https://doi.org/DOI: 10.1109/ICTACS59847.2023.10390302

CIO Council & C&I CoP. (2020). Application rationalization playbook (Version 1.1). U.S. Federal CIO Council. https://www.cio.gov/assets/files/Application-Rationalization-Playbook.pdf#:~:text=business%20applications%20across%20an%20organization,whole%20to%20eliminate%20redundancies%2C%20lower

City of Johannesburg. (2024) Oversight Report on the 2022/23 Annual Report and Its Annexures. Johannesburg: City of Johannesburg Metropolitan Municipality. Available at: https://joburg.org.za/documents_/Documents/Oversight-report-on-the-2022-23-Annual-Report-and-its-annexures.pdf (Accessed: 22 May 2025).

Cloud Security Alliance. (n.d.). "AI Safety Initiative." Cloud Security Alliance. "https://cloudsecurityalliance.org/ai-safety-initiative"

Coffi, J., & George, B. (2022). The Fintech Revolution and the Changing Role of Financial Advisors. *Journal of Applied and Theoretical Social Sciences, 4*(3), 261–274. https://iccsor.com/index.php/jatss/article/view/147. DOI: 10.37241/jatss.2022.66

Colorafi, K., & Evans, B. C. (2016). Qualitative Descriptive Methods in Health Science Research. *HERD, 9*(4), 16–25. DOI: 10.1177/1937586715614171 PMID: 26791375

Cooke, I. (2019). Developing the IT audit plan using COBIT 2019. ISACA Journal, 3. https://www.isaca.org/resources/isaca-journal/issues/2019/volume-3/developing-the-it-audit-plan-using-cobit-2019#:~:text=The%20IT%20Assurance%20Framework%20,can%20this%20be%20improved%20upon

Cordella, A., & Paletti, A. (2019). Government as a platform, orchestration, and public value creation: The Italian case. *Government Information Quarterly*, *36*(4), 101409. DOI: 10.1016/j.giq.2019.101409

Corruption Watch. (2024) *The state of South Africa's municipalities revealed in 2024 GPI.* Available at: https://www.corruptionwatch.org.za/the-state-of-south-africas-municipalities-revealed-in-2024-gpi/ (Accessed: 19 May 2025).

Costa, D. G., Peixoto, J. P. J., Jesus, T. C., Portugal, P., Vasques, F., Rangel, E. O., & Peixoto, M. (2022). A Survey of Emergencies Management Systems in Smart Cities. *IEEE Access : Practical Innovations, Open Solutions*, *10*, 61843–61872. DOI: 10.1109/ACCESS.2022.3180033

Coyne, C. (2025, February 4). *COBIT: A practical guide for AI governance.* ISACA Now Blog. https://www.isaca.org/resources/news-and-trends/isaca-now-blog/2025/cobit-a-practical-guide-for-ai-governance

Curtis, D. (1999). Performance management for participatory democracy: Thoughts on the transformation process in South African local government. *International Journal of Public Sector Management*, *12*(3), 260–273. DOI: 10.1108/09513559910267413

Daily Investor. (2025, April 15). *One threat bigger than load-shedding in South Africa.* Retrieved from https://dailyinvestor.com/business/85980/one-threat-bigger-than-load-shedding-in-south-africa/

Das, D. K. (2024). Exploring the Symbiotic Relationship between Digital Transformation, Infrastructure, Service Delivery, and Governance for Smart Sustainable Cities. In Smart Cities (Vol. 7, Issue 2, p. 806). Multidisciplinary Digital Publishing Institute. https://doi.org/DOI: 10.3390/smartcities7020034

Dastidar, S. G., & Chatterjee, S. (2013, May). Distributed software development: Experience and recommendation. In 2013 3rd International Workshop on Collaborative Teaching of Globally Distributed Software Development (CTGDSD) (pp. 11-14). IEEE.

Deloitte. (2017). Blockchain technology and its potential impact on the audit and assurance profession. *Deloitte Insights.* https://www2.deloitte.com

Deloitte. (2023). *Third-party governance and risk management.* Deloitte Insights.

Deloitte. (2024, January)"AI Presentation for the Audit Committee - Second Draft." *Deloitte*. https://www2.deloitte.com/content/dam/Deloitte/se/Documents/audit/AI%20presentation%20for%20the%20Audit%20Committee%20-%20Second%20draft.pdf

Deloitte. (n.d.). *Continuous monitoring and continuous auditing practices*. https://www2.deloitte.com/content/dam/Deloitte/uy/Documents/audit/Monitoreo%20continuo%20y%20auditoria%20continua.pdf

Deni, S., Husain, T., & Deni, A. (2020). Bureaucracy and Challenges in Digital Era: A New Concept of Information Technology Integration in the Archipelagic Country. *Journal of Public Policy and Administration*, *4*(4), 71. DOI: 10.11648/j.jppa.20200404.12

Dhopte, A., & Bagde, H. (2023). *Smart Smile: Revolutionizing Dentistry With Artificial Intelligence* [Review of Smart Smile: Revolutionizing Dentistry With Artificial Intelligence]. Cureus. Cureus, Inc., DOI: 10.7759/cureus.41227

Dhotay, M., Mitra, A., Suryawanshi, A. S., Bangare, S. L., & Tiwari, A. (2024). Securing cloud infrastructures: A multi-layered approach to data protection. *Computer Fraud & Security*, 126–133. Advance online publication. DOI: 10.52710/cfs.69

Dillard, J. F., & Yuthas, K. (2001). A Responsibility Ethics for Audit Expert Systems. *Journal of Business Ethics*, *30*(4), 337–359. DOI: 10.1023/A:1010720630914

Đ , T. T., & Tr n, K. (2021). The combination of robotic process automation (RPA) and chatbot for business applications.

Dobrinić, D. (2020). *Conceptual model for cloud computing acceptance in the audit profession*. Informatologia., DOI: 10.32914/i.53.3-4.6

Doshi, H. K., Balasingam, S., & Arumugam, D. (2020). Artificial Intelligence as a Paradoxical Digital Disruptor in the Accounting Profession: An Empirical Study amongst Accountants. *International Journal of Psychosocial Rehabilitation*, *24*(02), 873–885. DOI: 10.37200/IJPR/V24I2/PR200396

Drata. (n.d.). *Automate your compliance journey*. https://drata.com/

Dunleavy, P., Margetts, H., Bastow, S., & Tinkler, J. (2006). New public management is dead—Long live digital-era governance. *Journal of Public Administration: Research and Theory*, *16*(3), 467–494. DOI: 10.1093/jopart/mui057

Durodolu, O. O., & Olumide, O. (2016). Technology Acceptance Model as a predictor of using information system' to acquire information literacy skills. Library Philosophy and Practice. https://digitalcommons.unl.edu/cgi/viewcontent.cgi?article=4029&context=libphilprac

Dzomira, S. (2020). Corporate Governance and Performance of Audit Committee and Internal Audit Functions in an Emerging Economy's Public Sector. *Indian Journal of Corporate Governance*, *13*(1), 85–98. DOI: 10.1177/0974686220923789

Edu, J.. (2022, October). Exploring the security and privacy risks of chatbots in messaging services. In *Proceedings of the 22nd ACM Internet Measurement Conference* (pp. 581–588). DOI: 10.1145/3517745.3561433

El-Maissi, A. M., Kassem, M. M., & Nazri, F. M. (2024). Resilient critical infrastructures: An innovative methodological perspective for critical infrastructure (CI) integrated assessment models by inducing digital technologies during multi-hazard incidents. *MethodsX*, *12*, 102561. DOI: 10.1016/j.mex.2024.102561 PMID: 38292313

Emily, M. M., & Muyengwa, G. (2021). Maintenance of Municipality Infrastructure: A Case Study on Service Delivery in Limpopo Province at South Africa. *American Journal of Operations Research*, *11*(6), 309–323. DOI: 10.4236/ajor.2021.116019

Erasmus, L. J., & Matsimela, T. (2021). The Municipal Audit Committee Self-review Threat: The South African Dilemma. *Southern African Business Review*, *24*. Advance online publication. DOI: 10.25159/1998-8125/6332

Eskom (2024) Eskom has attached Emfuleni Municipality's bank accounts to recover R8 billion in arrear debt after the municipality failed to comply with the Debt Relief Program. Available at: https://www.eskom.co.za/eskom-has-attached-emfuleni-municipalitys-bank-accounts-to-recover-r8-billion-in-arrear-debt-after-the-municipality-failed-to-comply-with-the-debt-relief-program/ (Accessed: 2 May 2025).

European Commission. (2022). *2022 European Semester: Country Report – Estonia*. Brussels: European Commission. Available at: https://commission.europa.eu/system/files/2022-05/2022-european-semester-country-report-estonia_en.pdf (Accessed: 3 April 2025).

European Parliament and Council. (2016). *Regulation (EU) 2016/679 of the European Parliament and of the Council – General Data Protection Regulation (GDPR)*. https://eur-lex.europa.eu/eli/reg/2016/679/oj

European Parliament. (2023, December 9). *Artificial Intelligence Act: deal on comprehensive rules for trustworthy AI.* https://www.europarl.europa.eu/news/en/press-room/20231206IPR15699/artificial-intelligence-act-deal-on-comprehensive-rules-for-trustworthy-ai

Faccia, A., De Lucia, C., Eltweri, A., Sawan, N., & Cavaliere, L. P. L. (2020). Extended Audit Report: Enhancing Trust and Reputation in IT Processes and across E-business Industries. *Extended Audit Report: Enhancing Trust and Reputation in IT Processes and Across E-business Industries*, *23–27*, 23–27. Advance online publication. DOI: 10.1145/3446922.3446927

Face, H. (2023a). Flan-T5. Retrieved from https://huggingface.co/google/flan-t5-xl

Face, H. (2023b). all-mpnet-base-v2. Retrieved from https://huggingface.co/transformers/all-mpnet-base-v2

Faddom. (2023). Application portfolio management: Essential elements and 7 critical best practices. Faddom Blog. https://faddom.com/application-portfolio-management-essential-elements-and-7-critical-best-practices/#:~:text=Mitigate%20Security%20and%20Compliance%20Vulnerabilities

Fahmideh, M., Beydoun, G., & Atif, Y. (2016). Cloud migration process: A survey, evaluation framework, and open challenges. *Journal of Systems and Software*, *120*, 31–69. DOI: 10.1016/j.jss.2016.06.068

Fajriyah, N. O., & Djunaedi, A. F. (2021). The Transformation of Smart City Concept in Urban Development (Case Study: Semarang City). *IOP Conference Series. Earth and Environmental Science*, *764*(1), 12028. DOI: 10.1088/1755-1315/764/1/012028

Fayyazi., ... (2024). ProveRAG: Provenance-Driven Vulnerability Analysis with Automated Retrieval-Augmented LLMs. arXiv preprint arXiv:2410.17406.

Fedyk, A., Hodson, J., Khimich, N., & Fedyk, T. (2022). Is artificial intelligence improving the audit process? *Review of Accounting Studies*, *27*(3), 938–985. DOI: 10.1007/s11142-022-09697-x

Fernandez, M., Cukier, J., Jones, T. S., & Khurana, R. (2012). Privacy and security in the cloud: A healthcare perspective. In *Proceedings of the IEEE HealthCom* (pp. 187–192). IEEE. https://doi.org/DOI: 10.1109/HealthCom.2012.6379435

Fiore, M., & Mongiello, M. (2023).. . *Blockchain for Smart Cities Improvement: an Architecture Proposal.*, *1*, 1–5. Advance online publication. DOI: 10.1109/ICCSM60247.2023.00009

Fitrani, L. D., & Ginardi, R. V. H. (2019). Analysis Improvement of Helpdesk System Services Based on Framework COBIT 5 and ITIL 3rd Version (Case Study: DSIK Airlangga University). *IPTEK Journal of Proceedings Series*, *1*(1), 28. DOI: 10.12962/j23546026.y2019i1.5102

Floridi, L., Cowls, J., Beltrametti, M., Chatila, R., Chazerand, P., Dignum, V., Luetge, C., Madelin, R., Pagallo, U., Rossi, F., Schafer, B., Valcke, P., & Vayena, E. (2018, November 26). AI4People—An ethical framework for a good AI society: Opportunities, risks, principles, and recommendations. *Minds and Machines*, *28*(4), 689–707. DOI: 10.1007/s11023-018-9482-5 PMID: 30930541

Folorunso, A., Babalola, O., Nwatu, C. E., & Adedoyin, A. (2024). A comprehensive model for ensuring data compliance in cloud computing environment. *World Journal of Advanced Research and Reviews*, *24*(2), 3514. Advance online publication. DOI: 10.30574/wjarr.2024.24.2.3514

Foster, E., Mphil, M., Nkyi-Asamoah, J., Klutse, E. K., & Kwadwo, M. (2020). Technology in Music Education: A Survey of Computer Usage in Teaching Music in Selected Colleges of Education in Ghana. *Journal of Education and Practice*. Advance online publication. DOI: 10.7176/JEP/11-3-15

Frej, M. B. H. (2020). Light-weight accountable privacy-preserving protocol in cloud computing based on a third-party auditor. *[Conference name or journal missing]*.

Gadhi, A., Gondu, R. M., Chaudhary, H., & Abiona, O. (2024). Cyber Resilience through Real-Time Threat Analysis in Information Security. *International Journal of Communications, Network and Systems Sciences*, *17*(4), 51–67. DOI: 10.4236/ijcns.2024.174004

Ganapathy, V. (2023). AI in auditing: A comprehensive review of applications, benefits and challenges. Shodh Sari-An International Multidisciplinary Journal, 2(04), 328-343. Retrieved from https://icertpublication.com/wp-content/uploads/2023/10/29.-AI-in-Auditing.pdf

Ganesen, R., Bakar, A. A., Ramli, R., Rahim, F. A., & Zawawi, M. N. A. (2022). Cybersecurity Risk Assessment: Modeling Factors Associated with Higher Education Institutions. *International Journal of Advanced Computer Science and Applications*, *13*(8). Advance online publication. DOI: 10.14569/IJACSA.2022.0130843

Gao, Y., ... (2023). Retrieval-augmented generation for large language models: A survey. arXiv preprint arXiv:2312.10997, 2.

Gartner. (2025, February). Market Guide for AI Trust, Risk and Security Management.

George, B., & Wooden, O. S. (2023). Managing the Strategic Transformation of Higher Education through Artificial Intelligence. *Administrative Sciences*, *13*(9), 196. DOI: 10.3390/admsci13090196

Gerber, A., & Matthee, M. (2019). Design Thinking for Pre-empting Digital Disruption. In Lecture notes in computer science (p. 759). Springer Science+Business Media. DOI: 10.1007/978-3-030-29374-1_62

Ghorashi, S. R., Zia, T., Bewong, M., & Jiang, Y. (2023). An Analytical Review of Industrial Privacy Frameworks and Regulations for Organisational Data Sharing. *Applied Sciences (Basel, Switzerland)*, *13*(23), 12727. DOI: 10.3390/app132312727

Ghosh, P., & Ghosh, S. (2024). Neural Network and Neural Computing. In R. Jaganathan, S. Mehta, & R. Krishan (Eds.), Intelligent Decision Making Through Bio-Inspired Optimization (pp. 131-175). IGI Global Scientific Publishing. ChicagoDOI: 10.4018/979-8-3693-2073-0.ch009

Glisson, B. G., ... (2021). A survey of artificial intelligence in cybersecurity. In Proceedings of the IEEE International Conference on Artificial Intelligence for Cybersecurity. Retrieved from https://ieeexplore.ieee.org/document/9458190

Global Affairs Canada. (2022). Application portfolio health index (APHI) description. https://www.international.gc.ca/transparency-transparence/audit-evaluation-verification/2022/2022-11-it-ti.aspx?lang=eng

Global Affairs Canada. (2022). Audit of IT application portfolio management. https://www.international.gc.ca/transparency-transparence/audit-evaluation-verification/2022/2022-11-it-ti.aspx?lang=eng

Goncalves, G., & Berner, M. (2024). Application portfolio assessment strategy for AWS cloud migration. AWS Prescriptive Guidance. Amazon Web Services. https://docs.aws.amazon.com/prescriptive-guidance/latest/strategy-application-portfolio-assessment-migration/introduction.html#:~:text=At%20a%20high,priorities%2C%20and%20accelerates%20business%20outcomes

Govender, N., & Reddy, P. S. (2019). Effectiveness of governance towards digitalisation at eThekwini Metropolitan Municipality in KwaZulu-Natal province, South Africa. *Africa's Public Service Delivery and Performance Review*, *7*(1). Advance online publication. DOI: 10.4102/apsdpr.v7i1.336

Grant Thornton Bharat. (2021). Simplifying the enterprise application portfolio. Insights Blog. https://www.grantthornton.in/insights/blogs/simplifying-the-enterprise-application-portfolio-to-make-the-most-of-your-organisational-investments/#:~:text=Gartner%20estimates%20that%20organisations%20following,significant%20saving%20in%20IT%20budget

Greiling, H., & Kend, R. (2024). Artificial intelligence in auditing: Shifting the role of the auditor. *Administrative Sciences*, *14*(10), 238.

Guarda, T. (2019). EU General Data Protection Regulation Implementation: An Institutional Theory View. www.academia.edu. https://www.academia.edu/77963189/EU_General_Data_Protection_Regulation_Implementation_An_Institutional_Theory_View

Gu, H., Schreyer, M., Moffitt, K., & Vasarhelyi, M. (2024). Artificial intelligence co-piloted auditing. *International Journal of Accounting Information Systems*, *54*, 100698. DOI: 10.1016/j.accinf.2024.100698

Gul, I. ur Rehman, A., & Islam, M. H. (2011, June). Cloud computing security auditing. In The 2nd International Conference on Next Generation Information Technology (pp. 143-148). IEEE. Retrieved from https://ieeexplore.ieee.org/abstract/document/5967489?casa_token=lsIwW-gEZN0AAAA A:NuYnEVH7a3UW1jok-bYykHQZpux3ctA7CUv3G_E2RTBbvl9eWCjzDbKqWt3ZOUkG04AuZY89HXQ

Gunasekaran, K. P. (2023). Exploring sentiment analysis techniques in natural language processing: A comprehensive review. https://arxiv.org/abs/2305.14842

Gusher, T. (2024, January 30). *AI and ML are cybersecurity problems and solutions*. EY. Retrieved from https://www.ey.com/en_us/insights/cybersecurity/ai-and-ml-are-cybersecurity-problems-and-solutions

Hamzah, P., Yeba, E., Maithy, S. P., & Poetra, G. B. (2024). Opportunities and Challenges in Integrating Artificial Intelligence into Financial Auditing. *Journal of Economic Education and Entrepreneurship Studies*, *5*(4), 591–600.

Han, H., Shiwakoti, R. K., Jarvis, R., Mordi, C., & Botchie, D. (2023). Accounting and auditing with blockchain technology and artificial intelligence: A literature review. *International Journal of Accounting Information Systems*, *48*, 100598. DOI: 10.1016/j.accinf.2022.100598

Harper, N. (2023, April 7). *Regulating AI tech is no longer an option: It's a must!* ISACA Now Blog. https://www.isaca.org/resources/news-and-trends/isaca-now-blog/2023/regulating-ai-tech-is-no-longer-an-option

HashiCorp. (n.d.). *Sentinel – Policy as code framework.* https://www.hashicorp.com/sentinel

Hashim, W., & Hussein, N. A. K. (2024). *Securing cloud computing environments: An analysis of multi-tenancy vulnerabilities and countermeasures.* SHIFRA., DOI: 10.70470/SHIFRA/2024/002

Hazela, B., Gupta, S. K., Soni, N., & Saranya, C. (2022). Securing the confidentiality and integrity of cloud computing data. *ECS Transactions.* https://doi.org/DOI: 10.1149/10701.2651ecst

Hoda, R., Salleh, N., & Grundy, J. (2018). The rise and evolution of agile software development. *IEEE Software*, *35*(5), 58–63. DOI: 10.1109/MS.2018.290111318

Hu, K.. (2022). Supply chain characteristics as predictors of cyber risk: A machine-learning assessment. arXiv. https://arxiv.org/abs/2210.15785

IBM. (2023). Watson Discovery. Retrieved from https://www.ibm.com/products/watson-discovery

IBM. (n.d.). *Compliance-Trestle.* https://github.com/IBM/compliance-trestle

Info-Tech Research Group. (n.d.). Rationalize your application portfolio (Blueprint). https://www.infotech.com/research/ss/rationalize-your-application-portfolio

Investopedia. (n.d.). "Black Box." Investopedia. "https://www.investopedia.com/terms/b/blackbox.asp"

ISACA News. (2024). Cloud data sovereignty: Governance and risk implications. ISACA Industry News. https://www.isaca.org/resources/news-and-trends/industry-news/2024/cloud-data-sovereignty-governance-and-risk-implications-of-cross-border-cloud-storage#:~:text=the%20global%20public%20cloud%20services,compliance%20measures%20to%20ensure%20successful

Isaca. (2012). Cobit 5. https://dl.acm.org/citation.cfm?id=2361913

Isack, M. (2024, March 28). *Replicating reason: The advent of human-like audit judgment by generative AI* (SSRN Working Paper No. 4716860). SSRN. Retrieved from https://ssrn.com/abstract=4716860 or DOI: 10.2139/ssrn.4716860

ISO/IEC 42001:2023. (2023). ISO. https://www.iso.org/standard/81230.html

Issa, H., Sun, T., & Vasarhelyi, M. A. (2016). Research ideas for artificial intelligence in auditing: The formalization of audit and workforce supplementation. Journal of emerging technologies in accounting, 13(2), 1-20. Retrieved from https://publications.aaahq.org/jeta/article-abstract/13/2/1/9209/Research-Ideas-for-Artificial-Intelligence-in

Issa, H. A., Sunyaev, A. M., & Vasarhelyi, M. (2016). Research ideas for artificial intelligence in auditing: The formalization of audit and the application of artificial intelligence. *Journal of Emerging Technologies in Accounting*, *13*(2), 1–20. https://scholar.google.com/scholar_lookup?title=Artificial+intelligence+in+audit%3A+Theory+and+practice&author=Issa,+H.A.&publication_year=2016. DOI: 10.2308/jeta-10511

Iverson, T., & Barbier, E. B. (2021). National and Sub-National Social Distancing Responses to COVID-19. *Economies*, *9*(2), 69. DOI: 10.3390/economies9020069

Jakkula, A. R. (2024). Ensuring Data Privacy and Security in AI-Enabled E-commerce Platforms. *Journal of Artificial Intelligence & Cloud Computing*, *3*(1), 1–3. DOI: 10.47363/JAICC/2024(3)288

Jaleel, A. (2023, January 18). *ChatGPT and Leveraging Artificial Intelligence in Auditing*. ISACA Now Blog. https://www.isaca.org/resources/news-and-trends/isaca-now-blog/2023/chatgpt-and-leveraging-artificial-intelligence-in-auditing

James, M. (2022). International Student Recruitment During the Pandemic: The Unique Perspective of Recruiters from Small to Medium-Sized Higher Education Institutions. *Higher Education Policy*, *36*(3), 510–528. DOI: 10.1057/s41307-022-00271-3 PMID: 35465058

Jamshidi, P., Ahmad, A., & Pahl, C. (2013). Cloud migration research: A systematic review. *IEEE Transactions on Cloud Computing, PP*, 1–1. https://doi.org/DOI: 10.1109/TCC.2013.10

Jesudoss, A., Lakshmanan, L., & Christy, A., MercyTheresa, M., & Jayaprakash, S. (2021). Public auditing in cloud environment for secure data sharing. *Proceedings of the First International Conference on Advanced Scientific Innovation in Science, Engineering and Technology (ICASISET)*. https://doi.org/DOI: 10.4108/eai.16-5-2020.2303943

Jordan, M. I., & Mitchell, T. M. (2015). Machine learning: Trends, perspectives, and prospects. *Science*, *349*(6245), 255–260. DOI: 10.1126/science.aaa8415 PMID: 26185243

Jo, T. (2019). Text mining. *Studies in Big Data*, *45*, 1–373. PMID: 31495561

Journal, H. I. P. A. A. (2023). *What is HIPAA compliance?* https://www.hipaajournal.com/hipaa-compliance/

Kahya, M. D., & Seneler, Ç. (2018, September). Geographical distance challenges in distributed agile software development: Case study of a global company. In 2018 3rd International Conference on Computer Science and Engineering (UBMK) (pp. 78-83). IEEE.

Kamara, R. D., & Rabie, B. (2021). The Efficacy of Policy and Legal Framework for Cooperative Governance and Local Economic Development (LED) in Small Towns in a Selected Region in South Africa. *Zarządzanie Publiczne*, *7*(1 (53)), 7–26. Advance online publication. DOI: 10.4467/20843968ZP.21.001.14134

Karp, D. (2024, March 14). *How AI is transforming audit, risk and compliance.* ISACA Now Blog. https://www.isaca.org/resources/news-and-trends/isaca-now-blog/2024/how-ai-is-transforming-audit-risk-and-compliance

Karpouzis, K. (2024). Artificial Intelligence in Education. *Ethical Considerations and Insights from Ancient Greek Philosophy.*, *1*, 1–7. Advance online publication. DOI: 10.1145/3688671.3688772

Kasmawati, , Aprilianti, , & Dauri, . (2022). Kasmawati, Aprilianti, & Dauri, D. (2022). Urgency of Electronic Licensing Management Licensing Services in Improving the Community Economy. Advances in Social Science, Education and Humanities Research. *Advances in Social Science, Education and Humanities Research.* Advance online publication. DOI: 10.2991/assehr.k.220102.013

Katsonis, M., & Botros, A. (2015). Digital Government: A Primer and Professional Perspectives. *Australian Journal of Public Administration*, *74*(1), 42–52. DOI: 10.1111/1467-8500.12144

Kempwad, A. (2024). COBIT APO05.04 – Maintain portfolios. ITSM Docs. https://www.itsm-docs.com/blogs/cobit-framework/cobit-apo05-04-maintain-portfolios#:~:text=COBIT%20APO05,optimize%20resources%2C%20and%20maximize%20value

Keskin, O. F., Caramancion, K. M., Tatar, I., Raza, O., & Tatar, U. (2021). Cyber third-party risk management: A comparison of non-intrusive risk scoring reports. *Electronics (Basel)*, *10*(10), 1168. DOI: 10.3390/electronics10101168

Khale, S., & Worku, Z. (2013). Factors that Affect Municipal Service Delivery in Gauteng and Northwest Provinces of South Africa. *African Journal of Science, Technology, Innovation and Development*, *5*(1), 61–70. DOI: 10.1080/20421338.2013.782143

Khanna, E.. (2021, August). Artificial intelligence-based risk management framework for distributed agile software development. In *Proceedings of the 2021 8th International Conference on Signal Processing and Integrated Networks (SPIN)* (pp. 657–660). IEEE.

Khanna, E., Popli, R., & Chauhan, N. (2022). Identification and classification of risk factors in distributed agile software development. *Journal of Web Engineering*, *21*(6), 1831–1851. DOI: 10.13052/jwe1540-9589.2164

Khoei, T. T., Slimane, H. O., & Kaabouch, N. (2023). Deep learning: Systematic review, models, challenges, and research directions. *Neural Computing & Applications*, *35*(31), 23103–23124. DOI: 10.1007/s00521-023-08957-4

Khorsheed, H. S., Ismael, N. B., & Shamal, H. O. M. (2024).The impact of artificial intelligence and machine learning on financial reporting and auditing practices. *International Journal of Advanced Engineering, Management and Science(ISSN: 2454-1311)*,10(6), 30-37. DOI: 10.22161/ijaems.106.4

Khther, R. A., & Othman, M. (2013). Cobit Framework as a Guideline of Effective it Governance in Higher Education: A Review [Review of Cobit Framework as a Guideline of Effective it Governance in Higher Education: A Review]. *International Journal of Advanced Information Technology*, *3*(1), 21–29. DOI: 10.5121/ijitcs.2013.3102

Khurana, D., Koli, A., Khatter, K., & Singh, S. (2023). Natural language processing: state of the art, current trends and challenges. Multimed Tools Appl;82(3):3713-3744. https://pubmed.ncbi.nlm.nih.gov/35855771

Kim, D., & Kim, K. S. (2022). Privacy-preserving public auditing for shared cloud data with secure group management. *IEEE Access, PP*, 1–1. https://doi.org/DOI: 10.1109/ACCESS.2022.3169793

Kim, J. S.. (2023). The impact of artificial intelligence on threat intelligence systems. *Information Systems Frontiers*, •••, 25.

Kohl, R. D. (2023). Key factors for advancing innovations to scale: Evidence from multiple country case studies of agricultural innovations. *Frontiers in Sustainable Food Systems*, *7*, 1053152. Advance online publication. DOI: 10.3389/fsufs.2023.1053152

Kokina, J., Blanchette, S., Davenport, T. H., & Pachamanova, D. A. (2025). Challenges and opportunities for artificial intelligence in auditing: Evidence from the field. *International Journal of Accounting Information Systems*, *56*, 100734. DOI: 10.1016/j.accinf.2025.100734

Kokina, J., & Davenport, T. H. (2017). The Emergence of Artificial Intelligence: How Automation is Changing Auditing. *Journal of Emerging Technologies in Accounting, 14*(1), 115–122. DOI: 10.2308/jeta-51730

Kotepuchai, P., & Limpiyakorn, Y. (2024). Machine Learning and Substantive Analytical Procedure in Financial Audit. Retrieved from https://www.academia.edu/124153258/Machine_Learning_and_Substantive_Analytical_Procedure_in_Financial_Audit

Kuleto, V., Ilić, M., Dumangiu, M. A., Ranković, M., Martins, O., Păun, D., & Mihoreanu, L. (2021). Exploring Opportunities and Challenges of Artificial Intelligence and Machine Learning in Higher Education Institutions. *Sustainability (Basel), 13*(18), 10424. DOI: 10.3390/su131810424

Kumar, M., Maple, C., & Chand, S. (2023). An efficient and secure identity-based integrity auditing scheme for sensitive data with anti-replacement attack on multi-cloud storage. *Journal of King Saud University. Computer and Information Sciences, 35*(9), 101745. DOI: 10.1016/j.jksuci.2023.101745

Kuo, A. (2011). Opportunities and challenges of cloud computing to improve healthcare services. *Journal of Medical Internet Research, 13*(3), e67. Advance online publication. DOI: 10.2196/jmir.1867 PMID: 21937354

Lamarca, B. I. J. (2020). Cybersecurity Risk Assessment of the University of Northern Philippines using PRISM Approach. *IOP Conference Series. Materials Science and Engineering, 769*(1), 12066. DOI: 10.1088/1757-899X/769/1/012066

Lazer, D., & Radford, J. (2017). Data ex Machina: Introduction to Big Data. *Annual Review of Sociology, 43*(1), 19–39. DOI: 10.1146/annurev-soc-060116-053457

Lean, I. X. (2022). EOL vs. EOS in software: Meaning & business impact. LeanIX Blog. https://www.leanix.net/en/wiki/trm/what-is-end-of-life-vs-end-of-support#:~:text=Using%20software%20after%20it%20reaches,EoL%20poses%20several%20risks

Lean, I. X. (n.d.). Gartner TIME framework for application rationalization. LeanIX Wiki. https://www.leanix.net/en/wiki/apm/gartner-time-model#:~:text=The%20Gartner%C2%AE%20TIME%20framework%20,planning%20and%20executing%20application%20rationalization

Lee Kuan Yew School of Public Policy. (n.d.). *The Six Principles of Good Governance in Singapore.* Retrieved from https://lkyspp.nus.edu.sg/gia/article/the-six-principles-of-good-governance

Lee, R. B. (2023). AI-based external risk posture assessments. Cybersecurity Review, 4(1).

Lee, R. F. I. (2025, January 3). *The synergy between generative AI and IS audit.* ISACA Now Blog. https://www.isaca.org/resources/news-and-trends/isaca-now-blog/2025/the-synergy-between-generative-ai-and-is-audit

Lee, J., & Banerjee, A. (2023). Explainability and ethics in AI for risk assessment. *AI Ethics Journal*, *5*(1), 17–29.

Leocádio, D., Malheiro, L., & Reis, J. (2024). Artificial Intelligence in Auditing: A Conceptual Framework for Auditing Practices. *Administrative Sciences*, *14*(10), 238. DOI: 10.3390/admsci14100238

Lester, B., ... (2021). The power of scale for parameter-efficient prompt tuning. arXiv preprint arXiv:2104.08691. DOI: 10.18653/v1/2021.emnlp-main.243

Li, C., ... (2023). Large language models understand and can be enhanced by emotional stimuli. arXiv preprint arXiv:2307.11760.

Ling, F. (2024) 'Efficiency and integrity: The pillars of Singapore's public service'. Medium. Available at: https://medium.com/@feiwuling/efficiency-and-integrity-the-pillars-of-singapores-public-service-55e0b186a727 (Accessed: 19 May 2025).

Ling, F. (2024). *Efficiency and Integrity: The Pillars of Singapore's Public Service.* Retrieved from https://medium.com/@feiwuling/efficiency-and-integrity-the-pillars-of-singapores-public-service-55e0b186a727

Lin, J. W., Hwang, M. I., & Becker, J. D. (2003). A fuzzy neural network for assessing the risk of fraudulent financial reporting. *Managerial Auditing Journal*, *18*(8), 657–665. DOI: 10.1108/02686900310495151

Liu, Y. (2024). Build an audit framework for data privacy protection in cloud environment. *Procedia Computer Science*, *247*, 166–175. Advance online publication. DOI: 10.1016/j.procs.2024.10.020

Li, Y., & Goel, S. (2024). Making it possible for the auditing of AI: A systematic review of AI audits and AI auditability. *Information Systems Frontiers*. Advance online publication. DOI: 10.1007/s10796-024-10508-8

Lois, P., Drogalas, G., Karagiorgos, A., & Tsikalakis, K. (2020). Internal audits in the digital era: Opportunities risks and challenges. *EuroMed Journal of Business*, *15*(2), 205–217. DOI: 10.1108/EMJB-07-2019-0097

Luo, J., Meng, Q., & Cai, Y. (2018). Analysis of the Impact of Artificial Intelligence Application on the Development of Accounting Industry. *Open Journal of Business and Management, 06*(04), 850–856. DOI: 10.4236/ojbm.2018.64063

Luo, M., Xue, B., & Niu, B. (2024). A comprehensive survey for automatic text summarization: Techniques, approaches, and perspectives. *Neurocomputing, 603*, 128280. DOI: 10.1016/j.neucom.2024.128280

Luo, X., Wang, X., & Jiang, T. (2025). Application of AI technology in audit risk assessment and control: Taking internal audit of higher education institutions as an example. Journal of Infrastructure. *Policy and Development, 9*(1), 10125. DOI: 10.24294/jipd10125

Lyu, J., Zhou, S., Liu, J., & Jiang, B. (2023). Intelligent-Technology-Empowered Active Emergency Command Strategy for Urban Hazardous Chemical Disaster Management. *Sustainability (Basel), 15*(19), 14369. DOI: 10.3390/su151914369

MacGlashan, J. (2017, July). Interactive learning from policy-dependent human feedback. In *Proceedings of the International Conference on Machine Learning* (pp. 2285–2294). PMLR.

Mah, D.-K., & Gross, N. (2024). Artificial intelligence in higher education: Exploring faculty use, self-efficacy, distinct profiles, and professional development needs. *International Journal of Educational Technology in Higher Education, 21*(1), 58. Advance online publication. DOI: 10.1186/s41239-024-00490-1

Ma, J., & Zhao, Y. (2020). NLP applications in compliance monitoring. *Journal of Cybersecurity Intelligence and Cybercrime, 3*(1).

Majumdar, S., Chawla, G., Alimohammadifar, A., Madi, T., Jarraya, Y., Pourzandi, M., Wang, L., & Debbabi, M. (2022). ProSAS: Proactive security auditing system for clouds. *IEEE Transactions on Dependable and Secure Computing, 19*(4), 2517–2534. DOI: 10.1109/TDSC.2021.3062204

Manoharan, A., Melitski, J., & Holzer, M. (2022). Digital Governance: An Assessment of Performance and Best Practices. *Public Organization Review, 23*(1), 265–283. DOI: 10.1007/s11115-021-00584-8

Maota, T. (2024). A conceptual framework for private higher educational institutions to respond to disruptions in South Africa. Available online: https://researchspace.ukzn.ac.za/items/404b7a1f-e593-490a-a749-09c00f6d9e07

Marcela, E. D., & Fianty, M. I. (2023). Performance Evaluation IT Governance on Universities: COBIT 2019 Approach with Measurement Capability Levels. *Indonesian Journal of Computer Science*, *12*(4). Advance online publication. DOI: 10.33022/ijcs.v12i4.3353

Marri, R., Dabbara, L. N., & Karampuri, S. (2024). AI security in different industries: A comprehensive review of vulnerabilities and mitigation strategies [Review of AI security in different industries: A comprehensive review of vulnerabilities and mitigation strategies]. *International Journal of Science and Research Archive*, *13*(1), 2375–2393. DOI: 10.30574/ijsra.2024.13.1.1923

Marzban, C. (2008). Basic statistics and basic AI: neural networks. In *Springer eBooks* (pp. 15–47). DOI: 10.1007/978-1-4020-9119-3_2

Masmali, H. H., & Miah, S. J. (2022, July). Emergent insight of the cyber security management for Saudi Arabian universities: a content analysis. In Proceedings of Seventh International Congress on Information and Communication Technology: ICICT 2022, London, Volume 2 (pp. 153-171). Singapore: Springer Nature Singapore.

Mbonye, V., Moodley, M., & Nyika, F. (2024). Examining the applicability of the Protection of Personal Information Act in AI-driven environments. *South African Journal of Information Management*, *26*(1). Advance online publication. DOI: 10.4102/sajim.v26i1.1808

McHugh, M. L. (2012). Interrater reliability: The kappa statistic. *Biochemia Medica*, *22*(3), 276–282. DOI: 10.11613/BM.2012.031 PMID: 23092060

Meiran, G., Unkašević, T., Banjac, Z., & Milosavljevic, M. (2021). Automated compliance system for service organizations. *Sinteza*, 21–27. https://doi.org/DOI: 10.15308/Sinteza-2021-21-27

Menon (2021). *Volume 4 How can AI drive audits*. ISACA. https://www.isaca.org/resources/isaca-journal/issues/2021/volume-4/how-can-ai-drive-audits

Menon, S. (2024, February 21). *Broad, regulatory frameworks needed to responsibly harness AI*. ISACA Now Blog. https://www.isaca.org/resources/news-and-trends/isaca-now-blog/2024/broad-regulatory-frameworks-needed-to-responsibly-harness-ai

Mhlongo, T. P., & Thomas, P. (2024). An examination of the Fourth Industrial Revolution in the context of the South African local government. *Africa's Public Service Delivery and Performance Review*, *12*(1). Advance online publication. DOI: 10.4102/apsdpr.v12i1.807

Mirandilla-Santos, M. G. (2008). Promoting E-Government in the Context of New Public Management: The Case of the Local Government of Cebu, Philippines. SSRN Electronic Journal. DOI: 10.2139/ssrn.1558948

MIT Media Lab. (2024). *Generative AI for Personalized Learning & Self-Development.* Retrieved from https://www.media.mit.edu/projects/generative-ai-for-personalized-learning/overview/

Mofolo, M. A. (2012). Strengthening Performance Management System Implementation in South African Municipalities. *Africa's Public Service Delivery and Performance Review*, *1*(1), 73. DOI: 10.4102/apsdpr.v1i1.25

Mohamed, M. M. (2024). The impact of cloud computing on activating the role of risk-based internal audit and its reflection on the organization's financial performance - An empirical study. https://doi.org/DOI: 10.21608/atasu.2024.348955

Mohamed, E. A., Elshareif, E., & El, . (2019). Designing a Generic Information Systems Audit Framework to Improve the Quality of Audit in Higher Education. *Journal of Computational Science*, *15*(5), 664–672. DOI: 10.3844/jcssp.2019.664.672

Mohta, Y.. (2024, May). NLP-enabled bot for managing third-party risk. In *Proceedings of the 2024 International Conference on Computational Intelligence and Computing Applications (ICCICA)* (Vol. 1, pp. 131–135). DOI: 10.1109/ICCICA60014.2024.10584983

Mökander, J.. (2023, February 6). Auditing large language models: A three-layered approach. *AI and Ethics*. Retrieved from https://arxiv.org/abs/2302.08500

Mökander, J., Curl, J., & Kshirsagar, M. (2024, July 7). A blueprint for auditing generative AI. *arXiv*. https://arxiv.org/abs/2407.05338 DOI: 10.2139/ssrn.4887768

Morgan, H. (2022). Conducting a Qualitative Document Analysis. *The Qualitative Report*. Advance online publication. DOI: 10.46743/2160-3715/2022.5044

Motubatse, K., Ngwakwe, C., & Sebola, M. P. (2020). Internal Control as a Catalyst for Clean Audit Outcomes in the Local Government. The Moderating Role of Information Technology. In International Journal of Recent Technology and Engineering (IJRTE) (Vol. 9, Issue 4, p. 204). DOI: 10.35940/ijrte.B4036.119420

Mudzusi, T. N., Munzhedzi, P. H., & Mahole, E. (2024). Governance challenges in the provision of municipal services: In the Vhembe District Municipality. *Africa's Public Service Delivery and Performance Review*, *12*(1). Advance online publication. DOI: 10.4102/apsdpr.v12i1.749

Muller, S. R. (2023). An analysis of the design of the Cybersecurity Maturity Model Certification (CMMC) and its direct effect on supply chain management. In *Real-World Solutions for Diversity, Strategic Change, and Organizational Development: Perspectives in Healthcare, Education, Business, and Technology* (pp. 220–243). IGI Global. DOI: 10.4018/978-1-6684-8691-7.ch014

Munoko, I., Brown-Liburd, H. L., & Vasarhelyi, M. (2020). The ethical implications of using artificial intelligence in auditing. *Journal of Business Ethics*, *167*(2), 209–234. https://link.springer.com/article/10.1007/s10551-019-04407-1. DOI: 10.1007/s10551-019-04407-1

Murphy, D., & Brown, C. E. (1992). The uses of advanced information technology in audit planning. *International Journal of Intelligent Systems in Accounting Finance & Management*, *1*(3), 187–193. DOI: 10.1002/j.1099-1174.1992.tb00020.x

Murtaza, M. A. (2024). Cloud ERP and audit reliability: An empirical study. *SSRN.*

Nadiyah, F. A., Maharani, B., & Rahmatika, D. N. (2024). Pengaruh Audit Teknologi Infomasi Terhadap Kualitas Audit. *Ekonomi Keuangan Syariah Dan Akuntansi Pajak.*, *1*(3), 236–253. DOI: 10.61132/eksap.v1i3.278

Nah, F. F., Zheng, R., Cai, J., Siau, K., & Chen, L. (2023). Generative AI and ChatGPT: Applications, challenges, and AI-human collaboration. *Journal of Information Technology Case and Application Research*, *25*(3), 277–304. DOI: 10.1080/15228053.2023.2233814

National Institute of Standards and Technology (NIST). (2018). *Framework for improving critical infrastructure cybersecurity, version 1.1.* U.S. Department of Commerce. https://www.nist.gov/cyberframework

National Institute of Standards and Technology (NIST). (2024). *Cybersecurity Framework.* Retrieved from https://www.nist.gov/cyberframework

National Treasury. (2021) *Final Financial Recovery Plan for Lekwa Local Municipality.* Pretoria: National Treasury. Available at: https://www.treasury.gov.za/comm_media/press/2021/LekwaFRP/02%20Final%20Lekwa%20LM%20FRP%20Report.pdf (Accessed: 12 May 2025)

Navarro, F. J. (2024, June 7). *How to audit your generative artificial intelligence.* LinkedIn. Retrieved from https://www.linkedin.com/pulse/how-audit-your-generative-artificial-intelligence-francisco-j-navarro-kmouf/

Naveena, P., Soundarya, R. S., & Mohanapriya, K. A. (2020). Light weight secure auditing scheme for shared data in cloud storage. *International Journal of Engineering Research & Technology (Ahmedabad)*, •••, 8.

Ndevu, Z., & Müller, K. (2018). Operationalising performance management in local government: The use of the balanced scorecard. *SA Journal of Human Resource Management, 16*. Advance online publication. DOI: 10.4102/sajhrm.v16i0.977

Nel-Sanders, D. (2018). Risk management in the South African local government and its impact on service delivery. In International Journal of Management Practice (Vol. 12, Issue 1, p. 60). Inderscience Publishers. DOI: 10.1504/IJMP.2019.096683

New Horizons. (2024). Multi-cloud challenges: Best practices and strategies (T. Karl, Ed.). https://www.newhorizons.com/resources/blog/multi-cloud-challenges#:~:text=,cloud%20management

Ngumbela, X. G. (2022). *The relationship between policy, governance and service delivery in local government in South Africa*. International Journal of Innovative Technologies in Social Science., DOI: 10.31435/rsglobal_ijitss/30062022/7810

NicCanna. C., et al. (2021, June). Globally distributed development during COVID-19. In Proceedings of the 2021 IEEE/ACM 8th International Workshop on Software Engineering Research and Industrial Practice (SER&IP) (pp. 18–25). IEEE.

Noordin, N. A., Hussainey, K., & Hayek, A. F. (2022). The Use of Artificial Intelligence and Audit Quality: An Analysis from the Perspectives of External Auditors in the UAE. *Journal of Risk and Financial Management, 15*(8), 339. DOI: 10.3390/jrfm15080339

Now, I. S. A. C. A. (2024, June 10). *AI for auditors: Challenges and opportunities for career advancement*. ISACA Now Blog. https://www.isaca.org/resources/news-and-trends/isaca-now-blog/2024/ai-for-auditors-challenges-and-opportunities-for-career-advancement

Nurdin, A., & Lubis, M. (2023). The IT Governance Measurement using Cobit 5 Framework in Quality Assurance Department. *Jurnal Informatika Dan Rekayasa Perangkat Lunak, 5*(1), 80. DOI: 10.36499/jinrpl.v5i1.7963

Nzewi, O., & Sibanda, M. M. (2023). Local Government's Existential Challenge: 25 Years of the White Paper on Local Government (1998–2023). Journal of Local Government Research and Innovation, 4. https://doi.org/DOI: 10.4102/jolgri.v4i0.168

O'Dea, X., & O'Dea, M. (2023). Is Artificial Intelligence Really the Next Big Thing in Learning and Teaching in Higher Education? A Conceptual Paper. *Journal of University Teaching & Learning Practice, 20*(5). Advance online publication. DOI: 10.53761/1.20.5.06

O'Donnell, J. B. (2024). Auditing Transformation: A Model of Artificial Intelligence Adoption. *Journal of Applied Business and Economics, 26*(6). Advance online publication. DOI: 10.33423/jabe.v26i6.7390

Odzaly, E. E., Greer, D., & Stewart, D. (2018). Agile risk management using software agents. *Journal of Ambient Intelligence and Humanized Computing, 9*(3), 823–841. DOI: 10.1007/s12652-017-0488-2

OECD. (2023a) 'Government at a Glance 2023: Finland'. Available at: https://www.oecd.org/en/publications/government-at-a-glance-2023_c4200b14-en/finland_d1080a88-en.html

OECD. (2023b) 'Government at a Glance 2023: Switzerland'. Available at: https://www.oecd.org/en/publications/government-at-a-glance-2023_c4200b14-en/switzerland_8f88ce47-en.html

Omoteso, K. (2012). The application of artificial intelligence in auditing: Looking back to the future. Expert Systems with Applications, 39(9), 8490-8495. Retrieved from https://www.sciencedirect.com/science/article/pii/S095741741200111X?casa_token=R0r ohONtAoIAAAAA:ZI89YFkRHRpVSzBXBuM2ZT4-mgP6sbiotR1A6UoO-QrSiPPT8n WAfezvZi13CbNXjDtP_X4KrWA

Omoteso, K. (2012). The application of artificial intelligence in auditing: Looking back to the future. *Expert Systems with Applications, 39*(9), 8490–8495. DOI: 10.1016/j.eswa.2012.01.098

Onwubuariri, E. R., Adelakun, B. O., Olaiya, O. P., & Ziorklui, J. E. K. (2024). AI-Driven risk assessment: Revolutionizing audit planning and execution. Finance & Accounting Research Journal, 6(6), 1069-1090. Retrieved from https://fepbl.com/index.php/farj/article/view/1236

Open Policy Agent (OPA). (n.d.). *Policy-based control for cloud-native environments*. https://www.openpolicyagent.org/

OpenControl. (n.d.). *OpenControl – Compliance made simple*. https://github.com/opencontrol

Oqaily, M., Jarraya, Y., Mohammady, M., Majumdar, S., Pourzandi, M., Wang, L., & Debbabi, M. (2021). SegGuard: Segmentation-based anonymization of network data in clouds for privacy-preserving security auditing. *IEEE Transactions on Dependable and Secure Computing, 18*, 2486–2505. DOI: 10.1109/TDSC.2019.2957488

Owoc, M. L., Sawicka, A., & Weichbroth, P. (2021). Artificial Intelligence Technologies in Education: Benefits, Challenges and Strategies of Implementation. In IFIP advances in information and communication technology (p. 37). Springer Science+Business Media. DOI: 10.1007/978-3-030-85001-2_4

Oyeniyi, L. D., Ugochukwu, C. E., & Mhlongo, N. Z. (2024). Transforming financial planning with AI-driven analysis: A review and application insights. Finance & Accounting Research Journal, 6(4), 626-647. Retrieved from https://www.fepbl.com/index.php/farj/article/view/1037

Palada, B., Chandan, V. S., & Gowda, C. P. (2024). The Role of Augmented Reality (AR) in Education. *International Journal for Research in Applied Science and Engineering Technology*, *12*(3), 1400–1408. DOI: 10.22214/ijraset.2024.59079

Pandjaitan, R. H. (2024). The Social Media Marketing Mix Trends in Indonesia for 2024: Communication Perspective. *Jurnal Komunikasi Ikatan Sarjana Komunikasi Indonesia*, *9*(1), 251–269. DOI: 10.25008/jkiski.v9i1.1005

Parimi, S. S. (2018). Optimizing Financial Reporting and Compliance in SAP with Machine Learning Techniques. Available at *SSRN* 4934911. Retrieved from

Patel, S., & Ragolane, M. (2024). The Implementation of Artificial Intelligence in South African Higher Education Institutions: Opportunities and Challenges. *Technium Education and Humanities*, *9*, 51–65. DOI: 10.47577/teh.v9i.11452

Patil, D. (2025). Artificial Intelligence In Financial Risk Assessment And Fraud Detection: Opportunities And Ethical Concerns. DOI: 10.2139/ssrn.5057434

PCI Security Standards Council. (2022). *Payment Card Industry Data Security Standard: Requirements and Security Assessment Procedures, version 4.0.* https://www.pcisecuritystandards.org/

Pennington, J. (2023). Singapore's Administrative Service – a model from which ASEAN should adopt? https://www.aseantoday.com/2017/09/singapores-administrative-service-a-model-from-which-asean-should-adopt/

Pérez-Calderón, E., Alrahamneh, S. A., & Montero, P. M. (2025). Impact of artificial intelligence on auditing: An evaluation from the profession in Jordan. *Discover Sustainability*, *6*(1), 251. DOI: 10.1007/s43621-025-01058-3

Pieterse, H. (2021). The Cyber Threat Landscape in South Africa: A 10-Year Review [Review of The Cyber Threat Landscape in South Africa: A 10-Year Review] [AJIC]. *The African Journal of Information and Communication*, *28*. Advance online publication. DOI: 10.23962/10539/32213

Polokwane Municipality. (2024) *Final Draft Annual Report for 2022–2023*. Polokwane: Polokwane Local Municipality. Available at: https://www.polokwane.gov.za/wp-content/uploads/2024/02/FINAL-DRAFT-ANNUAL-REPORT-FOR-2022-2023.pdf (Accessed: 12 April 2025).

Popenoe, R., Langius-Eklöf, A., Stenwall, E., & Jervaeus, A. (2021). A practical guide to data analysis in general literature reviews. *Nordic Journal of Nursing Research, 41*(4), 175–186. DOI: 10.1177/2057158521991949

Power, M. (1997). *The audit society: Rituals of verification*. Oxford University Press.

Prasad, V. (2024, August 2). *AI algorithm audits: Key control considerations*. ISACA. https://www.isaca.org/resources/news-and-trends/industry-news/2024/ai-algorithm-audits-key-control-considerations

Prescott, M. B. (1995). Diffusion of innovation theory. *The Data Base for Advances in Information Systems, 26*(2-3), 16–19. DOI: 10.1145/217278.217283

Process Wiki, I. T. (n.d.). ITIL service portfolio management. https://wiki.en.it-processmaps.com/index.php/Service_Portfolio_Management#:~:text=Service%20Portfolio%20Review

Prosci. (2023). Managing Disruptive Changes in Higher Education. Retrieved from https://www.prosci.com/blog/managing-disruptive-changes-in-higher-ed

Qader, K. S., & Çek, K. (2024). Influence of blockchain and artificial intelligence on audit quality: Evidence from Turkey. *Heliyon, 10*(9), e30166. DOI: 10.1016/j.heliyon.2024.e30166 PMID: 38720713

Radford, A.. (2019). Language models are unsupervised multitask learners. *OpenAI Blog, 1*(8), 9.

Raji, I. D.. (2020, January 3). Closing the AI accountability gap: Defining an end-to-end framework for internal algorithmic auditing. *Proceedings of the 2020 Conference on Fairness, Accountability, and Transparency*. Retrieved from https://arxiv.org/abs/2001.00973 DOI: 10.1145/3351095.3372873

Rane, N. (2023, August 30). Role and challenges of ChatGPT and similar generative artificial intelligence in finance and accounting. *SSRN*. DOI: 10.2139/ssrn.4603206

Ray, I., Ray, I., & Kulkarni, N. (2013). Information assurance and security in healthcare cloud computing: Survey and challenges. *International Journal of Healthcare Information Systems and Informatics, 8*(3), 57–74.

Reddy, H. M. (2023). *Cloud security compliance: Challenges, solutions, and impact on enterprises*. International Journal for Multidisciplinary Research., DOI: 10.36948/ijfmr.2023.v05i04.19118

Riany, K. G. (2021). Influence of Electronic Administration on Public Service Delivery among State Agencies in Kenya. *European Journal of Business Management and Research*, *6*(2), 39–43. DOI: 10.24018/ejbmr.2021.6.2.712

Rizki, P. A. N., Wijaya, A. F., & Mustafid, N. H. (2024). Impact of cloud computing on IT audit practices: Challenges and opportunities. *MRS Journal of Accounting. Business and Management*, *1*(1), 4–7.

Rodgers, W., Murray, J. M., Strashnoy, L., & Lande, D. (2024, April 19). Ethical auditors' framework for generative AI cybersecurity. *SSRN*. DOI: 10.2139/ssrn.4800215

Rogers, E. M. (1962). Diffusion of Innovations. https://blogs.unpad.ac.id/teddykw/files/2012/07/Everett-M.-Rogers-Diffusion-of-Innovations.pdf

Rojas, Ó. A. C., Contero, M., & Hincapié, M. (2025). Personalized and Timely Feedback in Online Education: Enhancing Learning with Deep Learning and Large Language Models. *Multimodal Technologies and Interaction*, *9*(5), 45. DOI: 10.3390/mti9050045

Roshanaei, M., Olivares, H., & Lopez, R. R. (2023). Harnessing AI to Foster Equity in Education: Opportunities, Challenges, and Emerging Strategies. *Journal of Intelligent Learning Systems and Applications*, *15*(4), 123–143. DOI: 10.4236/jilsa.2023.154009

Ryoo, J., Rizvi, S., Aiken, W., & Kissell, J. (2013). Cloud security auditing: Challenges and emerging approaches. *IEEE Security and Privacy*, *12*(6), 68–74. https://ieeexplore.ieee.org/abstract/document/6662349. DOI: 10.1109/MSP.2013.132

Sachan, S., & Liu, X. (2023, December 16). *Blockchain-based auditing of legal decisions supported by explainable AI and generative AI tools. Expert Systems with Applications*. Retrieved "https://www.sciencedirect.com/science/article/abs/pii/S095219762301850X"

Sadgrove, K. (2016). *The complete guide to business risk management*. Routledge. DOI: 10.4324/9781315614915

Saifudin, S., Januarti, I., & Purwanto, A. (2023). The role of artificial intelligence in the audit process and fraud detection: A literature outlook. *Journal of Ecohumanism*, *4*(1), 4185–4203.

Samsinar, S., & Sinaga, R. (2022). Information Technology Governance Audit at XYZ College Using COBIT Framework 2019. *BERKALA SAINSTEK, 10*(2), 58. DOI: 10.19184/bst.v10i2.30325

Sánchez, M. A., & Zuntini, J. I. (2019). Digital readiness in government: the case of Bahía Blanca municipal government. In International Journal of Electronic Governance (Vol. 11, Issue 2, p. 155). Inderscience Publishers. DOI: 10.1504/IJEG.2019.101500

Sayankar, V. N. (2024). A review on information systems audit. *Research Journal of Engineering and Technology*. https://www.researchgate.net/publication/381653679_A_Review_on_Information_Systems_Audit

Scarfone, K., & Mell, P. (2021). Guide to intrusion detection and prevention systems (IDPS) (NIST Special Publication 800-94). NIST.

Schiff, D. S., Kelley, S., & Camacho Ibáñez, J. (2024). The emergence of artificial intelligence ethics auditing. *Big Data & Society, 11*(4), 20539517241299732. DOI: 10.1177/20539517241299732

Schön, E. M.. (2020, May). Improving risk management in a scaled agile environment. In *International Conference on Agile Software Development* (pp. 132–141). Springer International Publishing. DOI: 10.1007/978-3-030-49392-9_9

Secureframe. (n.d.). *Compliance automation for modern enterprises.* https://secureframe.com/

Seethamraju, R. C., & Hecimovic, A. (2020). Impact of artificial intelligence on auditing – An exploratory study. In *Proceedings of the 26th Americas Conference on Information Systems (AMCIS).*

Seethamraju, R., & Hecimović, A. (2023). Adoption of artificial intelligence in auditing: An exploratory study. *Australian Journal of Management, 48*(4), 780–800. DOI: 10.1177/03128962221108440

Seetharamarao, R. Y. (2023). A unified approach towards security audit and compliance in cloud computing environment. *2023 16th International Conference on Developments in eSystems Engineering (DeSE)*, 623–629. https://doi.org/DOI: 10.1109/DeSE60595.2023.10469536

Sengik, A. R., Lunardi, G. L., Bianchi, I. S., & Wiedenhöft, G. C. (2022). Using design science research to propose an IT governance model for higher education institutions. *Education and Information Technologies, 27*(8), 11285–11305. DOI: 10.1007/s10639-022-11088-3 PMID: 35528756

Serpil, H., & Kesim, E. (2024). Understanding the Application of AI in Higher Education Systems: Global Perspectives From a Local AI Ecosystem. *Open Praxis, 16*(4), 645–662. DOI: 10.55982/openpraxis.16.4.725

ServiceNow. (2025). Application portfolio management – Cloud assessment (Vancouver release). https://www.servicenow.com/docs/bundle/vancouver-application-portfolio-management/page/product/application-portfolio-management/concept/apm-cloud-readiness-score-prof.html#:~:text=Log%20in%20to%20get%20a,better%20experience

Shahrabi, A., & Ghaznavi-Ghoushchi, M. (2021). Application of machine learning in cloud computing security: A survey. *IEEE Access : Practical Innovations, Open Solutions, 9*, 20732–20749. DOI: 10.1109/ACCESS.2021.3054783

Sharma, S., & Jain, A. (2020). Role of sentiment analysis in social media security and analytics. *Wiley Interdisciplinary Reviews. Data Mining and Knowledge Discovery, 10*(5), e1366. DOI: 10.1002/widm.1366

Sharmeen, N., & Hassan, M. M. (2018). Machine learning and deep learning methods for cybersecurity. *IEEE Access : Practical Innovations, Open Solutions, 6*, 33752–33781. DOI: 10.1109/ACCESS.2018.2848966

Shen, Y., & Zhang, B. (2024). Advancing the Emergency Industry: Policy, Innovation, and Implications for National Security. *Journal of the Knowledge Economy, 16*(2), 1–23. DOI: 10.1007/s13132-024-02018-4

Shrivastava, S. V., & Rathod, U. (2015). Categorization of risk factors for distributed agile projects. *Information and Software Technology, 58*, 373–387. DOI: 10.1016/j.infsof.2014.07.007

Sibanda, M. M., & von Solms, R. (2018). Devising a strategy for IT governance implementation in municipalities. A case study of South Africa. *The Electronic Journal on Information Systems in Developing Countries, 85*(2), e12067. Advance online publication. DOI: 10.1002/isd2.12067

Simmons, K., & Miller, D. (2022). Third-party data breaches: An escalating risk. *Cyber Risk Review, 10*(2), 33–41.

Singh, A. (2023). Secure auditing and deduplicating data in cloud. *International Journal for Research in Applied Science and Engineering Technology, 11*(5), 6530–6534. Advance online publication. DOI: 10.22214/ijraset.2023.53343

Singh, T., & Kumar, A. M. (2023). Analyzing security and privacy issues for multi-cloud service providers using Nessus. *2023 Fifth International Conference on Electrical, Computer and Communication Technologies (ICECCT)*, 1–8. https://doi.org/DOI: 10.1109/ICECCT56650.2023.10179727

Sityata, I., Botha, L., & Dubihlela, J. (2021). Risk Management Practices by South African Universities: An Annual Report Disclosure Analysis. *Journal of Risk and Financial Management*, *14*(5), 195. DOI: 10.3390/jrfm14050195

Smith, L. C. (1976). Artificial intelligence in information retrieval systems. *Information Processing & Management*, *12*(3), 189–222. DOI: 10.1016/0306-4573(76)90005-4

South African Local Government Association (SALGA). (2024) *Annual Performance Plan 2024–2025*. Pretoria: SALGA. Available at: https://www.salga.org.za/Documents%20and%20Publications%20APP.html (Accessed: 18 April 2025).

Stancheva-Todorova, E. P. (2018). How Artificial Intelligence Is Challenging the Accounting Profession. ideas.repec.org. https://ideas.repec.org/a/isp/journl/v12y2018i1p126-141.html

Stanford University. (2024). *Data Governance Center*. Retrieved from https://datagovernance.stanford.edu/

Stanford University. (2024). *The AI Index 2024 annual report*. Stanford University AI Index. Retrieved from https://aiindex.stanford.edu/report/

Stoker, G. (2006). Public value management: A new narrative for networked governance? *American Review of Public Administration*, *36*(1), 41–57. DOI: 10.1177/0275074005282583

Subashini, S., & Kavitha, V. (2011). A survey on security issues in service delivery models of cloud computing. *Journal of Network and Computer Applications*, *34*(1), 1–11. DOI: 10.1016/j.jnca.2010.07.006

Sulasula, J. (2023). Exploring the viability of Smart Public Universities in the Philippines' Zamboanga Peninsula Region. DOI: 10.31219/osf.io/tu5qs

Suleiman, N., Amneh, N., Borgi, H., Phung, N., Muhammad, N., & Ali, N. (2020). How Artificial Intelligence Changes the Future of Accounting Industry. *International Journal of Economics and Business Administration*, *VIII*(3), 478–488. DOI: 10.35808/ijeba/538

Sun, W., Huang, L., & Wang, Y. "Exploring Customer Behavior Patterns: A Process-based Perspective" (2020). *WHICEB 2020 Proceedings*. 31. https://aisel.aisnet.org/whiceb2020/31

Sun, Y., Li, J., Lu, M., & Guo, Z. (2024). Study of the Impact of the Big Data Era on Accounting and Auditing. *Frontiers in Business, Economics and Management, 13*(3), 44–47. DOI: 10.54097/0fa7xk79

Swiss Federal Department of Foreign Affairs. (n.d.). *Switzerland promotes governance*. Retrieved from https://www.fdfa.admin.ch/content/dam/deza/en/documents/themen/anwaltschaft-regierungsfuehrung/FS-Gouvernanz_EN.pdf

Systems, A., ... (n.d.). ComplyScore signs partnership with Qualys. Retrieved December 11, 2020, from https://www.atlassystems.com/recent-update_news/complyscore-signs-partnership-with-qualys/

Takabi, H., Joshi, J. B. D., & Ahn, G. J. (2010). Security and privacy challenges in cloud computing environments. *IEEE Security and Privacy, 8*(6), 24–31. DOI: 10.1109/MSP.2010.186

Tamersoy, A.. (2021). Vendor risk scoring using public data sources. *IBM Journal of Research and Development, 65*(2/3).

Ter, K. L. (2018). Singapore's cybersecurity strategy. *Computer Law & Security Review, 34*(4), 924–927. DOI: 10.1016/j.clsr.2018.05.001

Terraform Compliance. (n.d.). *Terraform compliance framework*. https://terraform-compliance.com/

The CAQ. (2024). "Auditing in the Age of Generative AI." *The Center for Audit Quality*. https://www.thecaq.org/wp-content/uploads/2024/04/caq_auditing-in-the-age-of-generative-ai__2024-04.pdf

The Ethics Institute. (2024) *Code for Ethical Leadership in Local Government*. Pretoria: The Ethics Institute. Available at: https://www.tei.org.za/wp-content/uploads/2024/02/LGELI-Code-for-Ethical-Leadership-in-LG.pdf (Accessed: 1 April 2025).

The Open University. (2024). *Distance Learning and Online Courses*. Retrieved from https://www.open.ac.uk/courses/what-is-distance-learning

Thesari, S. S., Trojan, F., & Batistus, D. R. (2019). A decision model for municipal resources management. *Management Decision, 57*(11), 3015–3034. DOI: 10.1108/MD-05-2017-0500

Theseira, D. (2024). What is application portfolio management (APM)? The guide to success & best practices. Ardoq Knowledge Hub. https://www.ardoq.com/knowledge-hub/application-portfolio-management#:~:text=Application%20Portfolio%20Management%20,overall%20value%20to%20the%20business

Thomas, J., & Harden, A. (2008). Methods for the thematic synthesis of qualitative research in systematic reviews. *BMC Medical Research Methodology*, *8*(1), 45. Advance online publication. DOI: 10.1186/1471-2288-8-45 PMID: 18616818

Thomson Reuters. (2023, October 25). *Auditing AI for transparency*. Thomson Reuters Technology Blog. Retrieved from https://www.thomsonreuters.com/en-us/posts/technology/auditing-ai-transparency/

Thomson Reuters. (2024, September 3). *Embracing change: Auditors' views on generative AI. ThomsonReuters Tax & Accounting Blog*. Retrieved from https://tax.thomsonreuters.com/blog/embracing-change-auditors-views-on-generative-ai/

Thomson Reuters. (n.d.a). Navigating the new era of auditing with AI technology: Meet Audit Intelligence. https://tax.thomsonreuters.com/blog/navigating-the-new-era-of-auditing-with-ai-technology-meet-audit-intelligence-analyze/

Thomson Reuters. (n.d.b). Are you harnessing the cloud to its full potential? https://tax.thomsonreuters.com/blog/are-you-harnessing-the-cloud-to-its-full-potential/

Tian, H., Wang, M., Quan, H., Chang, C.-C., & Vasilakos, A. V. (2025). TEEMRDA: Leveraging trusted execution environments for multi-replica data auditing in cloud storage. *Computers & Security*, *150*, 104250. DOI: 10.1016/j.cose.2024.104250

Tiron-Tudor, A., & Deliu, D. (2022). Reflections on the human-algorithm complex duality perspectives in the auditing process. *Qualitative Research in Accounting & Management*, *19*(3), 255–285.

Tonmoy, F., Hasan, S., & Tomlinson, R. (2020). Increasing Coastal Disaster Resilience Using Smart City Frameworks: Current State, Challenges, and Opportunities. *Frontiers in Water*, *2*, 3. Advance online publication. DOI: 10.3389/frwa.2020.00003

Torii. (2023). Application rationalization: How to optimize your software stack. Torii Blog. https://www.toriihq.com/blog/application-rationalization-made-easy#:~:text=Elimination%20of%20Redundant%20Applications

Toslali, M., ... (2024, July). AgraBOT: Accelerating Third-Party Security Risk Management in Enterprise Setting through Generative AI. In Companion Proceedings of the 32nd ACM International Conference on the Foundations of Software Engineering (pp. 74–79).

Tounsi, A., & Temimi, M. (2023). A systematic review of natural language processing applications for hydrometeorological hazards assessment. *Natural Hazards, 116*(3), 2819–2870. DOI: 10.1007/s11069-023-05842-0 PMID: 36776702

Ucoglu, D. (2020). Current machine learning applications in accounting and auditing. *Pressacademia, 12*(1), 1–7. DOI: 10.17261/Pressacademia.2020.1337

Udeh, E. O., Amajuoyi, P., Adeusi, K. B., & Scott, A. O. (2024). The role of big data in detecting and preventing financial fraud in digital transactions. *World Journal of Advanced Research and Reviews, 22*(2), 1746–1760. DOI: 10.30574/wjarr.2024.22.2.1575

University of Edinburgh. (2024). *Learning Analytics - Information Services*. Retrieved from https://information-services.ed.ac.uk/learning-technology/more-about-learning-technology/learning-analytics

University of Maryland. (n.d.). Blockchain technology could bring benefits to the auditing industry. https://www.rhsmith.umd.edu/research/blockchain-technology-could-bring-benefits-auditing-industry

van der Hoogen, A., Fashoro, I., Calitz, A. P., & Luke, L. (2024). A Digital Transformation Framework for Smart Municipalities. *Sustainability (Basel), 16*(3), 1320. DOI: 10.3390/su16031320

Vasarhelyi, M. A., & O'Leary, D. Artificial Intelligence in Accounting and Auditing: Creating Value with AI, Volume 5. Retrieved from https://raw.rutgers.edu/MiklosVasarhelyi/Resume%20Articles/CHAPTERS%20IN%20BOOKS/C12.%20creating%20value%20with%20ai.pdf

VMware Tanzu Labs. (2023). Introducing the open source application portfolio auditor. VMware Tanzu Blog. https://blogs.vmware.com/tanzu/introducing-application-portfolio-auditor/#:~:text=consistently%20assess%20cloud%20readiness%2C%20quality%2C,up%20to%2015%20software%20analyzers

Wang, S., Yu, M., Zhao, M., & Wang, H. (2024). Blockchain-based cloud data auditing scheme in multi-cloud storage service environment. *2024 27th International Conference on Computer Supported Cooperative Work in Design (CSCWD)*, 669–674. https://doi.org/DOI: 10.1109/CSCWD61410.2024.10580186

Wewerka, J., & Reichert, M. (2020, December 22). *Robotic Process Automation — A systematic literature review and assessment framework*. arXiv.org. https://arxiv.org/abs/2012.11951

White Papers 2024 Understanding the EU AI Act. (2024). ISACA. https://www.isaca.org/resources/white-papers/2024/understanding-the-eu-ai-act?utm_campaign=ISACA+Main&utm_content=1732631880&utm_medium=social&utm_source=linkedin

Wiseman, R. (2025). List of standards and regulations requiring an application inventory. Orchid Security Blog. https://www.orchid.security/blog/list-of-standards-and-regulations#:~:text=Requirement%3A

Wu, C., Liu, S., & Zhou, Z. (2024). Intelligent Information Audit System Construction: Integration of Big Data and Artificial Intelligence Technologies. *Frontiers in Science and Engineering*, *4*(4), 163–167. DOI: 10.54691/23b70s23

Yang, X., Wang, M., Li, T., Liu, R., & Wang, C. (2020). Privacy-preserving cloud auditing for multiple users scheme with authorization and traceability. *IEEE Access : Practical Innovations, Open Solutions*, *8*, 130866–130877. DOI: 10.1109/ACCESS.2020.3009539

Yermack, D. (2017). Corporate governance and blockchains. *Review of Finance*, *21*(1), 7–31. https://scholar.google.com/scholar_lookup?title=Blockchain+technology+in+the+audit+profession&author=Yermack,+D.&publication_year=2017

Yu, S., Wang, C., Ren, K., & Lou, W. (2010). Achieving secure, scalable, and fine-grained data access control in cloud computing. In *Proceedings of the IEEE INFOCOM* (pp. 1–9). IEEE. https://doi.org/DOI: 10.1109/INFCOM.2010.5462174

Yu, T.. (2020). Behavior-based insider threat detection using AI. *IEEE Transactions on Dependable and Secure Computing*, *17*(1).

Zahedi, M. H., et al. (2023). Risk management framework in Agile software development methodology. International Journal of Electrical & Computer Engineering (2088-8708), 13(4).

Zemánková, A. (2019). Artificial intelligence and blockchain in audit and accounting: Literature review. wseas Transactions on Business and Economics, 16(1), 568-581.

Zeng, K., & Wang, C. (2022). AI-driven policy mapping for third party risk. *Computers & Security*, **•••**, 107.

Zhang, Y., Ma, Z., & Meng, J. (2025). Auditing in the blockchain: A literature review. *Frontiers in Blockchain, 8*, Article 1549729.

Zhao, H., & Wang, Y. (2023). A Big Data-Driven Financial Auditing Method Using Convolution Neural Network. *IEEE Access : Practical Innovations, Open Solutions, 11*, 41492–41502. https://ieeexplore.ieee.org/stamp/stamp.jsp?arnumber=10107399. DOI: 10.1109/ACCESS.2023.3269438

Zhen-qi, W. (2021). Review of Government Performance Management in the Big Data Era: Practice, Issues and Prospects. Advances in Social Science, Education and Humanities Research. *Advances in Social Science, Education and Humanities Research*. Advance online publication. DOI: 10.2991/assehr.k.210519.076

Zhong, C., & Goel, S. (2024). Transparent AI in auditing through explainable AI. *Current Issues in Auditing*, *18*(2), A1–A14. DOI: 10.2308/CIIA-2023-009

Zubizarreta, M., Ganzarain, J., Cuadrado, J., & Lizarralde, R. (2020). Evaluating Disruptive Innovation Project Management Capabilities. *Sustainability (Basel)*, *13*(1), 1. DOI: 10.3390/su13010001

Мюллер, В., Кузнєцова, А. Я., Христофорова, О. М., Карпачова, О. В., & Сулима, М. О. (2020). Accounting and Auditing according to International Standards as a managment function. *Financial and Credit Activity Problems of Theory and Practice*, *4*(35), 60–68. DOI: 10.18371/fcaptp.v4i35.221787

About the Contributors

Manish Gupta is Executive Vice President and Audit Director at one of the 10 largest banks in the United States, responsible for oversight of cybersecurity and technology risk management programs. He is also adjunct professor at State University of New York at Buffalo where he has been teaching graduate courses in IT auditing and IT risk management since 2012. His research has won best paper awards and has been published in MIS Quarterly, Decision Support Systems, Journal of Organizational and End User Computing, and various ACM Transactions, among others. Manish received his Ph.D. (Management/MIS) and MBA (Finance and MIS) from State University of New York at Buffalo, NY, USA.

John Walp is an experienced information security executive and cybersecurity risk leader with broad industry and technology background. With more than 20 years of financial services and health insurance security industry experience, John is widely known as a subject matter expert in the areas of online fraud and has served in a variety of roles where his skills and knowledge provide business clients with valuable insights into various areas of information technology and cybersecurity risk management. John's areas of expertise include IS Auditing, cybersecurity, strategic information security thought leadership and technology risk management.

Raj Sharman is a Professor of Management Science and Systems, Department of Management Science and Systems, School of Management, The State University of New York, Buffalo, NY Ph.D. in Computer Science and Master of Science in Industrial Engineering from Louisiana State University, Louisiana, USA; M.Tech and B. Tech from Indian Institute of Technology (IIT), Bombay, India Research Interests: Cyber Security, Disaster Response and Business Continuity and Healthcare IT Several research projects funded by agencies such as NSF, AFSOR and the University at Buffalo; Published over a 100 articles in top-tier journals and conferences.

***

Aanchal Ahuja is an experienced IT audit professional with over 9 years in the field, offering a unique blend through her hands-on experience in both internal and external IT audit roles. She currently works in the Internal Audit team, at a leading FinTech company. Before this, Aanchal was a Risk Manager at a major tech company, where she gained worked in Governance, Risk, and Compliance (GRC) space. Her career also includes several years at a Big 4 firm, where she specialized as an external IT auditor, working with a wide range of clients across various industries. This combination of internal audit, external audit, and GRC experience gives Aanchal a comprehensive understanding of risk management and IT audit domain, from both an organizational and regulatory perspective. She holds a Master's in Management Information Systems from the School of Management at the State University of New York, Buffalo.

Tanisha Ahuja is a CISA certified professional with expertise in IT Audit, Risk Management, and Cybersecurity. She holds a Master's degree in Management Information Systems with an Advance Graduate Certificate in Cybersecurity from the University at Buffalo. Tanisha has hands-on work experience in IT Risk and Operations, where she developed controls and automated critical workflows, including access management, change management, and segregation of duties, enhancing security while supporting compliance with SOX 404. Additionally, she holds a Bachelor's degree in Computer Science Engineering. She is passionate about safeguarding information systems, reducing risk, and driving compliance by enhancing the IT control environment and aligning processes with frameworks and regulatory standards.

Dinesh Kanna Aranganathan is a product management professional with a strong foundation in data analytics and product strategy. He holds a Master's degree in Management Information Systems from the University at Buffalo and brings over four years of experience leading cross-functional teams in analytics-driven product development. Dinesh has successfully driven KPI-focused innovations across sectors such as real estate and insurance, delivering measurable outcomes including increased adoption, efficiency, and ROI. His technical proficiency spans tools like SQL, Tableau, and Python, alongside Agile methodologies. He is a Certified Scrum Product Owner with a proven track record of transforming complex datasets into actionable insights and scalable solutions.

Muralidhar L B is a professionally qualified dental surgeon. He holds a Ph.D. from Canara Bank School of Management Studies, Bangalore University, after his MBA from Christ University. He is qualified in management at UGC - NET and KSET. He has 18 years of total teaching experience spanning across dental education, healthcare management and general management and 4 years of corporate experience. He has worked as a research associate in the Institute for Social and Economic Change, Bangalore in a project entitled as "Management By and For Common Man: An Exploration of the Concept and Direction for Future"post Ph.D. He had secured 28th rank in the S.S.L.C. examination for Karnataka State in 1993. His 25 patents have been published, and 2 design patents have been granted. He has 41 research publications to his credit, of which 15 are Scopus-indexed, 5 are ABDC indexed and 1 is indexed in Web of Science. He has co-authored 11 books and 7 book chapters.. He is supervising Ph.D. research of 3 research scholars at JAIN (Deemed to be University). He works as an assistant professor in the Department of Business Management Studies, School of Commerce, Jain Deemed to be a University in Bangalore.

Vijay Kumar Banoth received his Master's degree in Management Information Systems from the University at Buffalo, State University of New York, where he specialized in product management, IT audit, and cloud security. He also holds a Bachelor's degree in Computer Science from MNIT Jaipur. With nearly six years of experience in technical support and product operations, his work spans enterprise software architecture, ERP integrations, and customer-centric digital solutions. His interests include user-focused product strategy, agile delivery, and the application of AI in enhancing product scalability and compliance across fintech and SaaS environments.

Y.Fathima, BBA.,MFC.,MBA.,M.Phil.,DGT.,Ph.D.,is an Professor in the Department of Commerce, School of Commerce at Jain (Deemed-to-be University) Bangalore. An accomplished educator with demonstrated ability to teach, motivate, and direct students while maintaining high interest and achievement. Articulate communicator able to effectively interact with diverse population of students at a variety of academic levels. She has 18 years of Teaching Experience and 10 years of Research experience. She has published papers in reputed journal and authored 4 books.

Moksh Gupta is a sophomore at Williamsville East High School with a strong passion for science, discovery, and community service. He holds leadership roles in the Medical Outreach Club, Science Bowl Team, Indian Cultural Club, and his school's FBLA chapter, where he is a member of the FBLA Honor Society and a two-time national qualifier with multiple state-level awards. He is also an award-winning Science Olympiad competitor, with top regional placements in biology and chemistry events. Moksh has completed over 200 volunteer hours, serves on the advisory board of the Amherst Youth Engaged in Service (Y.E.S.) Program, and has received both the Gold and Bronze Presidential Volunteer Service Awards. As a Mental Health Ambassador for the Bridges from Borders initiative, he co-hosts a podcast promoting awareness and open dialogue around mental health. Moksh is also a co-author of two published cybersecurity research book chapters and was selected as a finalist for the International GENIUS Olympiad competition. In addition, he plays alto saxophone in his school's Wind Ensemble and has been selected for both the All-County and Area All-State bands.

Asmita Jain is a graduate student currently pursuing my Master's in Management Information Systems with an Advanced Graduate Certificate in Cybersecurity at the University at Buffalo (SUNY). She has completed her undergraduate degree in Electronics and Communication. She have over five years of experience in network security and cybersecurity, putting information security plans into action and protecting network infrastructure. She has worked with Citrix, Accenture, and HCL as a Senior Network Security Engineer. Products that she has hand-on experience are load balancers (ADC/F5), firewalls (Checkpoint), Cisco routers and switches, and WAF. She has strong interest in improving data privacy standards and investigating novel approaches to changing cybersecurity risks. Researching auditing in generative AI, governance, and risk management is what she is doing right now, and it excites her and makes her ready for the challenges of the future by encouraging her to look into the relationship of cybersecurity in other areas of technology.

Dollie Juneja is a Master's student at the State University of New York, studying Management in Information Systems with an Advanced Graduate Certificate in Cybersecurity and Information Science Security. She is currently employed as a Graduate Research Assistant at the institution, where she contributes to pioneering research and significant initiatives. Dollie has a Bachelor of Technology in Computer Science from The Northcap University, Gurugram, and over four years of professional experience as an Application Security Solution Advisor in the Risk and Financial Advisory domain at Deloitte Touche Tohmatsu Ltd. She has three research articles published in prestigious publications and conferences, with an emphasis on social network analysis, predictive analytics, and IoT. With her robust industry experience and academic pursuits, Dollie is deeply invested in the realms of cybersecurity, governance, risk, and compliance, IT risk management, and IT auditing. She is passionate about making meaningful contributions to industry collaborations and exploring innovative dimensions in information technology.

Aneesh Krishna is a Research Assistant at the University at Buffalo, where he recently completed his Master's degree in Data Science. His research focuses on the intersection of machine learning, cybersecurity, and explainable AI, with recent work exploring AI-driven approaches to third-party risk management. He has contributed to academic and applied projects in intrusion detection and generative AI applications.

Zishen Liao is a finance graduate.

Tshepo Maota is a leading expert in IT auditing, disruption management, and governance frameworks, combining his PhD research, industry expertise, and professional certifications (CISA, COBIT) to drive innovative solutions in IT governance and risk management. His contributions continue to shape audit methodologies, cybersecurity frameworks, and IT governance strategies that enhance resilience, compliance, and organizational performance. His commitment to academic research and industry best practices positions him as a key thought leader in technology-driven audit methodologies and digital transformation strategies. With a vision for enhancing IT governance, integrating AI into risk assessments, and fortifying cybersecurity frameworks, Dr. Maota remains dedicated to advancing the body of knowledge in IT auditing and governance while providing strategic leadership in the evolving digital landscape.

Aman Modi holds a Master of Science in Management Information Systems from the University at Buffalo, State University of New York, and a Bachelor of Engineering in Computer Engineering from Savitribai Phule Pune University. He has over six years of professional experience as an IT consultant, with a strong focus on IT governance, risk management, and compliance. His areas of expertise include SOX compliance, IT General Controls (ITGC), IT Application Controls (ITAC), and secure system implementation. Aman is also engaged in research on IT application portfolio optimization, aiming to improve enterprise risk posture and audit efficiency through data-driven strategies.

Shilpa R working as Associate professor, Department of Management Studies, RJS Institute of Management Studies, has 16 years of experience in teaching. She has worked with the T.John Institute of Technology for 6 years and Quantum Leap for 1 year. She has completed an MBA, M Phil and PhD at Jain (Deemed to be university) specialize in the area of OB/ HRM. She has also published research papers in Scopus, ABDC, and UGC care journals and presented papers at national and international conferences. Authorized Book chapters for international journals and project guide for MBA students. Attended FDPs, conferences, and workshops and also organized programs for the students. Member of ISTE and MTC Global.

Nishanth Holla Raghavendra received the Master's degree in Management Information Systems from the University at Buffalo, State University of New York, where he focused on cybersecurity, cloud security, and IT audit. He also holds a Bachelor's degree in Computer Science. He has over three years of experience in IT operations, with practical involvement in cloud platforms, regulatory compliance frameworks, and industrial IoT environments. Nishanth aspires to contribute to global initiatives that advance cybersecurity awareness, ethical innovation, and equitable access to secure digital infrastructure for all.

Varanasi Rahul, an Assistant Professor at JAIN University, Bangalore, holds three postgraduate degrees (M.Com in Accounting & Taxation, M.Com in Management, and MA in History) and is a semi-qualified Cost Accountant. He has cleared UGC NET in Commerce twice, AP SET in Commerce, History, and Management, and TS SET in Commerce. With 3 years of teaching experience and 6 months at PwC, he is also a freelance archaeologist, epigraphist, and numismatist. He has authored 3 books, published 6 research articles, contributed 9 book chapters, and written 30+ newspaper articles. Rahul has applied for 11 patents, with 1 granted and 09 published.

N Sathyanarayana has over 15 years of teaching experience at the UG and PG levels. He holds a Master's in Business Administration and Commerce and is pursuing a Ph.D. He currently holds the position of Assistant Professor in the School of Commerce at Jain (Deemed-to-be University), Bangalore. He has published 22 research papers in international journals (2 Scopus Index), 7 research papers in national journals, and presented 14 research papers at international conferences and 11 research papers at national conferences. He has co-authored 2 books at national level and 8 book chapters (Scopus indexed).

Zayan Shaheen is a graduate student currently pursuing my Master's in Management Information Systems at the University at Buffalo-SUNY. He is from the Buffalo-Niagara area and has done his undergraduate at University of Buffalo in Management Information Systems. He has experience as an IT Business Consultant where he developed in-depth solutions that helped businesses with their problems. This further instantiated his interpersonal and problem solving skills. The tasks done ranged from simple industry analysis to developing a complete user interface. Through his time in higher education, he has gained experience with database modeling, front-end and backend development. He is deeply passionate about enhancing data privacy standards and exploring innovative strategies to address evolving cybersecurity risks. This work equips him to tackle future challenges by delving into the intersection of cybersecurity, business analytics, and emerging technologies, enabling me to develop solutions that bridge technical innovation with strategic decision-making.

Anuja Ulhe is a graduate student currently pursuing my Master's in Management Information Systems at the University at Buffalo-SUNY. She has completed my undergraduate degree in Electronics and Communication from MIT Pune . Anuja has 7 years of total IT experience . She has worked with HCL Technologies and KPMG Global Services . Anuja has strong expertise in the data driven platforms working front end and back end. She has worked on several projects involving data analysis, automation and optimization . Anujs's core competencies include data management, problem solving and communication. She has a passion for applying technology to create value and impact for business and society.

Tianyi Zhang is currently pursuing a Master of Science in Finance at the University at Buffalo, SUNY. His academic interests focus on emerging technologies in auditing, financial data analytics, and the intersection of AI and assurance services. He has experience in empirical research and financial modeling.

Index

B

C

D

E

F

G

H

I

Z

www.ingramcontent.com/pod-product-compliance
Lightning Source LLC
LaVergne TN
LVHW062324300926
849161LV00007B/1558